The Bears Of Manley

Adventures of an Alaskan trophy hunter
in search of the ultimate symbol.

The world's most definitive and complete work on why men hunt.
Fascinating information and exciting entertainment for hunters.
Enlightening and absorbing answers to animal activists.
Stirring response to antihunters.

Sarkis Atamian

ISBN 1-888125-01-2

Library of Congress Catalog Card Number: 95-71680

Manufactured in the United States of America.

Publication Consultants
Anchorage, Alaska

Dedication

To Alison
My beloved wife and angel.

Whose love has been my great
treasure gifted by God's grace.

With your permission, kind reader, let me pay homage to my buddies with whom I shared the thrills of the chase before they plunged to death in their airplanes over the trails we hunted together:

Dean Barnard

Lynn Castle

Clark Engle

Hank Plante

Stan Thorsheim

Rest In Peace, dear comrades.

Acknowledgments

I have deliberately avoided trying to make this book a research monograph, an academic project, or a scholarly work, although there are some unavoidable elements of these. Hence, I have kept the usual footnotes, references, and scholarly impedimenta to a bare minimum—except when the few quotations have been direct.

While the hunter's mind is important to explain him, his soul is far more important to understand him, since he is the result of many cultures, civilizations, and the universal human spirit. I have preferred to concentrate on his soul and the meaning of the hunt which makes the hunter what and who he is. For better or worse, I have been my own study and the hunting trail is the laboratory of my experiments and experiences.

No one can spend 25 years teaching in the university, as I have, without preferring certain ideas over others since some are, obviously, of far greater value, integrity, and influence. Ideas are not of equal importance. The reader may be interested in some sources that are important to my thoughts. With one obvious exception, none of the small list of select thinkers below is a hunter, nor have they written anything about hunting as far as I know. But they have written extensively, and germinally, about culture, civilization, history, and human psyche. Oddly enough, these are things that tell us what hunting is all about. The spilling of blood does not. Also, some authors have expressed thoughts on the nature of sports and athletics in general. They too have been helpful to me and are included.

David Frost, *The Philosophical Scientists*

Jose Ortega Y Gasset, *Meditations On Hunting*

Johan Huizinga, *Homo Ludens*

Carl G. Jung, *The Portable Jung*

Dorothy Norman, *The Hero: Myth, Image, Symbol*

Pitirim A. Sorokin, *Culture, Society, and Personality*

Mihaly Csizkszentmihalyi, *Beyond Boredom and Anxiety*

George Leonard, *The Ultimate Athlete*

And some 800 books by hunters, from the world's greatest to the pretenders and spoilers; to mention even a few important ones would be too many.

I acknowledge, with special gratitude, six people who made this book a reality.

Dr. Arnold Griese, dear friend and colleague, for his encouragement.

Clyde Beutler, dear friend and gentleman extraordinaire, who pushed the magic buttons to find my publisher.

Evan and Margaret Swensen, who had the courage to publish this book despite its Political Incorrectness.

Ersa Kelley, for his dedicated hours of proofreading and kind suggestions.

Alison Atamian, beloved wife and worker of miracles, who never lost faith in me to finish this book, did the typing, and still got the meals on time.

I also express my gratitude to the following persons who gave so generously of their time, expertise, and suggestions: Dr. Rahim Borhani, Mrs. Linda Conover, Dr. James Ivey, Mr. Robert Lafferty, and Dr. Ron Williams.

Table of Contents

Preface

I t is necessary to make a few autobiographical comments to put into perspective the stories that follow. Since I subscribe to Wykes' (biographer of old time professional hunters) thesis that a hunting book is really about characters, I might as well say something about the character revelation that made a hunter out of me. I do not see how I can avoid this issue after saying so much about it in the Introduction. Critics and opponents need my own reasons—the real reasons—for my joining the hunting fraternity, not the reasons they concoct to make a case for me. I will make my own case.

I was born of humble parents who miraculously survived the first and worst genocide of the twentieth century when the unspeakable Turkish government, in an official policy of brutal extermination, deliberately massacred 90% of my Armenian ancestors in World War I. Today, that government denies the genocide ever took place, and the agony of my people, who have had a 4,000-year history, is all but forgotten.

The significance of this fact is that my parents migrated to this country and had all they could do to survive and raise three children. Papa did any menial job he could find, and we knew poverty long before the Great Depression. The best job Papa eventually got was in an iron foundry, where primitive work conditions wreaked havoc on him. He clung desperately to that job because it gave him a small, but steady paycheck, and he didn't have to know much English. They say hard work never killed anybody. It killed my father at age 49, before I finished high school.

I make this painful point so many who think trophy hunters are born with golden spoons in their mouths with an Anglo-Saxon ancestry who followed the royal sport, will realize the truth. It is true, trophy hunting is a terribly expensive affair, and it has its share of millionaire aficionados. It is also true many trophy hunters are men of modest means who can afford only limited, once-in-a-lifetime hunts.

There is a sad consequence to this. Those who manipulate or incite our culture wars or social class struggles, love to stereotype the millionaire hunter as a crook made wealthy by ill-gotten gains, who delights in sadism of killing animals for fun. Of course this invites the scorn, envy, and ill-will of the vast majority of us who are not blessed with all that money that should be taxed by a rapacious government who promises to tax (legally plunder) only the top 3% of the money-makers. This figure quickly grows into three-fourths or more of the population who are surprised to learn how rich they were without suspecting it.

Most middle-class persons who climbed up the hard way, as I did, don't care how millionaires squander their money. That's their business. We care about how we spend ours, and its tough to afford one or two safaris to Africa as I did. I mortgaged my house, borrowed on my insurance policy, and spent 6 years to pay for a 3-week hunt and subsequent taxidermy bill. I have no connection with European imperialism that may have produced all sorts of trophy hunters. I will never qualify due to circumstances of my birth, over which I had no control. Any ordinary man who does what I did for my hunting does not have fun, recreation, or sport on his mind. There are less expensive and less dangerous ways to amuse oneself.

If one could not afford such expensive hunts in faraway places and he were an American citizen, the next best thing used to be moving to Alaska, except that politics have made that into a losing proposition these days with all kinds of discriminating legislation, especially against nonnative American hunters. Yet, I moved to Alaska in 1961. There are those who suspect my sanity, given the extravagant expenses for trophy hunting, but as they say in Latin— "De gustibus non disputandum est," or, "you can't argue tastes," roughly translated. Anyone can do what I did if he just sacrifices other things.

To go back to the beginning. I didn't know a single word of English because my parents didn't. By the time they learned enough to get by, it was too late to do me much good. I had already learned the hard way. Early in my elementary schooling, they gave me, what I later knew to be, an I.Q. test. I stared and stared at a picture of a bed and a choice of three words with which to identify it: cat, bed, and hat. I knew the word for bed in two other languages, but not English. I couldn't do the test.

The greatest breakthrough in my life came when I finally learned that squiggles on pages made words, in right combinations. I had learned to read at last. I discovered there were no other books to read except the ones used in class.

Another major breakthrough came in the fourth grade when a branch librarian showed up to say we could borrow books from the public library free if we signed up. I was the first in line. In the wintertime, when we couldn't play outside, I haunted that library. In many ways, one of the most significant experiences of my life occurred there, although I didn't know it at the time. The librarian, Miss McNarney (that's the way her name sounded to me), probably didn't know it either. She became my guardian angel, not only because she was pretty, but because she was also a kind, understanding, and caring person. She showed a kid like me, who was in a fist fight every other day because of the cruelty, taunts, jeers, and gang attacks of those who called me a foreigner and a dummy, the world was not as bad as I thought.

She encouraged me to read and showed me how to use the encyclopedia and dictionary. Some of my chums had early brushes with the law. If I avoided a similar fate, it was not because I was an angel. It was because I had someone who made a great difference in my life. After the big war (the second one), when I fully understood that difference, I went to see her, but she was gone and no one knew where. When I go to heaven, hopefully, she had better be there so I can tell her how much I love her—how grateful I am to her. If she isn't there, God and I are going to disagree, although I know in advance who will win.

I read every book in the juvenile section, some of them twice, but new ones did not come in fast enough. In my desperation, I committed my first criminal act. I sneaked into the adult section, and like Robinson Crusoe, stood thunderstruck in front of shelves marked Adventure. The titles scrambled my brains with excitement, so I grabbed the first three I could reach, and got out of there fast, before someone caught me.

Then, I did something shameful. I took them to the checkout desk where my angel was sitting. She smiled, said hello, and without opening the book she told me the orange call card inside meant the book was for adults and these must have gotten into the juvenile room by mistake. Saying that, she looked at me kind of funny.

I stood there with my blue juvenile card in my hand, caught blue-handed. How did she know it was an adult book before she even opened the cover? Of course, I knew nothing about orange cards. She must have seen more than my dismay. She said I could not borrow the books, but if they were for my school research, I could read them in the adult reference room. Her eyes told me to say yes although I wasn't sure what the word research meant. I said, "Yes," and immediately charged to the reference room to do my research. For the next several years, I spent most of the winter months there. They were some of the happiest days of my life.

I devoured every book on adventure, travel, African and arctic exploration, natural history, archaeology, and wildlife. Apart from Armenian freedom fighters, my heroes were Cherry Kearton, Authur Radclyffe Dugmore, Martin Johnson, and Carl Akeley. Photographs in their books were more real to me than the real world I lived in. There were all kinds of pictures but my favorite ones were of lions. Everywhere there were lions. They looked so free, so indifferent to cares of the world. They didn't have to hide their heads in shame because they could always feed their young, and besides, they looked so invincible that obviously no one could pick on them. Did they know how free they were? I did. Then there were the painted black warriors with their spears and shields. They always looked like they knew what they were doing. How I wanted to hunt with them just once and feel life as they did!

There were not many pictures of polar bear in the frozen Arctic wastes, but they told me the same thing. They were free. They could roam anywhere they pleased. Lion or polar bear were born free, as a popular song observes. They also died free. I not only stared at those pages, but in my mind's eye, I got into them and stood by my lions and polar bears and talked to them, pleaded with them to take me along on their wanderings and out of my Great Depression poverty.

The worst of poverty came one afternoon when I returned home from the playground and saw a crowd gathered before our house. I was too young to understand what was happening, but I remember the red flag and the stranger standing on our steps. He was taking bids as he auctioned off our home right before Pappa's eyes. Our mortgage payments were in arrears despite Pappa's best effort to meet them. There were no entitlement programs or helping services. It's the only time I saw my father cry. Yet, in spite of all that privation and misery, we knew many moments of real joy and happiness because we were family. We had love and respect for each other, the courage to keep going, and always the hope that tomorrow would be better.

All at once, billboards and posters all over town bedazzled us. A brand new movie had arrived, one of the first to be shot on actual location in Africa. It was *Trader Horn*, starring Harry Carey. The garish illustrations showed snarling lions, intrepid trader and hunter, and painted black warriors. I was only 8 years old then in 1931 at the peak of the Depression, and could not find 25¢ to save my life, but that's what it cost to see the film at Loew's Theater in Providence—one of the most luxurious movie palaces in the country. I waited on pins and needles nearly a year until that movie came to a second-rate, rerun theater, and I had worked hard to scavenge the dime to get into the Bijou.

Years later, I hardly remembered the white, blond, jungle goddess ruling an entire tribe of natives—another, *She Who Must Be Obeyed*. But the wild animals that went racing across the screen still ran wild through the forests of my mind. I never forgot the charging lion. Trader Horn's right-hand man was a valiant, noble black hunter, Mutia. (Mutia Omoolu, in real life.) He speared the hurtling lion and brought it down at arm's length from the others who watched helplessly. When Mutia was killed by a stray arrow from a band of charging enemy tribesmen, Harry Carey hugged the lifeless form of his comrade and fought back a tear. I couldn't stop crying for that brave warrior who would hunt no more.

At movie's end, Trader Horn, in love with the white goddess, gallantly gives her up to his younger partner, who also loves her. With a stoic look in his eyes and a smile on his lips, he shoulders his rifle and heads out into the tall grass for his beloved animals. I applauded him ecstatically because he had made the right choice. Ah, for the sweet innocence of childhood! I then returned to my books in the library for the tall grass and my beloved animals on the printed page.

Because of all that reading, I got into some trouble in the ninth grade. The class had taken the national grade placement test—a thing called the co-ops. The principal called me to his office. Although psychiatry had two more decades to go before it became the in-thing, he started shrinking my head. After a long time of word games, he hit me on the noggin with verbal sledgehammer blows—he accused me of cheating and wanted to know how I had stolen a copy of the test when it was under lock and key.

I was flabbergasted and told the truth—I had never seen the bloody thing until it was given in class. Then, he wanted to know how come I knew all those big words because my score had gone off the chart after it had passed the scores for a college senior. I wasn't that smart since I didn't even know what a college senior was, so I figured he had to be pretty dumb, no matter who he was—but I didn't tell the principal that. He had to be on the senior's side since, obviously, he was not on mine. Instead, I told him another truth. I did a lot of reading, I said.

He looked at me incredulously and then at the book I had in my hand—second volume of Fridtjof Nansen's *Farthest North*. I was rereading parts of it because I wanted to memorize temperatures of arctic waters, their salinity and light refraction indices in those places where polar bear had their habitat. I spewed back some technical data to prove I really knew what I was talking about. He just gaped at me, but after that, whenever I went past his office and he saw me, he looked as though I was about to toss a nuclear grenade at him, which hadn't even been invented yet.

First, they called me a dummy because I didn't know any English. Now, I was accused of using big words too advanced for me. I was a failure again precisely due to the kind of success for which I was being educated. I realized right then the futility of progress. Of course, I walked out of those pages as I grew older and the rest of life got in my way. But those pages never walked out of my life and forced a showdown some 30 years later—the pictures and stories had won. The direction of my life had been set early with those books.

Modern teachers and librarians are correct. If you are going to control adult males, you start by censoring and controlling the kinds of books active young boys can have access to. You must stop them before they get the kind of start I did, or they go out and kill animals. That's why there are few books in school libraries about hunting. Boys are not allowed to become men. They are encouraged to be wimps with books on safe sex.

Today's psychologists tell us to get childhood memories out of our minds for easier programming into modules for new world input. They always tell us what childhood does to our adulthood. They never tell us what adulthood does to our childhood. In the first place, I doubt we can turn our childhood past on and off like a faucet. Any sudden experience can take it out of cold storage for the microwave whether we want to or not.

In the second place, if childhood was a happy one, why should we give it up even if we could? Its joyful memories give us a right sense of direction when we are adults. Then, we don't give our children bad memories they cannot run away from. The past is always with us because without it there is no present pointing to a future. If that past was a bad one, we have to face it and fight. If it was a good one, we embrace it with fond memories. The one thing we cannot do is run away from it, future fantasies notwithstanding. I came to Alaska to become a real hunter.

My future started with my past. It started with happy memories and books of my boyhood. I believe it was a far better deal than what kids are reading today, if they can read at all.

When the uninitiated ask me what fun can I get out of hunting, or why I do it, and want my answer in a half-dozen words, I laugh so hard I could cry. Can they tell me in a half-dozen words how their dreams eluded them, or of success and failure in pursuing them, or the joy and pain of their fulfillment? They have had the same struggles of the spirit I have had, the only difference being the symbolic treasures we have sought and the paths we took in finding them.

I have forgotten many innumerable hunts I enjoyed, but taught me little. When hunts were truly memorable, I wrote them in a journal I kept only for that purpose—to recall moments important to me when memory would eventually grow weary and dim. I never thought I'd want to publish them. In fact, I sent out only one story to two different publishers. I needed the money. As I suspected, I was no writer, because both publishers sent the story back to me. The comments were vexatious. One publisher said there was no fun in my story. The other said I was too funny for a story otherwise too ghastly.

I researched and published several articles of an academic nature concerning hunting, and made lots of speeches in a few parts of the country Outside (as we say in Alaska). I was trying to sound the alarm on the coming destruction of our nation in which hunting would invite another breach in Western culture, so hated by those who secretly craved its success.

I never wrote or spoke publicly about my own hunts, however. They were too intimate, too precious to part with for the admiration or damnation of the anonymous. Sometimes, it's hard to share things like this. I knew what I was proud of and what I was ashamed of on those hunts. Of what possible interest could this be to other hunters? Antihunters would have a negative interest only—it would give them one more target so, in the name of loving animals, they could strike another blow in undermining the foundations of Western culture whose sport hunting was another consummate, bourgeois evil.

I had my own ideas about politics, philosophy, psychology, and sociology of hunting. As a professor of psychology and sociology, I had a long-standing academic interest in hunting, did some serious research on it, and hunted quite avidly, besides. This put me in an awkward spot. A few in the hunting fraternity who depended on game for subsistence thought I was too much of a theorizing egghead intellectual, writing highfalutin articles on sport hunting (a.k.a. head-hunting) instead of concentrating on the blood-and-guts issue of killing in order to eat.

On the other hand, there were too many intellectual elite among my colleagues who thought my pro-hunting statements were not politically correct. I defended what they thought were outmoded Neanderthal rituals with too much blood and guts desecrating the hallowed halls of ivy. I was thinking "A plague on both your houses," when one of my dearest friends and colleagues suggested I write a book on some of my hunts. He thought they were exciting from some of my experiences I had shared with him. What? Another book on the stalk, kill, and jubilation? Thanks, but no thanks. I had too many other things to do.

My friend tightened the noose with things about my sense of duty to my passion for the hunt, the need to present the other side of the story to rebut the monstrous lies by television producers with a political axe to grind, my sense of gratitude to the giants of hunting who had bequeathed to me the honor and dignity of the sporting fraternity, and so on. My rejection of his arguments was based on one simple fact: there was a mountain of hunting literature with superb writing comparable to any literary genre. What could I add to it?

Then he used my favorite phrase against me, "the soul of the hunter." I had used the word soul in the old traditional Armenian sense that had been around long before its current connotations. It meant something special to me, and, of course, he had me checkmated. The hunter does not live in a vacuum until he suddenly appears on the printed page doing his wilderness thing. He brings to his hunt, the entire life he has lived before the hunt. He will take back into the rest of his life everything the hunt has done to him long after it's over. This connecting linkage is a spiritual thing, making the underlying theme of his life different than it would have been if he had not hunted. Because that life is different, the man is different. In that difference lies "the soul of the hunter."

Most of my hunts had given me thrill of achievement, reward of overcoming a tough challenge, joy of having beaten the odds, and excitement of high adventure. Was there a common denominator? I went over my journal, asking which hunts had taught me anything about life that made me different than I would have been without them. I realized they were hunts in which something had gone wrong, from minor hazards to major catastrophes that threatened my very life. These were hunts that taught me something. They had torn my soul to shreds, one way or another. When it had regenerated into a new spiritual growth, I sensed what the phoenix must have felt shaking off the ashes so he could fly again.

Why was it so difficult for decent, fair-minded, and intelligent people to see the hunter in his true light? Why did they always hint of the stereotyped monsters portrayed in television shows and antihunting literature, even when they suspected propaganda intent of those sources? Why was the hunter being given a stigmatized identity to set him apart for easy denial of his humanity? Did the hunting fraternity do this to others?

My discussion of all this with so many people over the years gave me many answers, but a central theme emerged. All they read in the hunting literature was the stalk, kill, and jubilation. There was no indication anything else was involved in the action-packed, objective telling of these stories. Such readers didn't understand our side telling them what hunting really meant to us because we our side telling them what hunting really meant to us because we didn't tell them. We hunters simply omitted the soul of hunting and the subjective side of it because that was understood by fellow hunters. Did it ever occur to us that our opponents would go to our writings and make their case not only on what we said, but on what we didn't say when we should have said it?

Reviewing notes I had kept over 25 years, I saw unevenness and lack of continuity among them. They looked like experiences of several different men during different lifetimes. The lifetimes may have been different indeed, but they all belonged to one man. Or did they? Had I changed so much through the years? I was halfway through rearranging that material when life got in the way again. I retired, moved to a milder climate in Alaska, married the best student I have ever had and finest woman I've ever known, built the castle of my dreams for our retirement home, had a quadruple bypass, took a trip around the world with my wife, and hunted and fished. I returned to my manuscript 8 years after I started it.

I do not claim to explain "the soul of the hunter." I merely say, I have searched for it and found more than my wildest dreams. I bare my soul here (which the perceptive reader will see through, anyway) in support of Wykes' thesis and try to show something of the other side of hunting and about one hunter who has seen glimpses of that other side.

Too many fine hunters who are decent men, besides, increasingly doubt who and what they are under the overwhelming assault of the media. They tell me they do not know what to say to standardized and well-rehearsed attacks by critics who are paid to create propaganda and big lies that are repeated often enough to feign credibility. For nearly a century, too many hunting books have wrestled with the why of hunting. We still need answers. I do not pretend I have them, but I insist I have quested for them and have found some inklings after much travail.

Those answers have to do with the human soul and true hunting spirit that is so difficult to know, and even more difficult to reveal. I have tried to show it here in the way I have experienced them. I have written the actual hunts in separate chapters, where all the action is. Following each chapter of a hunt, I have written another section entitled *Reflections*. This is where contemplation tells what lessons and answers those hunts taught me. To me, these sections are more important than the others, for what they taught me, is still with me, and gave me insights I have found nowhere else. I hope they will help the reader if he has been intrigued by the same problems. They are central to understanding what the hunt is all about and what the hunter is up against in the cultural war and decline of our times.

I have kept *Reflections* separate because some of them may be too heavy, though I have kept them as light as I could for the sincere critic of hunting who never understood the hunter's position and what a real hunt is all about. There is no getting around this because the ideas discussed are at the heart of the hunting controversy. For the politicized antihunting critic who knows very well what he's doing, it is high time the roots of his own position are exposed. By keeping such chapters separate, the reader may return to them later if he prefers to read the hunting stories by themselves.

I share what I have found, hoping this book will contribute to the true spirit of the hunt. It is the only way I can show my gratitude for what hunting has given me. Let the reader judge my success or failure.

Foreword

I was born and grew into manhood when hunting was politically correct. Looking back, with a half-century of hunting perspective, convinces me honorable hunting and ownership and use of sporting firearms have been desecrated by enemies of freedom. As a single parent, my mom told me stories of my dad's great hunts. She arranged with worthy men to take me afield. These men—men like my Uncle Ivan, Uncle Randal, and cousin Carl, became my early heroes. As we camped and hunted together, I learned high values and great lessons. When I became a father, I took my boys and girls into the wilderness in search of game, and tried to teach them the valued traditions of my heroes.

Then came Pied Piper animal activists and antihunters, blowing their horns and persuading youth, and adult alike, to abandon time-honored traditions of hunting. Many listened and believed the false and fabricated tunes played by these anti-tradition purveyors. These troublemakers, pawning themselves off as peacemakers, have succeeded in convincing almost a whole nation to give up its sporting arms. They are persuading people to elevate animals above man—man, who was created in the image of God.

Now comes Sarkis Atamian with the beginning of the final answer to the question of why men hunt, and why hunting is honorable. Principled people have always known hunting is moral, noble, and honorable, yet, they lack a ready response when confronted with lies of those who chant against hunting. Sarkis' book speaks of what honest hunters have felt in their hearts, but were unable to express.

When I finished my first reading of The Bears of Manley, I knew I'd been in the presence of excellence and had partaken of truth. The Bears of Manley calls for hunters to take the higher trail. Its paragraphs are packed with wisdom. Its pages plead to this generation to hold on to their integrity and identity as men. The book petitions people to not follow those whose roots are falsely secured in systems designed and destined to enslave and to plunder.

Sarkis helped me remember things I never knew. His enlightened ideas have not only won the commendation of hunters, they are a welcome answer for the non-hunting, true animal lover. Every hunter needs the information in this book to rightly respond to animal activists and antihunters. To discuss animals and hunting without the knowledge contained in this book, is like sending smoke signals in the wind.

Evan Swensen
Publisher and Editor
Alaska Outdoors magazine

Introduction

An ancient Chinese philosopher is supposed to have said, "It is a well-known fact that one horse can run faster than another. Why go to the race track"? No doubt he jested and knew the answer—we go to the race track to see which horse wins and how good he looked doing it between start and finish, when anything could have gone wrong.

It is something like this when reading big-game hunting books and, henceforth, my use of the word hunter shall refer to the big-game hunter, the trophy hunter, especially, unless otherwise designated, although much that is said here applies to hunting, generally. This is because I am a trophy hunter, derisively known as a headhunter (every man to his own tastes), and do not know enough about other kinds of hunting to comment on them. I hope I have given the reader enough advance warning.

In any event, the reader of any kind of big-game hunting book must play a kind of game with himself. He pretends he does not know in advance what he knows full well—no matter how enormous and frightful the odds against the intrepid hunter, he will survive nicely or he wouldn't have been around long enough to write of his exploits. Yet, the reader remains engrossed with one such book after another. Why?

Alan Wykes, the author of at least two good biographies of old-time professional hunters, says the reader of big-game hunting books gets tired or bored after his fifth or sixth book on the subject. This is because all big-game hunting books become routine after a time since they all have the same thing in common—the stalk, kill, and hunter's jubilation. There may be minor variations, but the major theme is common to all the literature. What a good hunting book is all about, says Wykes, is character—the hunter's character, of course, as it unfolds from stalk, to kill, to exultation, and all that happened in between, which is what reveals the character business. This is why we read on after the fifth or sixth book.

There are a few things, of course, which complicate Wykes' thesis and my support of it. It is true enough that the hunter's adventures, excitements, dangers, and challenges may jade our tastes after a time—but the unfolding of character? The truth is, any literary work, classical or otherwise, is a study of character in some way. This always fascinates us because, one way or another, we are always fascinated with our own.

Our character is always a mystery because we do not come into this world with it full-blown, all in one quick shot. It develops or comes to us in slow increments, in random bits and pieces in such a way that often we are not even conscious of it developing until it reveals itself, sometimes as complete surprise, during moments of great ecstasy or despair, courage or cowardice, nobility or ignominy, and all other feelings that flesh is heir to. This is why we are admonished—"Know thyself."

We all know, however, that really knowing ourselves is about the toughest thing there is to know. This is why we are fascinated by reading about another's character—whether Mother Teresa, the Sainted Heroine; Abe Lincoln, the President; Tarzan the Ape Man; Marilyn Monroe, the Sex Goddess; or Nimrod, the Babylonian Hunter and Builder of Cities. Saints, sinners, celebrities, knaves, crooks, geniuses, actors, actresses, swindlers, tycoons, military heroes, and all sorts of characters written about on a daily basis in our nation's countless newspapers, periodicals, and books, or shown on countless television programs and movies—these all warrant our fascination.

We hope if we can understand someone else's character, we may find clues that help us to understand our own. Perhaps at no other time in history have there been so many people as in our modern mass societies, torn loose from their spiritual roots, seeking a sense of identity and purpose, looking for their own characters. This may be why so many popular psychology publications and audiovisual programs produce self-discovery entertainment.

We learn how difficult it is to unravel, clarify, and understand who and what we really are because it takes unsparing honesty and courage to do so, which themselves are a part of character. Paradoxically enough, it takes character to understand character. Maybe that's why it's so tough. Besides, all this takes time, if we are to do it seriously, and we are too busy with other, more immediate things. So, we often wind up with the ignorance of pleasant self-deceptions rather than knowledge of traumatic truths. This is why we have so many identity crises in adolescence, middle age, and old age. Just when we thought we knew who we really were, we weren't. So, we stumble to the next self or character we are searching for. Often, we remain mysteries to ourselves to the very end, although many others have known too much about us all along.

There are some catches when it comes to the study of hunting character which is unlike any other character study, except possibly that of matadors and soldiers. No other persons engage in such sustained, high-intensity action, repeatedly, with high degrees of risk involving life of one and intended death of the other in a two-way relationship. It is one thing for an accomplished author, who is also a shrewd judge of human nature, to write about some other hunter's character, and something else for a hunter to reveal his own character through his writings. For one thing, he may not want to, and for another, he may not know himself well enough to be accurate. Then, again, he may know himself so well he'd rather not let anyone else in on it.

There are first-rate writers who hunt, and first-rate hunters who write, but there is a difference in them, of course. Marshall, Ruark, and Hemingway are writers who hunt, and their writings have a large appreciative audience who would read them if they never wrote a word about hunting. Then, there are all sorts of hunters who write, and here a whole host of problems emerge which do not trouble the first group of writers as much or as often.

Most hunters who write a book or two of their experiences cannot or will not reveal their innermost feelings, emotions, sentiments, attitudes, and thoughts, or what I call the "soul of the hunter." To try ferreting these out may lead to little more than guessing by the reader. Results are all too often fantasies and projections of such a reader's own prejudices. Sometimes, these prejudices become downright vicious when the reader has an extreme hostility toward hunting or hunters for any number of reasons, and is searching for support of these reasons in what he reads, for he, too, is looking for something else.

Why do hunters not bare their souls? There are several reasons. The main reason is, a hunter is part of his culture like everyone else, and he, too, reflects the world view or basic assumptions his culture makes about the nature of the world. This view, or world appearance, is what older anthropologists and historians used to call a *Weltanschauung* if it is necessary to get technical. It's a German word, of course. Germans, like Greeks, have a word for everything.

Some cultures are fatalistic, and their view is that a distant God foreordained everything. "What is written, is written," and one submits to that all powerful fate, and there is nothing anyone can do about it. Other cultures are contemplative, believing desire is the ruination of man, and all that exists is merely illusion, so it is better to renounce everything in this world, including self, and wait to be absorbed into some great, collective spirituality in the next world and escape bondage from this unreal one.

Then, there are other cultures, like ours of the West. Our world view is that nature can be understood and bent to our will. We are not a withdrawn, contemplative people. The essence of our reality is action, and we believe that dynamic becoming, not static being, is the reality and only change is real. Change must lead to a better thing than that which was—so we are the first civilization that invented the idea of progress for better or worse. All this is, of course, terribly oversimplified but this is not the place for hair splitting. It is sufficient to make the point, which follows.

Again, why do hunters in our culture not bare their souls? Because, the big-game hunt by its very nature is packed with action in certain key moments, and the hunter must meet challenges which are often intense, dramatic, and even dangerous. He is motivated to win, or survive, in the objective world out there, not the subjective world in here. The reader continues to read because he wants to share vicariously in precisely the same action, drama, excitement, and adventure the hunter experienced; it's the next best thing to doing it yourself, if you could. The hunter who emphasizes subjective contemplations and does not emphasize objective happenings, loses his reader. Our vernacular automatically asks, "Hey, where's all the action around here?" The writer loses more. He loses his publisher, who needs a readership to stay in business. He's not into psychological counseling; there are others who do that better.

There is a paradox here. Why should the reader, who is fascinated with discovering his own character, want to read only about objective happenings to the hunter? Would it not be easier to read about some hunter whose subjective contemplations overtly and easily provide the obvious character lesson? The answer is no, for many reasons. First, the reader is not usually aware of what fascinates him—the search for his own character—and, in all probability, neither was the hunter for that matter.

Second, there are only a few authors who have revealed their souls, and then only in small glimpses here and there. Robert Ruark, Elgin Gates, and Peter Capstick come to mind. There were more of them in the 19th century—R. Gordon Cumming, William Baldwin, Paul Du Chaillu, and Jim Corbett for example—and their writings are hard to find, even in reprints. Hunting literature of the 20th century gives scant attention to character for other hunters to find much encouragement. This is another irony of our times—the more we really need character in every area of our deteriorating culture, the less we can find it.

To return to our question—why does the reader not deliberately seek out the hunter's character? Because, even if that character is spelled out, it is too private. The reader does not want ready-made answers clobbering him like a sledgehammer. He wants only clues to construct his own answers to fit his own private world of reality. Although he may not know factually what answer he has found, he will sense intuitively that it fits the puzzle of who he is when he has found it.

There is a last and paramount reason why a reader does not deliberately seek out a character study. While reader and writer share a common language, culture, symbols, meanings, desires, and understandings, there are limits to how much of this is transferable. Both minds do not meet at the same stages of their lives, or have an identical background, or the same experiences. A part of each of us is unique because our unique experiences make us that way—and this is the part that cannot be duplicated or synchronized. Our inner worlds of reality in which we live are ours alone. Since we can never know ourselves completely or with absolute certainty, there is an element of mystery about who and what we are.

It is this mysterious tendency that animates and vitalizes so much of what we do unconsciously, and puts us into contact with greater realities that work profound changes in us which we sense or feel without always knowing what or why. I call this spiritual, because it cannot be measured or quantified, but it is felt and perceived as something beyond us. Modern psychology avoids the word like the plague (it smacks too much of religion) and substitutes other names sounding less religious, even if more phantasmagoric and equally unmeasurable or unverifiable.

There is not a hunter worth his salt who does not feel awe, grandeur, and mystery of the wilderness and what it does to the innermost recesses of his soul, or who will not admit there is something spiritual about it, no matter what other words he uses. That's one of the unknown forces that keeps enticing him out there like a haunting melody whenever he talks about being one with nature, and so on. On occasion, we luck out when we read of an obvious novice on one of his first hunts who says with innocent candor, "It was like being in church," or "It was kind of religious," or "I found God out there," or "It felt so mysterious," and so on. On occasion, even seasoned veterans, like Robert Ruark, drop such hints of their beguilement, so blunter talk will not offend those who worship the created wilderness instead of the Creator above it. To look past the symbols which point to the ultimate and final reality would prove exactly what some psychologists and most atheists suspect—hunters suffer from paranoid delusions of grandeur or schizophrenic withdrawal from reality, and are very dangerous to themselves and to society.

Apart from these broad philosophical aspects of the problem, there are some practical considerations no less important. Sometimes a hunter does not write of subjective aspects of hunting because he cannot or will not. The hunter cannot easily get introspective or subjective about what a particular hunt did to him because he is not quite sure of all that happened in a few tense, action-jammed moments when man and animal confronted each other face to face, and a ton of spiritual TNT exploded in his soul and created an instant rebirth of character, or blasted his sense of humanity orbiting into outer space for a more belabored rebirth.

Forsooth, as it used to be said, it is difficult to recognize or respond to all happenings even when there are only firecrackers going off. This is not because the hunter is an ignoramus. It is because he must be highly selective to what he will respond and to what he will deliberately ignore, especially in moments of extreme pressure when everything is happening all at once. His actions are automatic and reflexive; the consequences to the wrong moves may be terminal. The prize at stake here is not a handful of nickels and dimes clinking out of a slot machine, but a magnificent trophy the price for which is life and death—either way. The prize can also be his life when a sudden natural exigency of the wilderness threatens him without a single animal present.

All sorts of things can be happening simultaneously around the hunter at the critical moment, yet his white-hot concentration on only the most pressing of these things arrests his attention. Even then, there is another factor—how well will he remember or recall these arresting details when the action is over and he sits to write? Levels of awareness, alertness, perception, and memory are highly variable among human beings. Obviously, a hunter may be able to reconstruct fairly accurately what else must have happened based on what he knows did happen. Of course, if there is a hunting companion along, he may make it easier to know or infer what else happened the hunter was not aware of.

The point is, if the hunter knows solid-sure what happened, then he can stand firmly on his story with a clear conscience no matter how he may be doubted or discredited—he knows what he knows and never mind the guffaws of the poltroon who has never hunted but knows all about it anyway—he thinks.

If the hunter restructures his thoughts on inference as logically and honestly as he can, he knows there might be an error that could have escaped his surety. If he cannot in good conscience swear to his version of the happenings and says so, he will not be given the benefit of the doubt. His detractors will have a donnybrook—then again they may, anyhow, no matter how many witnesses testify to the truth of the matter. In this day and age, the hunter's enemies (who are legion) are loaded for bear (if I may), and as an old country Armenian proverb will say about any one of them, "He is looking for a hair in the egg," which means, of course, he will find it no matter what.

Yet another condition in which a hunter may refuse to reveal what really happened, although he knows it beyond a shadow of a doubt—that is when his behavior was illegal, unethical, unworthy, unsportsmanlike, or otherwise thoroughly dastardly. He will have reason enough to conceal the reality of what he did, or didn't do—what happened or didn't happen. On the other hand, occasionally there are hunts where the hunter's honor is worthy of the *Croix de Guerre*, or any other medal of merit, and the trophy is simply a magnificent world record which ought to be written about, but the hunt was too routine, too uneventful.

The hunter who gets his world record moose or grizzly bear on the second day of the hunt in the field where he and his giant prize nearly walked into each other and a single shot dead-eye-dicked the animal without a twitch—that hunter knows the entire affair does not leave much to write about. The temptation to make a story out of it results in a padded and contrived account. It is better to leave the trophy unsung in prose than run the risk of fakery, no matter if the trophy turned out to be numero uno in every record book worldwide.

The intensity of passionate desire which leads to good or bad risk is always present and the closer one reaches the moment of confrontation, the more it influences the hunter, especially if he does not yet easily admit his limitations. This is compounded by another factor often overlooked—duration of the hunting season. It is not uncommon to have a season not much more than a couple months or even a couple weeks out of which the hunter may not have more than 10 days or so. A miss or a mishap now and it's a long, long wait until next year or 10 years from now depending on how much the rest of life gets in the way. What seems to him like a reasonable risk given these impositions of fate, may make him look like a madman or a braggart to the reader, so the most exciting parts of many a hunt are often omitted, or toned down to banality, with editorial finesse rather than risk being tagged with either label.

All these factors sketch the big picture, which explains why the hunter reluctantly bares his soul, or not at all. There is a secret buried in that soul. He knows he does not go into the wilderness to kill an animal for the sake of killing it, as every mother's misbegotten son or daughter of his critics contend. Killing is not the goal. It is only the means by which he can attain a symbol of paramount importance in his life—his search for the meaning of life. The trophy hunt is not some superficial, whimsical act of killing for the "fun" of it. It is a serious and profound event with great emotional and spiritual reasons at the very center of the hunter's life—of all human life, for that matter. All life is a search for symbols that give meaning, and to be human is to make that search, each in his own way.

On this point, let there be no callow or specious reasoning about the morality of this issue. In the last analysis, this is what the hunter-hater concocts, though normally he detests morality, to make his case—killing is killing and nothing justifies its cruelty, which is an offense to civilized society.

The critic is shooting a dead horse (if I may), since the avoidance of cruelty is one of the hunter's main objectives. The critic's unfounded charge makes him a defender of public morals, nevertheless, and here, he is either deliberately hypocritical or innocently contradictory. It may be politically incorrect, but I must reluctantly point out that such a critic is often the defender of abortion which, by any other name, is the murder of a helpless human baby by tearing it to pieces and ripping it out of its mother's womb. What are the critic's moral grounds for being self-righteous when he charges hunters with cruelty who kill an animal, often one with lethal competence, when a neatly placed bullet produces painless, instant, and merciful death? It turns out that killing is not killing after all, but it depends on who does it and why. Surely, a society which condones killing human babies but frowns on killing animals shows something irrationally wrong in its value system.

The hunter's quest for the trophy gives him the symbols for the larger meaning—what life is all about. To be human is to make that search, each in his own way. It is at once the blessing, and the curse, which separates man from other animals. Like any animal, man too must eat, but food is for the belly and symbols are food for the soul, and it is more difficult to be human without the latter than the former. Right here and now is where the spirit is involved, and the hunt is a spiritual quest through those symbols. Let the hunter breathe those mysterious words, spiritual quest, and the bugle blares the call for a spirited war on the hunter by precisely those who detest violence and do not believe in the spiritual.

There is one truth about the human being which holds anywhere at anytime—he is always looking for something, and most of the time that something is an ultimate of some kind—a symbolic treasure beyond compare, priceless, unique, and worth any ordeal to find it in the wasteland of human agony. Only a few succeed in finding it, and fewer still are satisfied when they do. This is enough to arouse resentment of those who also tried, but failed. Still, the search must go on.

In this day and age of mass democracy gone wild, the compulsion to equalize everything can only vulgarize anything. It reduces even the highest sanctity of anything to the lowest profanity of everything else. This perverted process of profanation, unfortunately, must be made into a public affair. If it were not, the sacred would remain inviolate. What is the secret whose revelation fills the hunter with dread? It is fear—not of man-killing animals, or the unexpected calamities of nature in the wilderness, or of Herculean effort ending in naught, but the chilling fear the wrong public will know who he really is sitting around his campfire. Outwardly, he may look like some Neanderthal caveman—coarse, unshaven, and grimy with wood smoke. Inwardly, however, the man turns out to have the soul of a nobleman in the finest sense of the word.

Noblesse oblige—nobility obligates. The hunter's allegiance is to higher powers that obligate him to the spirit of mercy and generosity with the world. That's why he is noble, for he gladly pays the price which, all too often, is exorbitant. Therefore, he demands little from this world and gladly allows it to make demands upon him, because it is in the nature of his spirit to give and not to grab; but when he wants something fairly, then there is no compromise—it must be the best, and there is precious little of that left anymore in a society that extols the commonplace.

Herein lies the agony. In a democracy like ours, which has legalized equality of opportunity for all, some become infuriated to discover that this does not guarantee equal results for any. The hunter sticks out like a sore thumb where there is no equality among thumbs—they are all different. The hunter has no objections to others who differ from him—they are entitled to their differences. Why, then, do others object to the hunter who is different from them and who is equally entitled to his differences? Because that which aspires to excellence always indicts that which is content with mediocrity. If one has something which the other wants but cannot have, then the one should not have it either; it is the only way envious resentment can get even.

Though the trophy hunter be a country bumpkin, he will be envied and resented because he is seen as an insulting alien in the noble pursuit of excellence in defiance of the vaunted average. The hunter does not see himself this way; he is not a snob. Why should he be? He is competing with nature, not fellow man. He is not opposed to the legitimate interests of others; others are opposed to his legitimate interests. He is seen as a snob by those who resent him because the worst form of discrimination is that of the anti-snob snob who looks down on everything.

The object of the trophy hunter is to pursue the quality of excellence. If the trophy does not go above the average, it is hardly a trophy, is it? That trophy must reflect the best the hunter could do in getting the best. Failing this, there is no trophy hunt worthy of the name.

There is another consideration which is more materialistic, but the hunter must take it into account. The total expenses involved in that hunt are sometimes enormous, but that is not all. Since the whole object of the hunt is the trophy, it must be mounted or there is no point in such a hunt—after all, the trophy is an irreplaceable symbol. There are no substitutes for it. No one else has, or can have, that specific trophy with its experiences surrounding it. It cannot be purchased anywhere. There is not enough money to buy it at any price. No one else can duplicate it. It has only one invisible signature on it, and it is signed with the hunter's name. That is what the trophy has in common with an art object in a museum master-piece. It is a work of art which belongs only to its owner and no amount of equal rights can lay claim to it. That's what infuriates every egalitarian from professional intellectual to professional prole-tarian. If anyone else wants one, he has no choice but to go out and earn one himself. That's where we separate the men from the boys.

Then, there's the rub. That trophy, to be completed, requires a taxidermist whose fees are usually almost as high as the cost of the hunt, and sometimes more. Now, comes another catch—the trophy room, which can be a real problem since it is, after all, a limited space, and it cannot be used up by mediocre specimens of a routine effort when the objective was achievement of the highest order. The trophy room is the hunter's pantheon; it will accept only the best, finest, most revered—in a word, the ultimate.

The hunter engages in some of the most private, personal, and intimate experiences in the wilderness, and they are all his—no one else can claim them or rob him of them. He, alone, can recall them from deep pools of memory years later, when there is little time left to collect memories anymore. That wilderness gives him the adventures and the oneness with the mystery of all being, including his own. It is his escape, his temporary flight from the most agonizing debilities which life pours on the human spirit—boredom, tedium, the lack of engagement.

It is these which lead to the human wasteland of agony and futility. But, what is boredom except living the while which lacks worth, and the moment we discover that, we devise anything worth-the-while—some good, some bad—so life can continue before we give up on it in despair. For the hunter, it is the wilderness which gives him the brief search for reality. It is better than the constant mirage of life in the humdrum of everyday existence in the concrete and steel jungles of downtown, which man has built as a memorial to his folly. This is modern man's pantheon, and who is to say he is not entitled to it?

The hunter finds his real wilderness more honest, more honorable with its stark realities of foreboding, terror, grandeur, majesty, and mystery. Somewhere between breathtaking vistas and somewhere between silent adorations, his awe of all creation before him becomes humble discovery and worship of the Creator who made all this magnificence, then made him, too, and found him worthy to be placed in the middle of it. It is then that infinite mystery enfolds the being of the hunter's ephemeral reality. It is then that man, the hunter, knows the stirrings of his spirit returning him to his roots for a few moments. That is when he drinks deeply of the elixir of life, revitalizing himself for the journey back to more oppressive time where things less near to his heart's desire must be endured. One way or another, we all do this. We all return to some beginning for a fresh start. Some have a little more style, a little more class in bringing it off, that's all.

Here lies a subtle reality that the hunter's critic responds to with unconscious contempt. He feels that when the hunter prefers the wilderness, that choice rejects the artificial values of urbanism to which the critic is committed and, therefore, it is a rejection of the critic as a person. He doesn't see the modern trophy hunter is also a part of urban artificiality. The difference is the urban sophisticate, devoted to life of the metropolis, does not renounce it when bored. He immerses himself deeper into variations of the same old theme and only becomes bored in different ways. He would not know what to do in the wilderness, or how to do it even if he chose to go there. It is the hunter who makes the radical break and becomes, without wanting to, the symbol of envy and difference. Different is strange, which in people, makes them strangers. And the stranger, all too often is perceived as danger.

The end for which the hunter hunts is all remembered, it all comes to life again, in a fleeting glance at that trophy on the pantheon's wall, for it is a symbol which, like all symbols, refers to something else; and that something else is the symbolic treasures locked in the soul of the hunter which that trophy made possible with the gift of its life. That is why it lives, why it never dies, in the eyes of those who understand and behold it with respect and reverence, awe and gratitude. How else can one find his way back to the spirit except by visible symbols which, in this case, are the wilderness icons lighting the way from whence he came? The hunter is only a voyager of the spirit searching for some ultimate and final radiance in the darkness of this world.

An entire volume can be written on the mystique of hunting and the soul of the hunter who pursues it, but this introduction can give no more than the few hints it already has. It is easy to forget hunting is older than the first man millions of years ago, and, in all probability, our apelike ancestors may never have crossed the sapient threshold without the hunter, and hunting has existed since then without interruption. When it no longer became essential as a method of obtaining food with the emergence of the first agrarian civilizations, it became ritualized as an art, or what we today call a sport, and has remained that way for thousands of years.

There is no older and more continuous tradition than this, and the modern hunter is, therefore, its defender and symbol of this continuity. Both he and tradition have subtle interconnection with nearly every major institution on which our society rests. There are those who hold our society and its Western cultural basis in contempt, seeking its destruction. This is why the hunter is seen as another traditional obstacle to the revolutionary New World Order of the utopians—as the danger to be destroyed.

Monarch Of The Polar Ice

**P**olar bear! What fascination there is in seeing those two words. What magic in the sound of those three syllables! Instantly, word and sound project a spectral image—a floating, weaving, ghostly form, moving eternally through limit less desolation of polar ice—invincible, grand, and awesome in power and beauty. There isn't a true hunter anywhere who has not confronted polar bear in his secret fantasy world and yearned to see that dream become a reality.

The dream and aching yearn for that reality had been a part of me since I first learned to read. It was an ultimate symbol giving my restless imagination no rest until it became real. It was my North Star giving me bearings to fantasied treasure when harshness and futility of life misled me to the wrong path. There were dreams worth living for, and that compass point never failed to beckon me toward the horizon where it shone over treasure I could not see. There were those with different dreams who laughed at mine, but that didn't matter. What mattered was that all of us needed some dream to lure us on or we would give up too easily on life when it became a nightmare. I was even willing to tolerate the foes of hunting their dreams and let fate decide who had the better one.

Repeatedly, I felt with growing anxiety the vast distance between dream and reality moving further apart with each passing year, as life taunted me with one obstacle after another. When determination wavered, my dream grew more intense. Circumstance, my constant enemy, suddenly became my instant friend when it unexpectedly changed in the twinkling of an eye. Surprise stunned me for several moments before my benumbed state realized it could be done. It all came about by another miracle. There is a prologue to that miracle worth relating, because I got to the polar bear by way of a mountain goat that started the chain of events.

The Fairbanks newspaper carried an ad by an Anchorage pilot who was flying hunters in for mountain goat. Mountain goat continues to be the most underrated trophy in Alaska. Horns of *Oreamnos americanus americanus* were great prizes, but if one went into Alaska's mountains, one would go for Dall sheep instead, because its horns are more spectacular, making the hunt for sheep more popular.

There was one more factor, but it made little difference. The law still allowed hunting on the same day the plane landed. Goats inhabited such precipitous topography, it was often more difficult to reach them than sheep, and when hit, a goat was more apt to fall into inaccessible places, making its retrieval a good bet for suicide. The bet for sheep was just a hair less suicidal. This digression is necessary to show how I met the pilot who was to become my guide for *Thalarctos maritimus*—polar bear—alias ultimate verification for life that still vibrated.

I got George, self-advertised pilot for mountain goat, on the phone, nailed the deal instantly, and met him in Anchorage. As I had intuited, he turned out to be the salt of the earth, the very stuff of which the story-book noble Alaskan is made, and they don't make them like George, anymore. He was not only a superb pilot, but a decent, honest human being. He was a top-notch guide when he didn't have to be, since our agreement was, he'd let me off to my own devices and pick me up later.

But he decided to guide and set a blistering pace up a 2,000-foot mountain side with its breath-vacuuming air currents. By the time we reached the location of the two locomotive-sized billies, they had grazed their way down the other, steeper side. Even if we got them lower down, we'd never be able to climb back up again.

Disappointed, we returned to the plane in late afternoon.

George found another likely spot, landed, and headed toward timber. I followed, and when he pointed to the skyline along the mountain range, with its rock face reflecting the roseate glow of setting sun, I saw the critter more than 1,000 feet up, rapidly walking on the rim. It was sharply silhouetted against the pink sky. I guessed a spot in the sky above his heart, led him by several hair breadths and squeezed the trigger on my Winchester .308. The billy jackknifed into a sideways dive and plunged down a couple hundred feet, bounced high off a crag and plummeted down the rest of the way, landing onto loose shale and rolled almost within 100 feet of us! It was one of the most spectacular sights I'd seen on any hunt. We rushed to him and George groaned with dismay and I did, too. The goat's horns had popped off somewhere when he had landed.

I am not embarrassed to repeat what George said. "Now ain't that a goldarned crime? That was one of the greatest shots I've ever seen, and look where you hit him—right in the pump (he poked his finger into the blood-trickling hole), but you don't have a trophy because there are no horns, goldarn it! And the sun's goin' down too fast. There's no time to hunt for a needle in the haystack, now."

We didn't have time to skin the goat, so George motioned me to help him pick up the carcass and get it to the airplane. I balked. "Aw, please, George, just 2 minutes," I begged and, before he could answer, crawled up the shale a bit, stood up, and my eyes frantically searched the uneven surface of shale rubble and stones. My heart nearly broke with such a cursed stroke of fate. Without those horns, the head could not be mounted. Had I killed a beautiful animal only to waste it because of an uncanny accident beyond my control? It seemed hopeless, scanning that ocean of rounded stones choking larger shale chunks scattered among them.

I had asked for 2 minutes and now knew it would take 2 weeks. Then I barely saw a small black oval shape standing out in the sea of dull gray rubble that didn't belong there. It was about 50 feet away, and it could be anything. I charged to it in desperation. It was my treasured horn! A rapid survey in the vicinity a little higher and the other one turned up, too! They were better than average, just missing record-book size. It was the luckiest find in the shortest time-span of my life.

I leaped down, war-whooping with Comanche abandon all the way, jammed the horns back onto the stubs of the goat's head for a quick picture that George took, and we hustled to the plane, a half mile down on the beach. All the time, George kept saying, "You've got eyes like an eagle! You've got eyes like an eagle!"

I had to respond with the truth. "No, George," I said, "I've got the luck of the Irish." Indeed, finding those horns was either pure luck or a miracle, but my elation was that I had not wasted that animal, after all.

While we waited at the Anchorage air terminal for my flight home, we sipped coffee and made small talk. George kept saying, "What a shot that was, what a shot—and I still can't believe you found those horns."

"George, it was pure luck on both counts," I insisted, knowing how badly I've shot on other occasions. That was the context in which the miracle occurred. Out of a clear blue sky, George asked, "How would you like to hunt polar bear?"

There are moments in life when one's breath stops halfway in or out, the objects all around become hazy and far away, and one feels dazed, ready to hit the deck. It was such a moment for me, and I sat stunned and speechless for a change. George saw my glazed stare and said he guided for polar bear, his bookings were full for the coming season, but he would take me on his preliminary reconnaissance flights before the big-money Nimrods showed up. When I asked him, very cautiously, how much it would cost me, he quoted half the usual price, which in the 1960s was nearly $3,000; an awful lot of money back then, and still is today.

I juggled some figures in my head for a few moments, thanked him very much for the offer, more than generous, and refused because of an emergency financial priority that was par for my course. "Pay me whatever you can monthly," he said.

Another wave of suffocation swept over me. "This way," George said, "it will help cut my gasoline expenses for all the looking around I have to do for other clients and give you a break at the same time."

It was too good to be true. There had to be 10,000 guys waiting in line for such a deal, so why me? I was indelicate enough to ask! He told me he needed a good pair of eyes in the back seat as a look out, and then made some complimentary remarks about the kind of hunter he thought I was, and would be too immodest even for me to repeat here. All I know is George gifted me a great kindness I could never really repay. He was a kind, generous, and decent man. Still, I had some doubts when I got home.

Airplanes for hunting polar bear? It sounded like a mechanically blundering way to wreck a dream of adventure on polar ice. I preferred the romance of dog-sleds and natives—it seemed more primal, more in the spirit of human strife against elemental things. I had heard some natives offered dog-sled hunts more to my liking, but one needed a month for hunting from a dog sled, and much more money because there were few natives offering this service. Besides, dog-teams could not work much beyond a 20-mile radius from a village site—more than that created logistics problems when risk of violent weather changes forced a hasty retreat to the safety of a village. This limited radius meant coastal travel, sighting fewer bears, smaller in size, and reportedly of a more yellowish coloration according to the popular folklore. Still, I would have preferred that, I think, for the sheer adventure of it.

On the other hand, the plane could cover a 200-mile hunting radius over polar ice on the Bering Sea, way out where bears were bigger, of a whiter color, and more highly prized; at least that was the expert scuttlebutt. The real clincher, however, was the much cheaper price, although I couldn't afford that either, but that's why 99 out of 100 polar bear hunts were done by plane instead of dog-team.

Like the walrus hunt, where engine-powered craft could not be avoided, so, too, in polar bear hunting, airplanes couldn't be avoided—for all practical purposes. I didn't think I could ever afford a dog-sled hunt, or even an airplane hunt, for that matter. But here was George giving me the affordable break of a lifetime, and it was not the moment to ponder imponderables.

George called me to say it was green lights all the way if I wanted to go, but would understand if I didn't. How could he understand my not wanting to go? Rather than risk losing the chance, I heard myself saying, "Damn the torpedoes, full speed ahead," and grabbed on for dear life. And that's how a poor immigrant's boy, growing up in the Great Depression with dreams of Nanook of the North, had fortune smile on him in adulthood. The rest was up to me.

From Nome, I flew to the native village of Teller. Teller was solid-socked with ice and snow, although it was late March. George, bless his soul, met me at the landing strip running alongside the cemetery with its tilting wooden crosses jutting through the snow. Judging from the way the plane landed, the cemetery's location was convenient.

George's command post was a small, rented house also doubling for a hotel and Las Vegas casino. There were 10 hunters in the village, each with his pilot and copilot. While all of them were waiting for the right weather conditions to float around, everyone visited every one else to kill time. That's why George's place looked like a misplaced Mardi Gras when I walked in.

In a room 15 by 15 feet, the air was viscous with blue tobacco smoke. Static-riddled music loudly gurgled out of a radio. At least four cliques were formed shoulder to shoulder, drinking, playing cards, or yelling with louder gurgles than the radio to hear each other. I squeezed into a corner, sat on a sagging couch that was to be my bed, took coffee offered by a shy, good-looking blond, and started reading Haggard's *Alan Quartermain* for the tenth time, which I never seemed to finish.

Sometime later, the return of the shy blond was accompanied by a sullen looking man, behind whom was George. Somehow they squeezed through the human mass surrounding me. George introduced me to the man and woman. They shall be named Jim and Jane for this story. It turned out Jim was to be our copilot for the hunt. There was something about his looks that set me on edge. Jane was his dearly beloved. Jim didn't stay too long, wisely retreating from my suspicious glare, and George followed him with accommodation. Jane stayed for a chat, obviously why they had brought her to me. She was point-man, shyness notwithstanding.

Hesitantly, she told me her story. She had survived the terrible ordeal of a divorce, but she and Jim were serious about each other and their relationship was perfectly honorable since they intended to marry soon. She said she knew I would understand. Why is she telling me all this, I wondered?

I assumed the clinical mode with Jane and at long intervals I staged the profound psychoanalytical strategy of muttering, "Ah, I see," or just plain, "Ahh-hhh-h," or more mysterious and profoundly, "Hummm," until she got to the underlying motive. Since the only other room (actually cubicle) in the house was George's bedroom, there was no where else she and Jim could sleep, except on the floor right between my couch and the kitchen table, just an arm's length away. All the while I had thought, erroneously, they had domicile at the far end of the village. Now I found out they would be sleeping right below me, where even proper breathing could sound like Bacchus and Bacchante gone ape.

Assuring me she and Jim were proper people, she hoped the arrangement would not embarrass me. I was indelicate enough to tell her bluntly, that it did. After all, I had never slept in a room with a man and woman—strangers at that. I instantly regretted my tactless retort, and assured her it was okay, given the situation. No matter how things may have seemed, she was a woman and deserved respect. After all, she didn't have to give her explanation. My reassurance gave her a boost of morale and, somewhere in the small talk, she let a cat out of the bag. When my hunt was over, Jim was taking her on her hunt for a polar bear. It was his pre-nuptial gift to her.

Jim's sullen behavior now had a plausible explanation. I was in the way, and the sooner my hunt was over, the sooner the torrid romance would go on without the chilling effect of my presence, and before the arrival of the next client, right around the corner. Flying his own plane as George's copilot, there were a couple ways Jim could speed up the hunt and still make it successful and still legal, but against my sense of fair play. Jane must have realized my preoccupation with other thoughts as my responses grew less and less frequent, and soon she went to join Jim, leaving me to my concerns—not about sleeping arrangements (after all, they did have separate sleeping bags), but about the possibility this dream hunt of mine at a moment's notice could explode into a fight to the finish between Jim and me. If he didn't see the implications, I certainly did, and it could spoil the entire hunt for me, so something had to be done, fast.

I caught George's eye, pointed to my rifle and the outdoors and he waved assent. We donned our parkas and stepped out into the frozen wannigan, lighted the kerosene lamp, and found a safe place to prop my rifle.

I had already cleaned all lubricants from it to prevent their freezing. The metallic temperature had to be acclimatized with the outdoors overnight, otherwise all kinds of mechanical troubles could occur if the rifle had to be used during abrupt temperature changes. This was the proper time and place to collar George about my problem.

"What's with this copilot of yours and his future bride?" I asked. "I'm sorry about that," George said, "but my regular pilot is in the hospital. Busted leg. Snow machine accident. I was lucky to get Jim at the last minute, or I'd have lost my entire season's earnings. There's no one else around I could find."

Then he threw up his hands and said, "Goldarn it, how did I know he'd bring his girl with him? I'm sorry if she's bugging you."

"I can live with that," I said, "but I'm afraid Jim may try to hurry this hunt with hotshot shenanigans, and we have a previous agreement."

"I gave you my word," George said, "and I'll guarantee it will go as we agreed. I've already told him all about it. Don't worry."

I heaved a sigh of relief and returned to my reading.

Shortly after midnight, visitors finally turned into pumpkins and went home one by one. We turned in. I couldn't sleep, tired as I was, because the problem which stressed me went around and around in the couple million miles of association fibers in my brain.

I never bothered about hunting ethics in the beginning of my hunting career, largely because I didn't know such a thing existed except for a few vague references. Moral subtleties are not for youth who do everything without second thoughts. Besides, to have hunted, one must kill his animal, and killing is killing, isn't it? So, what's the problem?

At the start of my hunting career I had innocently and stupidly committed my own breach of hunting ethic, fair chase, and sportsman's code on three occasions (go ahead, antihunters— gloat) until retrospectively, the moral problems cried out for resolution. I studied philosophical aspects of the hunting ethic, refined it with my own experiences, established my own answers, where literature was inadequate, and hunted with a clear conscience, thereafter. I never made those early mistakes again, once I figured out why sport hunting was different from all the rest. That's how and why I became a fanatic about the ethic. To violate it out of ignorance is one thing. To violate it intentionally is something else.

When I'm caught in argument with antihunting fanatics whose logical critique of the art boils down to their own prejudices and they grow wild with anger, I am not only amused, I can actually hug the dumdums out of sheer gratitude. Their fallacious reasoning and accusations are what forced me to seriously consider the whole ethical problem in the first place. I owe them for my understanding of a problem they have never understood. I knew what they would say about polar bear hunting. Odd, wasn't it, the very presence of any copilot, without whom the hunt was legally impossible, also became the very grounds on which the hunt could be made unethical, playing right into the hands of the enemy?

Rumors abounded that unscrupulous pilots chased polar bear, flying low over them, pushing them into exhaustion and collapse, then landed and the poor helpless animal was heroically "hunted" by the millionaire sportsman, who just stepped out of the plane and blasted away with a high-powered rifle. No one I knew, who repeated such tales, could identify such a hunter or guide, nor did I ever read of an authenticated case, but it would be foolish to believe it couldn't be done.

The very situation invited the possibility. A hunter after polar bear has spent a small fortune, and the guide is under enormous pressure to produce. Moreover, a few pilots and hunters are all by themselves in hundreds, even thousands, of square miles of very dangerous, frozen surface on the polar icecap. Who else will be there to see them? An occasional law enforcement official may show up in the village for a nominal check with no way of proving what really happened out there. It would cost a fortune to cover the necessary territory for a chance sighting. Besides, everyone in the village knows he's present, and there are no hideouts or stakeouts possible on the ice cap.

The problem was the copilot—any copilot who was required to be there by law. It was a good law, though it made the hunt twice as expensive. There had to be two planes in case anything happened to the one that landed with the hunter. The greatest and very real danger was in landing and taking off on the icecap. No one could be sure if that ice layer would remain stable under impacted weight at that time of year. If anything happened to the plane carrying guide and hunter, it was the copilot's job to effect a rescue if possible, or pinpoint the location, and go for help on the double if those below had survived. That was the good part of his being aloft to watch the proceedings at critical moments. The bad part was, being aloft, he could herd the bear to the hunter if both were unscrupulous. That worried me.

I had told George at the outset, with no punches pulled, that absolutely under no conditions, should any copilot hassle, herd, or interfere in any way with my bear, although the law allowed it at the time. I didn't care about the law as much as I did about the ethics of fair chase. The plane had to stay away from the encounter. This was between my bear and me and if I lost him, so be it. I was paying for it. I knew George had relayed my message and that was the point of umbrage. Jim resented such a crazy demand by an upstart polar bear hunter, and, frankly, I couldn't blame him. However, that's the way it had to be. We understood each other. I knew George would see it through.

We were ready for the hunt, but the weather was not ready for us. For 5 days and nights it stormed and winds howled from the bowels of hell as they passed over Teller. Each day, hunters and natives came to visit and kill time with monotonous regularity. Irritation gradient climbed visibly like the mercury column in a thermometer. We awakened each morning to whines and howls of that infernal radio with George hovering over it like a protective mother, turning knobs and dials trying to eliminate screeches and wails for weather reports.

If winds on the polar ice were calm enough, the temperature was 50° below zero, Fahrenheit, or lower. If the temperature shot up to a warm 20° below zero, the winds reached 50 knots or more. Temperature and winds shifted constantly. The right combination of both were crucial to avoid chill factors of 70° below zero or lower—where only the polar bear could survive—not men or machines.

When George concluded there would be no hunting that day, there was nothing to do but kill time, and at last I finally finished *Alan Quatermain*. Then I visited other houses trying to find a trade-off for it, and settled on a detective mystery, the kind where you correctly guessed who did it in the first chapter. The high expectation for each tomorrow grew to boredom by evening, and it was having its effect on all of us, but that was polar bear hunting.

On the 6th morning, I cautiously peeped out of my sleeping bag. My neighbors downstairs were still in deep slumber. I squinted at George. I'll be goldarned if he wasn't grinning widely, twisting and turning the radio knobs to hold the communique on steady course.

Finally, he said, "Guess what? Maybe we hunt today." In fact, he had the plane's engine oil warming up on the stove.

I can't believe it, I thought, going mad with utter delight.

We ate a hearty breakfast—no telling when we'd be able to eat lunch. Then we began to haul our gear to the plane. On my second trip with an armful of things, it became obvious to me something was wrong. George and Jim were huddled together, looking at something. Jim's plane had blown a nose cone seal.

What grief! It was better here, however, than in midair.

Better luck held out when George found a spare one among a barrel full of parts in the wannigan. A couple of heavy tarps reaching ground level from over the plane's cowl and a couple of primus stoves inside the improvised hangar warmed flesh and metal enough to work. I handed tools, mostly, and some hours later, cramped and frozen in our makeshift workshop, the boys had the trouble fixed. But now it was too late to go hunting. We hauled back the stuff we had hauled out. Our frustration was more intense than ever. The batch of constant visitors streaming in and out showed the same look of worn out fedupness.

The next day brought blessed good luck. Wind and temperature were just right. We quickly ate, loaded our gear and got aloft as soon as the engine warmed up. Fifteen minutes out of Teller my eye caught it—polar bear, far below, ambling along! It was my first sighting of the animal in his native habitat. The little boy in me would have cried with joy at that gorgeous sight if my spine-tingling sense of awe had not interfered. It did seem odd, though, to find him so close to Teller.

I leaned over and shouted, "Do bear come this close, often?"

George shouted back, "Naw, never happen. We gotta go a long way yet—be patient."

It was a nasty thing to do, but I poked my finger into his shoulder and then downward at the right wing. George jerked his head twice in a quick double-take, banked, and zoomed lower.

"Goldarn," he shouted, "It's a bear! Never seen one this close in before."

I thought it was a good omen and felt good about spotting it first. Maybe George's faith in my eagle eyes justified his taking me along.

By this time, my whole being was totally enthralled by that magnificent animal, but George dismissed him, saying it was only an average 8-foot bear. Although we stayed high enough, the little guy's curiosity got the better of him. He would look up every so often as he ambled along, and then finally stopped, pawed the air, gave us a piece of his mind, and took off, lickety-split.

He was headed right toward an open lead of ice. From our elevation, we could see it long before he could. When he finally saw it coming, his front legs stiffened, and his momentum threw him into a skid, spraying slush and snow in a trail. The spray trail looked a mile long and like it was chasing after him full bore. He must have had good power brakes because he screeched to a halt just in time at the edge of water. Nothing short of a silent Keystone Cops movie could have had such a comic reveling in sheer exuberance. I laughed uproariously finally dispelling the anguish of the preceding 6 days. We left him behind still gawking upward at us between stops.

Sometime later, George shouted and pointed ahead. I recognized them a moment before he said, "The Big and Little Diomedes." From our angle, they looked exactly like the shapes on maps and charts. The exotic names suddenly took on a new meaning for me. These were real, not just shapes on a map. Between them ran the imaginary International Boundary Line separating our country and the U.S.S.R. I suddenly realized, as never before, how close Alaska was to the Soviets, and wondered if the rest of the United States knew we were still united. My mind returned to more important things. I knew we were approaching real polar bear country at last.

Topography below was something else, even breathtaking. It looked like The Giant had swept from heaven, in an angry moment, a trillion pieces from an infinite, frozen jigsaw puzzle right off a cosmic table, dumping them right below us in a kaleidoscopic jumble of color and form.

Open leads flashed steely-blue looking like canals gone berserk. Ice pressure-ridges tumbled into countless slashing splinters following open leads of newly fractured ice, with flat, thick sheets randomly tossed between. Stark coloration of a thousand shades of blue and white spelled out only one message—nothing could survive on the surface—except polar bear, mighty monarch of the North, lord and emperor of all domain and territories he surveyed.

We began to see tracks even from our altitude, so clear was the air. If the imprints were dark, we knew they were freshly made, the indentation swallowed in shadow surrounded by higher, whiter snow. If shadows framed a light-colored imprint, we knew they were old, the compacted track resisting the angry sweep of howling winds that eroded surrounding snow covered by the shadow of pedestaled tracks.

Sometimes, there would be two or three sets of tracks crisscrossing each other. We would follow them. Often they stopped at the edge of a fresh lead where wind and pressure had fragmented huge sheets of ice into floating islands. George would circle wider and wider until tracks appeared on another leading edge. We then knew where the bear had been before wind and pressure had pushed things around after his passing, or where he had landed after swimming a lead.

In a short span of time we saw four sows, each with a cub or two. It was fascinating to watch the little guys meandering around. When they suddenly realized that mamma bear had kept going, the little ones would hustle, roly-poly, to catch up. On a couple occasions, mamma bears looked back at their tardy, errant off-spring, walked over and cuffed them sharply. Obviously, these were not permissive mammas who would tolerate children doing their own thing in the name of "creative self-expression'.

We had been following a set of large tracks so intently, we were surprised at a long shelf of land suddenly looming ahead of us. George estimated it to be less than 10 miles off. Reluctantly, we gave up the pursuit of our tracks. That was Soviet territory up ahead. Since we were so close to that mound of land they call Siberia, we wondered if MIGs really were stashed away with Soviet pilots ready to give chase.

We turned around, headed for home. It was getting late and a long way back. I was enthralled with the gold, orange, yellow, red, and pink colors the waning sun splashed across the sky. Where they spilled onto the horizon, they glistened on the gray, unending sheet of ice that was the lid on the polar seas beneath. It was another masterpiece of art, inseparable from vistas and souls of all who hunt and are hunted. It was deep dusk, nearly dark, when twinkling lights of the village appeared straight ahead. What a welcome sight as we approached for a landing on the icy strip next to the tilting, wooden-slat crosses of the native cemetery.

All things seemed to end here. It was a day I had spent in fantasia, a world of sheer magic, awesome and dangerously beau-tiful, images beyond imagination. Nothing can ever make me forget it. I thought I had witnessed the first primal scene before God put man on earth.

Now our appetites were whetted, bad weather the following day was especially distressing. The vigil began again. Two days later, we got our second break in weather and took off with high hopes. This time there was no roundabout scouting and exploring. We headed straight for the Diomedes and beyond, somewhere over the ice atop the Bering Sea—with the Chukchi Sea beyond. It was going to be a long, hard day of hunting. I had seen Jim's plane twice on the first flight. Now, I had not seen him at all. If he was staying that far away we must be getting into real bear country. George confirmed my guess and urged me to stay lookout sharp. I did, and in less than 2 minutes we each saw two lone boars within moments of each other. They were not big enough. Hopefully, they'd grow to full magnificence and fight old age to the end. Five sows, with their cubs in tow, seemed to be wandering all over the place. Had we finally found polar bear stomping grounds?

It was very cold in the plane. The heater up front was anemic at best in this weather. There was a skinny, Jerry-rigged hose pipe, bringing engine heat to the rear of the plane. Despite my heavy footwear, my toes were numb enough with cold to require frequent adjustment of the free end of the hose first under one foot, then the other.

We began to see snow cones, actually more ice than snow, surrounding blow holes formed by seals coming up for air. They'd gulp lungs full, then dive under the ice again searching for food. In turn, they became food for polar bear waiting for them the moment they shoved their heads into view.

We searched for some time before George circled the plane and dropped slightly to make sure of what we were seeing. There was no mistaking it. Curled lazily around a snow cone, there was our bear patiently waiting for a head to appear, announcing dinner would follow immediately. We didn't get too low and risk startling him, but the look was good enough to tell us he was a beauty! He had spirit, too, since he finally got irritated at the drone of the plane, stood up and looked us over, circled the blow hole a few times, loped back and forth as though he wasn't going to leave, and then decided to shake us.

He took off in an easygoing amble, arrogantly indifferent to the world around and above him. We climbed higher so not to distract him from his flight pattern. Far ahead, we could see the open lead he must inevitably reach if he stayed on course. We had to get far ahead of him for interception.

We spotted a flat expanse of ice, just large enough for a landing. It was next to the open lead along which the bear should be taking his stroll, if we were lucky. George circled the ice pan a few times and very gently put us down. We tumbled out and pushed the plane up against a ridge of pressure ice to conceal it from a chance sighting by the bear, but more to protect it from sudden gusting winds. There was no time for elaborate anchoring. We checked to make sure our cameras were still warm inside our parkas, checked bolt action on the rifles, and hurried toward the open lead.

It was my first time on polar ice and the sensation was immediate. There had been a lifetime dreaming of this, but now it was here, all the reading I'd done had hardly prepared me for it. It was a feeling of total desolation and a sense that no human being really belonged here except the Eskimo. Soon, he would not belong here, either, as his experiment with modern democracy destroyed his priceless heritage and natural equality. Right now, in a sudden emergency, he would know what to do. I didn't.

I thought of what could go wrong with George and me and it had nothing to do with enraged polar bears. A storm from nowhere with 100 knot winds, a fall through a sudden, splintering crack of rotten ice into freezing water, another blown nose cone seal, a leaky engine oil line, inability to get lift-off from that barely adequate ice floe, and a hundred other things could go wrong—and it was all over. Names and images flashed through my mind: Peary, Nansen, Kane, Franklin, Amundsen, Scott, Byrd, Shackleton, and all those who fought ice and cold at either pole. Did they feel what I felt? How insignificant life was in this foreboding vastness of frozen desolation, disrupted only occasionally by life itself. My family and friends would know if something happened to me. Jim would tell them.

Jim? Where was he? I looked up and around but could see or hear nothing. Suddenly, I wanted a hundred Jims to be around flying overhead to remind me there was another world I had run away from. A world that wanted me, which I needed, and which I disliked. Unconsciously, I had been fumbling a fourth cartridge into the chamber while hurrying along with George ahead of me.

I shook thoughts loose out of my head about the possibility of instantaneous, unexpected, unwanted death. It enhanced my profound gratitude for the duration of life, minute by minute, which was still mine. I hurried my pace to catch up to George, who was as unconcerned about all this as the bears themselves. He'd been through it a hundred times.

We reached a barricade of pressure ridge ice—a gigantic tumble of huge slabs and chunks, lifted off the ocean's surface by wind and wave when there was no room for expansion. They rammed into each other, creaking and groaning, forming a chaos of crushed, frozen labyrinths.

The wall towered over us by some 8 or 10 feet. If I could climb it, I'd have all kinds of view, but there was a good chance that constant gusts of wind, blowing erratically, would diffuse my scent all over the visible world from atop that icy perch. George thought so too and signaled me to stay low, afraid wind could carry our voices for miles.

Directly in front of us, below a rampart of ice, was a low, lopsided, diamond-shaped opening formed by huge slabs of ice, 2 to 4 feet thick. They had been rammed together so their tips, leaning against each other, formed the rough diamond-shaped opening, on top of which was piled tons of icy slabs and blocks. The opening before us tunneled into a peep hole that allowed a good view straight ahead. In effect, this created a long, crooked A with the pressure ridge on the left of us, the open lead on the right, the diamond in front where the cross bar of the A should be, the peep hole at the apex of the A, and the diagonal sides going to the back of us, boxing us in.

I did not like the set up, frankly, and shook my head negatively at George, pointed to the sides of the pressure ridge slabs hemming us into a kind of corral, and drew a square in the air with my mittened hands and then pointed to him and me. I felt just a touch of claustrophobia.

Now, it was George's turn for pantomime. He shook his head negatively, shrugged his shoulders in a sign of futility, pointed to his sleeve covering his wristwatch, and waved his hand toward us in a rapid, chopping motion. I got the message before he drew his hand across his throat as a final gesture. Well, he knew time, distance, terrain, and polar bear habits better than I, so there was nothing to do but agree, yes, the bear was closer than I thought, and we simply had no time for fancy scouting around to find a better location.

Crouching before that opening, no more than 4 feet high at its apex, I knew I'd see *Thalarctos* all the way if he came straight on. The open lead glinted a steely-blue ribbon, only a part of which I could see. The ridge to the left was visible for a good bit longer. I was now satisfied that he had two avenues of escape, and I'd never get a shot if he got into either one. I could only hope he would come straight on. If something went wrong and he chose fight over flight, coming over the top of my diamond, we were virtually boxed in and there was no place he, George, or I could go, except backward for us and forward for him. He could be on me before my backup, who was not far enough back, could shoot fast enough to protect himself, never mind me—or reverse order, making me George's backup. All I could do now was play cat and mouse or polar bear and snow-coned seal.

No sooner had I surveyed all this, crouched, and taken my position, than I became aware of another world of sheer fantasy inside the opening of that diamond entrance. The inside surface of those slabs glistened with light, giving them an eerie, luminescent glow of yellow-green blending into a light and dark blue like some giant gem refracting cold, polar light. It formed an ethereal outline that would frame the bear right in the center. It was a stupendous, mind-boggling display of nature's art from which hunting can never be separated. It is always there, but the soul of the hunter rarely responds to it under the pressure of concentrated pursuit.

George was standing up beside me, but he stooped down, periodically, to squeeze next to me and see what was happening ahead. Without movement to keep blood going, we were freezing again, although it couldn't have been more than 30° below zero.

It was an agony of suspense. Would Nanook come toward us or not? Had he crossed the pressure ridge to our left far ahead of us, or even swam the open lead across to the other side, unseen?

I was looking through my scope, turned high, straight ahead, straining my alleged eagle eye, and could see nothing but pure air, with nothing else in it for several minutes, and in the next ten-thousandth of second, he materialized out of pure, thin air. He was coming right into the center of the glowing, icy frame. The effect was electrifying. It was mind boggling. It must have short-circuited all neuronal connections in my brain at once. The scene was a bigger-than-life painting suddenly come to life. I felt myself dissolving into an accidental dab of color which didn't belong there, somewhere at the edge of the frame.

I wanted to shout at the top of my lungs, "At last! It's real! It's real!"

It seemed as though I could just reach through that tunnel and close my fingers around him to be sure he wouldn't disappear as magically as he materialized. I was in the picture of reality, not the reality of a picture mutely staring at me from the pages of a book.

I had lived for this moment most of my life, and now it was here, my entire consciousness was focused into a pinpoint of acutest concentration.

Every detail of that magnificent beast was sharply visible. His long neck lowered, his huge, tapered head close to the ice, sniffing for telltale scent of prey or danger. The slow, shuffling gait was punctuated with a rhythmical thump-thump that barely echoed off the ridge as his huge paws landed softly on the snow, bouncing masses of hair enveloping them.

I could see his rippling muscles beneath his shaggy coat, and beneath muscles I could sense the incredible power and fury of his might. From time to time, he swung his head from side to side. Dark shadows cast by jagged ice revealed a trace of vapor from his breath clouding his shiny, jet-black nose. He lumbered closer, filling my luminescent frame of ice.

George had long since nudged me to shoot, and when I didn't respond, he whispered so softly right in my ear, "Shoot!" I didn't want to do it! I thought I had a few more moments to let him get closer. There was so much more detailed reality to be seen and felt! I was entranced with a sensation of floating "out there" as a part of wind, ice, snow, cold, and bear—completely lost to my own sense of "being back here." I would ponder that experience again on another hunt.

If I had refused to hear George's whispering, "Shoot," I sure heeded the next sound he made—the soft, metallic slither of the bolt he moved to chamber his cartridge. I was full alert. Apparently, he had had enough and didn't appreciate my appreciation of the bear. Poor George! He told me later, he was worried out of his wits, not knowing why I was stalled with total inertia.

The bear filled my entire scope and looked close to me because of that enlargement. I knew he was much further away. George, who had no scope, saw him with naked eye and guessed the white, ghostly form to be much nearer than I thought. He estimated about 70 feet (he later said) with the gap closing rapidly.

When my backup buddy nudged me to inch aside so he could fit in beside me, and I heard the slithering of his bolt, I knew George had given up on me. I either shot now, ready or not, or he would. Gripping my mitten between my teeth and yanking it off, I understood his point of view instantly. I looked over my scope and saw the bear with several yards he still had to traverse, wondering why George was in such a hurry. I spun the scope hard to starboard to see the entirety of the animal and find the best target circle. My entire world collapsed at what I saw next through the lens.

Directly in front of me, the only thing visible through the opening of that icy tunnel was the bear's forelegs. His chest, head, and rest of him was blocked by the upper rim of the tunnel's opening. In the brief moment I had lost his image as the refocusing lens blurred it, he had stepped on a pedestal of elevated slope, or slight hummock on the ice and snow, just high enough to conceal his engine room with its pump and pipe fittings. To make matters worse, there was a shard of ice right in the way of my reticles. I had seen neither icicle nor pedestal that had sunk below my field of vision. The earlier magnified view looked right over them, focusing on pretty pictures of ice, reflecting jewels, tunnels, and polar bear that entranced me.

Forelegs, frozen stark still without a trace of motion, now looked like two columns of concrete painted white. From his frozen, immobile stance, it was obvious, he must be sniffing for scents having little to do with scotch or cognac. What had brought him to such a sudden halt? Had he heard the slither of George's bolt or my turning scope? Had a stray wisp of air carried our scent to him? Or was it the supremacy of primordial instinct over belabored cogitation?

One does not kill bear by shooting at its legs. If he only walked forward one or two paces, he would be off that pedestal of ice and lower down, where I could see him in proper alignment.

I didn't have a shot; that's all there was to it. The thought hurled a bolt of panic and desperation through me. Realizing the game was all but over, I squirmed and snaked backward, rolling over as George eased out of my way (he later said he was dumbfounded at my maneuver). When one doesn't know what to do next, he checks out what he was doing before. I snapped my head around and got instant confirmation that the ice parapet above me was too steep and difficult to climb instantly. To the right, the pressure ridge extended too far for quick clearance. To the left, slanting slabs blocking us abutted into another labyrinth of tumbled icy walls.

Now I knew what to do—squirm forward to my earlier position to figure out what to do next with equal futility, cursing my stupidity for having watched my bear for too long. I threw the scope to my eye, only to see the bear's hind legs moving to my left. Dreams of a lifetime were disappearing within virtual grasp and I aimed as high as the tunneled edge of ice would allow. It was a simple 50-50 risk. Either I hit and slowed him down for a sorely needed extra moment and a more telling shot, or I would miss clean because there was nothing else that could be hit when all of him disappeared in a fraction of a second. I knew one other thing for certain. Since I was lying down in the wrong position that could not be helped, the scope on the rifle's recoil would smash my skull right over my eye.

I squeezed the trigger at the leg just as it moved out of sight. There was no hoped-for sound of the soft thwack hitting flesh and sounding back to me. Instead, I saw the sharp splintering of ice a second before the ear-shattering boom of my .338 came back to me in peel after peel of thundering reverberations echoing through that tunnel. The tunnel had become a gigantic resonator. From the briefest retinal afterimage and George's total silence, I knew I had missed him clean. He had scampered up that mountainous wall of tumbled pressure ridge ice like a wraith and disappeared for good into the frozen wastes. All I had left was a skull-shattering ringing in my ears.

I sat there in total shock, numb and devoid of all feeling and thought, the full agony not yet setting in. I was unaware even of the mundane nuisance of blood trickling into my eye from the gash in my brow and mechanical motion of cupping snow to staunch it. I don't know how long I sat there frankly not giving a hang about what happened next because there was no next. Everything was has been.

A lifetime of dreams and miracles bringing me to this point were blown away in a single shot. I felt total emptiness inside. No millionaire who lost his fortune, no emperor who lost his empire, could feel the loss I did for my polar bear. Life could go on without millions and empires as it had for millennia. Mine could not go on without my dreams. I had lost my dreams right in grasp of my palm.

Was I, to use the "in" phrase, overreacting for a mere trivial symbol? But importance of life itself is a collection of symbols, any one of which can become trivial depending on other trivia we compare it to when anything is relative to everything else. I did not feel my loss to be relative. That's a cop-out for word-weaslers. My loss was absolute. I knew of no substitute for polar bear. There are no substitutes for the unique and ultimate in anything. I had lost, and there was no weaseling out of my pain. Time might heal my wounds of the spirit, but there was no escape from enduring it until the end.

Poor George just stood there watching me. He knew what I must be going through. I finally stood up with embarrassment and looked into both his eyes with one of mine. Of all guys, I had to let a man like George down after all his efforts and generosity. He had given me a magnificent chance and I had blown it. What's worse, it was the first time in my life I had missed a first shot for anything I wanted that badly. And, it had to be a once-in-a-lifetime polar bear. Was there no end to the irony in this fiasco?

George looked at me with kindness and in a gentle voice asked, "What happened?"

There was no use trying to explain details that could sound like whining excuses—there was no excuse for what had happened. "Nothing," I said. "I just blew it."

Naturally, I thought my hunt was over. He had given me more than my money's worth, and it wasn't fair to expect another chance. How many chances are there when stakes are this high? I thanked him, told him what I felt and said I was ready to go home. As a mighty Nimrod of the North, I felt less than a fat, useless zero.

He looked at me, flashing one of his big, broad grins and said, "What's the matter with you with that kind of talk? You're not the first guy I've seen who has missed a shot at polar bear. It just happens."

When I looked at him searchingly, he said, "I've seen you shoot before, remember? It's just going to take another try, that's all. Let's go upstairs and try to find him again while we still have some daylight left. Okay"?

He started moving out, and I followed him mechanically, dazed, and dubious, but knowing how much I owed this older brother of mine when he could have quit right then and there.

We pushed the plane out of its hiding place and took off in a few minutes. Blood flowing over my eye had stopped, but I was deep in a fit of indifference to all else except nursing inner wounds. I became aware that George had been jabbing his finger at the window for a while. When he finally got my attention, he began pointing below, banking the plane at the same time. Out the window, and way, way down, was my bear! I didn't know whether I wanted to hug him or punch him in the eye. As soon as we got over him, he immediately started moving ahead at a faster clip.

He stopped occasionally to look up at our red-and-white mechanical bird carrying two madmen over his polar desolation, one of whom did not deserve a second chance. Ahead was an open lead. The bear charged toward it and plunged into icy, blue water without a moment's hesitation. I could see a long yellow-green wake trailing behind him until he reached the opposite side and clambered out. He shook himself like a giant shaggy dog, and took off again. Without doubt, he knew we were after him. George climbed higher, so to worry him as little as possible.

Suddenly, the radio crackled and Jim's voice broke through— I had forgotten all about him and had not seen him since before the Futile Fiasco at Thundering Tunnel.

"It's getting late," his garbled voice said, "Are we heading back?"

"Naw," George drawled, "we got time, yet. Let's go a little more."

I strained trying to locate Jim and finally spotted him for a moment, way back and overhead. His flight pattern made me feel comfortable, but his conversation didn't.

He sounded irritated when he said, "He knows we're after him and he's dangerous, now. You still want to do it your way"?

"That's right," George drawled. "We're going down when we can."

"Then tell the old man to get on the stick," Jim snarled.

Obviously, this was for the old man's benefit. We had waited a week for bad weather to clear and lost a lot of time. If I didn't connect now and had to hunt again tomorrow, it would cut into Jim's romance time, already short enough. Maybe Lady Jane was getting to him. Was this the beginning of his shenanigans?

I was simply in no mood for it or his insult and didn't hesitate cutting him down to size over the microphone. George was smiling. He held up his microphone and twiddled his finger. He had shut it off, and Jim had not gotten my message. How I wished I had George's finesse!

Down below, the bear was grinding out the miles, heading straight into the sunset like the Lone Ranger, minus Tonto. It seemed like a long time before George found the place where he thought the bear would show up. He finally selected a large, flat expanse of ice surrounded by a pressure ridge. He circled the pan a few times, figured out his angles, and put the plane down.

We both noticed a 10-inch wide crack in the ice not too far from where the plane had taxied to a stop. It was a fresh lead, opening up just a few feet long. Our landing probably did it. "We gotta hurry," George said, looking at the sky growing to a deeper crimson. He looked at that split section of ice again without saying anything.

For a few moments, I really considered calling it off for the day. I just didn't feel comfortable with the time pressure, and despondency over the last calamity had not left me. I halfheartedly helped George push the plane behind a ridge. He grabbed his rifle and camera, and with a burst of enthusiasm headed straight ahead for a small hummock about 100 yards away. I shoved a fourth shell in the chamber, and in a kind of daze, started walking slowly behind him while he poured it on. I didn't want to spoil his enthusiasm.

It took less than a half dozen paces for me to realize we were in a different world from our first landing, although we were barely 5 miles from there. Back there, it was claustrophobic. We were choked in by gigantic walls of the pressure ridge ice forming that long tunnel. Now, it was agoraphobic; for as far as the eye could see it was flat, open vastness full of emptiness and desolation, laced here and there with pressure ridges. Instead of a corral, it now felt like a gigantic saucer, and we were in the hollow of it with the horizon above us and winds blowing gusts of dry, powdery snow with nothing to stop it.

A distant ridge looked like a toppled, limitless Stonehenge. Nothing, anywhere, was of familiar design or shape to give one depth and perception of distance or size. It was all flat, like I wore a patch over one eye. When I looked out, I saw George, who looked like a cartoon moving in circles behind the hummock, no doubt to stay warm. But he looked strange and out of place. The contrast between his form and limitless space all around made him look funny. So funny, I suddenly broke into laughter knowing I would look that way in a few moments.

My despondency and anguish suddenly melted. I knew I wanted to reenter the real world around me. Just in case that bear showed up again, I vowed there would be no more trances, wonder, and art appreciation. It was down to brass tacks from now on, and "no monkey-business," I scolded myself.

Had George picked the right spot? I was halfway to the hummock when the answer came with total surprise. At the top of distant Stonehenge, about a quarter mile away, there appeared a seemingly detached, tiny, black, shiny spot bobbing up and down in the middle of vast whiteness. The wind had momentarily died down, and in the crystal clear atmosphere, I was willing to wager that nose could have been seen from 5 miles away.

Polar bear have much keener sight than their black or brown cousins. Could he have seen me? I looked at George walking behind the hummock, totally unaware of what was way up ahead. There was a large shallow depression between me and the hummock, and crawling on my belly, I rolled myself into it. When George looked for me and found me, I waved my hand frantically, signaling him to stay put and drop behind the hummock.

He got my meaning immediately and did so. It was vital to keep that hummock between me and the bear's line of sight. When I was close enough to the hummock to be hidden by it, I ambled for it, and George's grin told me I had not been seen.

The spirit surged through me, and I felt in command of myself again. If that bear got into my sights, he'd never get away again. The hummock was providential. If I were standing up, it was just the right height to use for a gun rest. The bear was now fully visible behind his coal-black shiny nose. His huge hulk appeared to be, not climbing, but oozing down the jagged blocks and slabs of ice until he squeezed straight out when he reached the bottom of his zigzag descent. He stopped, lifted his head, and seemed to look right and left, deciding the coast was clear. Shuffling toward us, he entered that vast arena of desolation with the most majestic demeanor ever given to man or beast.

I could see him against that background much better than in the narrow tunnel. Again, electricity crackled through the marrow of my bones, only more supercharged now than before. I thought I heard an airplane's drone, but looking over the scope, there was nothing overhead in front of me so I ignored the impulse to look back where the sound had to be. My battered skull ached too much, and later I was to recall the irritation.

The wind gusted erratically, and bright, clear air would be dusted with obscuring, powdery snow one moment and then clear into crystal clarity the next moment. My sights were right on him and I was waiting for him to get closer, much closer. He was still about 200 yards away when he suddenly stopped in midstride. He jerked up his head in such a powerful arc, it seemed to yank his entire body up with it in one smooth motion and come full upright on his hind paws. What a gorgeous sight for just a second looking like a marble statue in a museum without walls! Just for a second, though. Immediately, he spun to his right, dropping on all fours at the same time, and quartered away, full bore. The speed of his executed maneuver was unbelievable. He must have whiffed our scent, I thought, with the first renewed gust of wind.

"Aw, naw," George's voice wailed, "Goldarn it! We'll never get him now. It's all over for sure."

My sights had never left the bear, however. The moment George expressed his dismay, something inside me said it was a dead ringer. Didn't George know I never missed? I held my breath as the reticles led him slightly given the angle at which he was quartering away. I followed for another moment knowing it was going to be a tough shot and hoping that a sudden gust of wind would not alter the bullet's momentary flight, I squeezed.

He went down hard on his haunches, spinning like a top three or four times. He was half turned backward with his paw raking his side and I knew his back was broken, paralyzing his hind end. He was now nearly broad side, and in an instant I got off the next shot into his engine room. He flattened out, lifeless. There was no quivering to be seen through the scope.

George apparently didn't believe it, so he shouted, excitedly, "Hit him again, hit him again!"

I felt it was needless, but he was right. It was always the dead ones that got up and ran away or charged. My next shot was a careless miss and the next one hit him in the lower leg, but he didn't move. I had lost the concentration for sharpshooting. It took a stunned moment for me to realize it had been done. George sensed it and said, "Okay, let's wait 5 minutes and make sure." I liked that better and besides, it was standard procedure for dangerous game.

Suddenly, Jim's plane zoomed over us from behind, headed for the bear, and circled over him. Apparently convinced the monarch was dead, he came back, found the pan hiding our plane behind us and dropped low for a landing. I hadn't seen him for ages, it seemed, and was surprised at his sudden appearance. I suddenly realized I couldn't account for his presence at the exact moment of my shooting. I was positive he was nowhere in sight, but had I somehow missed seeing him over my bear? The thought nagged me.

George and I stood there waiting, our backs turned to the biting winds. I was buried in my thoughts when George broke the silence.

"I can't figure you," he said.

"What did I do wrong now, George?" I asked thinking of Thundering Tunnel.

"Nothing wrong," he said, "but it sounded like a machine gun. You got two killing shots in about 3 seconds, two more in the next 3 or 4 seconds by my reckoning, all at a tough angle with that bozo going lickety-split at better than 200 yards away. I thought nothing could ever stop him. Goldarn it, that was some shooting."

George wasn't given to cheap flattery, and coming from him, this would have been welcome praise, indeed, but what made me feel uncomfortable was the absence of his broad grin saying it.

There was something else he wasn't telling me so I asked, "What, then, can't you figure out?" George said, "Why and how come you missed that shot back there under your nose when he was standing dead still. Why are you not war-whooping like a wild-man now you got him and what a beauty he is."

"George," I said, "please don't ask. I just goofed and feel real badly about it."

"Goldarn it," said George, "it was a little thing that went wrong."

Yeah, I thought, it was "just a little thing," like a lifetime full of dreams that was nearly lost forever. Slowly, it sank in that my dream had come true, and it was hard to believe.

George scanned the horizon. "We've got to move fast," he said. "It'll save time if you start the skinning. I'll go to the plane and get the game bag and gear. Be careful when you approach him and make sure he's dead."

He turned and headed for the plane. I headed for the bear.

The wind had died again for a few moments. In the deathly silence, I could hear the crackling of my mukluks sounding like muted thunder on the ice pack. Soon, I reached the bear, approached from behind, and nudged him with my rifle. He was quite dead.

This close to him at last, I stood there awestruck at his magnificence. I, more alone now than he, enveloped in the Arctic nothingness. Even in death, he was an intimidating majesty. The winds began to pick up their wail, again. The years rolled back in the magic mirror of my mind, reflecting pictures and adventure stories of Nanook and Arctic wilderness, which so excited the imagination of a little boy who thought life was forever and there was no ugliness in this world. There had been years of dreaming and hoping for the moment that confronted me now with its stark reality.

Gazing at the monarch of the polar ice at my feet, I felt humbled by that magnificence and potential fury now lying in stillness forever, his fur rippling in the biting gusts of wind with its savage, bitter cold so much a part of his real world he could no longer know. His inertness now was the end of all living things, except the bear looked so intact, complete, and eternal in majestic dignity, even in death, surrounded by his mausoleum of ice and snow.

Gazing at him, my soul struggled with emotions my mind could not comprehend. A profound sense of sorrow gripped me, not because all living things must die, but because all that is magnificent, noble, and glorious deserves to live longer than it does.

Looking at what I had killed, I felt the mystery of its death and sensed something else, but could not identify it easily. Then, it hit me in a flash of insight. How intact and dignified he looked lying peacefully on his side in full repose.

That was it—its manner of dying and its appearance in death. The mirror of my mind reflected a revolving montage of images all too familiar with the dying on battlefield—images that often haunted me at the most inopportune moments, and this was such a moment—broken bodies of dead and dying fellow soldiers during war—my comrades in arms, torn, mutilated, ripped open with jagged holes and tattered flesh, missing limbs and body parts, internal organs spilling out, black, pustulant, stinking, necrotic flesh caked with vomit, blood, and excrement. Moans and screams. Unconsciousness, through which, sobbing voices of grown men, who would receive medals for valor if they survived, made them infants again, calling for their mothers, not knowing who or where they were. Bodies piling up outside the surgical tent faster than we could mend, repair, anesthetize, or pack them, or what remained of them. Packing them in garbage bags by other names, as gruesome caricatures faintly resembling what had once looked like us. Spewed out on the edge of the battlefield, it become a nightmarish hell, too grotesque, too bizarre for mortal comprehension.

How intact, undefiled, and dignified my polar bear lay in peaceful repose in solitude of his wilderness. The animals I had killed on many a hunt rolled through the magic mirrors of my mind, and I saw the common denominator of their deaths—they all lay with their bodies intact, with dignity even in death, in untroubled sleep unspoiled by the trickle of blood from one or two neat, unobtrusive holes. The neatly placed bullet always seemed to produce a peaceful death without mutilation and agony. Death was the end of all who lived, about which nothing could be done. It was the manner of dying that mattered.

Sorrow and regret dissolved and I became overwhelmed with contentment for this dream fulfilled, for life's misfortunes wiped out with this prize making up for it all. I wanted to shout my gratitude to the entire world and all its past humanity—humanity whose travails had enabled life to survive through centuries to bring me to this present moment.

I just wanted to say thank you, to someone, to anyone who would listen, but there was no one here in the desolation of the moment to hear me. The overwhelming urge had to go somewhere, so I tried to shout it to my bear, but I couldn't. My throat was choked with conflicting emotions of sadness, joy, and gratitude.

I knelt and tried to lift his massive head, just to give him a hug for finally coming into my life. It had been a long, long time from those dreams of the boy and his books to the present reality of man and animal. Tightness in my throat would not even let me utter the simple words, thank you, but they had to come out somehow. For the first time in many, many years, hugging that shaggy head and enveloped in howling winds and whirling snows, I broke down and wept shamelessly, like a child, to utter thanks in the only way I could out of the depths of my soul. A few moments ago, I had wanted to shout my gratitude to the world. Now, I was glad there was no one around to see my loss of self-control.

How long I knelt there sobbing, buried in my thoughts, I do not know, but out of nowhere, above the wind's howl, a voice called my name and said, "Don't cry, please don't cry." It was Jane.

I had forgotten all about the others, let alone her. And now this! Tears are not meant for public display. One of my life's most sacred moments was assaulted by a woman who was a total stranger to me in the midst of Arctic desolation. What is privacy invasion except the anonymous intrusion into one's solitude that disrupts the gentle presence of God?

I rose slowly, flushed with humiliation and anger, unclenching my fist that would have pulverized her in a wave of fury were she a man for having had no regard for sanctuary. Then I tried to shrink into my parka, my anger becoming a shame I knew not how to handle. Here I was, macho me, caught crying by a modern, emancipated woman. I couldn't believe it! She was caressing my face, smothering me with her eternal motherhood act reducing my being to an object for her intrusive scrutiny!

It took all the courage I had to slowly lift my head, prepared to

70

tell her off for what she had really done. Our eyes met. She was crying, too. She brushed aside her tears, reached up and kissed me like my kid-sister.

"I understand, please believe me. I understand, don't cry," she said.

I didn't know what she understood, but something inside me fell apart. This was no phoney display of modern caring and sharing to hide the macha broad seeking the jugular of the macho jock. If this were a lie, there was no truth anywhere. This was intuitive understanding, genuine kindness, and compassion which we men so rarely show.

It was the priceless gift good women give so freely without asking for anything in return. It was the bottom line to all that was beautiful and eternal in womanhood being betrayed by modern feminism. Any man readily resented the radical feminist with her vulgar self-assertion, her strident, aggressive, power-seeking dominance she denounced in the male, while secretly craving it for herself. She was resented not because she competed with manhood, but because she lacked class to bring off her imposture. I was not looking at such a female. I was looking at one whose integrity as a woman commanded instant respect.

I had just enough sense left to realize that no matter what I had thought of her earlier, here, in this encounter, was another soul better than mine earning my immediate admiration, and exactly that kind of rare and radiant womanhood which this soulless twentieth century was annihilating.

There are things more shameful than a grown man crying alone in the wilderness. One of them was to reject the gift of human kindness given in midst of this frozen eternity. The contrast was stark between this gracious womanhood and Mother Nature in the raw. The last words locked in my throat, I could not utter to my precious bear, were the first ones now tumbling out to this lovely lady. "Thank you," I said, since she had become the world who listened and understood. I gave her that hug of gratitude I owe to all who lead me closer to the mystery that is God.

It has been difficult to write all this because it's still embarrassing to reveal such a private truth to the reader now, when I didn't want anyone to know it back then, but there is no way around it. It is a truth and cannot be omitted from all that happened that day.

In a way it's funny—I mean the image of a supposedly tough, mean, cold-blooded, vicious, plug-ugly killer, who should have been laughing hilariously and enjoying "fun" at the death of this animal. Instead, here I was weeping like some orphaned waif with sheer gratitude for the treasure of my dreams this bear gave to me at the cost of his life. One just cannot laugh at such a thing. (I have never laughed at any animal I've killed, but I cried once more years later when I got the second of my twin dream treasures—my lion.)

I've heard, and read, of other hunters overwhelmed by the same impassioned tears. Maybe critics who always boast of compassion for animals will forgive us merciless Neanderthals for what follows years of waiting, yearning, effort, and sacrifice until it happens. When it does, in a split second or two, realization of it is so mind-boggling that one goes crazy inside and the craziness comes out tears of joy, sorrow, and gratitude all mixed together. When the soul overflows with instant infinity of fulfillment, it has to spill out, somehow.

Over Jane's shoulder George and Jim hove into view. Nodding in their direction so she would understand, I walked off to compose myself before returning to the aid of the men who, hopefully, suspected nothing. If they did, they were good enough not to let on.

With three of us working rapidly and the waning sun spurring us on, we had the skinning done in about a half hour; record time. He was a magnificent bear of record class, squaring the magical 10 feet, in prime pelage, with scars of a dozen battles on its muzzle and neck. We stuffed the hide in the gamebag, dragging it over the ice, our shadows slanting like gargoyles ahead of us.

We had to take a slight detour to get around a lead too wide to cross. A little further on, we noticed the 10-inch fissure we'd seen earlier had opened to a 6-foot-wide lead.

We changed direction, found an opening through the ice pack, and crossed over to the solid side, losing precious time. We made it to the planes. Jim and Jane hurried to theirs and got aloft, circling overhead, watching George and me. I suspected they got out of here so quickly because the call of crackling ice was getting too close. We spent more valuable minutes making room in back of the plane for the hide, which was an enormous bundle to squeeze and stuff into that small space, and then repack the rest of the things.

George looked up to the circling plane above, said, "I'm sure glad they're up there," bounced up and down a few times on the ice and muttered, "I don't like the feel of this. Let's go, fast." I squeezed into the plane and doubled over into a cranny.

He revved the engine, and taxied into position. Ahead, I saw what I had sensed and what worried George. Earlier leads we'd seen had split much wider, going around nearly in a circle. Undoubtedly, two planes landing on the ice and all our movements were the cause of it. If we didn't make it, we'd probably be cut off and adrift. My innards tightened into a knot, but it was needless to nudge George. I looked out the window and felt the wide ski blades of the landing gear hit the edge of ice. There was a thudding bump, but the plane kept going.

We had cleared the open lead, but just barely. There was plenty of room now for a good take off. I heaved a sigh of relief, settled back, and for the first time, felt the glow of satisfaction, of contentment for mission accomplished and well done—okay, reasonably well done, but my dream was fulfilled.

We were comfortably aloft, when I asked George how he judged that spare foot or two when the skis barely bridged the gap. Maybe there was some electronic secret, I thought. George just grinned and said one word, "Experience."

If his judgement had not paid off, he later told me, the ski tips would have hooked into the edge of the ice. Then, if we were lucky, we would have struggled out before the plane submerged and tried to survive overnight until Jim came back with help.

All this squared with what I had read and heard. The most dangerous part of polar bear hunting was landing and taking off on polar ice. Only human judgement, and the art of those geniuses who handle such aircraft, spell the difference between life and death. There is no other way. You take the chance. Danger is all around you on every hunt even when there are no animals around.

A few weeks later, I got some mail from George with a piece of 8 mm movie film and a note apologizing for its short length— the camera had frozen. I measured that miserable piece of short-change a hair below 26 inches. It had to be spliced at both ends with blank film to make it long enough to thread it through the projector sprockets. The movie was disappointing. It was barely in focus, with poor exposure in the waning dusk, but I could see three things: myself hunched over the hummock and in the distance what must have been my bear. It looked small and blurred. If I didn't know what should have been out there, I could have mistaken it for a microscopic UFO. It was slightly darker than the rest of the surroundings, moving full bore, suddenly stopped, and became a blur spinning around (that was my first shot), then tilted and fell over (that was my second shot). It did not move before the film ran out. That much agreed with what I had seen through the scope.

Then there was the third thing. For less than 5 seconds in the upper left hand corner Jim's plane suddenly appeared, circled over the bear, and flew out of view. The bear was already dead. I ran that film over and over again to be sure. The plane, with its red-striped fuselage, more clearly visible than anything else on the film, was flying fully broadside with all of its 22.6 feet of Piper Cub length. My watch said from the first shot, to his toppling over, from the second shot, was between 3 and 5 seconds.

The blurry, out-of-focus image would not allow for greater precision. From the first projected image to the first shot, Jim's plane was not in sight over a lot of territory filmed at that distance. Before that first shot, I had not seen Jim anywhere. Nor could he be seen over a lot more territory after that bear toppled and the plane flew out of sight just before the camera froze.

I remembered my irritation at the engine's drone I had guessed to be behind me, somewhere, the nagging doubt about where it was exactly, and then ignoring it because of my concentration through the scope. Now I knew exactly where it was not. It was not anywhere near my bear before, during, and after my shot. Maybe the bear had scented us as I thought. Now it seemed probable he had heard or seen Jim's plane behind us.

The next thing fell into place and verified what I knew I saw without the movies. The bear had quartered back toward the pressure ridge away from us and the plane behind us. If anything, that wretched plane had probably made my shot needlessly more difficult as the bear started fleeing back toward the icy ridges from whence he'd come. That's how I knew the bear's escape route was unobstructed. If the plane were behind him, he would obviously have come straight toward us or gone in another direction. Had he reached the pressure ridge ice, from whence he came, the hunt was ended right then and there.

Moreover, if the plane had been anywhere near the bear in those crucial moments, George would never have groaned at the outset that we "had lost the bear for sure, goldarn it." If anything, all indications were that Jim had faithfully served my wishes and best interests, through George's directives, no matter how much he may have resented them. Only then did I realize how easily I could have lost my bear on the last minute just to live by my code.

Given all the odds, I was lucky to have gotten away with it. I knew what George and Jim had tolerated just to please me. I owed Jim an apology and a tremendous gratitude to both men. They had come through for me like champs. They had class. They were true professionals.

I was satisfied with three things: first, even discounting George's superlatives about my shooting, I had done well enough, everything considered; second, the bear had a fair chance to escape; third, he had not been hassled in any way from our first sighting to the last moment. I felt I had been more than fair in how I had shot that noble beast, in spite of the way we had reached him by plane. Fact is, there was no other practical way to do it for me.

How glad I was I had not waited for a dog-sled hunt. I would have never made it. Shortly after this, the white man was prohibited by law from hunting polar bear.

It took me a year to pay my bill to George, and a year-and-a-half to pay off the greater costs of the taxidermy bill. On an artificial block of blue polar-ice, my glorious bear stands on all fours, his nostrils flared, sniffing for the telltale scent of prey. He is a constant reminder of what I owe him, and there is no way I can say thinks except by my undying respect and gratitude. Out of thousands of bears, this was the one who made my lifetime dream come true.

I'm sure my father and mother knew nothing about hunting, had no desire to see a live polar bear, except possibly in the zoo, and the thought of a "stuffed" one in the house would have driven them mad.

They didn't live long enough, however, for me to tell them this treasure of mine symbolized my triumph, on their behalf, over the poverty of the world we knew when they tried so hard to keep us kids alive. In an odd sort of way, it was my priceless gift to them, undelivered. Had I really tried to give them this gift, I know they would have laughed at their son who again had "left his mind," but they would have understood what he was trying to say. Now they were gone. I dedicated it to them. It was the most precious thing I owned. I could give it to them in gratitude.

An archetypal hunt never ends. Almost 10 years later I was invited again to give another address to an international sportsmen's conference in Las Vegas. They billed me as the "voice of the

American hunter," and it was another "blockbusting speech," said the press, which won a "standing, rousing ovation." I fully appreciated that honor by hunters who were better than I, but that was not the real thrill for me that afternoon. The real thrill, while shaking hands with the well-wishers, was to see Jim and Jane standing there! The joy was instantaneous.

She gave me a hug in tearful remembrance, and it was my turn to give her a kiss, delivered long after it was due, in gratitude for memories past. Jim smiled and his handshake was warm and sincere. They were happily married. In a way, two strangers, who had played such an important part in one of my life's great moments, felt like my family to me. Hopefully, they did not think me impertinent.

My friends and guests who visit for the first time stand in awe and envy of my polar bear. If they are fellow hunters, they will usually say, "What I would give to hunt such an animal." It always saddens me that they will not have that chance, not because polar bear is an endangered species, but because nefarious politics have made it off limits for the white man, even if he is an Alaskan. It is an exclusive native prerogative now, to preserve a traditional life style, it is said, but it is so sad to see some natives who are caught trading polar bear hides for cocaine, which was never part of any Eskimo tradition. I know I am twice blessed for having had my hunt just in time before the curtain of "justice" was lowered on the rest of us.

I have been asked, often of course, if I would like to hunt polar bear again, assuming it were allowed once more for white trophy hunters. I would not do so for three reasons: first, I have had my fair share and would like to see someone else have his chance. Second, stalking on open ice is negligible, permitting little for the hunter to do; he is either at the right place at the right time or he is not, and it is not he but the pilot who determines that. This leaves the hunter little to do but aim and shoot. Third, whether critics believe it or not, I have known the ultimate, and I will not risk spoiling the memory of it. I want to think of polar bear as I remember my bear stalking toward me, framed in blue-green luminescence of that diamond-shaped opening in the icy slabs beneath a shattered pressure ridge, both of us embraced by the awesome desolation of Arctic wilderness. Dreams like that come only once to any man. I am more than grateful that mine came true.

Reflections

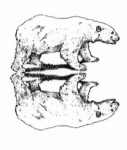

Years after that hunt, the memory of it is still with me. Two things stand out sharply in my mind: the moving magnificence of the polar bear, heading right toward me in the center of that luminescent frame of ice; and on our return to Teller at day's end, the waning sun with its gold, orange, yellow, and red splashed over glistening desolation of the polar ice cap.

Those memories reached into the past and snagged me into a much earlier bear hunt, when I sat exhausted on a mountain top in Valdez looking at the opposite range. The sky above was a water-colored wash with deep greys, blues, and purples against a pitch-black sky. The fury of a storm was lashing the coast below it. The only other sky like it I'd ever seen, was in El Greco's painting, Storm Over Toledo, as I watched the unfolding of its surrogate in Valdez. With two Spanish names like that, the association was simple and permanent. With that permanence, the association between two vistas like stormy Valdez and the frozen Bering Sea, both bathed in dramatic color and form, viewed from a higher vantage point, enhanced the essential reality of both experiences. Nothing could have been more dramatically esthetic.

All thoughts and memories incubated between those two hunts, now obsessed my imagination with art in general and the art of hunting in particular. If art is as old and as central to the human spirit as is hunting, then why were hunters and artists, with whom I had many discussions, so far apart in their views about nearly everything? It was a big question. My inadequate answers to it threw into sharp contrast the world of elemental nature and its exigencies, I loved, with the once great civilization I live in, and which is rotting before my eyes and nagging my soul with pain.

The urbanized world is full of things big and little, full of sounds, smells, and sights which, when perceived, trigger off unlimited images, thoughts, and memories that come alive in the brain. There are those fortunate enough whose brains automatically shut out the unpleasant sensations that energize negative symbols in our souls constantly bombarded by the irritants of metropolis. Unfortunately, I am not blessed with this gift.

I drive past the polished granite walls and glistening glass of a modern skyscraper, and I appreciate its architectural genius, but only for an instant. In the next instant, my wretched mind reminds me I owe a mortgage draining my hard-earned salary month after month, year after year, while I grow old, still waiting to do things I cannot do because money for doing them went to an office somewhere in the bowels of that building with polished granite and gleaming glass. My anger is at interest rates once denounced as usury.

I wait at the traffic light, and some of the autos and trucks coming and going past emit the heavy, brain-fogging stench of burned motor oil and gasoline, and I wonder if their drivers got stuck with the cost of "emissions control" like I did, while the car waiting next to me, with open window, has its radio turned on full blare emitting a raucous, cacophonous "musical" savagery, and the driver is bent on forcing auditory pollution on all ears within 10 miles.

Then there is the nightly newscast on television, which I hate to watch because it is demoralizing an entire nation with its reports on crime, drugs, perversion, revolution, riots, hunger, assassination, and insanity. Why do I do it? Because each time I hope against hope to hear something good, something encouraging to tell me that maybe our corrupt, degenerate society is turning a corner, that something has improved, that there is hope beginning to emerge somewhere.

But it's not yet time, and one must keep fighting inside to stay strong, to hope, to keep the faith until it is time, and in the interim, one needs spiritual renewal. If one is a hunter, he renews the spirit, where else, but in the world of elemental nature that knows no deception, cunning, fraud, and injustice? So I go to the wilderness, part of that wilderness the government is trying to take from me. I go to renew other sights, sounds, and smells energizing different symbols nearer to the longings of my soul. There is not a hunter anywhere who fails to experience the central reality of every hunt—beauty.

Countless times I have seen sights of spectacular, breathtaking beauty, each with its own arresting uniqueness. The wilderness is eternal, but never the same from season to season, day to day, and even hour to hour. Once, I happened to be at the right place at exactly the right split second when a rumbling sound shattered the stillness, gathered momentum and a cascading avalanche of snow and ice plummeted down a 4,000-foot drop, settling in a swirling, rising mist below, seeming to float the world away from where I stood firmly planted to a pinnacle of rock.

Many times, I have seen a waterfall tumbling down from great heights. Sometimes a thin, wispy veil floating off a rocky wall, sometimes a roaring, mighty, white-spumed cascade, plunged onto the boulders below and foamed into a turbulent river headed out who knows where.

How many times have I stood on some mountain top, looked out at the endless ranges winding faraway, their craggy peaks melting into a pale and hazy bluish-purple, where the horizon reached up to bolster the sky? Always the wind was there, sometimes gentle and sometimes fierce and blustering, over landscape and myself alike.

When reaching the valley below, there are small enchanting glens of leafy bough and uncurling fern, and in early morning hours, the pendants of bejeweled dew on grass and leaves scintillate like diamonds, emeralds, rubies, sapphires, and topaz—treasures for which Sinbad would have sailed the seven seas, no matter the storms or demons.

And the moon. There is no moon anywhere else on earth like the Alaska moon in the fall when it is full. It is a gigantic ball of bright, burnished gold floating low over the horizon, only to sail high and far away. In a little while it becomes a silvery disc of mirror, daring one to reach out and grasp it before it hides behind some lost shred of cloud.

And the forests with their dead, wizened tree trunks, gray and ghostlike, angling upward every which way from ancient forest fires that denuded them, reaching a quenching river or rocky divide on the other side. Other trees, now green with leaves or needles and rough corrugation of bark full of gnarls and wrinkles, bury their roots through undergrowth centuries old. Through the dank, matted vegetation there grows the green wispy fronds of fern and foxtail. Far off, the low, rolling valleys are covered with acres of wild flowers of every hue and color, each in its own season, living its brief lifetime of a few weeks or days to become the seared and withered shroud covering which had once been vibrant life, waiting for its resurrection.

Higher up, the tundra—unending miles of tussocks, clumps of dead grass a foot tall, and so much again in girth—and sometimes the wrong step in the spaces between them, filled with brown, stagnant water, have thrown me sprawling. The withered, strawy expanse of tan and brown splashed with the red and yellow leaves of berry bushes ready to take their winter's sleep.

Once, I sat bone weary on the edge of a flat boulder, its surface barely poking above ground high up on a hilltop. It was covered with lichen, light verdigris in color. White, scalloped edges and a darker green moss curled around a slight depression on the rocky surface curved exactly like a big question mark and filled with a tiny pool of water. An occasional dragonfly whirred by with gauzy wings athwart a slender needle-body of bright blue. It is risky to drink from still water, but my thirst was great, and the water was so delicious and cool. It turned out to be just fine. I shall never forget the beauty of the scene surrounding me as sunlight broke through clouds in bands of luminescence.

There were always brooks and streams, cold, sweet, and crystal clear, babbling and swirling over a bed of rocks or pebbles, surely the escaped runoff from some fountain of youth. There were nights when it was not raining, snowing, or blowing storms with whistling furies of hell, when chilly autumn evenings made welcome the campfire with its glowing embers on which sat the pot of coffee after dinner—and the quiet conversation with trusted comrades.

Often we watched, entranced at the Northern Lights shimmering and dancing, or skipping and leaping across the skies, and one knew, "God is in His heaven and all is well with the world." His fingers were writing celestial runes across the tablet of the heavens to say so. Once, I saw another example of divine calligraphy in broad daylight as we flew our Piper Cub through the center of the brightest, most perfectly circular rainbow I'd ever seen suspended over a mountain range!

The hunter is constantly surrounded by beauty of wilderness in all its infinite varieties—sometimes gentle and elegant, like a lovely sylvan muse strumming her golden lyre—sometimes, dangerous and terrifying like a hissing Medusa, her eyes paralyzing all who look at her. Like femininity everywhere, Mother Nature in the wilderness changes her appearance and moods from moment to moment. Without experiencing it directly, it is hard to realize that an idyllic moment of tranquility can change to instant volatile danger, and danger has its own terrifying beauty, and beauty itself can be a terrifying danger.

The wilderness is, among other things, a treasure house and a haunted house of countless, changing symbols. The greatest symbol of all that is wild and dangerous, yet beautiful and serene, is the trophy on the wall, symbolizing the wilderness shrines where the hunter worshipped and communed with furies and angels. What else are the birds and animals he sees, but beauty in motion? When he hunts for his trophies, what else is he trying to do but freeze beauty in space and time to stop its fading away? What else but to be in the presence of its beguiling, hypnotic effect, where symbol points the way to the reality of spirit? If he fails to see a single creature, he is still surrounded by beauty in its pristine, original state—the wilderness.

There is no such thing as great beauty without an ugliness that threatens to mar it always. There is no such thing as triumph unless wrested from the clutches of danger and risk. There is no such thing as joy without release from some agony or despair. There is no such thing as life without death. The trophy is the connection between these opposites telling the hunter that he has taken the challenge to live life, not to feint at its shadows.

There are psychologists who think the hunter is trying to give himself immortality by leaving behind some semblance of himself in the trophy. This is solipsistic nonsense. There are easier, safer, and less expensive ways to do that. Besides, every hunter knows what happens to his "immortality," soon after his death when he is no longer around to stop his trophies from being sold, abandoned, discarded, or taxed.

However, there is an "immortality" involved—the one the

hunter gives to his trophy, whose animal remains have not been swallowed up in the wilderness, entirely. It is the trophy which is immortal, having outlived its natural life expectancy but only as long as the hunter lives. After he is gone, the symbolic life of that trophy, so significant to the hunter, no longer exists. It becomes another object, another thing symbolizing something completely different to the detached beholder, depending on who he is. If the immortality of that thing exists a few years after the hunter, in this throwaway society, it will be an accident of fate.

At any moment, the hunter enters the magic threshold of his wilderness; he is in the world of art and beauty. He is in nature's gallery. She has collected her own treasures for millennia, and nothing done by the hands of man can boast of being its equal. Man, the hunter, surrounded by this living art, can only respond to it in the language of art, with its spiritual and emotional nuances. He becomes an artist himself, a creator of beauty, whether in the crude medium of the country bumpkin or the sophistication of the courtly aristocrat, but an artist in either case.

Nowhere is there more freedom for the soul of the hunter, or anyone else's, to create its own realities of the spirit. People used to say that man is created in the image of God. Male academic yahoos and female steroidal chauvinists reduced this to the cheap arguments about physiognomy, sex, and intelligence as though animals, too, do not possess these attributes, no matter how little. No one says that animals are in the image of God except mistaken pagans and polytheists who never understood the mythology of their ancestors.

Animals do not possess the one single, vital attribute of God's image, which was gifted to man alone, the single spark of divinity making the crucial difference between all living things on the one hand, and God and man on the other—creativity. There is no religion that has denied God as the original Creator of all creation, except the new theology of current American political correctness—the new liberal tyranny, seeking the ultimate in total thought control while denouncing tyrants. Even the lamentable excuses for ordained clergy who choke on the word God, breathe easier with the substitute olive-branch word Creator, with emphasis on the last syllable sounding like tawr to rhyme with door, which betrays what they have subconsciously slammed shut on divinity.

Modernism denies the essential reality of being human, which is the unquenchable thirst in yearning, searching, and hunting for the sacred. We only use different symbols to find and make the path leading to it. Why else do we have the gift of creativity? Even if it's true that, in the absence of God, man must create Him, from whence did he get his creativity? Dissection of brain tissue and examination under all electron microscopes in the world, does not reveal where and how creativity lies buried in the microcosmic mass of electrochemical processes writ infinitesimally small. It only intensifies the mystery until finally even the blasphemer makes a sanctity out of blasphemy.

There is a spark of the sacred in all humanity. No one is denied the divine gift of creativity, from the prehistoric engravings on the cavern walls of Dordogne by an unknown artist deifying the hunter and his bison, to the Sistine Chapel where God's finger reaches out to touch Adam's hand and transfer a spark of that divine creativity, as Michelangelo's hunt for the sacred found it. It is a far cry from a Rembrandt masterpiece to the child doodling with globs of color on the living-room wallpaper, or the cannibal decorating the handle of his primitive skull-smasher with wavy lines and dots, but they are all the results of the artistic urge in response to the creative spirit. Some simply have more of it in finer quality than others.

On that point, I once fell out of grace with a knee-jerk liberal supervisor when I unwisely said there is music and music. There was Harry Truman, good man though he was, who still couldn't play the Missouri Waltz on the piano with any class after 50 years of it, and then there was Mozart who not only played the piano at the age of 3 with spellbinding genius, but was composing the world's great music shortly thereafter. I can't prove it, but sometime later, when I was denied my promotion, I had the strong feeling my supervisor's revenge was behind it. He was a political genius with great creative artistry in interdepartmental intrigue, and may God illumine his soul, as we say in the old country.

Creativity is the most fundamental of all urges in mankind, each person having a little or a lot, perfectly or imperfectly, with routine intelligence or a touch of genius in every culture and historical epoch. It is difficult to imagine anything done by human hands or brains which does not contain some element of creativity. Anything created can be a work of art, the only question being the esthetic excellence of what is created to determine whether it is good or bad art.

For better or worse, the human animal (if animal he be) is a creator at any time in any place. If products of his creativity have any degree of esthetic appeal, then he is an artist for better or worse. To write one's name is a simple act of creativity which has become a mechanical routine. It is a work of art depending on whether the letters are an illegible scrawl or a lovely scroll. There is good art and bad art. This gets us to some difficult problems in the area of art, creativity, and esthetics which can only be discussed briefly, for they are involved at the heart of hunting.

If art is the product of creativity, what then is creativity? We have not gone far in answering this since Plato took on the problem with creative thoughts in his Symposium, a work of intellectual art, some 2,500 years ago. His thoughts boiled down to the basic premise that creativity and originality are the combining and recombining of old elements into new and different totalities or forms, whether they are things or ideas.

It is from this context that the artistic and esthetic emerge. Anything created can be an artistic creation, from a functional tool like a streamlined claw hammer, to a tasty, eye-catching loaf of bread. Or rusty tin cans piled in a certain modernistic way—all it needs is someone to think it is beautiful, which is a highly subjective evaluation.

This is the case in Alaska, where dry moose droppings, about the size of large Manzanilla olives, are painted gold and made into items of jewelry or souvenirs. This art is a far cry from the fine arts of painting, music, literature, architecture, sculpture, ballet, drama, and dancing, where there are arguable cannons of taste and propriety, the sole purpose of which is to create esthetic appreciation and expression.

There are many conflicting theories about the nature of art and beauty, but they are creative recombinations of the basic ideas of Plato's original creation, which is sometimes reversed. It is possible, but only in theory, to take apart a fancy loaf of bread and search for the combined ingredients. In actual practice, this will destroy the bread, of course.

A variation of this theory was created in the 19th century by the Russian anarchist, Mikhael Bakunin, who, said, in his *The Godless State*, the destruction of everything, including God and bourgeois society, was a highly constructive and creative act in preparation for totalitarian state socialism. Since then, all socialist states have suffered a shortage of bread. What was destructive for Plato was constructive for Bakunin and vice versa. There is good art and bad art depending on one's point of view. Creativity has social consequences, obviously.

Long after Robert Oppenheimer presided over the creation of the atom bomb, which was not completed in time to nuke the Germans, and after he finally recanted his Communist affiliations, he had strong pangs of conscience for what he had done when he saw the social and moral consequences of Hiroshima and Nagasaki. The social criticism that some creativity and art is good while others are bad is true enough, but this does not change the fact that both are the results of creativity. Electricity is the common element used in both the electric shaver or the electric chair, and one is free to evaluate the goodness or badness of either, but they are both the results of the creative process with electricity.

So it is with hunting. It may be denounced or acclaimed as good or bad, but it is the result of creative effort. Where there was only wilderness, there is now an added trophy resulting from the venatic art which is what hunting is all about. The quality of the animal and the actions of the hunter determine the excellence of the hunt and its esthetics. A morally relativistic and multicultural society should easily grasp the emerging point—any artist is free to evaluate his own creative process because he creates primarily to satisfy himself, and not to hurt his critics.

The painter of wildlife or seascapes creates and hangs up his paintings for his own enjoyment or achievement. Maybe, he can even find a market for them and win great fame and fortune and become a professional if he so chooses. The trophy hunter may be the only artist or creator of the venatic art who knows in advance that he will not sell his creation; it is too personal and important to him; it is his masterpiece no matter what the social evaluation of it may be. After all, he did not hunt his trophy, often risking his life, for social approval, public display, or monetary gain. It is his symbolic quest for the ultimate and the sacred, and there is no price tag on that. His original intent in contesting for that trophy had nothing to do with selling a commodity or utility. It was to create a sacred icon which spoke to his soul and his only. It is a symbol that expresses the esthetic and spiritual, which anyone can appreciate, but he created it primarily for his own appreciation, for the mortality of his own life expectancy. One does not easily squander such a thing for profit or public appraisal.

There is sad and tragic testimony for this appearing more and more often in hunting periodicals these days. The trophy collections of older hunters from another generation suddenly appear for sale because the hunter has died and his next of kin either need the money, or cannot afford to pay taxes on inherited gifts, or do not have the same appreciation for "stuffed heads." The trophies had been the nonnegotiable treasures of the hunter's lifetime. It is negotiated by others that destiny has thrown into the cauldron of chance who prove there was no "immortality" after all. These days, rumors have it that the government is considering legislation to outlaw the sales of all such trophies to discourage future hunting. Ah, the delights of our democratic freedoms!

Hunting, as I shall detail later, has a kinship to all sports related to the contest, without being any one of them in particular, but a little of many of them in general. It has recombined separate elements or characteristics of many sports into a unique contest more than the sum of its parts. It goes beyond itself and enters the realm of esthetics to become the art of venery as the ancients had seen. Here, too, it recombines elements and characteristics of different arts, without being any one of them in particular, but a composite of several of them to become a unique art form. Then, it combines the contest and the art into a unique creation. How else is it possible to create the trophy?

What other sport or art has had, and still has, such universal devotion, spiritual transcendence, mystical apotheosis, and creativity from more unpredictable and uncontrollable elements which involve decisive human action for the outcome between extremes of chance or routine? All creativity requires two things—mental activity of thought, and imagination and material things on which the mental operates. Before material elements have been combined or recombined, the mind has already combined and recombined the mental elements of preexisting ideas, thoughts, and images, through reason and imagination, to create a blueprint or mental picture that is continually revised, modified, and fused together until that which is being created fits the blueprint.

There is reciprocity here, sometimes the emerging creation forces a revision of the mental picture, because there are practical problems or unforeseen consequences requiring revision of the mental blueprint. Always, there is a fusion between the material things being combined and the mental processes that do the combining.

There is a real difference between sensory reception of stimuli and their perception, which structures, combines, fuses, and interprets what was sensed. This is the origin of meaning. No two painters, equally skilled, will paint exactly the same ocean because their mental organizations, with which they perceive and extract meaning, are different.

There is a rough analogy between hunting and the graphic arts. An artist who wishes to paint a stormy seascape, for example, does not have to sit with his easel for days in the storm to paint what he sees. He can see that storm for 5 minutes, or 5 seconds, and his memory and imagination take over until he is safe in his studio and his mind makes new combinations of mental elements, or thoughts and ideas.

He knows how to create the illusion of three-dimensional space, depth, nearness, or farness by foreshortening lines that are actually on a flat surface. There is light, dark, and shadow, with foreground and background to account for. There are colors that complement, contrast, and harmonize with different hues, tints, and values. Textures must look smooth or rough enough so water, foam, sand, rocks, coastline, or sky overhead seem to have their own distinctive characteristics. One should intuit the different feel without having to touch the representations on canvas.

All these and other things must be brought together in the mind in such a way that what the artist intended as his creation becomes a reality on canvas. All these subjective ideations must now be transferred from the activity of the brain, mind, or soul to the objective material reality of the painting through the use of material elements like paint, mixed colors, palettes, brushes, spatulas, canvas, easel, and studio. Where there was nothing before on that blank canvas, now there is a seascape.

The inevitable questions arise—is it truly a work of art, or is it another picture? Is it good or bad? Will it survive the test of time, or disappear into oblivion like another fad or accident of history in the space/time continuum? Does it matter? Why? To Whom?

There are many schools of thought on the issue, so there are no final answers, and each to his own tastes. I have my own answer. Any real work of art must instantly move the mind and soul into understanding and feeling its symbolic intent. The function of any symbol is to refer to meanings outside of itself. It is a rung on the ladder we climb on our way to the top looking for the greater insight and greater refinement of meaning and reality. The more universally symbols speak to the mind and soul of man, the greater the art. It transcends narrow cultural limitations. It refers to lasting values and universal truths we all recognize, intuitively. It moves us. It matters. It is of consequence to what we are and what we become. It is, in short, spiritually uplifting and puts us into contact with the mystery of our lives.

The problem with too much of abstract modern art is that it can mean anything and everything, which is why a narrative account is often necessary to explain what the artist really meant in his private world of reality. But it is so private that no one else can enter it without explanation. It is self-defeating. Most of what real art can say has been said already, long since. It requires extra effort and talent to create different and better expressions for older universal realities of the human spirit. The modern artist, if he is not a genius with penetrating insight to uplift the human spirit higher than before, must say something, nevertheless. His art doesn't have to be better; it just needs to be different—change for its own sake. That's modernism which forces gimmickry and novelty to create something, anything new. It does not uplift spiritually. It merely entertains.

To illustrate my point, let me give an example. Once I visited a modern art museum and read many of the narratives explaining the paintings. The explanations were necessary, since the paintings could have meant anything. It was frustrating to learn that every meaning I imagined had not the least semblance to what the narrative said the artist meant. Then, I found my self staring at a painting without a narrative. Surely, I thought, I had found meaning at last. It was a canvas about 2 feet by 3 feet, painted completely solid black. On the extreme left was a tall, thin pylon painted solid white. The frame was attractive. On it was a small plate bearing the name of the masterpiece. It was entitled, "Soon." I vented my frustrated soul by writing on a slip of paper the only meaning I could think of. Then, I fixed it below the frame—"Not Soon Enough."

Since masterpieces are already in museums and private collections, art dealers need new masterpieces all the time. Their livelihood depends on it. They manipulate the market, hype the discovery of a "genius', and a third-rate piece of junk becomes a masterpiece which one wants because the other guy has an original. Because the effete elite need socially competitive status symbols to maintain prestige, an artificial market of supply and demand creates a new school of art.

Post-modernism is born, and it bewails the alienation of the human spirit and proceeds to alienate and derail it even more with its gimmickry and faddish novelties. Anything becomes art. It does not spiritually uplift. It entertains by advances to greater degrees of the bizarre and gruesome to say something original and different until the abnormal, perverse, and unwholesome become the new standard, surrounded by a new cult of elite devotees.

Once, in a discussion with a connoisseur, he told me he thought Picasso's *Guernica* was the greatest masterpiece ever painted. I asked whether it was art or one-sided political propaganda. His jaw fell, but no words came in answer. I didn't learn anything from him.

Let us return to the seascape which depicts an ocean. But what does the ocean symbolize? To me it refers to what the soul can feel, even if the mind boggles at descriptions. The ocean symbolizes at least the elemental, the grandeural and majestic, the foreverness of its mystery between glassy calm and demonic fury. It changes constantly, yet it remains eternal. It is one of the few things I know more restless than I and far calmer than I can hope to be. It was here before I came and will be here after I go. It made life, history, humanity, and cultures possible. It has also destroyed large portions of them. What secrets are still hidden beneath its surface when it changed the course of destinies?

Did the artist who painted the seascape feel any of this? If not, what did he feel, and in either case, how well did he translate it to canvas? Does he connect with my soul, winning my gratitude for saying better than I could what we both feel and know about the ocean? Of the countless seascapes I have seen, there are many that are technically competent, but lack soul or spirit. I am merely looking at a representation of water, not art.

Then there are masterpieces, and one of them has left a profound impression on me. I heard of it long ago from my father's unschooled compatriots who knew all about it. I finally made the trip to see it late in life, but see it I did. It is greater than they said it was. It hangs in the Armenian Mekhitarist Monastery standing on the island of San Lazzare, a short distance from Venice, on the site of a former leper colony closed in the 1600s.

The painting is a seascape by Ayvosovsky called *Chaos*. I'll wager that 99% of the artists, connoisseurs, academics, and cultural elite have not seen it, nor heard about it. It appears in no textbooks I know of, and yet, it is surely a great masterpiece. It instantly rivets the eyes and transfixes the soul. The dark, tempest-swept waves are a chaos of fury leaping at you right out of the frame, and the storm-tossed clouds above tell you nothing can survive out there. Yet, high overhead, there is a strange and beguiling light etching the cloud tops into almost a superhuman form hovering over that maelstrom below, promising calm, peace, and tranquility in a moment. You not only see water (you can do that with any seascape), but you feel the essence of the oceanic and what it means. You feel the salt spray and mist. You smell the brine-scented winds scudding off those waves. For a frightful moment, you can almost feel those waves engulfing you, and then you know you're safe—the light and calm above caught your eye and told you so.

That painting not only symbolizes the eternal mystery of the oceanic, but it reflects the human soul, which is also an eternal mystery changing from fury to tranquility, from despair to hope, from death to life. The painted symbols are a linkage to a piece of reality.

There are other realities of the soul with universal meanings that come to light, no matter how different the symbolic forms, for expression emerging from the soul-stuff of human drama. The hunter is also responding to that universal mystery understood only by God. Does He chuckle when hearing our shouts of triumph at a new solution of the old mysteries which will require more triumphal shouting at newer solutions while the mysteries remain unchanged, after all?

In crafts, trades, and technologies there are schematics, dia-grams, or blueprints, and established standards and operational procedures, that tell a functionary how to tackle his task and what to expect or predict with reasonable confidence concerning the outcome, which is not in doubt. Even the average time limit for completing a certain task is standardized. If something occurs to upset the apple cart, then one can start over again from where the task was interrupted, hopefully with better insight and corrected procedure.

The hunter has none of this, which is why his art is analogous to painting, for example. Beyond a bare minimum, his most important tasks are unstructured, non-standardized, spontaneous, and reciprocal. There may be a dozen ways to do each thing, or there may be no way at all in the sequence of actions aiming at a successful conclusion of what was intended all along. Anything can happen. There may be several trials and errors and many unknowns. What is done and how it is done is a purely creative process along each step of the way. That's why the hunter is engaged in an art—the venatic art, or the art of venery (as it was known for centuries), which has some elements in common with all art—the perception of which was sidetracked with the emergence of sport and sporting holidays.

The hunter also has a mental and material interaction which takes place in his studio—the wilderness. Like the artist who paints seascapes, the hunter, too, must visualize his own plan or mental blueprint. He scrutinizes the terrain, natural barriers, topographic advantages, and probable location of his quarry. Out of many options, he develops the best mental diagram or imagery for getting within shooting distance. The elements which must be combined for his diagram are: spoor, trails, tracks, droppings, crushed leaves, broken twigs, bent grass, the imprint of hooves, paws or claws on gravel, snow, sand or mud that read like a book to the tutored eye.

He must do this in a constantly changing studio. Unlike the painter who has control over all his elements, the hunter has no control over some of his, and in fact is at their mercy—the elements of nature. He can't control the rain, snow, storm, light, dark, and wind. But somehow he must adjust all his thoughts and actions to the real elements so that subjective intent steered by mind, instinct, and imagination can reach fruition in the objective reality of the wilderness world.

Now he must evaluate the best, and most likely way to make his stalk and calculate the risk to reach objectives. Since no two hunts can be exactly alike and often are totally different, given the nature of the animal and natural exigencies, the hunter combines and recombines in a hundred different ways all the old mental elements—his images, memories, knowledge, signs, signals, and cues in order to create a plan of action and strategy. There is no standard or predetermined way to do it. The way must be created anew in the progress of each hunt where each action and phase intuitively fits into another by its own internal logic without labored cogitation. The material elements are not brushes and paints, but rifle, ammunition, knife, rope, pack, compass, and whatever. This is the creative process, which hopefully results in a created product—the trophy, which was an elusive or infuriated animal.

Like any art form, the hunter's art has a crucial element best characterized by the idea of encounter. The encounter is essentially the sudden, unexpected meeting with something or someone resulting in opposition, conflict, challenge, or obstacle. There is a disruption of the immediate activity or a potential threat to the person encountered. Beethoven, while composing a symphony, unexpectedly encounters a problem of harmony or counterpoint disrupting the smooth flow of notational progress in his composition. He must stop, rethink his way through, and devise or create the solution.

The hunter also experiences encounters, but they often have an added element which no other art form has—the exigent. The encounter becomes an exigency disrupting or opposing the smooth flow of action with its threatened failure, loss, or disaster—in short, a catastrophe. To prevent it, immediate, urgent, and critical action is mandatory. There is no time for prolonged cogitation.

When the hunter suddenly and unexpectedly comes face to face with a grizzly, and that grizzly woofs and runs off with surprised alarm, that's an encounter—for both of them. When the hunter gives chase expecting to head the grizzly off at the river bank a half mile away, hears a commotion behind him, turns around to see the grizzly coming at him full bore from 10 feet away—that's an exigency. Since the hunter made the difference in the outcome, his actions are not the result of sheer chance or mechanical routine. They are the result of his creative art.

The hunter may never know it, and may not be interested in knowing it, but at heart he is a philosopher. His view of life, especially in the wilderness, is that ponderous reasoning spins one around in circles, forcing one to come out the same door through which he went in. In the exigencies, the hunter does not have time for reason, nor can he guess the unknowable. His entire being, therefore, is reflexively and instinctively geared to decision and the will to action when there is imminent danger from his quarry who decides to attack, or imminent and irretrievable loss if it escapes, or from the hazards and dangers from the elements of nature gone wild.

A hunter may hunt a lifetime and never face such exigencies. That's possible, but highly unlikely. He doesn't need too many hunts before such exigencies occur. They literally go with the turf.

It requires a certain type of personality or character to face these exigencies. Many who oppose hunters are of an opposite personality type—not better or worse, but merely different. Because the creativity of the hunter is inseparable from motion and action, it is analogous to another art form—drama. An actor on stage or screen must translate the emotions he feels, or imagines, to influence the feelings and minds of his audiences. He has learned a preexistent script. He knows how the play will end and exactly what he must do in advance. He has rehearsed every step of the way. The audience knows this but suspends judgement (as the critics say) and makes believe the actor is undertaking his action for the first time and the play is real.

The actor must give the make-believe enough verisimilitude so it is perceived as if it were real. The actor, Mercutio, does not really kill the actor, Benvolio, in a sword fight. It is the characters Romeo and Tybalt, acted by Mercutio and Benvolio, who act out the killing with dramatic flair. It is hard to tell whether it's Romeo or Mercutio who comes to life at the end of the play for a curtain call and applause.

Make believe becomes real again, and sometimes the "real" is make-believe. Ah, the play's the thing! Depending on how convincingly Mercutio and Benvolio acted out their parts, they were either good or bad actors. The vendetta between the Montagues and the Capulets suffers the full agony of grief when their children Romeo and Juliet die in so untimely, tragic, and dramatic death.

The hunt is real, tragic drama; unlike the play on stage, the hunter and hunted are playing for keeps, not make-believe. There are no rehearsals. It's for real the first time around, which may be the last time. There is no audience and no curtain call. There is no prepared script or suspended judgement. In place of verisimilitude, there is the reality of agony, encounter, exigency, contest, joy and sorrow, life or death. There is no other art form like the venatic art, because it is not created by sitting at a desk, standing at an easel, or moving on a limited stage. The quarry is free to move with great speed and stamina anywhere in a boundless wilderness. Where he goes for escape and safety is often the most inaccessible places for the hunter to reach, but that is where the latter must go to close in if he can. It is the quintessential action performed with a real outcome in doubt for the contesting hunter and hunted.

Whether the hunter asks for it or not, he is the stellar performer whose task is to overcome often heroic odds. There is no audience, and the wilderness is his stage. His conscience is the critic who rave reviews or pans the performance, who puts thumbs up or thumbs down. The trophy hunt is the real enactment of tragic drama. The goal is the search for the icon, the sacred art, and trophy on the wall is its symbolic expression.

Once, a friend, who was a serious student of art philosophy, was critiquing my thoughts on the art of hunting and its creativity. We were sitting in my trophy room. He understood what I said, but could not accept my conclusion.

He said, "All art and creativity results in some created product. Where is your product"?

I was dumbfounded. "It's right there in front of you mounted on the wall," I said. "Can't you see it"?

This argument had come up before with others, but it had gone the other way. Seeing the beautiful mounted trophy, most critics wonder what the hunter has to do with art or creativity since the taxidermist produced what's hanging on the wall. But those who riveted steel beams and poured concrete do not get credit for the skyscraper; it is the creation of the architect. While both hunter and taxidermist are involved in a final result, they are both doing different things. The taxidermist's role is complemental. He completes what the hunter began, who would have hunted even if taxidermy had not been invented. But the reverse is not true. Without the hunter there is no taxidermy.

In taxidermy, first there's the tanner, who must chemically so treat the hide it will be pliable for working and retain its hair and fur without slippage. When it gets to the taxidermist, often there are two or three different craftsmen working on different phases of the same trophy. A master taxidermist will, of course, check each phase according to his satisfaction and complete the finishing touches. Then, again, he may do the entire project himself.

In either case, the objective is to return cape, horns, antlers, and other distinguishing features to their original state as lifelike as possible, for which there are prescribed procedures. The techniques and technology are so standardized, that any number of competent taxidermists can take the same hide and come up with roughly the same results. A few taxidermists go beyond the "same results." Too many Dall sheep trophy heads look dull, lifeless, with wooden expressions, one eye looking at you and the other past you all too often. Somehow, they seem to insult you.

Some Dall sheep trophies seem to be alive, with a distinctive character all their own, looking right into your soul. You know you are seeing Dall sheep as though no hunter or taxidermist ever touched them. You are privileged to see the image of a reality unspoiled. The line between artist and artisan or craftsman is very fine, and the degree of excellence attained erases that fine line. The degree of mediocrity magnifies it. One way or another, a finished product will be a certainty for better or worse.

While a well-mounted trophy is a beautifully handcrafted product, it was preceded by another product of creative effort which had no prescriptions or standardized procedures and no certainty of outcome—the hunt. If successful, that hunt produced its own product—the skinned cape or hide; no matter how unfinished or even repellent, it is the result of an unique hunt, which has been created once and for all in its entirety. Nobody, not even the hunter, can replicate it. The hunt and hunter create the trophy; the trophy does not create them. The visible completed trophy symbolizes the invisible hunt. It is part of the greater reality now past. It freezes in time and space a part of a once tremendous, total experience, now gone forever.

The consummate skill of the taxidermist provides the means for remembrance. It is the hunter who has the memory of the creative achievement which that trophy represents. It is he who resolved the high-risks of doubtful outcome in his favor. His was the unique experience of agony or joy. He is the ultimate creator of the product. There is none of this in the routine outcome of taxidermy. To give the taxidermist his due in an art project is only fair; but to deny the hunter the greater credit for creating that art to begin with is gross injustice. But that's what the usual critic does looking at a trophy, not because he appreciates what the taxidermist's art symbolizes (in fact, he hates it), but because he wants to degrade the hunter, one way or another.

We don't know who quarried the limestone or carved, polished, and fitted it, but we know that somewhere between 2686 and 2613 BC, one of the greatest architectural geniuses who ever lived, Imhotep, created the first and only step pyramid, which inspired all the others. The Pharaoh, Djoser, who commissioned it, is hardly known; the artists, artisans, and skilled craftsmen who built it are unknown. But that symbol still stands, and when we see it, inevitably we wonder who created it. Imhotep was its creator, even if we never heard that name before and will promptly forget it.

I don't know how many taxidermists worked on my African lion, or who they were. I don't have to know to admire the superb work they did. However, they did not hunt it. I created the hunt and the art which made the trophy possible.

What I did has no importance to anyone but myself, or possibly to some antihunters angry at what I've done. I hunted my lion for myself, not for the taxidermist or the world's admiration. It is in the record books, even though few who read it know me, or are concerned about such elusive things as mortality and immortality. But I have it full-body mounted, rearing with outstretched paws, just as he begins his leap, as he did on that day of destiny when our paths crossed. I know I created the reality of the hunt, art, trophy, and icon. It is my symbol, still alive in my mind and soul. When I leave this world, I shall carry its image with me in gratitude and reverence as my offering to Him who made me a hunter. All the rest doesn't matter.

The One That Got Away

o hunt is ever really finished, and the bear I faced on the highway is proof of it. It was not quite 5 AM as I drove at high speed to get home to Fairbanks. My wife was dozing beside me while I tried to stay awake. We had slept for barely 3 hours before our mad dash home had begun. I was cutting it close, but I had to make the commencement exercise at the university.

We were in a different world, it seemed. Storm-swept Valdez and the wild ocean were already a hundred miles behind. Here the whole world was bright with sunlight, the road totally deserted, and a sweet-scented cool, gentle breeze caressed the green forest on either side of the highway. My mind drifted with the ambience gliding past the wide open windows, and my memory screen was beginning to fade, dimming the images and emotions of a reality I had experienced scarcely 6 hours earlier.

I had killed my black bear and survived the most incredible and bizarre thing that has ever happened to me in my checkered lifetime. Something similar must have happened to other hunters, but I've never read anything quite like it in big-game hunting books, and I've read at least 1,000 of them over the years (no brag, just fact. Over 800 are in my own library, and I guess at the rest).

It was not only the miraculous survival of near death in the wilderness, but the fifth such survival, consecutively, from 1964 to 1967. Those stories are related in the last three chapters of this book because of their single underlying theme, which makes it a fitting conclusion to the sequels narrated here.

It was that last happening, less than 6 hours previously, which put together the other pieces now obsessing me with the unrelenting why?, when my thoughts were suddenly interrupted. An immense splinter of mountain side angled down to the road, pushing it out of the way in a wide arc.

I had no sooner careened around the asphalt curve when far ahead, in the middle of the road, there was a glistening black lump. It was instantly recognizable as a black bear. I braked gradually, letting the truck roll closer, and came to a gentle stop. By this time, it was obvious this was one big bear, a lot bigger than I had just taken a few hours ago. After all I had gone through for it, why did this taunting, tantalizing thing happen now right in front of me?

I was about 50 feet from him when I took my rifle down from the rear window rack, quietly opened the door and took a step forward. He just stood there eye-balling me. I took another step, very slowly, so as not to alarm him, and made no other sudden moves. Another step.

He just stood there eye-balling me. When about 20 feet from him, I figured I was close enough, even if my sprained ankle were no distraction. My stance froze in his full view. Still, he stood there, and so did I—eyeball to eyeball. I knew if I took my eyes off him for a split second, he would do one of two things—bolt or attack, probably and hopefully the former. My voice came out in a soft, deliberate monotone. "Hi, guy."

At the first sound, he cocked his head aside to listen. What came to my mind for a second was an old Victor phonograph record with the red label showing a dog, head cocked to the side, listening to the horn from where music came. The logo said, "His Master's Voice." I didn't feel like this bear's master, but he sure listened, anyway, as I said again, "Hi, guy," knowing my voice disguised the click of the safety as I slid it off on my rifle.

A fresh, fragrant morning breeze rippled his lustrous black fur. He was a superb bear, and I wanted him, but how could any bear, discovered by chance in the middle of a highway be a trophy? Where was the stalk, the contest, the risk that transformed any animal into a trophy that had been earned and deserved by the hunter?

"You big, dumb, magnificent brute. What am I going to do with you, eh," I asked softly? He just stood there.

The requirements of the law crossed my mind. It required only that I be 1 foot off the asphalt before shooting and that spot could have been reached with two or three sidesteps from where I stood. If he didn't come at me, he would go down that embankment and I would be above him with unobstructed visibility for several seconds before he reached cover. It would be a lead-pipe cinch to bowl him over as he fled unaware of the odds against him.

The law said it was legal, but my conscience said it was not fair, given the chance meeting in the first place. I would not disobey the law, but I would not take advantage of it, either. Law, these days, was passed by politicians who had long since betrayed the moral basis for it. Appeasement of the more powerful pressure group over the interests of another was the "lofty" basis for corrupt jurisprudence. There were better guides for conduct.

What I would have given to get into that bruin brain for just a few seconds and see what he was thinking—or if he could think at all. I said softly, "Hey you, if I leave everything I have and join you, will you teach me to hunt as superbly as you can? Will you show me how to survive murderous winters without steam heat? Will you show me how to climb, endlessly, these bloody mountain ranges without fatigue"?

I was so intent with these thoughts that I jolted myself when I heard my own voice ask loudly, "Will you teach me these things, huh? Will you?" He refused to twitch a muscle or bat an eye lash.

Then, for the first time in my hunting career, I had a strange and unique sensation that I was to experience again in later years a half dozen times. I sensed a complete detachment from myself, a kind of weightless floating, a oneness with the bear and everything else around us—breeze, swaying trees, and bright sunlight. I no longer felt or knew who, or where, I was—where I ended, and everything else began. There was no sense of passing time. It was just being without a sense of duration. Later, I wondered if this mental and spiritual state were a normal and constant condition for the prehistoric hunter on the trail whose instincts took the place of complex reasoning.

Something took me out of my trance and back to the reality of bear and man. I became aware that a state of tension had emerged and reached the breaking point. He was ready for the showdown. I was too.

Any sudden movement or loud sound on my part would galvanize him into instant, reflexive action. Either he would turn and dash down the 30-foot embankment to my left or he would come at me. If he bolted to the embankment, the undeserved advantage would be mine. In order for me to be fair, it occurred to me that I would have to take the disadvantage. I asked him, softly, "Will you charge? Please charge. Either you take me or I take you. Right?" I realized at that range I'd have a split second to hold low and fire.

Even if I pulverized his heart, his momentum would carry him to me and his reflexes could savage me. It had happened before to others, many times. What would my reflexes do at such close quarters? The risk was high, but possible. It gave the bear the advantage, and there was my handicap. It was more than a fair contest, I felt. Could I do it? It would be worth finding out and I hoped my self-confidence was not misplaced. That, after all, was the only way to resolve the doubtful outcome. That is the very essence of the contest, is it not—to resolve that doubtful outcome in one's favor under conditions of fairness? Is that not true of any venture, involving a win or loss, whether it be a chess game, a war, a new recipe, or a bad marriage? Is this not what we say of life itself, that it is a contest?

We both heard the distant, high pitched whining of tires on asphalt behind me at the same time. He twitched his head the slightest bit reflexively, while I fought the same instinctive urge to turn around, for then, while I could not see him, he could still see me.

"Hey, brute," I said. "We're going to look very silly in a few minutes just standing here. You'd better do something."

The whining of tires grew softer and came to a slow stop. A soft metallic sound announced the opening of the door. Then, silence. It had to be Tom and his wife, our companions with whom we had shared yesterday's episode, who were driving behind us. No one else would participate in the drama without meddling instantly.

Unfortunately, the bear had finally taken his eyes away from me! He was watching whatever was behind me. The dumb dodo!

He'd not only shifted the advantage to me again, he'd left himself wide open. He was forcing me to make the first move in this battle of nerves with the odds again in my favor. Could he know what a sporting gesture he just made? What a tragic way to end his life and rob the wilderness of his lordly presence!

Where was his instinct for self-preservation? Either he was too trusting, innocent, fearless, or all three. I was looking nobility right in the eye. There was only one honorable thing to do—out-sport him.

I said, "Look, you dope, never, ever stand in the middle of a highway, because you don't know what a trap it is; because some boob will take advantage and shoot you dead. Do you hear me?" I waited for a moment or two, but he didn't take his eyes away from whatever was behind me.

"Now, go! I'll never forget you. So long, ol' buddy."

I was choked up with mixed emotions, and my voice cracked just a wee bit. Maybe it was the change in pitch or the waver in my voice. Maybe he really understood. In an instant, he wheeled and charged down the bank.

I spun around to see what was behind me. It was Tom, and that figured. He had walked quite a bit in front of his parked vehicle and had been standing barely 70 feet from me all the while. He sprinted down the bank, brandishing his rifle. He cut to the right, parallel to the bank, where it was fairly clear of brush, so he could see.

I had a marvelous view of the whole thing. The bear had cut to his left and got in back of some alder screening. It would be good for Tom to get that bear—it was certainly fair chase, henceforth. Yet, I also wanted the bear to get away. It was sure some contest, now—Tom, with long, lanky legs sprinting desperately, and the bear with his low-slung gait, moving like a juggernaut.

They ran right past each other, going in opposite directions, separated by an alder thicket where neither could see the other. My bear vanished behind the alders, and I waved good-bye, part of me vanishing with him, forever.

A few minutes later, Tom climbed the embankment winded and heaving for air. I knew that as soon as he got his breath this was going to be a delicate situation.

"What's the matter with you? Why didn't you shoot"?

"What—in the middle of the road"?

"Yeah, I guess it wouldn't have been very sporting."

"Glad you feel that way. You had lots of time waiting behind me. How come you didn't shoot, either"?

"Same reason, I guess," he said, after a moment's reflection. "Hey, were you talking to that bear"?

"Talking to the bear? You gotta be kidding."

"I heard a voice. I'm positive you were talking to that bear." I knew he'd think I was crazy.

"Tom, do you hear such voices often? Tell me something about your dreams. Maybe I can help you."

"I heard voices," he said slowly and emphatically.

"Okay," I said. "You win. It was the bear. He just said 'Goodbye' in a roundabout way."

It was my turn to look at him the way he had been looking at me. I knew exactly what he was thinking—one of us was crazy and it wasn't he.

I walked back to my truck, and my secret remained with me and the bear. If bruin wanted to blab, let him. I wasn't going to talk. Who would believe me?

Reflections

**H**unters often swap yarns and compare notes; they learn much from each other this way. I had traded my highway bear story occasionally to encourage others to talk with bears, and see if they would get the same kind of reaction. A few times, when talk came up about it with non-hunting visitors or acquaintances, I knew what they were thinking from the way they looked at me—how could a bloodthirsty hunter like me, lusting for cruelty and running right into a nifty opportunity like that, let the bear go?

A couple of them asked me point blank. I told them what I really felt about it, and still do to this day—it was the only decent thing to do since I had not hunted for it, but merely blundered into in the middle of the highway while driving a truck. How could anyone possibly deserve a trophy under such conditions? To let it go was the only decent thing to do, since I didn't want it for food. (By this time, a promotion had increased my salary, and I was eating more comfortably.)

In heated discussions that often followed, I once said it was the only "sporting" thing to do. I got the most common put-down. "What's so sporting about killing a poor animal? Why is such barbarism called a sport to begin with"? I never liked the word sport, either, not because it was barbaric, but because it referred to so many different things, poles apart and recklessly lumped together. Anyway, that's the thing that got me started on my hunt to learn why the simple word "sport" was used to mean anything from highly skilled athletic team play to nocturnal activity like hanky-panky when it was raining in the park.

I knew what the law said about the conditions of the hunt. They were precisely spelled out in voluminous rules and regulations. But where were the outlines stating what hunting ethic and fair chase were and why they were sporting? These phrases suggested, more than they defined, what they referred to in a general sort of way. I had seen dozens of references to these concepts, no two of them alike, each with a piece of the whole picture, but the whole picture was missing.

Statutory rules and regulations are enacted by duly constituted legislative bodies, or agencies of a state, subject to change from time to time. (In the case of Congressional crooks, elected officials organize new ethics committees every 4 years or so to create new opportunities for crookedness not yet outlawed by the previous ethics committees.)

For hunters, statutory law spells out such things as hunting season, sometimes to the hour of opening and closing; the kinds of hunting weapons that may or may not be used; which game may be taken, depending on numbers, sex, age, and even the size of horns, antlers, and so on. Laws may include areas within which boundaries may be hunted, what kinds of transport may be used up to, and within, specific areas, what the penalties are for infractions of the law, and so on.

Wildlife is considered a public trust or resource, accessible to all, though much Federal and State legislation excludes too many publics, except special interest groups that have powered such public-good legislation.

The objective here is, or should be, sound conservation, wildlife management, and equitable treatment of the various publics involved. There are many kinds of hunting regulated by such law: commercial, subsistence, sport, predator control, and so on.

The concept of the hunting ethic, however, applies only to sport hunting—again, a term I am not especially fond of. Without that ethic, there can be other kinds of hunting, but there can never be such a thing as sport hunting. In other kinds of hunting, the objective of taking an animal may be done by the most practical, efficient, and cost-effective methods, depending on the reasons for the hunt. Ethical or moral considerations are incidental, if they exist at all.

In sport hunting, especially trophy hunting, a certain quality of conduct must be maintained at any cost. That quality is not incidental, but central to such a hunt. It is not only what is being done, but how. It has little to do with efficiency and practicality, but everything to do with right and wrong which is why the whole thing is tagged as a hunting ethic. That's what ethics are: a code of right and wrong conduct or behavior, which is not an issue in any other kind of hunting. Here is where the problem starts.

What's the difference between ethics and morals, since both words are actively used, and the dictionary defines them interchangeably? Both refer to right and wrong principles or to proper conduct. Books on the subject do a lot of double talking, but, as I see it, morals go beyond ethics.

Ethics have to do with conduct between persons, and between people and the state. They serve as the basis for legalisms. Ethics are invented by people and change with the changing times and manners. They are relative. Infractions may be penalized by the state; where there are two sides to the question, it is resolved by the shrewdest attorney or judicial pedantry. It tries to satisfy one or another contentious side. It is characteristic of modern, secular societies. As law, it is decreed by formal, legislative enactment.

Morals also pertain to right and wrong behavior or proper conduct. They not only regulate behavior between men and the state, but between them and gods or God. Morals are not made by men, but revealed by divine authority and are absolute in nature. Infractions may, or may not, be legal violations, but they are always sins. Penalty is atonement to God, not the payment of fines to the state. Morals are always grounded in religion.

One can have ethics without God, but one cannot have morals without God. This is characteristic of religious and traditional societies, and it is decreed by faith, custom, and usage. Then, there are societies which are an unequal combination of both types trying to coexist or lock in mortal combat.

Modern law is cumulative and changes constantly because its ethics are relative. Take every law, which is a change from a previous one, and trace it back to its beginnings and out comes morals. When people don't like morals, but still insist on fair play, or justice, new ethics emerge, but they can not get rid of the underlying morality where all laws started.

One of the great intellectual hoaxes of our times is that we can't legislate morality. Of course we can and we do all the time. There is no question about that. The question is—whose morality? If it isn't ours, "there ought to be a law against it." The bottom line is always morals, no matter how well disguised. The next to the bottom line is ethics. We stop here because to go further would get us into the religious thing of morality, and we know there is a separation of church and state notion which discourages that.

The separation clause can then be applied so that, while the church (morality) must not interfere with the state, the state (coercive power) can interfere with the church, or morality, any time it feels like it by arguing an ethic, or a law, which is moralizing without God. In a godless state, morality does not count, which is why ethics do. Right and wrong disappear. Legal and illegal intrude.

Any good legal philosopher will shoot down all I have said because he will say it is wrong, which is an ultimate resort to morals, not legality, thereby proving how right I have been all along.

The problem in our secular society is that what is legal may be immoral or unethical, and what is illegal may be moral or ethical. This is true in many areas of life, but it is especially true in hunting, and it is at the heart of the hunting and antihunting controversy. With this preface out of the way, we can get down to brass tacks.

Hunting ethics are a modern concept based heavily on a much older hunting morality, without the embarrassment of supernaturalism so distasteful to the modern, secular world. It is the devolution from the moral to the ethical that needs to be understood. Since all morality is grounded in religious belief, it is not surprising that the impact of religious values on a culture are often discussed, especially by ethicists. When the cultural pattern known as sport hunting is examined, inevitably some religious values come to the fore, as antihunters well know when they attack the one to get at the other. Hunters who ignore the fact that the attack on hunting is also an attack on values that make their culture and civilization possible, do so at their own peril. Destroy the one and, eventually, you will destroy the other.

It is the counterculture activist who raises religious issues that he wants to discredit, so as to undercut the moral basis that permits what is seen as environmental evil. The hunter has no choice but to respond on the same wavelength. The entire environmental movement, of which the antihunting movement is a part, raises the hue and cry that our way of life is inherently rapacious, exploitative, and otherwise abusive to our natural resources. It does not see these abuses despite the moral order, but because of the moral order it has long since subverted. It does not seek to correct abuse to preserve the integrity of the moral order. It seeks to eliminate the moral order despite its integrity. It's like chopping off the head to get rid of the headache.

No one disagrees with the fact that, in some regards, planet earth is abused and needs environmental protection—the desanctified label for responsible stewardship by all now becomes a specialized agency by a few who will do the protecting. The disagreement lies with the excessive, and often fraudulent, claims of extreme environmentalists who have a hidden political agenda buried in the protective agency. The liberal-humanistic denial to the contrary, the crumbling remnants of our value system inherited from the Judeo-Christian tradition, is the real target. What follows is neither a defense nor an attack on any religion. It is an analysis of certain values, emerging from moral conviction, to understand why and how the antihunter justifies his position, and for proof zeroes in on Genesis 1:26-28 which says:

> And God said, "Let us make man in our image after our likeness: and let them have dominion over the fish of the sea, and over the fowl of the air . . . and over all the earth, and over every creeping thing that creepeth upon the earth." So God created man in his own image, in the image of God created he him; male and female created he them. And God blessed them, and God said unto them, "Be fruitful, and multiply, and replenish the earth and subdue it: and have dominion over the fish of the sea, and over the fowl of the air and over every living thing that moveth upon the earth."

It is this dominion clause that sticks in the craw of the antihunter and his coterie, because, as they see it, dominion is in the wrong hands for the wrong reasons. If that isn't bad enough, Psalms 8:3-8 makes things worse. It says,

> "When I consider thy heavens, the work of thy fingers, the

moon and the stars, which thou hast ordained; what is man that thou art mindful of him? and the son of man, that thou visitest him? For thou hast made him a little lower than the angels and hast crowned him with glory and honor. Thou madest him to have dominion over the works of thy hands; thou hast put all things under his feet . . . the beasts of the field; the fowl of the air, and the fish of the sea . . ."

From this moral point of view, God has not only given man dominion over animals, but crowns him with glory and honor, making man a little lower than the angels, but certainly higher than any other life form on this planet. Clearly, man is superior in this hierarchy to the animals (and the environment), and there is no talk here of equal rights. This is what grabs the animal-rights activist, the antihunter, and the radical liberal egalitarian by the throat. What? Man is more important than the snail darter, but less so than God? Impossible—on both counts, no less!

The antihunter animal-rights activist is infuriated at the thought that God may think a sport hunter is more important than a household pet, that capitalists can plunder the planet for filthy lucre, and Western civilization can dominate this planet and conquer its Mother Nature, all because a sexist Father God gave man dominion and made him lower only than angels. That is the reality motivating the antihunting attack on the hunter for which loving animals is often a pretext.

There is a monumental injustice committed by antihunters who are fond of repeating the dominion clause *ad nauseam*. If they are going to quote Scripture, they have to go all the way. My copy of Strong's Concordance shows only three references to the dominion clause in Scripture. But, there are over 20 references to the responsible stewardship clause, which they never quote, and it looks as though they have never seen. Dominion is inseparable from responsible stewardship. One can enjoy the former privilege only by meeting the latter obligation. The very verse that is hatefully quoted as giving man dominion contains the precise word replenish—man may have dominion, but he must replenish and use wisely what he uses. This was a moral injunction long before it became statutory law.

What can be recognized as one of the earliest historical mandates for wildlife conservation is Deuteronomy 22:6

*If, while walking alone, you chance upon a bird's nest with
young birds or eggs in it, in any tree or on the ground, and
the mother bird is sitting on them, you shall not take away
the mother bird along with her brood; you shall let her go,
although you may take her brood away. It is thus that you
shall have prosperity and a long life."*

The text does not state, of course, why the brood may be taken.
Presumably, it is for food, but it may just as well be for sheer
vandalism. In either case, it mandates a true replenishing the earth
and responsible stewardship. This is what justifies the dominion
clause. This is not only good wildlife management for the benefit
of man, it is also a compassionate sparing of the source that
perpetuates the species as God's sacred creation—not as the
political tool of some state agency.

The Old Testament contains few references to hunting. Nimrod, Ishmael, and Eassau are great hunters who are approved and
lauded. The point is that, while nothing in the Old Testament
mandates hunting, nothing stigmatizes or prohibits it, either. It is
up to man to hunt or not, but if he does, then there are moral
conditions of right and wrong to be met. Otherwise, nowhere is
hunting denounced, which is why today's antihunter or animal-
rightist is up in arms.

Furthermore, cruelty and abusive treatment of animals is
nowhere condoned, but denounced instead as sin, long before it
became law. Their compassionate and merciful treatment is mandated clearly in Numbers 22:22-35 when Balaam beats his donkey
for some minor reasons and is suddenly confronted by the angel of
the Lord (who) said unto him,

*". . . Wherefore hast thou smitten thine ass these three
times? behold, I went out to withstand thee, because thy
way is perverse unto me."* Whereupon Balaam says, *". . .
I have sinned . . ."* and repents of his ways.

Cruelty, seen as a perversity, is a sin, in the eyes of the angel
of the Lord. Not only are domestic animals, in this case an ass, to
be shielded from it, but, by extension, refers to all animal life as
part of the responsible stewardship clause.

Scripture is replete with admonitions against the abuse of

God's creatures, including man, himself, and that morality, grounded in a religious faith, precedes, by some 3,000 years, the modern ethics against cruel and unusual punishment, which makes a mockery of the original moral intent. Centuries later, that moral mandate of responsible and faithful stewardship, which includes the prohibition of cruel treatment of animals, has been absorbed and taught by Christianity. St. Paul makes it crystal clear when he says, in First Corinthians 4:1-2:

> *"Let man account to us, as of ministers of Christ, and stewards of the mysteries of God. Moreover, it is required in stewards that man be found faithful."*

There is no room for equivocation here—either man (including the hunter) is accountable to God for replenishing what he has dominion over in full and faithful stewardship, or he isn't. This moral code of responsible stewardship, with replenishment of God's gifts we use, and with kind and compassionate treatment of his creatures, is the 2,000-year basis for what eventually became the moral grounds for the hunting ethics and fair chase.

It was this emphasis on mercy and compassion to all God's creatures, including animals, which left such a profound impact on hunting, even from the earliest days of the new faith, in spite of the fact that the word "hunt" does not appear a single time in all of the New Testament. Neither does a single word appear which forbids, stigmatizes, or makes sinful the killing of animals, or the hunt, or hunters. The prohibition is not against killing animals (that's a pantheistic tenet). Indeed, the sacrificial killing of animals was an important part of the religious rituals in the Old Testament.

The injunction in the New Testament is against cruelty and lack of compassion, with or without killing. The antihunter's pantheistic objection is to killing animals under any condition, and he opposes Christian morality because it does not outlaw animal killing to suit his position. Ironically, some mainline Christian denominations have modified Biblical tenets enough to have joined the foe in opposing the hunter. From this stand, other tenets of the faith have been inevitably politicized and undermined. Politics make strange bedfellows.

From our perspective, the moral problem of man's relationship to animals reached its nadir in imperial Rome with the infamous gladiatorial games. For example, the Emperor Trajan did such things as staging one combat lasting 2 days in which 11,000 beasts were slaughtered by 100,000 gladiators. Nero staged a spectacle in which a whole division of the Praetorian Guard fought to the death 400 bears, 300 lions, and a sundry collection of other beasts. Even a cursory survey of the Roman relationship to wild animals would require a volume. Here, only a few key points are made.

Killers of men and animals were categorized by their specialties in killing techniques: *ratiarii* who used nets and daggers; *secutores,* who used shields and swords; *dimachae,* who used a short sword in each hand; *laqueatores,* who killed with slingshots; *essedarii,* who fought in chariots; and the *bestiarii,* who killed beasts in any number of ways, using even whips, prods, and hot irons to infuriate them into greater ferocity born of sheer desperation.

The Emperor Commodus was born 44 years after Trajan's death and lived to the age of 31. It is worth a few comments about one of history's greatest psychopaths by our standards. Commodus, trained as a gladiator, had over 1,000 contests including 350 duels to the death with other gladiators. He was no coward, but he was a bully when it came to contests with animals. His alternate lifestyle included drunken orgies, transvestite appearances in the arena, 300 concubines and 300 boys, fiendish sexual tortures, and so on.

Why should such a man not use red hot irons to goad gladiator and beast into ferocity to stage his theatrical spectacles? He killed all sorts of beasts, including ostriches, of all things, by beheading them in combat. Why not? He could, and did, kill human cripples with arrows or sword. Once, he killed 100 lions or 100 tigers (references do not state whether these were two separate events or a confusion in identifying the animal). The important point is not that men and animals were killed for entertainment (although that is bad enough), but that they had to be killed with deliberate cruelty to satisfy the blood lust of the spectators.

A stone marker commemorating the gladiator, Publius Baebius Justus, verifies the fact that he killed 10 bears *crudeliter* or with a sufficient degree of cruelty. Failure to inflict sufficient cruelty made the crowds scream for the incompetent or recalcitrant gladiator's death which they did with the famous thumbs down signal. This was Roman morality.

There were only a few voices raised against such inhumanity, and even the great Cicero, who denounced the slaughter, said that when guilty men died such a death in the arena it provided good "mental discipline" against suffering and death for spectators. Pliny the Younger, renowned for his civility, praised Trajan for providing the games, and Trajan had excused the slaughter by saying it was ". . . cheap gore of common men spilled in the arena, and nothing to get excited about."

There is an important point to all this. In the popular Wonders of Man series published by the Newsweek Book Division with its nationwide coverage, there is a handsome, well-illustrated volume entitled *The Colosseum*,[1] authored by Peter Quennell, who is obviously a gentleman and a scholar. It is, therefore, difficult to understand why he commits certain literary transgressions. The following quotations are taken from his above-named book to illustrate the point: ". . . men who fought from chariots, and the highly trained *bestiarii*, who only appeared in the popular beast hunts . . ." (p.45) and when the sound of music came from the hydraulic organs, it ". . . must soon have been lost in the savage hubbub produced by 45,000 maddened sportsmen, each bellowing . . ." (p.47) "A particularly repulsive aspect of the shows in the amphitheater were famous wild beast hunts . . . The *bestiarii*, professional beast slayers . . ." (p.51)

Quennell quotes the renowned Gibbon, who says, ". . . in all these exhibitions, the securest precautions were used to protect the person of the Roman Hercules (Commodus) from the desperate spring of any savage (animal) . . . The dens of the amphitheater disgorged at once 100 lions; 100 darts (spears?) from the unerring hand of Commodus laid them dead as they ran raging around the arena . . ." (p.141), Quennell knows (because he says so) that crosswalls in the arena divided it in such a way that ". . . the beasts . . . might be more easily speared at short range from any point . . ." and that Commodus, ". . . Aiming down from railings of the podium . . . also shot 100 bears." (p.64) This is sufficient, perhaps, to examine what is happening here.

Quennell knows that the arena is crisscrossed with walls which make small enclosures within the arena, which itself is an enclosed space. The animal, no matter how ferocious, can only run around, trapped and totally vulnerable from any point. How could this be called a hunt? Why would highly trained *bestiarii*, known in translation as beast killers, engaged in the carnage within an enclosure be called hunters, while the spectacle of slaughter is called beast hunts?

Why would the index of his book say, *"Bestiarii*: see Animal hunts"? Why does the psychopathic animal killer, Commodus, a *bestiarius*, become a hunter in a closed arena with his prey being whipped or branded (with hot irons) into attacking a hunter who cannot be reached in his railed podium? How can 45,000 spectators be called sportsmen? Why do "particularly repulsive aspects of the shows in the amphitheater (become) famous wild beast hunts?" Why would the Latin, *venator*, which means a fighter of wild beasts, or a wild animal combatant, used correctly by the author in one context, suddenly become a hunter in all the other contexts? Why does the Latin *venatio*, which specifically means a wild beast combat, or spectacle of animal killing based on cruelty and torture for the entertainment of spectators, suddenly become a wild beast hunt?

The entire concept of *venatio* emerged from the *ludi saeculares* or from ritualized games and play, partly religious in nature, and became commemorative funeral ceremonies of a departed military celebrity. The game was a simple combat, or, these days, martial arts contests between soldiers in his honor. Within a couple of centuries from such beginnings, *venatio* became the national theater of the masses. Combat, as a test of valor, had become the slaughter of beasts and men alike. Most gladiators were former slaves, eager to have a fighting chance for survival in the arena to win fame and glory. Some of them did, and became very wealthy in the process, but they had little occupational longevity.

Other victims in the arena were criminals, the physically deformed, enemies of the state, and, of course, the Christians who were slaughtered for mere religious beliefs. And the animals— always the animals. To supply the games with enough animals, some species were wiped out in parts of the Empire: in North Africa the elephant disappeared; in Mesopotamia, the lion; in Nubia, the hippopotamus; in Caspian Persia, the tiger, and so on, filling the need for more and more of the most cruel and barbaric entertainment for the masses crazed with lust for blood.

Why is the word *venatio* not used to mean a wild animal killing spectacle, or show, or pageant, or entertainment? Why is it always used to mean a hunt? *In a true hunt, the hunter must seek his quarry and find it in an unenclosed wilderness so that an animal has a chance to escape. Captive animals are not dumped on him in an enclosure.*

None of this is to discredit Quennell or the many other writers, some of whom are internationally reputed scholars (like Durant, Breasted, and Maspero), and antihunting critics, who have done the same thing. I believe these writers use the English language in an innocent manner, without intending any pejoration. They could not be expected to see the future implications.

Regrettably, the same cannot be said of Mr. Cleveland Amory, archenemy of the hunter and founding father of the antihunting movement, who knows well what he says and why. Amory denounces the ". . . mindless savagery and heartless indifference . . ." of hunters, and degrades the integrity and reputation of R. Gordon Cumming, among many other hunters. Amory denounces Cumming by saying ". . . that each of his encounters with elephants gets the full gladiatorial treatment,"[2] (Surely, "gladiatorial" is not a slip of the lip.) and zeroes in on one episode that required 35 bullets before Cumming brought down his elephant. But the context is ignored and manipulated. All this takes place in 1843-48 (which Amory knows), and Cumming is one of the first safari hunters in South Africa. In fact, he is exploring the Bamangwato region. Arguably, he is one of the founding fathers of the African safari. His field-loaded shells are so ineffective, he melts the silver in his teapots, drinking cups, and candlesticks to harden his bullets for penetration. His inefficient rifles are black-powder burners. In the 35-shot elephant encounter, his rifle explodes in his hands, which Amory fails to mention. Cumming berates himself for not knowing elephant anatomy, but neither did any other hunter of the times. It is Cumming who learned the secrets of elephant hunting to pass on to future hunters.

Amory quotes from a lengthy paragraph to indicate Cumming's gladiatorial savagery, yet that very same paragraph describes exactly what is happening and why. Amory omits any mention of Cumming's true feelings, who said: "I was surprised and shocked to find I was only tormenting and prolonging the sufferings of the noble beast (the elephant), I resolved to finish the beast with all possible despatch . . . to put an end to its life and pain in the quickest manner possible. I had often lamented having to inflict so many wounds on the noble animals before they fell."[3]

Amory completely passes this by from the same paragraph he manipulates to make his case that Cumming is a heartless, cold-blooded, gladiatorial savage. Amory does this repeatedly to other great hunters of the past. What excuse can there be for this?

How many antihunters have been influenced by such canards? Constantly, one reads of the cruelty and butchery inflicted on animals by the pioneers of sport hunting until their experiences enabled the constant improvement in firearms and ballistics technology. This is how we got to the modern, efficient high-powered rifles, in the hands of competent sportsmen, which can kill cleanly, instantly, painlessly. Providing it is done correctly.

What now? Initially, the hunter is damned for savagery, butchery, and cruelty. Now, he is damned for modern high-powered rifles that were developed precisely to end that "painful butchery" and enable merciful, instant, painless kills. One would think the antihunters would at least refrain from venting their contradictory arguments and attitudes, but no such luck. They have different motives buried beneath their sympathy for suffering animals.

The foregoing is not a game of word playing. It is what is known among academics as psycholinguistics and semiotics. Words, language usage, and the vernacular often have hidden meanings and emotions behind them. The words hunt, hunter, and hunting are linked with the idea of bloody, orgiastic, gory, cruel, brutalized suffering, and intellectuals who use them do not know the first ruddy thing about hunting. They don't do it; they just read about it from other intellectuals who couldn't possibly have done it either, or they could never make such mistakes of elementary observation. And, the biggest mistake of all is to judge people and values by our present standards, which are embattled in our current culture wars.

At the same time, such innocence creates a pejorative use of these words which become stereotypes. There are enormous psychological, spiritual, and propagandistic consequences to all this in the politics of our times. Today, one sees the term sport hunter written as "sport hunter" in quotes. This is itself a subliminal technique for stigmatizing the legitimate hunter to set him apart from normal humanity for easy identification as an evil target to be persecuted. In fact, today's hunter is one of the most discriminated against and persecuted minorities in the country.

The uninitiated modern urbanite, who knows hunters and animals only from the television set or zoo, gets an instant mental image of depravity lurking in his own neighborhood—with all the other criminal threats or violence to his well-being. Is not a modern-day hunter the same thing as a cruel gladiator slaughtering beasts and innocent people with sufficient *crudeliter*? Well, not quite, but almost—no? And is almost not a good enough substitute for the real thing in the mental world of fantasy? Witness Amory's treatment of Cumming the "gladiator."

There were courageous pagan voices in antiquity that dared criticize the games as an evil deserving obliteration. Seneca, Lucian, Epictetus, Artemidoras, and a few others. Their orations and writings, however, left little, if any, impact on the illiterate masses, and the sophisticated upper classes, who could read and understand, were precisely those who cheered the loudest at the games and opposed any notion of reform. It was one of their chief diversions, some made great fortunes from it, and it kept the unruly masses out of the affairs of state.

There were, after all, at least 180 state holidays a year, and an additional 50 regional ones, that provided free entertainment as part of the public dole for the vast majority of the poor and unemployed. Besides, a handful of critics could hardly undo an institution entrenched for nearly 600 years in one of history's most powerful civilizations.

The change in Roman morals came about only after Christianity's triumph against paganism. Early church fathers like Tertullian, Augustine, St. John Chrysostom, and Anastasius, not only denounced the carnage publicly, but the Council of Nicaea in 325 A.D. formally anathematized the games. The games did not become extinct overnight, however. Even the Christian Martyrs could not easily do that to such an institution.

Some writers have damned—with faint praise—the contributions of the early faltering faith in its struggle against the *venationes*. After much verbal high-wire balancing, Michael Grant, for example, finally admits, no matter how begrudgingly (and should be credited for it) that ". . . in the last resort, and in spite of the longtime lag, its (gladiatorial) termination must be attributed to the spreading of Christian ideas . . . those who believed in the Gospel of Christ could not, and did not, forever tolerate the fighting of gladiators for public entertainment."[4] It is nice that believers did not forever tolerate the butchery. Does this mean that they tolerated it at all? The Gospel and its believers did not tolerate it even for a moment on moral grounds, but its termination was a completely different problem. Although the Romans fed all kinds of people to the lions, only the Christians were kitty-cat vittles for their religious views. If there were others who believed in the evil of the *venationes*, no doubt they calculated the risk/cost effectiveness, and refused the purchase price. The Christians, committed to their beliefs at all costs, bought the package-deal with its consequences. No matter what their other shortcomings may have been, there is no need to weasel around the fact—the followers of the Gospel stopped the carnage—no one else; whether quickly or slowly is a value judgement, depending on a host of other practical conditions.

In fact, the morality of the Christian faith got into the hunting business, indirectly, at least, long before 404 A.D., when Honorius formally abolished the gladiatorial games, with varied results. The first known instant of it involved Placidus, a general in the Roman armies under Emperor Trajan. Presumably, he was a hunter since he saw a vision of a magnificent stag with a crucifix between its antlers. He and his family were converted to the new faith. When he refused to pay homage to the idols of Trajan, the Emperor in a typical fit of rage, had Placidus and his entire family thrown to the lions of the arena, and, for some strange reason, the felines did not molest them—let alone devour them. As a more surefire substitute, the infuriated Trajan had Placidus and his family sealed inside a huge bull idol made of brass, a roaring fire was ignited underneath the statue, and Placidus and his family were roasted alive. Placidus went into church history as one its early martyrs and saints, known by his baptismal name, Eustacius.

There are references to at least six or seven different instances of this stag with the crucifix between its antlers in medieval history, but the most famous one of all, undoubtedly, involves Hubert, son of Bertrand, Duke of Aquitaine, in the 8th century. As a young man, Hubert did what most sons of wealthy, doting parents do even today; he wined, wenched, and wastrelled excessively, but always his dominant passion was the hunt, the chase, or *la chasse,* as his French would have it.

One day, during the chase, he, too, saw the vision of the stag with the crucifix, and a voice warned him of his coming perdition. He repented, distributed his sizeable fortune among the poor, was ordained a priest, went into the remotest areas of the Ardennes, preached the sacred word, founded a church, and started what later became the city of Liege. He died in 727 A.D. and was eventually raised to sainthood as St. Hubertus.

To this day throughout Europe, Hubertus is venerated as St. Hubert, patron saint of hunters. European hunting fraternities (membership in which is often mandatory to qualify for a hunting license) issue a small pin of the stag with a cross between its antlers as an honored badge of such membership. In art, the most famous rendition of this is the great Albrecht Dürer's engraving (about 1505) of St. Hubert, kneeling before the stag.

Many prayer books at the time were decorated with wild animals. Such a volume, belonging to Emperor Maximilian, had an engraving of an aurochs, again by Dürer. Cranach the Elder, has a breviary engraving of St. Chrysostom's Atonement, circa 1509, with a wilderness scene showing elk, roebuck, and what looks like a partridge. Undoubtedly, the influence of St. Francis of Assisi must have been enormous on art work and religious attitudes of the time toward animals.

Born in 1182, Francis became one of the giants of the Catholic Church, founding the Franciscan order after he gave his share of the great wealth from his father's estate to the poor. He took the vows of poverty and became famous for his rules of gentleness, compassion, and mercy—especially toward animals.

During a pilgrimage, he stopped at the town of Gubbio to prevent the townspeople from hunting down a ravenous wolf who threatened life and limb. Francis confronted the wolf, subdued it with gentleness, led it back to town where the people promised to feed and care for the animal who in turn promised to behave himself; the wolf and people lived happily thereafter, and when the critter died of old age, the townspeople, who would have destroyed him, wept for their departed friend, commemorating his death thereafter.

It may be that today's animal lovers are right after all; the wolf is not an evil, dangerous creature, but a gentle, sweet, lovable animal misunderstood by ignorant and evil human beings. Now that they have this documented fact to prove how right they have been, I would bet a million dollars they scoff in disbelief at this Medieval superstition.

The good saint also chanced on some mischievous boys taunting some doves they'd captured. He gave them a sermon on cruelty to God's creatures and taught the boys how to build nests to protect and care for the doves. From such beginnings, legend tells us, the friars of St. Francis' order raised and propagated the dove as a gentle, loving symbol of peace. When in our own times, the overblown modern artist and Communist spokesman Pablo Picasso devised the dove as a sign of peace, he showed it flying to the left—naturally. Did the campus activists who used that symbol realize old Pablo had sworn Marxist enmity to the church of his people whose faith had come to endow the dove as the symbol of love, charity, and peace without political intent?

St. Francis' love for animals is one of his most famous attributes. To this day, each October 4th, his church celebrates a blessing of the animals, especially the pets that are brought to the altar; he taught reverence and love for animals he called his "brothers and sisters," and became their gentle, loving patron saint. By example and practice, he taught responsible stewardship and protection of animals, used for man's benefit, as a service to God, not some ulterior political motive.

For an illiterate peasantry, and in the absence of mass-produced books and schools as we know them, the oral traditions handed down over the years by the good saint's teachings undoubtedly did much to disseminate Christian morality concerning man's relationship to animals some 300 years before the invention of printing and the libraries of books on animals.

Since the foregoing does not intend to be even the briefest outline of the history of hunting, it is perhaps sufficient to make the following observation. With the advent of agrarianism, the world's major civilizations developed sport hunting as a leisure activity for the royalty, nobility, and aristocracy. While the common man was allowed to hunt for food under strict regulations, certain game was set aside as royal, or off-limits to all but the privileged few. It may not have been fair from our perspective, but it sure prevented the wholesale destruction and extinction of species for food, or *ludi saeculares*. Usually, such royal game were the larger ones capable of killing the hunter.

It was the ensuing contest, excitement, adventure, and achievement that made the game worth while. In Europe, Africa, and Asia such royal animals were, notably, the aurochs, bear, boar, stag, lion, tiger, and elephant. In every culture and civilization, this class and caste distinction and separation, applied even down to the techniques of the hunt. In modern times, this inequality is a secret bone of contention for antihunters.

If European nobility hunted rabbit for the table, they did not use nets, as did the commoners. Instead, they chased on horseback.

When they hunted boar, they would close in with a pike, not long-distance bow and arrow. When the first wheel-locks and muskets came into usage, Emperor Maximilian of Austria, one of the great hunters of all time, expressed grave concern for the future of sport hunting, fearing it would be too easy. He instituted heroic hunting, or closing in on boar and bear hand to hand, as it were, wearing only a padded corselet, and using a short sword and dagger. He believed in cold steel, close-quartered, not flying projectiles through space. When he hunted the mountain chamois, which cannot be approached too closely, he preferred to use the more laborious crossbow to the quicker longbow. He shortened the length of the boar spear to let him "get closer to his work." He added unnecessary difficulties and self-imposed restrictions on technique than they had to be. This was in addition to those already self-imposed by his social class, long since. This may have enhanced the hunter's ego, if he survived, but it also gave the animal at least an even break.

The animal could not only fight back, it could flee if it so chose, and his escape avenues would not be cut off with nets, barricades, and man-made contrivances. Moreover, in the final *coup de grace*, it was normally a one-on-one encounter, no matter how many assistants had helped to bring the animal at bay. Could such an encounter be gory and savage? Undoubtedly. But it was also a fair one-on-one exchange, a give-and-take where the hunter was involved in a high-risk operation—to his life, that is—and his sharp weapons and raw courage were more than offset by the animal's ferocity, strength, speed, and stamina.

If it was gory, savage, and primordial, it was fated by the exigencies of the fight, fought to the finish as quickly as possible, lest the quarry manage to escape in an unenclosed area, or the hunter got himself killed while playing the prima donna with too many theatrical moves. There was no time for prolongation of agony. No deliberate *crudeliter* to satisfy blood-crazed spectators. No attempt at entertainment for others, just personal achievement for life made more precious by near-miss survival. No release of previously captured and tortured animals for sudden confrontation, but long and arduous chases, pursuits, and stalks for encounter and contest by the rules.

There were a few exceptions for an effete royalty, where staged "hunts" were extravaganzas and pageants for the entertainment of spectators. While these never reached the level of Roman *crudeliter*, they were bad enough and cannot be classified as authentic hunts. Pavilions were constructed, orchestras played, wine flowed copiously, and amorous adventures took place while deer were run through palisades and "hunted." In France, Louis XI and, later, Louis XIV hosted such spectacles. In Saxony, Elector John George III had 10,000 guests attending such a spectacle.

Heroic hunting, far from being typical, nevertheless set the standards from which the modern sporting ethic and fair chase developed. Obviously, such a hunter did not hug his bear or boar with endearing affection as he might a cuddly, furry bunny rabbit. Neither did he kill it with deliberate, protracted cruelty for the sake of enjoying the animal's pain and suffering. He may not have been St. Francis, but neither was he Commodus.

However, there was an important reason for such hunting propriety. On moral grounds, hunting was not forbidden and one could hunt with a clear conscience. But those same moral grounds enjoined against excesses, lack of stewardship, hatred and cruelty, and killing for the sake of killing. We modernists, who complain of moral rigidities, impermissiveness, and intolerance of the Age of Faith, cannot turn about and say those same morals did not haunt and regulate the hunter's conscience to prevent what would have brought immediate censure from peerage and priesthood, alike.

No doubt those moral precepts were violated on occasion, given human nature. At least, however, they existed as a reference point against which right and wrong could be judged. It was better than no moral guidelines, in which case anything could be permitted, as in the Roman arena. The code of chivalry, always a hallmark of *noblesse oblige*, was central to Medieval knighthood, and could be extended to any foe or opponent—including animals. It was part of the basis of social honor for which our modern pragmatism has no use. We scoff today at shame and guilt, but that is what made people do the right thing by their standards. What others thought of one did really matter.

Every civilization since the advent of agrarianism has set aside sport hunting for its upper classes and castes—Egyptian, Assyrian, Persian, Moslem, Chinese, Hindu, Greco-Roman, and so on. Every one of them was based on some moral code, without which, organized society would have been impossible. There has been much in common between many of these codes. *However, it seems only Christendom mandated a special moral relationship to ani-*

mals that could, and did, produce a code of fair chase and hunting ethic, especially in the West.

This ethic has not been spelled out formally like some Bill of Rights. The fact that it still exists informally as a tradition, custom, and practice, even without an awareness of its moral foundations, is a tribute to that morality, its value system, extent, and duration. Then came the Industrial Revolution in the West.

Until the 18th century in Europe, feudalism held sway, as it did in the rest of the world. In Europe, however, the idea of the state, the enacted law and the rights and duties of the person had become part of the concept of citizenship. In the Orient, despotism prevailed where the word of the despot was law, not for citizens, but over subjects. In European and Oriental feudalism, there were two main classes: the rulers with their retainers (priests, military, and government bureaucrats), and the vast majority of the people, who were serfs or peasants bound to the land by agrarianism. A small percentage were traders, craftsmen, artisans, and the like. The Orient stayed that way, but a large, middle class appeared in Europe due to the Industrial Revolution.

Rapid growth of industrial technology needed ever larger supplies of manpower to run the factories. At first, there were deplorable problems in the burgeoning cities, where factories had attracted many rural dwellers who escaped the uncertain and dire conditions of farm poverty. Marxists and Charles Dickens notwithstanding, the common man slowly but surely began to experience a rise in his standard of living. Working from 8 AM to 6 or 8 PM, or even longer, with a sure paycheck, was better than sunrise to sunset with the possibility of failed crops. The new factory system of mass production required more and more raw materials and markets.

European colonialism and empires may have produced some ugly moments of human exploitation, but by the 1850s the factory system and scientific technology were producing miracles for those lucky enough to have access to them. Communicable diseases were being controlled. The invention of the steam engine made the railway trains and steamship lines possible, making remote places in the world accessible. Handmade, split bamboo fishing rods and superbly handcrafted hunting rifles and shotguns, which cost a fortune, and only within the reach of wealthy few, gave way to mass-produced hunting rifles and fishing and camping gear, now serviceable and affordable by many. The camera made it possible to bring home pictures of foreign scenes and enticing memories for others to see—and take more pictures.

Colonies provided opportunity for many young men to seek military service, or positions in diplomatic corps, or careers with business and commercial enterprises. Completing the tour of duty was a perfect stepping stone to semipermanent residence and access to the fabled and exotic beasts virtually in the backyard. The royal hunting mantle of Ramses, Ashurbanipal, Hubertus, Charlemagne, Kubla Khan, Bahram, and Maximilian was now draped over the shoulders of John Smith. After 4,000 years, sport hunting of royal game, for the trophies—for the big ones, the dangerous and exciting ones—was finally democratized.

The nobility of Hungary, Austria, Germany, Italy, Spain, Russia, Poland, and France of 18th- and 19th-century Europe had produced great hunters nurtured in a 2,000-year tradition of morality that related man to animal. It was the Englishman, however, who spread the ethics of the hunting code based on his sense of sportsmanship—the sporting instinct, and being a good sport. He had a larger empire for that sort of thing.

The earlier terms for sport hunting, like the *art of venery* or the *venatic art* or *cynegetics* in use since the Middle Ages, seems to have lost its popularity by the 18th century. In their stead appears disport. Our modern phraseology is clumsy when it says that one "engages in sports" or "participates in sporting activities." Instead, the older phrase was, simply, to *disport oneself.* The Latin prefix *dis* (to be apart or away or separated from) and the suffix *portare* (to carry, or transport) becomes *desporter* in Old French, and the English changes it into disport. Presumably, one can get carried away, or carry himself away, or carry things away.

Disporting oneself probably originated in more genteel form in the Grand Tour. The well-bred sons of European aristocracy carried themselves and their sizeable luggage on extended sightseeing tours throughout the continent, visiting big cities to absorb history, culture, and refinement as part of the educational process of the true 18th century gentleman. Today, the average man who is disporting himself is taking a vacation.

The European, the Englishman especially, disported himself in any number of ways because he had lots of leisure time—a happy state of affairs enjoyed by aristocracies. Sport is the aphetic form of *disport,* in which the prefix was eventually dropped. One who engages in sports becomes a *sporter*, a word still in use when I was a boy but is now rarely heard. Today, the trouble with sport is it has too many meanings, at least 17 different ones. Its referents go from plant and animal mutations to gambling, derision, pastimes, play, frolic, athletic events, outdoor activities, recreation, relaxation, amusement, the search for exciting new experiences, and anything diversionary for the "fun of it."

By the middle of the 19th century, the steam engine, powering trains and boats placed the wilderness of other continents within reach. By that time, the word sport was used in tandem with the word travel. Sometimes it was a toss up whether hunting was part of other diversions, or other diversions were a part of hunting, but travel was certainly involved in any case. Books appear at this time with titles like *Sport and Travel Abroad*; *Adventure, Sport, and Travel in the Tibetan Steppes*; *Notes on Sport and Travel*; *Forty Years of a Sportsman's Life*; *A Sportsman at Large*; *The Journal of a Sporting Nomad*; *Sport and Travel*; *Travel and Adventure In South Africa*; *My Sporting Holidays*, and so on—and travel makes associated diversions possible.

These sporters, now called sportsmen, seek thrills and adventures, but also give us travelogues on climate, geography, ethnic peoples and cultures, historic sites, and fauna and flora not directly related to the hunt. Often, their books contain pages of photos, drawings, and engravings about exotically costumed peoples, their artifacts and activities, and wilderness scenes. Often all their trophies are shown in a single frontispiece photo. These traveling sporters are titled nobility, or later, military officials who, in the middle of nowhere, often chance on their social peers—dukes, counts, barons, viscounts, lords, captains, generals, and anybody who is somebody back home. They even take their wives with them, leaving them safely behind in a military outpost, an exotic city, or palace of a foreign king or potentate when they enter dangerous wilderness for actual hunting.

These sporters go the limit. Obviously, they are seeking adventure, achievement and social honor. They are reasonable facsimiles of *l'uomo universale*, the Renaissance man, since they do almost everything and do it well. Many of them are part-time trophy hunters, but they are all full-time travelers and sportsmen. Sir Claude Champion de Crespigny, Major Harding Cox, and

Count Henrik Apponyi are typical of dozens of their peers. They talk about angling, cricket, polo, bird shooting in club competition, trap shooting, breeding horses, horse racing and steeple chasing, dog breeding, coursing after wolf and boar in Albania, duck hunting on the Nile, lion in Africa, tiger in India, ibex, argali, and Marco Polo sheep in the Pamirs, the Himalayas, Nepal, and Mongolia, canoeing, sculling, boating, yachting, punting (aquatics, as they call it), bowling, boxing, ballooning, lawn tennis and hiking (from 26 to 45 miles a day in one case).

They volunteer for military action, just for kicks, even when some of them are not in the military. They fight in the Boer War, Anglo-Egyptian Sudan against Mahdi uprisings, or Sotik Punitive Expedition, or Crimea and elsewhere, seeking adventure between interrupted hunting sojourns.

This may appear as the reckless, wild adventuring peculiar to the domineering culture of white, European militarists. Culture however, has little to do with it. It has venerable roots in antiquity.

The Egyptian pharaoh, Ramses III (1198-1167 BC) showed the true hunter's dedication when he refused to let mere routine matters divert his passion. During his war of liberation from Libya, he defeated the Pulasatis in fierce battle. In giving chase to the retreating remnants he received word from his scouts that three magnificent lions had been spotted not far away.

He did what any decent hunter would do. He called a halt to the pursuit of the retreating enemy, raced his chariot to the lions' haunt, hunted and slew all three of them, hastened back, double time to the enemy, caught up with them, destroyed them all, and captured all the field booty he could lay his hands on. Now that is versatile dedication! Nothing stops the true hunter from the hunt. Times, civilization, and cultures may change, but the spirit of the hunt is universal, and boys will be boys even in adulthood. Long live the spirit!

Many 19th Century European hunters were respectable naturalists collecting insects, butterflies, rare and exotic birds and their eggs, seashells, and exotic flowers. Some of these specimens are discoveries unknown to science and collections are gifted to museums and academies. Often discoveries bear the name of the hunter. Some of them are authentic explorers mapping out virgin territories that, until recently, bore their names.

They are first-rate connoisseurs discussing fine arts, architecture, and literature. They are gourmets invited to sumptuous dinners given by royalty, and they even publish the menus in their books. They dance at lavish balls and cotillions and do all the other things disporting ladies and gentlemen do on such ventures, or adventures, in foreign lands. Most of all, this sporting activity gives our democratic age the envy and excuse to denounce those who surely knew how to live!

If *disport* denoted carrying away, what was it that got carried? In the absence of Holiday Inns, Walmarts, and Pizza Huts, just about everything had to be carried away, and we moderns perhaps fail to appreciate what this meant.

H. Z. Darrah hunts in Baluchistan and Ladakh in the Himalayas. It is an 8-month and 16-days "travel and sport." If shelter can be found in some villages, it is primitive and often unsanitary. Vegetables can be bought, but they are often below standard.

Porters are not always easy to obtain, and new teams must be hired from one village to the next. Distance and topography determine how many are needed. Darrah has five permanent personnel in charge of things, but an average of 7 to 9 coolies are hired and often 16 of them are employed. Each carries 50-pound loads. Ponies carry 247 pounds and yaks carry away 329 pounds. Darrah's tent is 7 feet squared, and he must provide two or three tents for his crew. He carries a folding tub, wash basin, tinned foods, medicines, rifles, arsenical soap, darkroom supplies for test developing his films, and nine different maps of the areas he travels. All the things that had to be carried, with helpful suggestions to would-be hunters, are listed in three chapters totaling 45 pages.

Of his total time spent on this hunt: 121 days are for travel; 97 days are spent searching for game, often in storm-tossed treacherous terrain above 16,000 feet; and 42 days are required for resting and camping, often pinned down by foul weather. Of 97 hunting days, 34 of them produce no game in sight, or game not worth shooting. There are 27 shootable days, but it is impossible to reach the game. Of 97 hunting days, no shots are fired on 61 days. Of 36 shootable days, 10 shots are missed and game is bagged on 26 days. Half his leave is spent traveling, one-sixth camping, and forced halts due to weather, leaving one third of the time for actual searching for game. By his own figures, he has taken 53 animals with average heads, and only 10 more he considers outstanding trophies.

If he doesn't tell us the total miles he traveled, William Morden does. He and his partner, James L. Clark, travel 8,000 miles in 10 months through India, Russia, China, and Mongolia. However, they are hunting for museums, so they have a big order to meet. They use six languages, requiring three translators, before they get to English.

Ralph Cobbold started his sport and travel on September 13, 1897, and ended it in "midsummer" of 1898. Assuming this to be July, his sojourn lasted approximately 11 months. No matter what foodstuffs and other items he acquired along the way, he started his travels with his estimate of 2,300 pounds of equipment being carried away.

P.T. Etherton covered 4,000 miles in 11 months, going through Siberia, Mongolia, Chinese Turkestan, Tibet, Afghanistan, and India (which is the usual route for these hunts) and got severe frostbite, requiring several skin grafts.

Captain F.E.S. Adair, while hunting in Baluchistan and Ladakh carried his golf clubs to an altitude of 16,000 feet, and set up a competition match for his camp personnel! He not only got fine trophies, he also took a fine collection of butterflies from Tibet and presented it to the South Kensington Museum.

Hunting in Africa had a different set of problems. Instead of dizzying high altitudes and snowcapped mountains buffeted by storms, the African savannah, hillside, and light forest made travel easier. But the problems of carrying away equipment had its own difficulties.

It took William Baldwin, one of the earliest hunters in South Africa, 92 passage days to reach the Natal from England. It took another 3 weeks to get his equipment and manpower together, which consisted of three wagons, seven white men, and "lots of Kaffirs" (natives). Two more white men join the party but, "They died, poor fellows, of fever, together with two others of the party . . . within 2 months of our start." He spent 8 years hunting, from 1852 to 1860.

One of the legendary figures was R. Gordon Cumming, who began his safari on October 23, 1843. He was to make five separate hunting expeditions in a 5-year period. His first 1-year expedition wound up with three wagons and 100 oxen, a span of 12 to a wagon, and two horses. He had four servants, one white and three natives. His equipment consisted of, among other things, 300 pounds each of coffee and sugar, 100 pounds each of meal and flour, two dozen sickles, five axes, one large bell tent, 10,000 bullets (he will add to these in the field, later), 2,000 gun flints, 400 pounds of black powder, etc. etc. It was carry away, or desporter, in grand style.

By the early 1900s the motor vehicle sounded its first sputtering starts on the African savannah and commercial safaris began with outfitters, professional hunters, and all the necessary equipment easily carried away for the hunter. For all practical purposes, all the hunter had to do was shoot. As one professional hunter, giving a status report on Sumatran tiger hunting to a 1975 Safari Club International conference said, in a very short speech, "You can see, I'm not much of a talker. About all I say to my clients in the jungle, when the cat charges is, 'Shoot, shoot, you damn fool.'" It was the crisp British accent behind his German name that did it. I laughed so hard at the imagery, one of my friends grabbed me so I wouldn't fall out of my chair.

Sport and sporting meant many different kinds of vacationing and recreational activities and included hunting as part of aristocratic *disport*. As the nature of vacationing activities and recreation changed with the times and a burgeoning middle class, I believe the term sport changed the *venatic art* or *cynegetics* of hunting to sport hunting as it became more specialized and separated from its former *disporting* connotations.

One not only hunted for sport, but one also sport hunted for trophies. And to do that on distant continents, confronted tremendous logistics problems as an inseparable part of *disport* (carry away) which became sport. The word stuck. However, it is used so loosely in so many contexts, it has regrettable results, as we shall see later.

The bottom line to all this is those who engage in sports must have the one quality making them a sportsman, or a good sport as we say—the moral or ethical sense of fairness. As the dictionary says of a good sport, "A person characterized by his observance of the rules of fair play."

We have gone a long way from carrying away whatever is necessary to enjoy a sporting activity to a quality of behavior. It is not only what is done, but how it is done, and there are rules that determine this.

Sport hunting, as practiced by Europeans, was based on a moral code emerging from a 2,000-year-old Christian tradition and practice, emphasizing fairness, mercy, and compassion for even hunted animals. A sense of responsible stewardship came from even earlier Judaic origins. This was the basis for the hunting ethic or the sportsman's code of fair chase as we have seen. It existed side by side with the law. In fact, the law all too often was the result of that ethic. One needs only to read the Appendix in H. L. Haughton's *Sport and Folklore in the Himalaya*. The "Jammu and Kashmir Game Laws Notification, 1913-14," engineered by the British, begins, interestingly enough with, "The Rules apply to all European and Indian residents and visitors, ladies as well as gentlemen, including all state subjects and officials, with the exception of those who have been specially exempted by order of His Highness the Maharajah." Fourteen pages of rules and regulations follow, most of them addressed specifically to sportsmen.

Sportsmen in Africa had even more regulations. Captain F. A. Dickinson's *Big Game Shooting on the Equator*, shows the 1897 "Queen's Regulations Under Article 145 of the East African Protectorate" containing no less than 25 pages of the laws, rules, and regulations that controlled sport hunting, conservation, responsible stewardship, hunting ethics, and fair chase. The irony is that, in those far away lands of the Himalayas and East Africa, the English who didn't even belong there with literal dominion, did what the indigenous populations could never do—protect the game from slaughter.

India's maharajahs could hunt any number of tigers, anytime, anywhere, not because they were fiends, but because they had no traditional sporting ethic to dampen their enthusiasm. Caspian and Bengal tigers faced extinction, not because maharajah or sportsman endangered them, but because native poachers had an insatiable native market demanding tiger bones and whiskers for magic charms and medicinal potions of doubtful value.

In Africa, 35,000 of the magnificent black rhino have been all but exterminated for its horn to make aphrodisiacs and dagger handles. That didn't occur in the golden days of sport hunting. It occurred in the turbulent 1970s, only after white professional sport hunting associations were wiped out (all 300 of them in Kenya alone), by the despots who took over the new peoples' republics to the cheers of the American campus Greens, Reds, and Assorted Dum-Dums. They did not have the foggiest idea how much the sport hunter had done to legislate and fund the programs that kept species alive one step ahead of poachers, bulldozers, and "statesmen." Animal-lovers who "protect" animal "rights" would have no rights to protect if the maligned European, and then the

American, sport hunter had not protected the animal to begin with, starting a hundred years or so ago.

It was not the Chinese mandarin who hunted in Africa or the Hindu maharajah who hunted in China. Nor did they have a hunting ethic or a sportsman's code of fair chase to disseminate, even if they had hunted abroad. The sport hunting ethic was spread anywhere the European, especially the English and then the American, sportsman went. And they went everywhere. For the few heads they took, their conservation practices and laws protected entire species.

We all know there is something we vaguely refer to as a hunting ethic. What exactly is it? Well, it's difficult to get exact about any ethic, isn't it? What follows are my opinions open to revision by others. Until then, I hold my own ground.

Again, all that is legal is not necessarily moral, and all that is moral is not necessarily legal. Since all ethics have to do with right and wrong conduct, the problem is—which can be legalized and which cannot? Fortunately, a critical piece of hunting ethic can be, is, and should be legalized. This has to do with the concept of fair chase. The term itself hints at its moral and cultural origins. Law and ethics largely coincide with agreement in this instance. Without fair chase, one can have any kind of hunting but it won't be sport hunting.

"Any" kind of hunting runs a great risk—it makes it too easy to over-hunt game beyond its capacity to reproduce or replenish itself at optimum levels. This runs the risk of extinction, which the American bison nearly experienced at the hands of market hunters before the cattle markets were established. Protective legislation was passed just in time, and sport hunters played a leading role in agitating for it. Here, the public interest required such protection. This is why states will outlaw the use of helicopters and machine guns, to use an extreme example. Suppose a state or country does not outlaw such methods? It would be legal but unethical, and while some hunters might take advantage of such a situation, sport hunters would not, at least not if they wanted to enter that trophy in competition, or live with it in clean conscience, or be tolerated by their peers.

Such sport hunting organizations as Rowland Ward, Boone and Crockett, Safari Club International, Mzuri, Game Coin and several other national and international organizations were established precisely to maintain high standards of the ethical hunt and reward those who live by them. Annual awards, to further that goal, are made for outstanding trophies, which are competitively judged, but only if the requirements of fair chase have been met. Fair chase, basically, means no mechanically powered vehicle can be used for direct pursuit, herding, or harassing an animal.

The statutory laws of hunting have little to do with most sport hunting, which is based on moral norms or standards, custom, and tradition beyond legalization. For example, the law usually has no interest in whether a hunter kills his big-game animal with a single shot, or with two dozen shots, as long as his rifle's magazine does not contain more than three shells at a time with an optional one in the chamber, or other restrictions. The law has no interest in whether a caribou is chased across the snow with skis, snowshoes, galoshes, or even snowmobiles, in some cases. But sport hunting ethics do, for reasons that make the crucial difference in different types of hunting.

Some critics (Roger Caras, for example) claim the sport hunter makes a special case to exonerate or distance himself from other kinds of hunting, when there is no difference, since killing is killing. But the critic makes his own over-generalized case to tar all hunters or animal killers or gladiators with the same brush. All hunting is not the same, just because the killing of an animal is involved, any more than all motor vehicles are the same just because they roll on wheels.

The crucial difference is this, however, among subsistence and market hunters, predator controllers, poachers, and sport hunt-ers—especially trophy hunters—it is only the sport or trophy hunters who self-impose the unnecessary standards or norms, deliberately making their task more restrictive than it has to be. This is required to uphold the moral imperative that the hunter give the hunted a fair chance to attack or flee. If it's a man-killing animal, it must be allowed to attack its pursuer if it can, as its pursuer is allowed to attack, if he can. If the animal chooses to flee, then the hunter can try to stop it, but not with obstacles, man-made or natural, which make further flight impossible. This is the ethic to which the hunter is obligated and about which the animal knows nothing. The hunter is in a contest where the rules apply only to him and which he voluntarily imposes on himself. These rules give the animal the benefit of the doubt every time such doubt becomes an issue. From this follow all other ethical norms to which the hunter consents.

If the animal is a dangerous one, capable of killing man, and is wounded, but does not press home the attack and chooses to seek cover, then the true sport hunter must follow him into that cover no matter how dangerously the odds are now tipped against him. He is rarely a match for such an animal in dense cover, especially intelligent enough to circle from behind and ambush the hunter. That exigency was a part of the package-deal before the hunter squeezed the trigger and he must take whatever consequences at all costs. Of course, a hunter may lose his nerve. No law asks, nor can it force, him to go into heightened danger in close quarters. But if he fails to go in, then he has violated the foremost tenet of an ethical code, not a statute. He knows what he is and must live with his conscience or the judgement of his peers, if he can.

This ethical, fair-play sporting requirement exists for two main reasons: first, the wounded animal can be in great pain and experience a lingering death. Even a domestic animal, such as a horse or dog, suffering from traumatic pain is shot, if possible, as an act of mercy, or a lethal injection is used these days. It is even more incumbent on the hunter, who placed a wild animal in that condition, to relieve it of its suffering as an act of mercy. Second, and of greater moral consequence, is the fear innocent human beings may become endangered by an animal infuriated by its wounds, or whose wounds have healed long since, but have left it incapacitated, especially if it is a carnivore. Such animals very often resort to easier-to-kill human prey. Many professional hunters believe this is the main reason why some animals become man-eaters.

For the sport hunter, there is a critical issue here. He wants to kill the animal as instantly, painlessly, and mercifully as possible. He wants to do this for at least three reasons: first, it is crucial to the quality of his hunt. He is after perfection that is nearly impossible in this world so, if he has to, he will settle for excellence. That is what quality is all about. Therefore, he does not want a noble animal botched up with butchery. He wants a single shot to do it, if possible. Respect for that animal demands at least that much. The instant, painless kill is the feedback telling the hunter how well he succeeded in passing the course.

Second, it is also the finest insurance he has against the need to go into the cover of a dangerous wounded animal, thus increasing the odds of the hunter getting killed. No hunter has the smell, sight, hearing, instincts, power, ferocity, and speed of a cornered animal capable of killing a man. If the hunter wins, it's because his rifle has the power to stop the animal, providing the hunter has courage and ability to risk getting off a split-second shot in close quarters.

Third, even if a wounded animal does not attack in close quarters, the odds are great that it can escape the hunter and get lost to him forever unless, of course, he was stopped cold on the first shot. I have known, more than once, a thing common to many Alaska hunters—a wounded moose in thick brush, 10 feet from his hunter, can move away so silently he disappears like smoke, leaving a hunter dumbfounded. It doesn't seem possible for an animal that is often larger and heavier than a horse, but it is.

Countless interviews with hunting critics reveal a sad truth. Most of them have never hunted and, therefore, do not have the foggiest notion of how an animal is killed. The very thought of "killing" an animal is enough to make them avoid the issue. Anyway, it leaves them with the results of some other critics' wild imagination. Repeatedly, critics imagine the hunter shoots "at the animal." What else? But as any seasoned hunter will tell you, that is the best way to lose an animal who gets away for keeps, or butcher an animal with total incompetence, or inflict pain and suffering by shooting "at the animal," or turn that animal into a man-eater. A dozen such shots, anywhere "at the animal" will not necessarily kill it, and it gets away, painfully.

The vitality of big-game animals is enormous, and to be stopped effectively, the hunter really has an average target not much more than 6 inches in diameter where a vital organ must be hit. What the hunter is aiming at is the heart, in the lower third of the chest behind the shoulder, usually, or the brain, spine, neck, shoulders, and lungs to stop the animal. So the hunter, among other things, must know the anatomy of animals. Even then, the ideal target is one thing, and the ideal conditions for hitting the target are something else far different from the ideal. It's amazing how little the critic knows about hunting realities and his verbal free associations are merely oneiric fantasies.

Ask a critic to tell you what picture he sees in his mind when you tell him you killed an animal. Dozens of times I have heard, after the shooting "at the whole animal" fantasy, a simple, single theme in an exasperating scenario. In the critic's imagination, the animal, somehow, magically appears out of thin air about arms length from a man with a rifle. The man happens to be at the right spot at precisely the right moment, as though time and space have collapsed and from nowhere, like a genie out of a bottle, there's your hunter.

The critic must think he hears the animal say something like, "Here I am. Please shoot me right in the heart while I stand perfectly still for you with all my love. Please shoot me with your high-powered rifle and laugh with joy at my cruel suffering." Most critics have a Freudian explanation for this and see sex symbols in everything except in what they just said, or thought, about themselves. I will amplify this, later.

The ideal target is one thing. What makes for the ideal conditions enabling the ideal shooting at the ideal target is something else, since real conditions at that moment are usually anything but ideal. There are too many variables involved from the moment the hunter puts the sights to his eye until he squeezes the trigger. This is the moment of truth that has followed days, sometimes weeks, of hardship and toil on the trail, to say nothing of money, and perhaps years of waiting. It takes a lot of cool to put this in the back of one's mind and pretend it doesn't count in the outcome, just before that trigger booms out the shot.

There are only five ways the uncertain outcome can come out, if I may. The hunter will either: 1. miss cleanly and watch his dreams follow that bullet into nowhere; 2. wound the animal with a bad shot and lose it; 3. kill the animal cleanly and instantly with a perfect shot and embrace ecstasy; 4. mangle the animal with too many poor shots and turn his fondest dreams into the ugliest of nightmares; or 5. get himself killed any old which way since the animal has no compunctions about morals or esthetics—only achievement motivation. That's why the first shot is crucial.

Nothing stings the hunter's conscience as much as the animal who took shot after shot which mutilated it, and robbed it of a dignified death. Nothing haunts the memory of a hunter like the recall of his incompetent shooting that turned his art into simple butchery. Nothing makes a nobleman with a rifle look more like a caveman with a stone ax. And yet, more often than not, when the hunter squeezes the trigger, he does so under less than ideal conditions.

The single shot is an ideal, however, which is often frustrated by real conditions. The angle of the shot is determined by the animal's position, and often there is nothing the hunter can do about changing his position to adjust for it. He must take his shot as it is presented. Is it head on, full astern, broadside, or at an angle? This determines which vital spots, if any, are accessible. Is it partially or totally concealed by brush, tall grass, trees, or defiles, and might the bullet be deflected? Or is it fully visible with no obstructions? Is it standing still, unaware, or is it running alert, full speed, and in which direction? How much should he be led with the sights so bullet and target meet? If the animal is at a higher or lower elevation, how much should the sights be raised or lowered to compensate?

Is the terrain flat and open, or uneven and closed, mountainous and craggy, thick with foliage, or deep with snow or sand? This will determine the physical condition of the hunter at the critical moment of the shot. Is he rested well enough to hold steady, or is he panting hard with exertion only to see an alerted animal ready to flee, and he can't hold his sights steady? His heaving lungs gasping for air require enormous control to hold a wildly weaving open sight or scope still at his eye as his animal speeds out of view. Does he have a convenient, natural object for a rifle rest, or must he shoot offhand?

Then there is the constant problem of lighting. Is it early morning, afternoon, or twilight? Sunny or cloudy? Raining, snowing, or foggy? Since distance will always vary from sight to target, light plays deceptive tricks on one's optical system. Animals appear far or near when they are not, and compensation for correct sighting is made difficult. They look small or large, where sex or trophy quality cannot be easily judged at longer distances. On a blazing hot afternoon, when the hunter's blood races through his vascular system after a strenuous run or climb, his temples pound and his head swims while heat waves radiate from the ground just enough so the animal, standing absolutely still, looks like he's vibrating in eccentric circles—that's one thing. In 50° below zero chill-factored weather, sitting or crouching motionless for 20 minutes so a polar bear will not detect movement, while the hunter, despite his best warm clothing, is shivering with cold just enough to numb his finger so it cannot gage the delicate pressure on the trigger, which is yanked back, while his reticles bounce all over the hypnotically white landscape looking like some gigantic blur— that's another thing.

What will happen at the moment the animal is hit? It's too

unpredictable and anything can happen. There are a dozen things that can and do go wrong. What if the first shot does not kill instantly? If the first shot is deliberately fired to stop, turn, or down the animal because a lethal shot is impossible, does the hunter think he has a reasonable chance for the *coup de grace* with another shot, or two, within a few seconds of each other, to prevent the animal from escaping or coming out of the hydrostatic shock to its nervous system that has numbed it into insentience?

The processes of pain, death, and killing arise, so I alert the gentle soul to what follows, which may seem gross, but it is also reality, which cannot be avoided. How much pain does the wounded animal feel, and for how long, if it does not die instantly?

I know of no scientific studies that tell us. Science has discovered much during these past 20 years about pain, but there remains much in mystery. Our problem is complicated by the fact that animals cannot tell us what they feel. Humans can, however, and fortunately the endocrine and nervous systems (crucial to our problem here) are similar in many regards to all warmblooded animals. These systems are virtually identical between mammals and man, who is, after all, a mammal, himself. Therefore, a brief discussion of the endocrine and nervous systems in their normal state may be in order. Then, we can better create a paradigm of what is probably happening to a big-game animal from the moment a hunter's bullet strikes it, and upsets its normal physiological state or homeostatic equilibrium.

The endocrine system consists of ductless glands (adrenals, thyroid, pancreas, etc.) producing chemical substances known as hormones. These hormones are secreted directly into the blood stream and reach various parts of the body to perform critical physiological functions in the failure of which death occurs.

The second system involved is the nervous system, which consists of nerves, spinal cord, and brain. Their basic cellular unit is the neuron, which is an awesome and wondrous thing. In the brain alone, its numbers are estimated to be from 10 to 100 billion. The number of their interconnections in the brain are beyond calculation in the most complex structure and function probably in the entire universe. The only thing more fantastic is the belief that it originated by chance or accident. The most sophisticated computer is not even in the picture by comparison. Like an electric circuit, operated by a switch, these neurons are either open or closed—they either fire an electrical charge carrying a signal to any part of the body, or they don't. They not only receive messages from the outside, they respond with appropriate signals to the outside where it's needed.

They are structured with a cell body that sends out long trunks called axons carrying the message out. The axon ends in a dendrite that looks like tree branches reaching toward another set of similar endings in the next axon. Between these dendritic ends, however, there is a space known as the synapse, or synaptic junction, which the impulse must now cross to reach the correct dendrites of the other axons to continue the journey to its destination. It's like an electric spark jumping across a gap from the tip of one wire to the tip of the next.

Some axons outside the brain, like the one from the spinal cord down the legs to the toes, are 4 or more feet long. Neurons in the brain are special. The brain may be only 2% of the total body weight, but it gobbles up some 25% of the body's oxygen supply and 15% of its glucose, or simple sugar, without which there is no energy production to fire the cells. By an electrochemical process, the impulse, or message, moves through the axon at the speed of some 270 miles per hour.

What facilitates the electrical impulse to move across the synaptic junction, or space, are chemicals known as neurotransmitters. While the brain contains these chemical neurotransmitters like serotonin, acetylcholine, and dopamine, so does the spinal cord and the adrenal medulla. The adrenal medulla is a functional part of the nervous system forming a bridge between the endocrine and nervous systems. The adrenal medulla also produces the hormones' epinephrine (adrenaline) and norepinehrine. Under conditions of stress to the body, like fear, pain, anger, hypoglycemia, physical or emotional trauma, etc. both hormones are differentially released, in a process not yet well understood, by signals from the brain's hypothalamus. The hypothalamus acts like a dispatcher which routes the impulses to their correct destinations. It is also the center which connects with the limbic system, amygdala, etc., and influences our emotions.

Under stress, the hypothalamus sends increased signals to the adrenal medulla, which releases its norepinephrine. This hormone elevates blood pressure and, with epinephrine, both produce increased force, frequency and, amplitude of vasoconstriction (read squeezing the blood vessels) as well as coronary arterial dilation. At this point of increased pressure, lungs are pumping like bellows, the liver is belching glycogen (stored sugar), the heart is pounding with enough force to blow a boiler gasket, and blood is flowing profusely to carry oxygen and glucose to cells everywhere to meet the increased demands of stress. The body is now energized for maximal effort.

This is when Superman can run faster than a bullet, leap over tall skyscrapers, or derail locomotives. For real life, this is exaggerated of course, but only a little. After all, most farmers chased by an angry bull are stressed enough to outrun it most times. The supercharged body is prepared to do one of two things: "fight or flight" as the Cannon-Bard theory labeled it. But this cannot go on forever. The energy burns out and the body slows to regain its normal balance—unless it dies.

All the while that the body was undergoing this response to stress, the brain was doing other mind-boggling things. Our interest here is only in one of these things concerning endorphins. Chemically, endorphins are simple peptide chains of varying links made up of amino acids. It turns out that these peptide chains are the messengers with specific destinations in mind. It's the Message To Garcia all over again. There are a few dozen of these peptides already identified and there may be another hundred of them—maybe more. Amazingly, some of these have analgesic effects more powerful than aspirin. Well, to be more exact, some of them are 100 times more powerful than morphine, whose action they mimic. Morphine, a derivative of opium that comes from the poppy, led to the name opiates for these chemical combos.

Two particular forms of the opioid peptide chain were named enkephalins from Greek words meaning "in the head," because that is where the brain produced them. Where else? There were other peptide chains, at least a dozen of them, with similar analgesic properties, and they were all classified as endorphins, a word coined after morphine. In fact, there are several families of endorphin systems interacting with each other, each with its own pathway in the brain.

It was found that opioid endorphins are related to stress. Shock is another name for extreme stress that has broken down the body. The hormone ACTH (corticotropin) and beta-endorphin, released by the anterior pituitary, join and circulate through the system, tending to increase stress. The target organs, however, are not known with certainty, therefore it is difficult to conclude they reduce stress. These beta endorphins may act on some mu receptors, which produce morphine-like analgesia, euphoria, etc.; or they may act on kappa receptors, which produce analgesia, sedation, etc.; or they may act on sigma receptors producing hallucinations, etc. Nothing seems to be clearcut here.

Long distance runners, during the moments of great physical agony, refer to getting their "second wind," or "hitting the wall" just when they thought they would collapse. When a football player charges through tackles and guards to make a brilliant end run to score a touch down after heroic effort, he slams the football into the ground and jumps for joy. The hunter, nearly exhausted from running full speed to a vantage point, and getting a successful snap shot, despite heaving lungs and weaving scope, may suddenly explode with joy. Not only psychological factors, but endorphins are also involved one way or another.

The big problem is that we do not know what other endorphins or chemicals are also involved, the amount of endorphins secreted, exactly where they originate, and where they go. Another problem is whether more or less endorphins are released during acute versus chronic pain.

Endorphin discoveries were made in the 1970s and within a decade there was an explosion of research articles on these natural opiates, as they came to be called. But to date, nothing seems conclusive. In a sense, the body manufactures its own dope despite which, there remains an aura of mystery about exactly how they work. Yet, one thing is certain, the endorphin system is inseparably related to stress and pain. In fact, it is activated by them.

The question invites itself: What is stress? The answers are tough to come by. It was not studied scientifically until the early 1930s by the great Hans Selye. Stress, he said, was the result of adaptive reactions of the body to itself when its homeostatic equilibrium was disrupted. The disrupters were labeled stressors. What's a stressor? It boiled down to almost anything depending on the way it was perceived. Not all stressors act the same way in different individuals beyond a certain point. It could be a bullet, a hypodermic needle, or a recurring nightmare. Psychology and the emotions are a critical part of stress, therefore.

Some stressors are common to us all. A broken leg will stress practically any of us—it will hurt mightily. On the other hand, hatred for one's mother-in-law will be a high-level stressor for one son-in-law, but not at all for another son-in-law. The former may develop ulcers because of his stressor. The latter may be contemplating homicide for the fun of it. Selye created the acronym GAS for General Adaptational Syndrome. The body, trying to adapt to prolonged stress (about two or three years), will break down at the weakest organ. For example, a weak stomach will come down with ulcers and a weak heart will come down with myocardial infarction. When and if the body recovers, it will not improve to quite the level of wellness before the breakdown.

The cumulative level of various stresses is an active contributor to the aging process. War, crime, drugs, poverty, and even wealth, can be stressors for persons and entire communities or nations, depending on how they are perceived. When repeated stress, or stressors, are perceived as being impossible to control or escape, they create a feeling of helplessness, submission, and depression. This requires greater and greater levels of analgesia to lessen the same level of pain, which was lessened earlier with lower doses of analgesia. Hence, the effect of tolerance.

Pain signals originate in nociceptors, or special receptors with free nerve endings in the skin or walls of internal organs. When these receptors pick up a pain signal, they travel up special pathways in the spinal cord to the thalamus, hypothalamus, brain stem, and cerebral cortex, which sends its signals by a different pathway down to areas loaded with opiate receptors. High densities of opiate receptors are located in the hypothalamus. Incoming signals are altered in the downward path in the spinal cord and in two other areas in the brain. These locations are abundantly loaded with opiate receptors and endorphins, probably enkephalins, which are immediately released to inhibit, alter, or modify the pain signals at these points. How we respond to pain and how much we feel depends on our perception of it. Our perception of it depends on how the brain is responding to the stress. Yeah—it's kind of crazy.

Some pathways, like the lateral neospinothalamic tract, create awareness of intensity and localization of pain; some pathways, like the paleospinothalamic tract, subserve the arousal and emotional components of pain. The high density opiate receptors in the hypothalamus mediate emotionally influenced deep pain and the amygdala, a part of the hypothalmic system, regulates emotional behavior. When endorphins are injected into rats, the observed effects include analgesia, hypothermia, hyperthermia, tranquilization, irritability, agitation, and, in high doses, violent behavior. Hopefully, medical science will figure out how to handle all these complex variables in massive traumatic shock so that if an animal rights activist should suffer the misfortune of a terrible automobile accident, his life may be saved as a result of the very experiments he now condemns. Meanwhile, the research monographs, journals, and books written by highly competent authorities show a wise caution, hesitancy, and hedging, in trying systematic and predictive explanations. They do an exemplary job in view of the complexities and lack of more crucial data.

The foregoing is, obviously, a greatly oversimplified picture of a far more complex situation, but I fear I may have gone too far afield, already. It will have to do to keep this relevant to the hunting problem. It is, very roughly, what happens when the system is intact. What happens when the system is disrupted with sudden violence from an outside stressor like a high-powered bullet? It depends on some variables among which two are most obvious: the weight, diameter and velocity of the bullet and the place where it hits. At the moment of impact, the bullet produces what is often called hydrostatic shock—a term that is often used ambiguously.

Hydrostatics have to do with pressure and equilibrium of liquids (blood, in this case) and shock. Shock, of course, is the sudden and violent collision, impact, or concussion to the body that upsets the body's entire functioning, immediately and radically. In my view, shock is the ultimate stress. A bullet penetrates only a tiny area, but it is difficult to comprehend what happens to the rest of the body absorbing the total impact when, for example, it is hit with a .338 caliber bullet weighing 250 grains at 100 yards with 3,348 foot pounds of energy. Obviously, the stress is different when one is ill with pneumonia, or pricked with a splinter in the finger where the body's systems are still intact. But when a bullet smashes and tears out body parts, the body cannot return to its normal functions for quite a while when it is in state of instant and massive shock—if it can recover at all.

Medical records of battlefield soldiers are replete with cases where a soldier has a hand or arm blown off and, who continues his movements unaware of pain and even unaware that he has been hit and traumatically amputated. Or the soldier who stuffs a couple feet of protruding intestines back into the gash across his abdomen and keeps running for several yards before he falls over dead or *hors de combat,* as it was said. These soldiers are a classic example of shock.

Animals who survive shock cannot report what they experienced, if anything. Hunters can and do. Obviously, individual differences in both man and animals must play a great role, but generally, the perception of pain is lowered by distractions from powerful emotions like rage and fear, which will influence the "fight or flight" response. Often, the laboratory cannot determine whether endorphins cause an absence of pain, whether pain is always there, but is not perceived in given situations depending on other factors, or its perception is altered in degree and kind by various factors, or how long analgesic affects last, or the amounts of analgesic agents necessary—or, dare I say it, that pain is perceived even when it's not there. Emotions play a crucial part in all of this.

What the laboratory cannot tell us, empirically, hunters can to some extent based on their experiences notwithstanding the perils of introspection and macroscopic observation. What common denominators do they have to serve as the basis for further empirical research? Regrettably, science has shown little interest in studying such phenomena. There are several accounts by some great hunters in Africa who have survived being chewed, torn, mauled, crunched, stomped, tossed, and battered. They relate that the hunter is conscious of what is happening, but little or no pain is felt even though some describe the sounds of their own flesh being torn, or their bones being crunched. It is difficult to believe that endorphins, other hormones, neurotransmitters, hypothalamus, amygdala, and the whole grab bag of gum-balls is not involved in producing some analgesia. It would be good to know whether pain is stopped, altered, modified, perceived, or imperceived. But that is academic in the real world of pain and shock during those split seconds when life or death hang in the balance for hunter and hunted. It is only several minutes (no one has taken actual time measurements in the field) after the shock when the analgesic affect wears off and pain slowly sets in to reach unbearable proportions.

Taylor, among others, refers to a feeling he describes as a dulled consciousness or stupor when he is savaged by a leopard. Akeley, who is mauled by a leopard, is also mauled and battered by an elephant and is barely aware of what is happening. Stigand, Blunt, Finaughty, and Neumannreport report similar reactions they experienced in themselves or otheres they directly observed. They knew what was going on, sensed it only barely, but didn't feel it. The question is: how long will this relatively insentient episode of shock or imperceptible pain continue? This is one question science cannot answer for us since no experiments have been conducted which, admittedly, would be difficult to design. Also, the ethics of such experiments may be repugnant.

In the absence of exact scientific knowledge, one can only rely on personal observation, experience, analysis, and consensus. One can extrapolate, roughly, what must be happening to a wounded animal since its endocrine and nervous systems are practically identical with those of a human being. It is obvious, even to those who have never killed an animal in the field, that an animal dies instantly if hit in the brain or spinal cord. The nervous system, ceasing to function, shuts down everything else—instantly. There is no question of pain, perceived or otherwise, since everything is out of commission. This is the catastrophic collapse of all internal systems, simultaneously.

What if the animal is hit dead center or in the immediate area of a vital organ like the heart or lungs with massive tissue damage, but does not die instantly? It is in a state of immediate hydrostatic shock. Massive tissue damage has destroyed nerve fibers and blood vessels preventing the immediate transmission of pain stimuli. But for how long? That is the damnably vexatious question for which there are no clearcut answers at present. We only know there is a brief period of insentience and the animal will soon die with loss of blood and vital fluids, which carry all the elements necessary for life; but there is a time lapse before this happens. It takes time, a few seconds or minutes, for the entire system to finally come to a halt. It is this time lapse, which is the most critical moments of the hunt, because any one of three or four major outcomes are possible.

Any animal, in this case, may stagger, fall, and lay down quietly to expire. Any animal may bolt reflexively and flee (if his legs are intact). He will run for a short distance (maybe 50 to 100 yards or so) and drop. Sometimes, the bullet is just a hair off its target but close enough to it producing all the same results. Many an impatient hunter, in the throes of exultation, has then walked to his kill, kneeled beside it, or sat on the carcass to be photographed. Nothing comes as a more stupendous surprise than to have the "dead" animal suddenly get to its feet and run off lickety split, tossing the hunter into his own state of shock. The animal, bowled over with the first shot, was so still and inanimate it looked stone dead. It looks comical—unless the animal tries to kill the hunter instead of running away.

Then there are the animals who may charge full bore with every intent to kill the hunter if they are capable of it. In each case, the animal does not necessarily perceive or respond to his pain for a brief time lapse. His reflexes take over since his stuporous, desensitized state does not sense what has happened to him. His instincts reflexively, unconsciously make him do the number one thing—try to survive with whatever it takes. The pain and attempt to recuperate will come later—if he survives. That behavioral tendency, based on instinct and reflexive endocrine responses, is ingrained through eons of evolution. It's automatic, allowing no choice. Not having reason to tell him the worst is yet to come, which might alter his behavior, he keeps going and hastens his own death.

Which of these responses in the animal are most likely? Again, we have only generalizations, but the exceptions still do not invalidate them. A less vigorous, powerful and pugnacious animal like a deer (or sheep) may stagger, stumble, fall, lie down or stand still, totally dazed, not knowing what to do next. Depending on his vigor, he may fall into analgesic sleep or stupor, and pass away. Then again he may stagger up and flee reflexively unaware of his wounds or pain. Or he may bolt at the first twitch of his reflexes when hit. He is doing exactly what the traumatically amputated soldier did on the battlefield. All the time, the animal didn't feel a single twinge of pain or barely sensed it, if his end came soon enough. It is my cautious guess that nine and half out of ten times the end did come soon enough because a competent hunter saw to it in advance by shooting at the right moment, at the bull's eye and with excellent skill.

A dangerous, powerful, and pugnacious animal capable of easily killing a hunter, even when mortally wounded, may seek flight like the inoffensive deer, especially if he had not sensed the presence of danger. However, if the animal had seen the hunter or the direction of danger, his perception could have instantly triggered the hypothalamus-adrenal medulla route, and supercharged him with adrenaline. Had his adrenalized, juiced-up mental set already decided to attack the source of danger, the bullet's impact need not alter the predetermined intent but aggravate it. He will charge, full bore, even with a bullet hole in his heart. Sometimes, he will charge when hit, even before he senses danger, if he's normally cantankerous, or if he has had previous experience with traumatic pain.

He has several seconds—my guess is at least 60 of them—of reflexive life. In those few seconds, he can accomplish hellish deeds of destruction; his aggressive actions make him completely oblivious to pain—endorphined, altered, or otherwise. Scientists, whose work is with laboratory animals and have never met big-game animals in the field under such conditions, would find it hard to believe the tenacity, stamina, and vitality of such animals—like the grizzly bear or the African Cape buffalo, and a dozen others. They can kill in the very act of dying. Moreover, even a gentle cow caribou can be a determined killer, especially in the protection of its young. One kick of her sharp hooves can disembowel a man. All animals will fight back under given conditions. Without it, the evolution of their species would not have been possible. There are no pacifists in the animal kingdom except man.

I do not know the maximum time a wounded animal can remain free of pain under the influence of shock. Nor have I found any scientific evidence, as yet, that establishes this, or whether it's possible to do so. Nor do I have any such evidence about the minimum time. But I have my own experiences with the way animals behave immediately on being struck with a bullet—how they move or run, how fast or slow their actions are, whether they will flee, charge or just stand there, or how close they will allow a hunter to approach them before and after the bullet's impact. All animals have a critical reaction distance which are species specific. Some kinds of animals will not let man approach closer than a quarter mile before they flee. Others will not allow one to get any closer than 50 feet before they flee or attack. Unfortunately, we do not know the critical reaction distance for many big game animals, or the conditions in which they apply.

Hunters have general knowledge and lots of intuition, which is another reason why their undertaking is an art. How close will a wounded animal allow the hunter's approach before and after it is hit? That alone is an indication of its state of shock, flight or fight responses, and insensitivity to pain.

In this situation, when the animal is downed, a critical psychological problem emerges for the hunter. If the animal does not get up quickly, then it is dead—hopefully—but the hunter doesn't know that for sure. Most hunters will wait 5 minutes or so, as a rule of thumb, to give the wounded animal the necessary time to expire if it is not already dead. But does that animal start to feel his pain during that 5 minute wait? Earlier or later? There's no way we can know for sure. That's what nags the hunter's conscience.

What if the animal staggers to its feet to charge or escape? The hunter must fire immediately, to save his life in the one case, and to stop the animal from flight in the other case. In the second instance, if the animal's escape into hiding is successful, he will probably suffer a certain lingering and painful death. That is the one thing the hunter wants to avoid most of all if he is committed to his ethic. It forces hurried shots, which may not connect, or wound even more, with disastrous results in either case. Right there the hunter has his own adrenal flow and psychological conflict. How does he resolve it? Responsible hunters I know, feel certain the animal is still insentient during those first 5 minutes after being hit. Some feel 20 minutes is more like it (which I think too long). What is constant, however, is the nagging conscience of the hunter to spare the animal's needless pain or suffering. It is that which requires an act of mercy, pity, or compassion—or the misericordia. _Noblesse oblige_. This, after all, is the venatic art, not wanton killing. In the venatic art of the Middle Ages, the hunter used a misericord, a small dagger with which to end the animal's life and pain, since the "hated" high-powered rifle, with its massive shocking power, was not around. Cynics, who do not have the moral stamina to face the issue of conscience, will scoff at the entire affair and argue for the elimination of hunting as disguised sadism.

Whatever the time limit, the issue is the moral one of responsibility—of sparing the animal needless suffering or pain. This, after all, is central to the hunting ethic and its code of honor. I have my own rule of thumb on the issue. If the animal does not die instantly with the first shot, then I feel that he is still imperceptive to pain, numbed with shock, and will stay that way for at least 1 minute and maybe more. That's why I believe the hunter has ample time for an extra two or three shots to complete the task.

Here, another psychological problem arises. The hunter himself is keyed up emotionally. His own epinephrine and endorphins are working, which influence his own perceptions. After that first shot, and until the hunter is convinced it's all over, every second can seem like an eternity and the minute or more may seem like 2 hours. Having reason, he is fully aware that the animal's apparent lack of pain perception will not last forever. He will be compulsive about shooting too quickly without accuracy. He may not down that animal before it reaches him in a charge, in which case nothing else matters, or puts it to flight and risks losing it to a lingering painful death. The experienced hunter can place his shots quickly, but accurately, within his self-imposed time limit, which he can gauge realistically. That kind of hunter is calm and cool in control of his own emotions. The critic sees this coolness as cold bloodedness devoid of human compassion when compassion is precisely why the hunter may shoot too quickly.

Sometimes, the animal moves unwittingly at the precise moment the hunter fires, thus spoiling an instant kill. Sometimes, the most careful aim is still off the vital mark. Sometimes, a split-second exigency louses things up. These things will happen and a wounded animal gets away. When a couple more rapid-fire, well-placed shots, still do not down the animal, there are two main reasons, as I see it: The most obvious is simple lack of skill, competence or an off moment. The next reason is controversial with experienced hunters I know. But I believe high velocity, light weight bullets and rifles are the reason. I know they have their advantages, like flat trajectories for long distance shooting at small or medium sized animals like sheep at high altitudes where there is no intervening brush or trees. There is no question that in this case such a rifle is a superb performer.

On larger or dangerous animals, I feel these bullets do not have enough knockdown power and if they hit the slightest twig in forest terrain, they may shatter or do not mushroom enough going through the body. Yet I know there are superb hunters who seem to do well with these rifles and swear by them. I swore off them after a half dozen occasions when I have hit caribou and moose with a single shot in the immediate area of the heart if not the heart itself. To my great surprise, they have stood perfectly still, without even a noticeable twitch on the bullet's impact, and yet I've felt I could not possibly have missed. One or two more make-sure shots in rapid succession and it still stands there. Just before I have reloaded, the animal falls over. An examination shows all the bullets have scored exactly were aimed.

Why did the animal not sway, or move to let me know I had scored? If he had not died instantly on his feet, he was in a state of enough shock to prevent neurotransmission of pain or impulse to move even reflexively. Of course, the bullet killed efficiently, but to take two or three more shots at an animal dead on its feet takes away from the satisfaction and joy of perfection attained with an instantaneous, single shot painless kill.

My worry is not about the first shot, which almost always connects, effectively. My worry is about the next shot or two in the self-imposed time limits if the first one misses, which is rarely the case but must be accounted for. My exception to this was my grizzly bear (next chapter) even with its extenuating circumstances. This is not the place for a technical discourse on ballistics, which is always a favorite argument between hunters. I simply say, "To each his own, based on his own experience." Give me a heavier, though slower, bullet that produces enough knock-down-and-out power for larger and dangerous game, so I can get instant feedback to know what to do next—just in case.

This condition of the self-imposed time limit is an added difficulty enhancing the standards to be met. But it should be one of the most cardinal tenets of the trophy and sport hunting ethic. When achieved, it is one of the great triumphs and satisfactions of the excellent hunt. I have yet to meet the sport hunter who is not aware that the animal's imperception of pain during shock does not last forever and that he'd better get with it to prevent immanent pain. All this does not say that some animals, for any number of reasons, will not have pain no matter how short lived, or that some hunters will fail to prevent it no matter their best efforts. But no sport hunter intends to fail and he succeeds nine and half out of ten times. That's because he has his own intuitive sense of time lapse and the ability to beat the odds.

Critics cannot say that the high powered rifle makes killing a lead-pipe cinch, but that it cannot kill quickly, cleanly, and painlessly in the hands of a competent hunter. The antihunter will never believe the intention to avoid inflicting pain on the animal as part of the quality and ethics of the hunt. The thought of hunting and the sound of the word "hunter" are the stressors immediately exciting his preprogrammed perceptions; his adrenaline, endorphins, and hypothalamus pump him up with enough hostility to charge the thundering brigade of 600 lancers at Balaclava.

We come to the bottom line. Most of the time the animal in shock perceives no pain, even if pain is there, he dies instantly or in a few minutes. His nervous and endocrine systems plus the hunter's skill and ethical code determine that. This is one of the reasons why the hunter hunts with a clean conscience. Critics who are sincere in feeling so much hurt and anguish over the animal's "pain" can now breathe easier. Most of the time the animal is in far less hurt than the critic's projected pain of his own imagination.

Any one, or several variables may be involved just when a shot must be taken or risk the loss. It is intuition, instinct, maybe some reasoning, and lots of experience that puts everything together in a split second and influences the decision whether or not to squeeze the trigger. That decision is based on an ethic which emerges from a moral code.

If it doesn't feel right, then the real sport hunter will not shoot and risk maiming or wounding an animal he cannot down for keeps. He will wait for some other time, some other hunt, no matter how it hurts to lose this one. That is the hunter's moral code.

There are weeks or years of waiting, and days of toil, effort, and expense on the trail. There are nerve-tingling, risky, meticulously careful stalks. There are poor weather and light conditions fouling vision. There is an alerted animal, who can run between 20 and 60 miles an hour, or one hundred yards in 4 seconds flat, who is blazing full speed ahead, when suddenly it's the moment of truth and now or never, and a perfect shot, with all the odds in the animal's favor, drops that animal cold-turkey dead before it even knew what hit it—the hunter will go absolutely ape over his accomplishment. He has attained perfection, or excellence, honorably according to the code.

How many times in a life time can anyone attain that glory in anything? Only a 4,000-year-old embalmed pharaoh can be expected to stand there unperturbed—or a hunter hater, perturbed to the maximum degree, who could make a mounted trophy out of the hunter. Here is where another problem emerges.

Any reasonably decent person will admit the hunter's euphoria is understandable, and he is entitled to exult in it. But let the hunter talk or write about it, and his critic will go on the attack, depending on how many shots were fired. His critic will ridicule him for being a braggart or a liar boasting of his super-macho, dead-eye-dick, single-shot killing that "proved his manhood." The critic will not believe it. If he does, he will insist the hunter was not even there, apparently, at the moment of the fireworks, and the ubiquitous high-powered rifle did it by magically levitating to eye level and shooting itself off, or that, obviously, the animal was a de-fanged, de-clawed, anemic old thing that couldn't run fast enough, anyway, and the shot was pure luck.

Let the hunter, on the other hand, take two or three shots in rapid fire order, and now it's different. It proves the hunter is an incompetent bungler, or the power and might of the animal could not stand up to a "modern rifle" with the force of a tank-destroying bazooka that inflicted on the poor animal what the Constitution of the United States protects all of living creatures from—cruel and unusual punishment. More than a single shot proved that to be the case, didn't it?

At the moment of the hunter's glory, his critic completely misreads the situation. He thinks the hunter's ebullience and unbounded joy results from a poor animal being killed with bloodthirsty *crudeliter*. The critic hasn't the foggiest notion of why the hunter is truly ecstatic. Nor does the critic see the reverential sadness and, yes, the occasional tears of salutation and gratitude, nor can he imagine the honor that trophy will receive for as long as the hunter lives—and who knows, perhaps longer. The critic is dead-sure (if I may), that only a sadistic love for cruelty is behind the whole thing and hunters should be hanged to end their menace to civilized society.

The critic's obsession with "cruelty," when it's not there, is an irrational phobia having a logical explanation and will be discussed later. Now, there is one final point to be made.

Confront a critic with these facts and there is a last cheap shot to discredit the hunter's accomplishments. If a hunter is with a partner, as he should be in case something goes radically wrong in the middle of the wilderness, who stands as backup while the hunter is confronting his dangerous animal, the critic always asks, "What's so brave about that? There's another guy in back of him, isn't there?" Yes, but that other guy in back is not an illusion. He, too, is a hunter who has the same shooting conditions of lighting, weather, position, terrain, and the rest of it, to which is added the anxiety of protecting his partner or client. The backup is even more endangered if the animal is enraged with wounds and is now only a bounce away from two hunters. Do we now get a backup for the first backup and a third and fourth for the others in front?

When a backup could be critically important in a dangerous split-second, there is absolutely no guarantee that he can, or will, be. First, because his partner or client is probably right in the line of fire, or second, because an enraged grizzly or lion can take on two or even three incompetent men before it is downed for keeps. The greatest fear of professional hunters backing up is that their clients, by unexpectedly doing the wrong thing in a critical moment, will jeopardize both of them. It would have been better in the first place if the client had dropped his rifle and run to give his backup a clear field.

Finally, a professional guide or hunter is along even when a hunter does not want him. He is along because the laws of a state or foreign country require his presence for a nonresident hunter for a host of legal reasons having nothing to do with the hunter's courage or cowardice. No one can deny how utterly valuable a backup can be. To assume this guarantees the hunter's success, courage, or his life is wishful thinking. To begin with, putting one's life with trust and faith in a backup's hands requires its own courage. The hunter who does not have the guts to stand his own ground in the critical moment, will probably not have it to let another stand ground for both of them.

The backup is no substitute for the hunter's own performance requirements; he is a complement to it. When the hunter performs with excellence, and makes the backup unnecessary, he will be discredited because "there was a backup present." When the hunter performs with excellence without a backup, then he is not skillful or brave, but a psychopath, lacking in normal fear, anxiety, and compassion and proving his manhood by acting like a real macho, tough guy.

The foregoing put-down of the hunter is based on possibility, however. Yes, it is possible that a backup may have to do the *coup de grace* to save a hunter's life. But this is a rare condition in reality. If the hunter lacks confidence in himself, and, assuming he is sane, he will never take such a foolish risk if he values his life. That he takes that risk at all is reasonable evidence of his competence to down his animal. If his backup ever had to take a shot, then nine out of ten times it is not to save the hunter's life, but to make sure the animal does not escape or suffer. That is the probability.

Wild animals, especially dangerous ones, have enormous vitality. The biggest and sorriest surprise many a hunter has had is to exult a few seconds too soon. His "dead" animal, lying there absolutely motionless, has all too often leaped to its feet and made for cover. If the hunter is reloading at that moment, or has an off day, or is too exhausted for a second or third rapid fire shot, or if any one of a dozen things that can and do go wrong to the best of hunters, the backup is worth his weight in gold if he delivers the *coup de grace*, mercifully, and puts the animal down for keeps. The hunter has invested too much of everything to risk the loss of that animal or to lacerate his conscience knowing a wounded animal will linger in pain, or it can turn into a man-eater.

If the hunter, in spite of his best efforts, finds himself in such predicaments, what should he do? Let the animal escape? He then faces a different set of charges from his critic for "mindless and savage butchery." The critic should be grateful for the backup who prevents the worst from happening, not only for the hunter's sake, or the safety of other human beings, but also for the animal's sake. It makes little difference who delivers the mercy shot, the misericordia, as long as it is done as quickly and humanely as possible.

Finally, the best reason why a backup is there; he and the hunter are probably the best of friends and hunting companions. They are enjoying a unique experience together that cannot be shared with just any old buddy. That is the bonding instinct that was there when the first caveman hunted. It is still here, today. Many heavy-duty details and chores in the wilderness require help when one man can't do it alone. Or what happens if one of the hunters suffers a serious accident requiring help? The buddy is there to do whatever he can or go for help.

There is yet the most important reason of all. It is a spiritual one. As I've gotten older and developed ailments and slowed down, I welcome the presence of a trusted companion. If something final happens to me, then hopefully my partner will survive to have my remains returned to my loved ones, and to tell them how it happened so they will be at peace. I owe them this too, and no other duty I may have on the hunting trail can take priority. If the reverse should happen, then my partner knows I will reciprocate. Each of us knows the other will do his best at all costs.

Almost every responsible hunter I've talked to feels the same way. In the event of death on the trail, from whatever causes, each hunter knows the most important treasures he will leave behind are his loved ones. They do not deserve to suffer the anguish and doubts for weeks or years until someone finally discovers the remains to end the waiting, hoping, and grief of those left behind. I believe the total trust between hunting partners is the conscious or unconscious certainty that the survivor will try to carry out this duty. I believe the so-called bonding instinct between hunting partners probably originates in the need for this trust since prehistory.

Hunting will forever be an art because there are no known formulae or fixed procedures in advance to predict success or the quality of the hunt. There are no assurances danger, safety, joy, sadness, life, or death may, or may not, happen because anything can happen. That's why the hunt is exciting and an adventure. No two hunts can ever be the same. No one can get bored.

The man who is a perfect hunter is still an imperfect human being. He is a sportsman and an artist— not a robot. He will make mistakes, despite his best efforts, but as my track coach used to say, years and years ago, "You're not a champ until you've lost a few." Those sad, regrettable mistakes or losses of an off day, known to every hunter, are sometimes the only way an average man, proud of his democracy which lets him follow the dreams of yesteryear's nobility, becomes an honorable trophy hunter. I am not entitled to say how honorable a trophy hunter I think I may be, because that is a judgement of my peers. But, I know how hard I have tried not to be a dishonorable one. I know there are some sorry excuses for trophy hunters, or any kind of hunters for that matter, out there on the trail, who know too little of the hunting ethic or the sportsman's code of fair chase, and care even less. I know that too many decent hunters are too ashamed to admit this, but that does not make the scandal go away. It must be faced and denounced by the rest of us who owe it to the honor of our calling.

It is bad enough for a profane society to misunderstand the hunter and mock his art and sanctities, but it is worse when some hunters themselves, do the same thing to the art of hunting. There are bound to be hunters who are bad actors and sportsmen, human nature being what it is, in any society. But in our "value free do your own thing" societal miasma, the problem is immeasurably worse. Good hunters have a debt of gratitude to antihunters, no matter how different their intent, who point out the scoundrels defiling our art.

If there is a morality, a code of fair chase, a sense of sportsmanship by which the trophy hunter must abide, how does he come by it? In fact, how does the average man become any kind of hunter? A few generations ago, this was no problem. Today, it is. A few generations ago, the family was intact, and a father, grandfather, or older brother accompanied the neophyte on his early hunts.

The youthful novice hunter had competent teachers in his next of kin who themselves had competent teachers from whom they learned good hunting values and were, therefore, qualified to teach them to their apprentices. This was when the now-hated religious values of church morality were in full force. During early years in our nation's history, an estimated 90% of human action and behavior in all walks of life were controlled by the same set of moral values, because there was no moral or ethical relativism. Religious, denominational, or sectarian differences did not result in class or cultural war. By example of deed and precept, neophytes learned the ethics and morality of hunting. If norms were violated, it was out of deliberate intent, not from ignorance of right and wrong.

How does the apprentice hunter learn his art and ethics today? Of what does his education consist? He probably learns it just as I did. He finds a friend who is a hunter and tags along to learn whatever he can. Such a friend may be highly skilled, indeed, but ethics is a scary word and its "relativity" to everything else makes a formidable educational task.

The apprentice learns all the errors, bad habits, and ethical ignorance of his teacher and passes it on to his apprentices down the line. Whatever else the apprentice learns, it has little to do with ethics, because there are none he is aware of. Everything being relative, anything goes. It is the result of value-free education and a permissive society. For some, this has given the individual freedom to do whatever he wants, or can get away with. For others, this has created chaos and anarchy which threaten him at every turn.

Some states have introduced hunter training programs, with some attention to ethics, but emphasis is on firearms safety, legal requirements, and survival techniques. But even minimally, attention to hunting ethics and esthetics are welcome indeed—let us hope it is not too late. However, enrollment in such programs is often voluntary, and my guess is that those who need them most are apt to be the ones who attend them least.

Sociologists have a word frequently used—anomie. It refers to an absence of norms or standards of conduct and belief which creates confusion and normlessness in personal and group behavior. It is the basis for aberration and worse. In short, we don't know what is right or wrong, normal or abnormal behavior. It creates conditions of social instability, stress, conflict, and tension. Behavior becomes anomic.

When we encourage "do your own thing" or be a nonconformist without restraining moral norms and emphasize our rights without regard for our duties, we invite anarchy. Social constraint is no longer based on voluntary, internalized norms resulting from moral or ethical convictions. It is based on external legal coercion encroaching more and more in areas of personal liberty.

To the extent that we do the right thing, laws are unnecessary. To the extent that we do the wrong thing, laws are ineffective. To find a happy balance is delicate, and in a supposedly value-free educational system that declares war on all morality except its own, we guarantee anomic behavior requiring more and more legal coercion with liberty for none and injustice for all. We have law based not on wisdom, justice, morality, or experience, but on special interest group pressure, illicit power, or corruption.

Because hunting is one of the most democratic of all sports or arts, anyone may try it. Anyone includes those who cannot read on a sixth-grade level, although a king's ransom has been spent on their education. But they are expected to understand the subtleties and complexities of legal language in an exhaustive handbook of hunting regulations that change on a yearly basis. Without internalized moral norms, most apprentice hunters have only the vaguest idea of what they ought, or ought not, to do in the pursuit of game. Often, they do the wrong thing out of sheer ignorance. Even when they hunt legally, they do it dishonorably. It is on that issue that vicious stereotypes of the hunter are created by the counterculture elite who have spent more than a half-century ridiculing honor.

One stereotype sees the trophy hunter as a spoiled, arrogant millionaire capitalist, preferably a Texan, a political reactionary, a porcine, cigar-chomping, heavyweight boozer, and a macho, womanizing jock, all rolled into one, and who has only contempt for animals. In fact, he gloats with cruelty in slaughtering them on safari. This rather common stereotype in television and movies, foments class antipathy from the bottom upward. With democratization of sport hunting, one did not have to be royalty, but one still needed a lot of money for safaris or shikaris in foreign lands.

Without doubt, some of this was pure social snobbery for the upper-upper class conspicuous consumers. But that did not make them vicious killers worthy of condemnation just because they were having a good time to the distress or envy of the rest of us. Earlier movies like "The Most Dangerous Game," "The Macomber Affair," "The Snows of Kilimanjaro," "Harry Black and the Tiger," and "The Last Dinosaur" are subtly antihunting because they are about characters who are aristocratic psychopaths, military men, wealthy business tycoons, and unabashed playboys. They are upper class.

The opposite stereotype, later fomented class antipathy from the top downward. One of the most scurrilous antihunting documentaries ever done was CBS's "The Guns of Autumn." This time, it was not fictional characters but real people who were stigmatized, and the real attack on American hunters of the middle and lower classes had begun. Among other things, the emphasis was on coon-huntin', tobacco-droolin' semiliterate Southern rednecks, and nothing in that show indicates the informants were told this would be an antihunting documentary. It was enough to make a strong man cry to watch those poor, innocent, honest, hard-working, rural dupes trying to explain the hunting mystique to journalists whose cleverly loaded questions got the responses so easily twisted into pejorative stereotypes. As bad as the mendacity of the program was, the transparent cruelty of how it was done, in the name of programmatic art, insulted any viewer's intelligence. One was embarrassed by the East Coast Liberal Establishment's "finest hour" looking down its anti-WASP (White Anglo-Saxon Protestant) nose.

If these two examples maligned the opposite extremes, there was another one that got it all. Regrettably, I do not know the name of the television movie, because I turned it on accidentally halfway through. What I saw began with an attractive, middle-aged woman who shouted at her husband that she was leaving him (apparently they'd had a quarrel), as she slammed the door on her way out of an affluent, high-classed home.

Next scene. She is driving a fine automobile on a lonely highway at night and stops to pick up a male and female hippy hitchhikers, complete with long, greasy hair (hers) and an unkempt beard (his), a guitar and a new born baby (theirs).

Next scene. The woman tells them that she is turning off the highway at the next junction coming up, and she will let her guests off where she is sure they'll get another ride. The bearded one whips out a pistol, orders the poor woman out, takes the wheel and drives the car off into the night. She crosses the highway, stumbles into a ditch, and crosses a gully thick with brambles and rocks, where she breaks a heel on her shoe (it looks like) and hobbles toward a dimly lighted truck stop cafe on the other side.

Next scene. The cafe is empty except for the owner, a large, burly Anglo-Saxon type male, who is closing up for the night. As the woman stumbles into the light, one can see she is bruised and dishevelled. Pathetically, she relates what has happened and asks for a coin (her handbag was taken) so she can phone for help. He calms her down compassionately, suggests she go upstairs to tidy herself, come down for a cup of coffee when she is ready, and he will help her.

Next scene. She has tidied herself up and is combing her hair when (yeah, you guessed it) the burly restaurateur walks in, leering, and before she can say, "Don't," he throws her on the bed and begins to rape her. The camera now alternately pans to the wall in back of the bed and back to the rape, intermittently. What is on the wall (hang on, please) is the American flag, a rifle, a mounted trophy deer head, and a crucified Christ. In that brief scene, without a single sound except for the whimpering of the victim, one gets an instant one-semester course in the Introduction to Western Civilization.

The brutal owner of the restaurant business is also a rapist, an American patriot, a hunter, a gun owner, a Christian (probably a Catholic), and a man of violent talents. Wow! What a triumph of stereotypy. In one fell swoop, everything is packaged together to show the real causes for injustice and brutality to women.

Regrettably, I switched channels and should have waited for the credits at the end—maybe I could have learned the name of the movie. It was one of the most vicious pieces of antihunting, antiwhite male, anti-Christian, anti-patriotic, antibusiness bits of propaganda let loose in the name of entertainment. The wall symbols in that scene were totally gratuitous to the central theme. In the old days, one got mostly entertainment from the movies. Today, one gets mostly hidden ideological messages (with the subtlety of an army tank), There have been countless bizarre scenes like this chipping away at our major values, institutions, and national identity for over a half century.

There is ample scientific evidence (the Lichter studies for one) which show producers of such films see themselves as social change agents (the politically proper phrase for counterculture activists or play-safe revolutionaries) bent on wrecking the old established order to usher in the New World. Everybody knows this except hunters, who are too busy living their lives to analyze these films. The critics, whose professional business it is to do so, won't. They, too, are part of the social change agencies.

The point is, critics go considerably beyond criticism to partisanship and advocacy. They have declared war on a perfectly legitimate activity because they are committed to an opposing ideology and want the destruction of that culture in which the moral system permits hunting, among other things. The pretext that wins converts to that ideology includes the animal-rights movement, because many people genuinely love animals (so do hunters), and many are easily turned against hunters, who are identified with villains who are "cruel" to animals.

In the first place, animals have no symbolic language and, hence, cannot conceive of rights, let alone legislate for them. Their rights are declared for them and coincide, exactly, with the prejudices and politics of those who bestow these rights on animals to subvert the larger culture, of which the hunter is a part. Antihunting groups are big business for doctrinaire anticapitalist administrators in the top six antihunting organizations, whose annual salaries are near, or above, the $200,000 range. If that is not enough, many of these groups are subsidized by taxpayer dollars (including hunters) to declare war on hunting. If that isn't enough, the public school system has formal courses in nature studies, rife with antihunting values, claiming to be value-free.

Never in history has there been a pro-hunting movement. But today there is an antihunting movement with the seeds planted in kindergarten on up as part of official policy, no matter how cleverly disguised. When I was in grade school, we were always taught to be kind to animals as a moral good in itself, without ever a maligning or laudatory word about hunters. Today, one must love animals as a means to the ulterior end of hating hunters who are a political enemy of humanity.

The worst enemy of hunters, however, are other hunters who are bad sportsmen. When they violate the law or the hunting ethic, they need to be weeded out by the honorable hunting fraternity itself and treated like the criminals and scoundrels they are. Ethical hunters, unfortunately, do the natural thing. They put their trust in the law to prosecute the unethical hunter who violates the law, but the law cares much more about the politics of hunting than about its ethics. This is so for a very important reason.

With increasing public awareness of endangered wildlife and the natural environment, college-level majors in wildlife management and related disciplines outnumber by far the number of professional employment opportunities, and the chief employer is, of course, government. Hence, the glut of such students creates a buyer's market. Graduate majors are introduced to the politically prevalent atmosphere first in the university's training programs, large portions of which are governmentally funded and controlled, then to the politically based program of the government agencies themselves. Now, an irony emerges.

The private sport hunting societies of the late 19th century which were so instrumental in pressing for legislation to protect some species from the verge of extinction (the bison, for example), eventually gave the impetus to governmental regulation and founding of permanent departments of fish and game with pro-hunting sentiments. Their primary purpose was the scientific management of game resources and conservation. This was totally supported by those who were footing a substantial part of the taxes placed on them—the hunters, themselves. The hunters, an important part of the conservation program, culled surplus animals and maintained the habitat's ability to sustain optimal game populations. Hunters still play that important role.

Today, the traditional esteem for the hunter has changed in too many departments of fish and game. Government personnel have become ambivalent under political pressures of antihunting groups. Too many public agencies reflect the prejudices and politics of such groups, yet they cannot disown hunters altogether who are the primary paying users of renewable game resources that the agencies are in business to conserve. The average, young government worker in a fish and game department teeters on the brink between hunting and antihunting pressure. His supervisors will tell him which way to go, depending on which political regime is in power. Hence, government is often seen by the hunter not as his friend but an enemy. A confrontational, instead of a supportive, attitude is generated.

Nowhere has this attitude created more problems than in the public relations link between the hunter and his public—the professional hunters, guides, and outfitters. I called attention to this problem as early as 1971 when the antihunting mass movement was not yet an embryonic twitch. It appeared in an article for *Alaska Big Game Records Book.* In this chapter, I can do no more than briefly outline the gist of that analysis.

Guiding is a profession because its practitioners, as in other professions, have special knowledge, expertise, skills, and facilities which the client does not have. The guide knows where the game is, their species-specific characteristics, how best to get his clients to the animals, and provide for safe and comfortable camp facilities, services and support. This means the client must have complete trust in his professional guide to do what is in the client's best interests, and not the guide's, at the client's expense.

A final and most important characteristic of any professional is the legally chartered society or association to which he belongs. The society establishes its own code of ethics, maintains discipline over the ethical conduct of its rank and file, participates in the legislation which effects it policies, establishes fair and equitable fees, and so on.

The great difference between the hunting profession and other professions is the factor of seasonality. Wild animals have birthing, mating, migrating, and climatological cycles which necessarily restrict hunting activities. All this makes the professional hunters' or outfitters' gainful employment a seasonal one, at best. Often the professional has to take on some other occupation to survive in the off season. The initial financial outlay to such an enterprise is substantial. To provide comfortable quarters in a base camp with food supplies, horses, vehicles, and airplane access is a very expensive and time-consuming logistics project of several years to reach solvency.

In the midst of this, statutes are constantly changing due to political pressures, administrations, game populations and, in some cases, international law, due to mammalian or avian migratory routes. The problem is exacerbated by clients who know little about this. They have paid a lot of money to hunt with a certain guide in a particular location precisely because he has a good reputation for producing satisfactory results. He, on the other hand, is in marginal position torn between several conflicting interests at once among client, conservation, law, and contrary or conflicting public interests. His survival as a businessman and a professional is under great pressure.

From his perspective, a bunch of young, college-educated bureaucrats, without any length of service and experience change and pass insane laws that do not easily win respect. Many of these professionals are old timers who entered their calling as young men when there was no labyrinth of regulations and laws. It is difficult for them to stay abreast of constant changes. Many of them are no longer young enough to learn some other occupation and leave their profession. Many of them lack a college education and cannot keep up with their opponents' sophisticated political subtleties. A few of them are outright polecats and crooks who should never have gotten into the profession to begin with.

If the difference between success or failure for his client depends on cutting a corner, some professionals, already viewing the government and its laws as the enemy, will take the risk and violate the law. The point is when federal agents or high-powered antihunting opponents enter the fray and catch a professional violator dead to rights, he will make headlines, locally, nationally, and, in some cases, internationally.

That is enough for front-page sensationalism to blacken all hunters with the same brush. What can an honorable hunter do except grit his teeth and bear the ignominy of betrayal by his own kind and the calumnious "proof" of his traditional enemies?

The general cultural decline and moral corruption of our society does not appear in a vacuum by magic. It is the result of years of deliberate and systematic assault from within by those who reject that culture and morality. To move from one stage to the next in the dialectical struggle, there is a transient period of instability, chaos, and anomie.

Why do we have so much crime, for example? Because there are those who want to allow its magnitude. It is an extension of political struggle by other means. It destabilizes society. When we have enough of it, we will soon beg for the totalitarian big-brother state that will promise to wipe out crime by destroying the civil liberties for the rest of us. We are nearly there now and all that remains is to deprive all of us of the only means we have for self defense—our right to bear firearms.

The hunter is a prime target in this strategy. In the American Revolutionary War, the Battle of Bunker Hill was won by hunters and pioneers called in from the frontier. It was their sharpshooting which defeated the red-coats. To prevent such resistance again, sooner or later, the hunters especially must be disarmed. When that happens, it will be easier to disarm the rest of the population by the precedent set.

In every area of contemporary life, there is an increase in the sociopaths, psychopaths, deviants, and abnormal types, many of whom have a legally protected alternate life style. The uppermost strata in society often lead the way in such deviance and social disorganization. Dignitaries, celebrities, business tycoons, government officials, clergy, and all the role models are routinely routed from their positions or covertly protected, depending on which political side has the upper hand. Given all this, is it not a joke to single out hunters as devils who have infiltrated the choir of angels? There is no choir; we destroyed that long ago in the name of constitutional rights. Now, we all whistle the devil's tune.

The wonder is not that there are so many unethical hunters, but that there are so few compared to deviants in other groups throughout society who are not stigmatized like hunters. We cannot have it both ways. We cannot say man is a product of his society, the system is at fault for all our shortcomings, man is not responsible for his actions due to his subconscious forces, and then turn around and hold hunters responsible for their criminality as though society and culture have nothing to do with the character types they develop. To hold the hunter morally responsible for his shortcomings is the duty of the traditional hunters who claim a moral code; it is not the privilege of progressivists who hold no individual responsible for anything, since that is already the fault of the social system. Whose social system? Those who have indulged in the creative art of destroying the old system now complain of the new system gone amuck. The barbarians in both camps remain the same.

There are hunters today who want to identify with the glorious romance and adventure of the hunt, but they want to do it at bargain basement prices. They will grab a rifle and shoot at anything that moves. They want to kill in order to have hunted without touching the transcendental and, what's worse, they turn their backs on it. The spirituality and esthetics of the hunt are lost on them, especially when they are young or novices. At this early stage, they must be convinced they can kill an animal to begin with and, therefore, anything goes to succeed.

Responsible sport hunters refer to them as "slob hunters," hoping they will grow up. Although the slob hunter may not have a sense of ethics because no one taught them, there is always hope they will learn its ethics and morality if they hunt for sport and are faithful to the hunt. Most of them become superb, mature sportsmen once they grasp the philosophy of the art. They learn that while one must kill in order to have hunted successfully, the kill is not the objective for the sport hunter. The objective is the quality of the hunt based on an ethical code. The symbolic importance of the trophy cannot be separated from the quality of the hunt, which makes it an art or a sport. None of this will deter the antihunter from insisting that "killing is killing," because he wants hunting wiped out. He wants his will imposed on the hunter. He wants to be the one who, in the name of freedom, controls the hunter

There is another class of hunters who are apostates of two kinds. One of them deliberately brings discredit to hunting, but both have one thing in common—both were ardent devotees of the hunt, but turn against it. Both have a deep emotional and spiritual crisis in the process of conversion from one kind of self to another. The question they ask themselves is, "How could I have acted this way?" But one of them wants self-reformation only in his private world of reality, and is content with being freed from the agonies of once pleasant memories now haunting him. His is a very private and personal soul searching. The other kind has the same problem, but he wants more than self-reformation. His is a very public affair. He wants to reform the world. Though his numbers are few, they reach many. If the true sport hunter remains devoted to the hunt, he has the emotional stamina to withstand the critical assault on his self esteem. The apostate hunter who may be technically competent, eventually succumbs to the social assault on his self-esteem, which becomes a truly unbearable emotional burden. Human life is nothing if it is not a social phenomenon.

The impact of the group or fellow associates on the individual's value and attitude system is too well established to adumbrate it here. If the norms of one's group memberships or associates do not support hunting values, one will have a tough time hunting. Personal values, in defiance of the groups' or associates' norms, sooner or later result in informal methods of control—like the cold shoulder of ostracism, ridicule, disrespect, etc. The group tends to conserve its own norms and membership characteristics without which it ceases being a group. Associates lose interest in the person whose values are significantly different, since there is no longer a basis for congeniality.

Obviously, if one values his associates more than his hunting, he will give up hunting sooner or later. If he values his hunting more, then he will leave the group, wondering how he got into it in the first place. If he still needs associates and friendships, he may join a hunting group, or go about his own business. The question hits one between the eyes. Why would a competent hunter with years of devotion to his sport, suddenly throw in the towel? The psychological factors are too complex to discuss here at length, but there are five situations I have observed in Alaska, one of which I experienced myself.

Risking oversimplification, here they are: 1) All to often, men coming to Alaska, to make their home or follow a job, have the fringe benefit of hunting as a top priority in mind. One of the important reasons for a high divorce rate in the state is that he hunts too often, she resents it, the arguments get more bitter ending in divorce or estrangement. If he wants the relationship badly enough, he will give up hunting. 2) The high cost of living in Alaska, which is among the highest in the nation, keeps getting higher and higher and one simply gives up on sport hunting because he can't afford it. 3) He opts for subsistence hunting. 4) Politics and the antihunting movement add more and more frustrating laws and place more and more prime hunting grounds off limits, taking the joy out of it. 5) One's life circumstances change for any number of reasons and he loses interest.

In these scenarios the hunter gives up his hunting, but there is no hatred or deep emotional resentments against hunting or hunters, nor is there a sense of shame or guilt for having hunted so it becomes emotionally crippling or neurotic. What does not happen in these instances is a rejection of one's self image or identity. One can still live with oneself and function normally in his emotional life.

Then we come to the apostate hunters who need self-reform. Guilt and loss of self-esteem is the driving force. The first type of apostate sees his former hunting as an error of his own choice to be corrected. He knows he is solely responsible for his predicament, relinquishes his emotional attachment to hunting as a wrong choice, and sees it as another mistake he made with life and accepts his humanity. He blames himself, does not blame hunting, and leaves it alone. The second type sees his former hunting, not as his own erroneous choice, but as an abomination into which he was seduced. He didn't make a mistake with life; life made a mistake with him.

He will never leave hunting alone as something which once was in his misled life. He will loathe it, try to destroy it, and since it is still in his life, the memory opens wounds every time the outside world gives him a reminder. That is what he will now attack. Which of us haven't felt this way with the world at one time or another, for one or another reason? Of the two apostates, it is this world-attacker, this malcontent, which is of concern here, because we—hunters and non-hunters alike—are part of this world under his assault. The first kind of apostate is in a situation which theory calls a sum-plus game. He gets what he wants and lets us get what we want. Neither side is hurt.

The second type is in a zero-sum game. In order for the apostate to win, the rest of us must lose even when it is not necessary. The rest of us are not depriving him. He is depriving us—for our own good, he insists. He is the real apostate of history. To change himself, he must change the world to the way he wants it to be. This is the quintessential do-badder in disguise as the do-gooder.

He comes to abhor hunting and himself for having hunted. He wishes hunting had never existed, making him a part of it. While the other ex-hunters can live with themselves, the true-apostate hunter cannot. His memory will not let him. The world responsible for those memories must be forced to change. He becomes the undercover tyrant.

This kind of publicized apostasy was virtually unheard of in the past because there was no collective, mass antihunting movement to give it ear or stimulus. If there was a change of heart, it remained private. Since the 1960s' "activism," there has been a concerted vilification of hunting and the hunter via mass media. As the public is saturated with more and more of the negative image of the hunter, some of it is bound to get to the hunter. When he has doubts about himself and admits it, he is a good candidate for fame, money, and social acceptance by those who need to exploit him.

It is no longer rare to read about hunters who have "seen the light" and denounced their former sport to feel "born again." Our identities are largely the product of what others have us think of ourselves. When we get enough feedback that makes us feel rejectable, we wonder about who we are and why we don't feel comfortable with the way we were. The support from others for our identity is no longer there. Some take others' opinion with a grain of salt, but some are not so sure.

Made to feel guilty by the antihunting movement, the rebellious apostate must now get rid of his guilt, and loss of self-esteem, by the renunciation of his former selfhood, whose identity is breaking down under emotional stress. The technique of breaking down one's identity by vilifying his values comes from everywhere: the media, the political circus, the educational system. It produces an anomic individual—one who is no longer sure of what is right or wrong, good or bad. (This is one of the basic reasons for the public schools system's emphasis on "value free" education and, of course, there is no such thing: to designate education as value free is to assign an opposite value to values being changed.) If the hunter does not have enough inner-strength to see through and resist the con job, then he succumbs.

Shorn of his values, norms, and identity, the apostate hunter is anomic—like an empty sack ready to be filled by virtually any set of values, norms, and attitudes. He is then "put together" again. The collective support for his new identity comes from his former opponents, now his friends, who shower him with love and attention and exploit him in the bargain. He is given top billing to tell the world how wrong he was in his former ways and beliefs. What's worse, he can now tell the world how bad his former associates are who still remain. Who can sound more authoritative?

This, after all, was the brainwashing technique perfected by the North Koreans on American G.I. prisoners of war. Since then, it has become standard practice in many countries during war or peace. It appears in many different institutions and practices. In our country, a favorite "battleground" is the American university system of liberal arts, where in 4 years, too many young minds are subtly conned into a 180 degree turnaround. This is one reason why the halls of Congress make it so easy for almost anyone to enter the halls of ivy. It is one of the most effective means for producing an endless supply of new recruits for the "New Order of Things." The same technique is used on hunters some of whom fall for it. They become the new cadres, and soon the ranks swell, until it takes heroes to stand their ground against those who were once their own brothers and are now in the ranks of standardized robots.

Human beings in this emotional crux need and deserve sympathetic understanding. After all, they feel the same real spiritual anguish and debility that we all do in different contexts at one time or another in our lives. That, after all, is the cost of being human. It is especially sad to see this in some hunters, who abandon their early impassioned commitments to the hunt, and develop diametrically opposite attitudes with equal passion—not by the genuine moral reform of soul searching, but by the victimization of the ego through political and social process. Normally, our unique experiences often make us see the same object of attachment suddenly become an object of estrangement. That which once filled us with pride, now floods us with shame or guilt; love easily becomes hate.

We have all wondered how some of our friends, now divorced, spend the rest of their lives hating a former spouse who was once loved beyond all measure—and yet the spouse is the same person perceived in a different way. Always the evaluation of the self image is involved. We accept or reject our self-images depending on who loves and hates us and why. Sometimes, this *volte-face*, this psychological obliteration of one's ego for the adoption of an opposite ego, is a good thing, a spiritual blessing. Otherwise, the 4th century profligate from Hippo would never have become St. Augustine.

Sometimes, it's a bad thing, like when the seminarian, Djugashvili, of the Russian Orthodox faith, becomes Joseph Stalin of the Communist Party, and kills millions of Christians whose faith tried to teach him the humility of service to others instead of to self. It enraged his insufferable ego, and turned him against his past as it had Marx and Lenin before him. Augustine never killed anyone, and his teachings still inspire to this day. Stalin had others serve him, even in the Gulags. He even destroyed thousands of churches in Russia to get rid of the hated symbols which so bothered him. He was tossed into the memory hole by his own kind less than a decade after his death.

Today's man of honor may have been yesterday's scoundrel, and tomorrow's murderer may be today's choir boy. We all face this challenge without which growth and maturation are difficult, if not impossible. Sometimes, the revulsion is so great at what we were, that we feel self-contamination. We undergo a ritual of self-purification with the new self-image, and can now live with ourselves. This seems, to me at least, entirely normal and reasonable. It happens all the time, and we accept it as a personal satisfaction. But sometimes, there is a critical aberration to this normal routine. Since changing the self-image changes the perception of the world, some of us want to endow the whole world with our new-found fascination, and we go public for verification.

Self-change is not always satisfied with mere separation or desertion from its former image. All the elements of that self have changed except the overriding, uncontrollable memory which integrates the mind with its myriad elements. Change to something is always change from something else, and that something else is impossible to imagine or conceive without memory. Hence, that change of self requires the change of others' and the world's appearance. It becomes the mirror reflecting the changed image he wants to see in himself. To do that, he must seek relief from his taunting memories, now constant and hateful. His mind cannot escape to freedom. Anything in this world can, and does, trigger those despised memories.

Freud talked about forgotten or repressed memories due to trauma in the so-called subconscious seeking expression. I dare say, more people have become neurotic or insane with conscious memories of haunting trauma too often expressed, which could be neither repressed nor forgotten. Some are not so lucky with blissful oblivion, the basis for which is probably not psychogenic, but biological and genetic.

Unless all memory can be removed, or destroyed, from the mind seeking relief, a neat trick is for the mind to destroy or remove those symbols from the outside world that trigger the painful memories inside. Apostate hunters, in fantasy or reality, might destroy sporting goods stores displaying firearms; they may spray ladies fur coats with paint; they may demonstrate for excessive taxation on guns and ammunition, or handgun control. But sooner or later, one gets tired or caught doing these things.

However, when the apostate hunter joins the enemy to vilify the art of hunting and degrades the self-respect, humanity, and integrity of the hunters he was once a part of, then he can talk it out, since the symbols become spoken words and exit the memory as sounds. The relief is only temporary, however. The symbols keep coming back unless one takes tranquilizers. Sometimes these create brand new symbols which also keep coming back. The apostate now betrays the benefaction and memories of earlier hunts, because he owes them an obligatory gratitude and he hates obligation. Obligation is what he thinks others owe him, not what he owes to others. The more he loved hunting then, the more he must despise it now. The scales will level in his mind and give him relief from the imbalance.

It is his business to denounce his former identity and memories of the hunt now that he's had his enjoyment. But when he publicly vilifies the hunt and hunters, who will not betray their love for the chase and are aroused to defend their honor and integrity of the hunt, then the demonizers make double time. They turn a personal experience into a public cause, seeking to destroy the legitimate rights of others. The apostate becomes the tyrant. He is out to destroy all external symbols whose imagery his memory cannot shake loose. He wants to destroy them, lest memory haunt him. The danger is, if he has enough talent and audacity, he might become a part of the Apocalypse sooner than expected.

I always admired Howard Cosell as a sportscaster, because he brought high intelligence, wit, and a superb command of the King's English to the sometimes shabby game of boxing. He elevated that art to a certain sophistication of imagery. There was an authentic passion to his commitment. No snob could feel boxing was beneath his dignity when Cosell's commentary, round by round, gave it a certain polish, even with wry hyperbole. And the sport was good to him. It gave him fame, fortune, and fanfare. Suddenly, he not only changed his mind, he apostatized. He went public with vitriolic denunciation of the sport's "violence," "brutality," and "primordial killer instinct." He had known this all through the years the sport was so good to him. Why then, the sudden denunciation, and the betrayal of all those boxers and fans, who for years had entrusted their love for the sport in his care? Why did he adopt the canards which his, and the sport's critics had been spewing for years? What a loss the unique old Cosell was to us even before he died. The Cosell of the new image was a variation of the old routine by predecessors, who did a more authentic job with the vitriol and venom in attacking the sport that was his friend for so long.

The apostate is compulsive. He must convince the world it must change just because he has. He comes to love the world of his former enemies, so now they will accept him. If you can't beat them—join them. A dishonorable capitulation is better than an honorable defeat. It is always thus, and so it is for some hunters who become antihunters. But were they ever genuine sport hunters? Was their "love" for hunting ever based on solid ground to begin with? If they could betray it in the end to the enemy, why did they embrace it in the beginning? Did they know themselves so poorly? Was it so easy to betray themselves?

A classical instance of this came to light, recently. I will not reference the quotation (the reader will have to trust me), since I will not betray an ex-hunter who knows not what he has done. I quote it here because it brilliantly captures the very essence of the argument used so often by others. I wish to make no criticism of the person, only the logic of his argument, which is the evidence making the point: "I was taught to take (wildlife) not only for food but simply to take: to kill for the sport of killing, a diversion beyond need. It was thought a weakness to feel a consideration for other life forms. I overcame that so-called weakness and soon learned to kill with the rest of the hunting fraternity as a primal heritage . . ." There we have it.

If the diversion was beyond need, what could such killing be except sheer wantonness? And how can anyone learn this if he really didn't want to? What kind of teachers would teach that hunting is a "sport of killing"? Right there any neophyte hunter is off on the wrong foot. A true hunter does not kill for the sake of killing. Again, any true hunter must kill his animal to have hunted successfully. But not every killer of animals is a true hunter. Any person who kills an animal for the "sport of killing" may be many things, but by definition alone, he is not a hunter, let alone a sportsman. We cannot put the cart before the horse and then say, because of it, the horse doesn't count.

To kill some living creature for the sake of putting an end to its life is the essence of the psychopathological. To stop killing animals for the sake of killing them is to recognize its inherent evil. To renounce such killing, and to renounce the self capable of it, is the first step toward recovery of mental health and decent humanity. The courage and integrity required to make that change is to be applauded and respected. It deserves sympathetic understanding. But then, such killing was never hunting to begin with, was it? If there is absolution in apostasy, so be it. It is to the good. But why does it have to be made into public retaliation against a former passion, which gave the apostate so much when he saw it through different eyes? Why must he now vilify hunters, who remain faithful to the sport just because he has lost his faith? It is he who has changed, not the sport. All this is why apostasy has been rebuked throughout history. It victimizes others for one's own absolution, which has become revenge.

How sad it is to see the apostate hunter's mistaken anguish. What authentic sport hunter with his respect for animals, with reverence for his trophies, with strict adherence to the tenets of fair play, ethics, and sportsmanship thinks it a weakness to feel consideration for life forms? What can show more consideration for "life forms" of big-game than the ethics of true hunters? Who has done more for the research, protection, and conservation of big-game animals with private funds, without begging for governmental largesse or intrusion? Whose fraternities have done more to establish, maintain, and reward ethical conduct and performance standards for their own memberships? Who pressed more for legislation to create game sanctuaries, preserves, and refuges long before the "protection" of wildlife became politicized as a pawn in the power politics of class warfare and international gamesmanship?

A new cliche is gaining increased popularity to charge the hunter. It wants me to believe I hunt just because the animal is out there. Baloney! The game animal is out there just because I want to hunt it—I and twenty million other Americans who made their survival possible by our taxes, expenditures, legislation, and conservation practices long before the arrival of the new utopians. We do not attack animals just because they are "out there." But apostate hunters attack us just because we are "in here"—the fraternal circle they enjoyed, betrayed, and went to the enemy who is also "out there."

One man alone, the Maharajah of Mysore, who was one of the great tiger hunters of recent times, donated thousands of acres of his private land for a tiger sanctuary and animal preserve in India long before the Marxist grabbed it. Which group of animal rights activists have donated a half acre of their own land for animal sanctuary? (Their pressures on government to commandeer others' private property does not count.) With all of this and more put together, how do hunters show a lack of consideration for living things? How do they show this not to be a strength but a weakness?

If one wants to be an authentic and honorable hunter badly enough, the first thing he denounces is killing for its own sake. The next thing he denounces is the mendacity of calling such killing a sport. The next thing he does is to swear eternal enmity to those scoundrels who exploit for their own nefarious purposes, the agony and emotional trauma of any human being—including the hunter—who couldn't make the grade, dropped out, and turned against his own fraternity for the salvation of his sanity. The agony of the true hunter is to endure and forgive the apostate, who is not content with his own conversion, but must convert everyone else into hating hunters for what he mistakenly perceived as sport hunting.

How unfair and slanderous to say that one learns the "sport of killing" with the rest of the hunting fraternity. Are the "rest of the hunting fraternity" really involved in the "sport of killing" just because the apostate was? If so, what kind of fraternity was the apostate involved with and who was responsible for the involvement? Why are the "rest of the hunting fraternity" degraded and stigmatized because the apostate detests himself for the sport he once enjoyed? What the apostate hunter needs to grasp is the difference in killing for food—both primal and modern—and sport hunting with its rules and regulations. The moral basis for sport hunting was totally absent in anything primal, because all primal hunting was for subsistence or defense. There was no sport based on ethics or morality to be handed down to us as part of any heritage.

There can scarcely be a better example of how semantic confusion can lead to mental anguish for anyone because of words which create the wrong images, as Korzybski labored so diligently to point out in psycholinguistics. This is what's wrong with all those pundits, who insist that killing is killing, to justify the destruction of all hunting, just because they don't like it, so nobody else should either. How much emotional stress and anguish have unfortunate human beings suffered who have fallen into such semantic traps? I have only sympathy for fellow human beings who have suffered needlessly for the faulty semantics others have created. I too have known suffering and know what they feel. I am only sad that fellow hunters have left our fraternity. I wish them well in finding what they search for. I am sadder still, when they declare war on that fraternity, which I shall never betray. I have lived as a hunter, and will die as a hunter. What can I say to those who leave the fraternity, except, "Peace, brother, and may God have mercy on both of us, since we don't seem to have it among ourselves."

In our culture, success is the product of our sensationalism and materialism. Novice hunters, like any novices anywhere, are not aware the true hunter searches for some ultimate spiritual reality in order to find the mystery of being human. Some animal lovers have at least this much in common with true hunters and search for the same transcendental meanings the mature hunter has already found. There is always hope that from this group of neophyte hunters, some will mature into authentic hunters with conscience and integrity, that they will understand and uphold a noble and honorable tradition.

Some will not. Those who are barbarians in the field while hunting, display the same attitudes in the rest of their lives, and their lives are lived in a society becoming undone at the seams by experts at undoing seams. The sporting ethic and, indeed, the traditional role of maleness in high-risk, high-skill, physically demanding sports have always been perceived as a character builder. And character in any culture is based on the socially valued norms which support that culture. Culture rewards the attributes of such character by assigning to them high status and prestige.

So it has been with the hunter in our Western civilization. Those who oppose the culture, automatically oppose the status and prestige of the incumbents in those roles, including that of the hunter. Such sports and such sportsmen have been ridiculed and censured for years by other males, especially those who have different physical, emotional, and temperamental aptitudes which do not augur well for success in hunting. Yet the natural desire for social status and prestige remain high. Nothing is sweeter than the other's grapes we called sour before we got them.

Often, the quickest way to an older prestiged status is by direct assault on its values, norms, and incumbents, thereby delegitimating it. Now it can be stigmatized, then displaced by new status seekers demanding more legitimacy and respect from society than before. The constant struggle for equality is won when we have a little more of it than the people we took it from. The time honored respect and prestige enjoyed by hunters is under assault by antihunters who always find a new outlet for the generalized malaise of malcontention.

Ironically, some hunters play right into the hands of the enemy. The primary fault lies with those of us hunters who, no matter our failures in other walks of life, must live by that code of honor on the hunting trail. We have not done enough to teach or enforce hunting ethics to all those who claim to be hunters. It is not only what these deviant hunters do that gains opprobrium for the rest of us. It is the attitude of disrespect and brutality to animals they defiantly display. They are nonconforming to "outmoded" social tradition that taught what respect was while gladly "conforming to doing their own thing," which hardly needed to be taught.

Many, without ulterior political motives, who love animals do so because of a genuine appreciation for the beauty and spirit of wilderness creatures. They do not resent the hunter for the killing of animals so much as they resent the demeaning attitude that some unethical hunters display, not because they are savages, but, because they don't know any better. Some animal lovers don't know any better, either, because their impression of hunters is based on the negative stereotypes created by the social change agents (an euphemism for counter culture revolutionaries or agents provocateurs) in the entertainment business. Treating an animal in the manner of the stereotyped hunter is a personal degradation of the real animal lover who identifies so closely with the creatures of the wilds. There is an odd coincidence here. That is exactly how ethical hunters feel also, and for the same reasons. Hunters need to know that they have this much in common with honest animal lovers who have no political axe to grind. Honest animal lovers need to know that the authentic hunter is the foremost champion they have in a common cause otherwise manipulated by an insidious enemy.

All of the foregoing may seem like a long way from a brief encounter with the bear I chanced across in the middle of a deserted highway. A sense of common decency and fair play was why I let my bear go long before I learned what the sportsmanship and ethics of hunting were all about. It was easy to do, since sportsmanship was such a common value taught in those days for human conduct in general. To let the bear go seemed routine and natural to me. But the looks of skepticism and doubts that questioned the "sportsmanship" of hunting took me far into fields of enquiry to understand rationally what seemed like a normal, routine instinctive response. I also learned why the antihunter will never understand. Boasting of his nonconformity to "outmoded traditions" on his way to becoming the "new man of post-modernism," he has learned nothing of fair play or sportsmanship. He does not think it exists, which is why he does not believe in it. What is worse, he will not let anyone else believe in it.

1 Peter Quennell, *The Colosseum* (New York, N.Y.: Newsweek Book Division, Newsweek 1971)

2 Cleveland Amory, *Mankind?* (New York, N.Y.: Dell Publishing Co., 1974) p. 31

3 Gordon Cumming R., *Five Years Of A Hunter's Life In The Far Interior In South Africa* (London: John Murray, 1850) Volume 2, pp. 9-10

4 Michael Grant, *Gladiators* (New York, N.Y.: Delacorte Press, 1967) p. 124

Grizzly Before Breakfast

Flames leaped back to life as I pushed glowing embers together and added a few more sticks to the dying campfire. Soon, warmth was a soothing caress in the chilly, crisp air of an early September morning in the Brooks Range. We had awakened later than usual, stiff and brittle from yesterday's exhausting and futile climb.

Sitting there alone for the moment, drowsiness still fogged my brain and played tricks with my mind. My mind was pretending that aches and pains wracking my body were really not real. What was real was the other pain—the mental anguish in recalling yesterday's climb. It was a tough climb for me and for the other two guys, judging from the way they paused with heaving lungs—but only when they stopped to wait for me. My performance had been a total failure, I thought. It took too much effort for me, too much violent breathing and dull, heavy plodding, upward with frequent skeptical glances from my companions who wondered, no doubt, if the old man could make it.

It dawned on me for the first time what my problem could be: Five-zero; 50. Age 50 was a few months away, and it bothered me. I had simply not responded well to the physical demands of the upward, torturous climb. Why? I didn't know and the question plagued me, though I didn't remember if it had ever occurred to me before.

Was this what aging was all about? There had been no previous sense of gradually slowing, or mellowing, as they say. The first time the signals reached me was yesterday—all of a sudden. It just didn't feel right or make sense.

By the time we reached the top of the mountain, the sheep, seen there earlier, had disappeared under lightly falling snow that started when we were three-fourths of the way to the summit. Reluctantly, we turned back before more snow made the descent a treacherous roulette game.

Now, sitting by the fire, I had troubling doubts which were distracted by the sound of rattling pots and pans. Lottie was fussing with the chop boxes on the other side of the tent, getting things ready for breakfast. Wes, her husband and master hunting guide, was again tinkering with the carburetor in the truck precariously parked a few yards down the slope.

The vehicle was of ancient vintage. Wes had modified it with oversized tractor tires. It's flaking red paint inspired me in a lighthearted moment to dub it the Red Dragon. The carburetor constantly malfunctioned, the radiator leaked badly, the engine wheezed, snorted, and coughed, but it had carried four of us and all our gear through 10 very rough miles from base camp, where the airplane was, to where we were now at spike camp. From here on, the mountain sloped sharply upward. It was all footwork and tough climbing yesterday, and it would be so from now on. I guessed we would try it again today, now that the sun had burned off yesterday's light snow mantle.

The fourth person with us was a hunter named Lou from Chicago. Wes told me Lou would be with us on the tail end of his hunt before my arrival, but he would stay in camp while I hunted and we could all leave together when I got my sheep. Lou had already taken his. I wasn't overly fond of the idea with a total stranger in my camp, but Wes told me not to worry—Lou and I would get along, he said. We did. We instinctively disliked each other and stayed out of each other's way. Yesterday was the exception, of course, when he came along, just for fun. He had boosted my morale with the promise he would not shoot at anything, although he carried his rifle. "Don't worry," he said, "I'll guarantee it."

"No," I said, "I'll guarantee it," looking him straight in the eye with as charming a smile as I could force. We understood each other.

I was nursing the fire when Lottie sidled up, stopped cold, and excitedly stabbed her finger at a lone caribou she spotted about a half mile away on the opposite slope. She gave a cry of discovery to her husband and Wes stumbled into view from the Red Dragon below, shouting for his binoculars. Lou tumbled out of the tent with the glasses, and I just sat there too tired to do anything except squint.

The caribou was behaving oddly. He ran around in circles several times, then loped off a bit, then circled again. This sequence continued repeatedly. I had seen such caribou behavior a half dozen times in bygone years and knew the probable cause of it. Only grizzly bear or mosquitos could make a caribou do that. And there were no mosquitos at that altitude this time of year. An animated discussion followed among husband, wife, and nonresident hunter to explain the caribou's antics. Wes insisted it was a grizzly bear behind it all, and I knew he was right. They tried to lure me into the discussion, but I just said, "It's mosquitos," and threw a fistful of coffee into the pot of boiling water, hoping no grizzly would show up.

Silently, I cursed myself for having shot my mouth off the first day in base camp when Wes said there were ample signs of grizzly bear all over the place. Professional hunters always say that to their clients, who, in turn, say what I said—"I'd give my right arm for a grizzly bear any day over a Dall sheep." It is easy for clients to say this, especially if they have successfully hunted Dall sheep and failed at grizzly bear.

By this time in my hunting career I had taken every major trophy animal in the Greatland I had wanted, placing some of them in the record books—except the grizzly. Not that I hadn't tried. For the past 5 or 6 years every season found me on the trail hunting for him the hard way—on my own—with too little time, and too much effort just to hike around looking for the right place.

Destiny had decreed against even seeing one. When a grizzly crossed my path, it was always out of season when I was hunting for something else. It had occurred to me that I needed professional services because that seemed to be the best way I could use maximum time on the trail in the right place at the right time without the worry and effort wasted in futile search, logistics, or lack of proper equipment.

Wes had a base camp set up in good sheep country, knew the territory like the back of his hand, charged a price I could afford, and I knew I could trust him without question. I hadn't even thought of grizzly. I wanted another sheep. Finally, after all those years, I was in the right place at the right time, with all contingencies accounted for, and without doubt, there had to be a grizzly somewhere up in the slopes—and now I didn't want to hunt it!

It was true yesterday's miserable performance had demoralized me, my muscles and bones ached, I felt total stupefaction, but I could explain all that. What I couldn't explain was my lack of spirit that should have sent me into intergalactic space with the thrill of the chase—after all, there had to be a grizzly bear out there ready to cross destinies with me.

When hunting prized trophies, especially if they are dangerous, a hunter must be spiritually fit for the task. He needs a sense of invincibility to take on the invincible. He needs a sense of awe with which to confront the awesome. He needs a sense of honor with which to pay homage to the honorable. He needs a sense of nobility to confront the noble. He needs a soul so full of vibrant life it overflows in joyous song to muffle the death knell of distant rumbling drums never silent. All I could feel was a leaden inertia totally disqualifying me for the desire that had dogged me for so long. That bear deserved a nobleman on his trail, and I felt like the keeper of the stables. I could not believe my refusal to get excited, preferring to stay paralyzed at the fire's edge.

Wes, with his confounded glassing, startled me out of my reverie when his voice blurted out, "There he is!" We followed his pointing finger. The caribou had disappeared over the rim rock, and in its stead there was a faint and distant form ambling as only a grizzly could. Maybe he was working off his anger at the dinner he obviously missed, judging from the good, steady clip with which he angled due west down the slope. My heart sank with dismay. In a few moments I could no longer deny the reality of what I had seen and what was to come. Wes dashed to his tent and almost instantly came out with packboard and rifle, just as I feared.

I must have looked a sorry sight because first he glared at me, and then said, too softly for him, "Well, you wanted a grizzly and there he is. He's a good one even if he ain't no world record."

He approached the fire and his eyes bored directly into mine, waiting for affirmation. My eyes trailed off. He must have sensed my ambivalence and, no doubt, my miserable performance on the trail yesterday was on his mind. "If you're not up to it, maybe we shouldn't try. This is how they die of heart attacks. I don't want you to keel over on me. That bear is almost too far away now—we should have taken off an hour ago."

He waited a few moments. When I didn't answer, he concluded, "I think we should try it, but of course, if you'd rather not . . ."

His words rattled around in my numbed brain. If he is worried about my keeling over with a heart attack, I thought, then why is he taunting me with if you'd rather not business? How could I say to him I'd rather not? It would make me sound like a donkey, wouldn't it, after I'd said what I had about giving my right arm for a grizzly when all I had to give now was nothing. Grizzlies just don't grow on trees. They are once-in-a-lifetime things.

Poor Wes! He really wanted me to have that bear because, apart from friendship, we now had a professional relationship. I was his client and he was the professional, and like all true pros in the business, he had the one thing without which no professional hunter could be genuine. He had a fierce pride in his duty that separated the true pro from the others. Once he saw the trophy for his client, nothing would stop him from getting his client into position for a shot. The rest of it was up to the hunter. That was Wes' reputation and why I had gone to him.

Pros feel this way because it is the only standard they have which tells them how good they really are. That's the only way a client knows, also. The client who gets a chance to shoot, no matter the outcome, knows his pro has honored the contract and earned his keep. The client's trust was not misplaced. The pro knows it, too. Wes did not betray that trust. That's class for anyone. He wanted me to get my shot. Many other professional hunters I know would have welcomed my hesitation, saved that grizzly for the next client at a higher fee, and gone sheep hunting with me on the morrow. After all, half the fee was paid in advance.

If Wes is trying to make me look bad, shame me, or goad me on, he sure is doing a nifty job, I thought, and in the next split second of reckless defiance, I mumbled, "Let's go."

He smiled as I hurriedly laced my boots and grabbed my pack board. "Take your blunderbuss," he said, referring to my trusty .338, "and I'll take a lighter rifle. We may need both."

In a few moments he started heading out, and mechanically and reluctantly, I followed. No time was wasted since the bear was moving too fast and was a mile ahead of us. We had a lot of catching up to do.

Wes did not know what effort it required for me to keep up. He was 10 or 12 years my junior, this was his third or fourth hunt with clients this season and he was in superb shape, tougher than nails. The trick was to stay up with him and worry about the bear later, if and when we caught up. We crashed through a thin screen of alders and into the edge of bushes skirting a wide, shallow creek. In a few moments we tore through seared and withered leaves, then broke through the thin layer of ice forming on the water's edge. There were no boulders to skip over in getting across, so we plunged into the icy, shallow water. The stabbing cold drove some of the fog from my brain. It teased me with a little hope. Maybe I'd be okay and fully alert in a few moments, then match Wes stride for stride.

Quickly, we reached the opposite bank and scrambled up, tearing loose rocks into a sharp clatter. Next, we slashed through a narrow stretch of denuded bushes and finally reached the tussocks on top of the rise. The grizzly was nowhere to be seen, since the ridge above us was a high, straight wall, but soon we got around it and moved up to the next steep slope.

The bear had to be ahead of us somewhere moving at a good clip in the rifts that gashed the slope. He could not be seen higher up. Now, we were racing diagonally, half ahead and half upward on the mountain's flank. Soon, Wes disappeared over a ridge, and my lungs and legs labored hard on his trail. When I topped a couple of ridges, there he was ahead of me by a quarter mile. By now, I could hardly breathe, no matter how desperately I tried.

True, we were at a decent altitude far above the valley floor and timber line; the air may have been thin enough to force anyone's breathing, but this was altogether too much. Every gasp fanned the fire hotter in my lungs, my throat rasped, and the blood pounded through my skull trying to push my eyeballs out of their sockets. This must be why the landscape rolled to and fro like an oil-slicked backwash in the North Atlantic in a winter wartime convoy I had lived through. But that was during WW II some 30 years ago, and a voice above my nausea said, "No, it can't be," and another voice said, "Why not, old man?" By this time, Wes had disappeared again, up ahead, leaving me to my misery.

My running full speed had long since slowed down to half speed and then to quarter speed, then to a walk double time. Now, I could barely creep along, but the fear of losing that bear goaded me to try running again, until I was sure my heart threatened to explode.

Everything around me seemed fuzzy, as though some unseen hand was sprinkling fog before my eyes. Vertigo grabbed me, bouncing my sense of presence everywhere and nowhere at the same time. Flashes of bright light shot out of my eyes between large dark green and black splotches, and I could see nothing clearly.

One gully after another, one ridge after another, and soon there was no sense of distance or direction, making me wonder if I were going around in a large circle. Wes was nowhere to be seen in whatever was left of my sight.

I tripped and sprawled several times as I moved up another rise, gained the top, and stood there weaving, unsteady, and disoriented, when, for the first time since leaving camp, I saw my bear between the green-black spots in my eyes. He looked like he was a million miles away, but for a moment before he disappeared, I could see the sun pouring brightness over him, and the golden gleam of his form rippled in the breeze and dipped out of sight. He must be heading to the alder thickets up ahead, I thought, and if he got there, I'd never get him. He'd be gone forever. I had to go faster and the fastest I could move was too slow. The effort formed the green and black spots before my eyes again, threatening to black me out, demanding my surrender.

Blurred images flashed on and off like a stroboscopic light on my mental screen, as the psychic projector randomly threw pictures from my past here and there. I made out the image of a high school kid in a track meet, running smoothly, legs striding and arms pumping, as he lunged into the tape for another victory or leaped beyond the towel marker in the long jump pit, bringing the crowd to its feet with a roar. I had won again and again and again. There was a cabinet full of medals, ribbons, plaques, and statues I still had to prove it. Could that bloody bear up ahead boast of that?

Good grief, but I'd give them all back now just to keep that dumb brute ahead of me in sight! Did he know the agonies of hell I was going through, while he just kept shuffling along not even aware I was "chasing" him? Where was he now? Where was Wes? He was nowhere to be seen during the last century and a half.

Nothing can tell me what made me keep going, stumbling, falling, crawling, getting up to keep going again until I reached the top of yet another embankment, and there was Wes sitting down, breathing hard even for him. My knees just buckled, and the rest of me slumped prone to the ground beside him, unconsciousness hammering at me once more and a gnawing fear telling me I would not be able to get up again.

"Don't worry," Wes gasped, "we've closed the distance. We'll get to him soon. The wind is steady in our favor."

We've closed the distance? We'll get to him soon? Ha! It didn't matter if he was 6 feet away. I was finished, done, terminated. I couldn't get up again to save my life, and it didn't feel like I had much of that left. My mouth felt like it was stuffed with sawdust, but my voice came out faltering, in broken syllables, when I asked how far we had come. What difference did it make except the futile hope Wes would tell me the truth—that we had come a hundred miles and there was something acceptable about that figure that would let me quit with a clean conscience. Wes was a truthful man, but this once he had to be lying when he answered, "Not far—2, 2½— maybe 3 miles at most."

Is that all, I asked myself in utter despair? The cerebral cinema went on again and I could see the kid on the cinder track tearing across the finish line—first place. He didn't stumble or waver. He stood there, arms akimbo, facing me and wanting to know what was holding me back. The near-comatose old man lay there with an inner voice berating him for not being able to get up. The psychic projector went out instantly when Wes blurted, "There he is!"

Lying prone, only my head came up, and the world swam again. But my eyes saw him turned upside down, with the mountains on top of the skies. I wanted to see him through my scope for a good look, but in my weakness I could not lift the rifle to my eye, so I pushed it ahead on the ground and aligned my eye to the scope. It looked brighter out there through the lens, and the green-black spots disappeared for a few moments. Who knows where will power is located in the brain, but somehow it stopped the wild weaving of the scope just long enough for the sky to hover over the mountains again.

In the magnification, *Ursus arctos horribilis* was splendor personified. His light chestnut color radiated sunlight like a burnished ball of gold moving ethereally in a glittering aura. The creamy blond streak of fur along his back and hind quarters shimmered every time he moved forward, just so. Then the sky flipped under the mountains again, and the bear went out of sight upside down.

Wes had seen all this, too, and when the bear reappeared, he groaned with dismay. His halting voice broke through the sibilation of the wind when he said, "He's somewhere between 400 and 500 yards. We can't catch him before he gets to the alders. You've got to do it from here."

Though his voice sounded like it was coming in from outer space, I understood every word. "No," I gasped. But he must have misunderstood, and I couldn't talk to clarify what I meant. He knew my trusty .338 was zeroed in for 100 yards using a 225-grain slug for anything on the Alaska trail including grizzly at close quarters. But this was not close quarters; it was long range, very long range and there was no way my bullet would reach him now—I might as well be using a sling shot. Wes must have thought ballistics were my problem, and that is why I had said, "No."

"Give me that blunderbuss," he said snatching my rifle out of my grasp and shoving his .300 sheep rifle at me. "This is zeroed in at 300 yards with 180-grain slug," he said. He had it adjusted for sheep. "You gotta do it."

He sure wanted me to get my shot. If it were possible for me to do so, I would have laughed uproariously. Here I was with an unfamiliar rifle, a technical discourse on ballistics, my utter helplessness, and the irrelevance of it all. My saying, "No," had nothing to do with all this. Wes misunderstood my problem.

My problem was, no matter the rifle or bullet trajectories, conscience told me the distance was too great, and I didn't feel sharp enough to risk a clean and instant kill. I just didn't want to wound the bear and inflict pain and suffering only to see it get away and maybe die a lingering death. Nothing is worse in hunting, unless it is the lingering guilt of the hunter's conscience.

My decision to let the bear go was made before Wes shoved his rifle into my hands. The bear was so grand a monarch out there that he deserved respectful death, instantly. He did not deserve death sneaking in like a coward claiming him a little at a time because of my incompetence.

Wes' voice broke through my inner struggle. "He'll be in the alders soon if you don't do it now."

A furtive glance showed the skepticism on his face. He was merely meeting his professional duty, giving his hunter at least a chance for a shot and no one could have worked harder than he to do it.

Suppose this was the last time I'd ever see a grizzly this close, I thought to myself? When my eye got behind the scope again, it was not to shoot, but to take one last look at my glorious bear before he disappeared forever. I just wanted to fix in my memory, one last picture of that majesty. At the rate I was going, that might have to do in sustaining my dreams for the rest of my life. He was quartering away rapidly and how I hated to see him go. The pounding and vertigo in my head made it impossible for me to distinguish among a dozen thoughts that seemed to strangle all sanity. I may have been delirious. I thought of failing Wes after all he had done for me and another thought crowded in. The paladins of political power were pressuring an end to grizzly hunting with one regulation after another. There may never be another chance. What if I tried a shot and missed?

Ah, but there was the answer! A bullet whistling past would alert bruin into instant flight and end the hunt and my agony, wouldn't it? Wes would be satisfied I'd had my shot.

The couple minutes of rest had slowed down the violent heaving in my lungs. It helped me to see him much more clearly through the scope, and how I wished he didn't do what he did in the next second. He turned leftward almost broadside and kept ambling down. I became aware he was in the crosshairs and the light was brighter throwing him into a sharp, clear relief and throwing me into a boggled confusion.

A wild, instinctive impulse said it might be done, destroying my previous rejection of hope. With desperate effort, the violent pounding of my heart stopped just for a moment, the landscape stopped spinning, and the bobbing reticles stayed put. I lifted them somewhere between 10 and 20 inches above his shoulder, but I was less than sure I could do it. I know I wanted to hit him desperately, and yet, I hoped he would instantly disappear, robbing me of a shot that might only wound and drive him into the alders.

Ambivalence is the worst thing possible behind a scope focused on a grizzly. I led him a little, and that destroyed all reason, and insanity said it was now or never. I don't remember squeezing the trigger, but was surprised to hear the rifle go off with its booming jolt. To my utter and total amazement he went down instantly. Wes exploded with pent-up passion. "You did it! You did it! Great shot!" he yelled over and over again, his fists pounding the earth in sheer, savage exuberance. I was glad he was glad.

Now, new doubts tormented me. Had the light bullet impacted with enough force to cause the merciful numbness or was it nearly spent when it hit? Was he dead or was he in pain? Wes didn't have to urge another shot. I let go the remaining three rounds, but no matter how hard I tried, I shot over or under. I did not have a drop of energy left to hold steady.

How long he lay there I don't know, but he did what I begged him not to do. He staggered to his feet and kept going. It was hard to tell whether he was weaving or not, but he seemed to be going perceptibly slower. I guessed I had hit him in the lungs. I cursed him, silently. I cursed him because he was going to fight on, daring me to kill myself off in more pursuit at top speed before he got into the alders.

I was breathing a bit more easily now, and asked Wes for more ammo. Couldn't I guess, he had only one cartridge left and said he needed it? He took his rifle, returned mine, and though exhaustion showed all over him, he didn't bat an eyelash, got up, and told me he'd have to keep the bear in sight. He needed that round just in case.

"Follow me as soon as you can," he said "I need you to cover me."

Cover him? I couldn't even cover myself, but didn't he suspect that, even if he didn't know it? It was obvious that at great risk to himself, he was forcing me to keep up.

Soon, both man and animal disappeared down an incline. I lay there trying to gather my strength, expecting to hear a shot any moment, and the thought of it rankled me to get up and try again much sooner than I wanted.

Sliding and staggering down the slope got me to another rift, and another surge of desperate effort enabled me to somehow reach the top. Then, I saw Wes sitting about 200 yards ahead of me, his rifle across his knees, watching the bear who was lying down again about 100 yards in front of him. I managed to stumble to about 20 paces behind Wes and folded prone on the tussocks.

It could not have been more than 15 minutes since my first shot, but it was an eternity of anguish for me. I was torn between giving him a quick, risky misericordia now or getting a little more rest for a closer, surer shot. Before I could decide, the grizzly got to his feet and headed toward the alders and forced the decision for me. Ready or not, I had to do it now. A split second before I squeezed the trigger, Wes' rifle boomed.

His angle for a lethal shot was no better than mine, so he must have tried to turn the bear from the thickets. A puff of dust drifted from the grizzly's hind end with the bullet's impact, and my first impulse was to hurl some cursing at Wes for trying to finish my job for me, but I didn't have the strength.

It was small comfort knowing the one who made the first hit is credited with the kill. What humiliated me was, Wes had to shoot to turn the bear. That was the evidence that showed how badly I had bungled the job. I should not have fired when I had so much doubt. Wes' extra jolt merely aggravated the bear, who now began to turn around and around again with apparent fury, and now I was certain I'd hit him in the lungs. Well, at least he was turned away from the thickets, but he was madder than a hornet trying to locate the source of his troubles.

Wes jumped to his feet, and turned around with an empty gun and a look of sheer desperation in his eyes. Nervously, he scanned the ridge to see what was holding me back; now the bear had seen him. In his attempt to get out of there as quickly as he could, he nearly ran over me. It was only then he discovered I had been lying there all along camouflaged in the grass stubble, and all he could say was a surprised, "Oh."

It dawned on me he had shot, not knowing of my presence. That took guts with no shells left, and he sure seemed glad his backup was there, even in a sorry state. The grizzly, meanwhile, had lunged left and right, turned in circles, and came straight at us. It lacked the sureness of a charge, and, from that distance, he could only have been trying to get closer to see what he could target on. I waited a few moments until he got to 50 yards or so, and got to my feet. Wes caught on instantly and dropped flat, crawling to one side to clear the target for me. Though groggy and totally exhausted, a jolt of exultation went through me. The bear and I finally faced each other.

Since my boyhood and through the years in Alaska, this had been my dream—the charging grizzly. Silently, I begged him to come on. I needed to acquit myself of my miserable performance thus far and end the agony for both of us. He deserved better than he had been getting. He came a few more feet, and then my dreams collapsed. He stopped suddenly, wheeled around, and headed for the thickets. He didn't go far before he started turning in a slow circle. I knew he was dying, but I wanted to hasten death for his sake. My breathing was easier now, and my own rifle in my hands felt familiar. My shot hammered into his hump which spun him around before he dropped. In a few moments I was amazed to see him stagger to his feet again, face me, and sway side to side, not knowing when to quit.

I know how the cynics laugh with scorn when a hunter pays tribute to his quarry at such a moment. They don't see what we do, but they mock the truth we feel. I felt it at that moment, and I will say it like so many others have before me. Never had I seen any animal take it so tenaciously, courageously, so defiantly. Yes, he was magnificent, and the way he looked at me, I swear he was begging me to give him back his life or hasten the end. Through misty eyes I squeezed the trigger again and he crumpled over. He shuddered hard and lay still. Silently, I begged him to stay down. I didn't have it in me to shoot again.

Wes cautioned me to stay close. I knew he was glad I had a blunderbuss. We approached and nudged him. He was quite dead. He had taken an enormous amount of punishment. I sank to my knees and silently thanked him with reverence for the moment. He had fought far more nobly than I—game to the very end, while I had wanted to quit a dozen times. I knew he was the better adversary; I was just a lucky, undeserving old man.

Wes thumped me with congratulations, but I was in no receptive mood. I think he was more pleased with the results than I. He looked quizzically at me, and I think he sensed for the first time I didn't look right. He decided to go back for the Red Dragon and admonished me to keep my eyes on the wolves—there were four of them who had materialized out of nowhere and were now slinking on the ridge a half mile away. Who knows how long they had been watching?

Wes had no sooner dropped below the ridge, than I sank to my knees and drifted off into unconsciousness. Whether I fell asleep or fainted, I don't know, but with the wolves within sight of me and the grizzly carcass, it was probably the latter. I didn't even have a chance to study my bear.

I came to with a start and didn't know how long I'd been out; my first thought was of the wolves, but they were gone. Down below the ledge was the reason why. The Red Dragon, snorting loudly enough to be heard below the Mason-Dixon Line, had arrived at the creek far below. Sometime after it stopped, Wes and Lottie labored up the slope. They had a thermos jug of coffee, but I asked a very stupid question, "Is there a store around here? I want to buy some candy." I had a sudden craving for it. Husband and wife stood there looking oddly at me and at each other. I don't know if they handed me a bar from their kit bag or I fished it out of my pack sack. Little did I know the significance of all this.

We looked over my bear. It was about 6½ feet squared, certainly not a big grizzly, but an average one for these parts. That didn't matter. His coloration is what made him such a prize. He had a gorgeous golden streak down his chestnut brown back and hind quarters, with silvery tipped ears—a grand old warrior of the tundra. Any grizzly, like any Dall sheep, is a trophy because they are so tough to get, and I had sure toughed it out to get this one.

Wes snapped some pictures, and we skinned the bear, although I was not much help. The bright sky overhead darkened almost in an instant, and from nowhere clouds rolled in and began to sprinkle what looked like the first permanent snow of the season. The upper ranges were clad in white by the time we finished skinning and the Red Dragon bounced and jolted us back to camp.

Once there, Lottie started to make breakfast. I felt an uncontrollable urge to sleep and she, bless her heart, urged me to catch 40 winks, assuring me I'd be called for breakfast. When Wes shook me awake, the coffee pot was perking and the pancakes were piled high. I glanced at my watch. It was quarter to high noon. The more I ate, the better I felt, and when we had all finished, we struck camp and headed for the base and the flight back home.

———————————————◆◆◆◆◆———————————————

We were barely 2 weeks into the new semester when funny things began happening to me, again. The lecture hall would sway erratically to my senses; sporadically, hot flashes would sweep up to my head, bathing me in a cold sweat; the green and black spots would return and vanish; and I could not hear many words I knew I had spoken as part of audible sentences, otherwise. I checked with the students, and they were hearing everything I said and indicated nothing was wrong. When the lectern began to sway under my hands, and I knew it was standing perfectly still, I worked up enough courage to go to my doctor. I was afraid of what he might say, but I finally went.

He gave me a complete examination and asked me when I had first noticed these symptoms. I told him of my ordeal on the grizzly hunt, and I knew the difference between normal exhaustion due to expended effort and what I felt that day, age Five-Oh, notwithstanding. He ordered lab tests and said he wanted to be sure before he told me what he already guessed. I got more anxious. A few days and a couple of lab tests later, his office called to say the doctor was ready to see me.

I was waiting nervously in his examination room when he walked in, looked at me intently for an eternity and then said, bluntly, "You have diabetes."

I sat stunned. But, of course. My mother and grandmother had both died of it long since, and the hereditary conditions for it went through my mind. The other thing that went through my mind was the current crop of feminist banshees in my classes who gave me lots of venom whenever I said there was no natural equality between the sexes, but in a way they didn't suspect. The precondition for diabetes was one of over 70 pathologies that offspring inherited only from their mother's genes. The father just does not have those genes to pass on.

Foremost in my mind was what had happened to me chasing that grizzly bear. I asked the doc if diabetes was behind what made me behave so strangely.

"Behave so strangely?" he repeated.

He paused for a few moments, shook his head and said, "You were delirious, in shock. Without glycogen, your brain was dying. I can't understand how you survived."

He's trying to scare me, I thought, because doctors tend to exaggerate, but something gave me away.

"I'm not fooling," he said. "It was closer than you think."

Put that way, it did scare me. But in a perverse way, the diagnosis left me with a sense of gladness. If I had performed miserably that day and made decisions I shouldn't have, there was some reason for it besides advancing age. Then the obvious occurred to me. "Doc," I blurted, "no baloney, give it to me straight. Are my hunting days over"?

He said my whole life would be different in many ways, henceforth, but, yes, I could hunt under certain conditions if I used caution, good judgement, and took proper care of myself, none of which I was very good at. Then he started explaining about proper diet, insulin injections, pills, and all the rest of it. I wasn't listening. I was grateful to be alive and on my mind's projection screen there flashed the agony of that chase for my grizzly; and I saw something which made me grin even though my grizz had nearly killed me without laying a paw on me.

"What's funny?" asked the doctor.

I apologized and mumbled something which he fortunately pretended to understand rather than pursue.

I have that bear in a full-bodied mount on all fours. It is probably the only grizzly bear ever hunted by a man, partially or almost totally in insulin shock, and not supposed to have survived what I had in a 2- to 3-mile chase over the tundra. The experience of that hunt, and the sheer beauty of that bear is the good part. So was Wes' support, without which there would have been no hunt.

There is another side to it, however. I shot when I was less than confident of the odds being in my favor. That I succeeded in scoring with an almost impossible shot, I attribute to a great deal of just plain luck. If I had been able to understand with a malfunctioning brain and body what was happening to me, I am certain I would have never chanced that shot. With the stubbornness of a mule, I had insisted that old age was not going to defeat me.

My shot did not kill that gorgeous golden bear quickly enough, and I'm sure he suffered pain. That still weighs heavily on my conscience. It was bad art. But even in my condition, and with some help from Wes, I gave it all I had and learned the ultimate limits to my being. I saw it through the best I could, even though it literally nearly killed me. I could not have done less. How I wish I could have done more.

I now know why I had asked for candy when Lottie and Wes returned to me and my bear. The body's own wisdom in craving certain foods made me want sugar to replace that which had long since burned away and made my body and mind function or malfunction the way they did. Who knows what else would have happened to me without candy on the way to camp?

The secret I kept from my doctor when he caught me grinning is a picture in my mind. It comes alive in the afternoon hours when the South wall cathedral windows of my trophy room let in the sun, and my bear, on all fours, is bathed in light again. When I see him thus, it is not the agony of the chase that comes to mind, but that shimmering mist of gold in the distance ambling along, eternally.

Jogging beside him is his pal in spiked shoes on the cinder track—the boy without a care in the world. Neither one knows anything about diabetes. They both turn, beckoning me on. I chuckle because both rascals are in cahoots, teasing the old man, and how I wish I could be running with them forever. 🐻

Reflections

Long after that hunt, the central idea of it has never left me. I sum it up in one word, and I do not think it hyperbolic—Agony. Of course, there was a good deal of that in my sheep hunt some 10 years earlier, but then I was in full control of my senses, despite the physical ordeal, with a trophy I had already taken. This time, the agony was an unsuspected medical danger to my life as I pursued my bear.

There is a popular bias—hunters hunt because it's supposed to be fun. Critics always ask, "How can there be fun in killing some poor creature?" One doesn't kill a "poor creature" in order to kill a poor creature. In the first place, nothing is poor about the Cape buffalo or grizzly bear (and many others), which have an abundant wealth of lethal capacity with which to destroy the poor hunter.

In the second place, one doesn't even hunt rabbits for the fun of killing them. In both instances, one hunts because it is a high level achievement with symbolic rewards that, in the first case, risks high level agonies. Clearly, there is more than fun involved. There is no other enterprise quite like it. It is unique. It must be praised or damned on its own grounds, not on relativisms to something else.

It was this clash in my mind between the notions of fun and

agony that took me on a merry mental chase, or hunt, for the next few years, on and off, and what seemed like a simple problem at first became a complicated cerebral puzzle. One of my life's great satisfactions was to get some answers, which gave me great joy, though little fun—there is a critical difference between the two, I discovered.

I found the real fun later in educating many antihunting critics who, to their credit, clung heroically to their passionate prejudices, although they admitted seeing my point of view. In abbreviated form, those answers I found are stated in what follows. I hope other hunters will find some reasons, despite my shortcomings, to get better answers than I could.

The first thing that nagged me was the fun I was supposed to have when agony was my lot. Fun is a pleasurable thing and pleasure is an agreeable sensation or emotion, as one dictionary says, and adds that pleasure is a general term ". . . and the weakest, often indicating little more than absence of pain." The dictionary continues by showing several degrees of pleasure, like joy, delight, delectation, rapture, and ecstasy, and ending up in feelings of satisfaction and happiness.

In trying to understand pleasure, from whence all Freudian goodies flow, one can hardly escape his monumental work and nonsense about the Pleasure Principle, that pleasure in all its forms is, ultimately, sexual libido or its many disguises. This makes every artistic, intellectual, dramatic, sporting, bibulous, and culinary delight a neurosis camouflaging sexual repression. But judging from today's orgasmic frenzy engineered by Freud for ideological power, we should be the world's happiest harp-plucking cherubs. Instead, our civilization is teetering on the brink of self-destruction, which is precisely what is wanted behind his "scientific" theories. We have jumped from the frying pan into the fire—to use a time-honored expression in which Freud would see a disguised sexual sublimation.

All this is not to say sex does not have its delightful place. It is simply to say there are places, times, and pleasures where sex has to wait its turn like everything else. Even Freud found pleasure in smoking cigars long after his libido died down. There are pleasures and pleasures just like there is killing and killing.

It is one kind of pleasure to listen to Lily Pons sing Una voce poco fa, another pleasure to see Sir Lawrence Olivier do Hamlet, another pleasure, still, to see the Yankees win the World Series pennant (again), and yet another pleasure to sip a glass of vintage wine, or to enjoy two bowls of onion soup—one with Bermuda onions and the other with Maui onions. After all, there's a difference between T-bone steaks and Pinto beans. To insist they are the same, because protein is common to both of them, betrays an uneducated palate, incompetent olfaction, wishful thinking, or all three.

If we assume a 7-day, big-game Alaska hunt to be an average, and allow an average 12-hour day of actual hunting time each day, we will get a total of 84 hours. Let me recklessly assume as much as 10% of that time is spent in actual, honest-to-goodness fun. That leaves 75-76 hours of effort, work, toil, and agony. I have gladly paid that price, but not for any fun that was canceled 'ere it began. The trade-off was worth it for the joy of fulfillment. Fun and joy are not the same thing. Fun tickles the senses. Joy uplifts the spirit.

Of course, I've hunted ducks, quail, pheasant, ptarmigan, and other things with whirring wings. I've also hunted varmints, squirrels, rabbits, and others with similar terrestrial habits.

There are critics who decry the killing of "poor little creatures" clad in fur or feather. In the former case, hunters refer to their game as "varmint hunting." Hunters pursue such a passion because it has its own mystique and its own psychic rewards.

Any devoted hunter, who has the hunting instinct in his veins, must satisfy those urges of the chase one way or another. He must not lose periodic contact with the great outdoors for spiritual renewal, the joy of staying physically fit, or keeping his marksmanship skills finely tuned. He enjoys the rewards on returning to his original nature when artificial civilization has separated him from it for too long. For many, small game hunting is the only kind available to them which is practical in terms of time and money.

While such hunting is an end in itself for many hunters, there is yet a larger number of them for whom it is a stepping stone to greater reality. It keeps alive the hopes and dreams for greater ventures. It serves as a substitute for the ultimate—when destiny will allow it— the big game hunt itself. I have yet to meet the rabbit hunter who would refuse a chance to hunt deer or bear, or even lion or elephant, if time and money were not the rain storms putting out the roaring flames of ultimate desire. If one cannot bathe in the azure waters of Acapulco (assuming it is not yet polluted), one takes the sting out of paradise frustrated by going to a less exciting beach nearby his home. If that should fail, the public swimming pool will have to do, if one wants to swim badly enough. It is better than nothing.

Even as a substitute, hunting such creatures has its advantages and unique delights. Such creatures are more accessible in easier terrain, and many kinds of birds and small game persistently concentrate in larger numbers than most big game. If one misses a shot at a duck, no problem. Soon, there is another flock alighting among the decoys. They come to the hunter. Or one goes to ptarmigan and sees a couple hundred of them in a single day within a 3-mile radius.

A hunter can improve or enjoy his skills because he shoots more times with a shotgun, or .22, in a single day than he does in 5 years shooting a big-bore rifle. There is an exhilaration and excitement in the quick and repeated action. The rewards of the successful shot are immediate and satisfying. It is a more leisurely hunt. Companions and dogs, if they are along, add to the zest of the outdoor adventure. One can easily carry out his game bag. There are no great logistics problems, and delight is a prolonged enjoyment. One hunts like a gentleman and goes home after a couple days of having been exposed to no great hazards or stress, and he is ready to go again next weekend. As one gets older, one appreciates the slower, steadier pace.

Hunting big game is different. The terrain and habitats are different, requiring strenuous effort. One must truly hunt, seek out, search, or go to his quarry. It will not come to him. Big game in Alaska are not often a herd animal. Black bear, grizzly bear, polar bear, and moose tend to be loners after the mating season. Dall sheep and mountain goat may hang around with cohorts, but two or three of them are a large enough group, if they are of trophy quality. Individual animals, especially trophies, are much more difficult to find and stalk, where terrain is difficult to downright dangerous, because that is where a pursued animal seeks cover, and the safest risks from the animal and terrain can be suicidal.

It is nothing but laborious effort to skin a large animal. The head of a trophy animal has its own painstaking problems. If the bag should be moose, for example, it is exhaustive, backbreaking labor to skin, quarter, cut, and bone 1,000 pounds of meat, and then backpack 100- to 200-pound packs. Usually, it will require from a half dozen to a dozen trips, covering anywhere from a half mile to a mile or more each trip, to get to camp or whatever conveyance for loading. I have never found this enterprise to be fun, and know of few hunters in this category who have found it so, either. Nor is it fun trying to stay warm and dry in a tent or makeshift shelter during rainy or snowy weather, without letup, for several days in a row with all the other wonders of romanticized environment.

Fun is pleasurable, but diversionary and superficial. It comes and goes easily without great loss or gain, without much effort, and without any pain. The fun of fun is precisely not having to do too much for it. There is an element of humor in it. There are few, if any, preconditions. That's why we like it, but put too much effort into chasing it, or holding on to it, and it becomes something else, entirely. Often, it ends in its opposite—tragedy. It may be the result of what is desired and sought after, but if it does not come to pass, it is no great loss, because one can try for it again without much effort, planning, or anguish.

It is difficult to imagine profound fun, because there are no emotional or spiritual antecedents or prerequisites to it. It leaves no lasting impact. It comes to us even when we do nothing to bring it about. Suddenly, it's there as part of the situation in which we find ourselves—sometimes directly opposite to what we anticipated. That is why we often remember the time and the occasion in which we had fun, while we can hardly remember what was so funny. In time, we even see nothing funny at all about something that was hilarious when it happened.

Joy is something very different and easily confused with fun. It is difficult to think of superficial joy, because when superficial, it is mere delight that doesn't go anywhere or become more than it is. Joy is deep and profound, going beyond the sensory and into the spiritual, because it either results from, or is released by, all the great passions. Usually, there is great risk and effort, or great desire and hope involved. One could have had a great loss, but, instead, there was a great gain. The consequences are important either way. There is nothing superficial or whimsical about it as there is in fun.

Joy explodes upon us instantly and we are overjoyed because we got what we so passionately wanted and hoped for, what we worked and risked for, when it could have gone the other way. We are elated and exultant in it. Had it not occurred, we would have been greatly disappointed or depressed. We would have lost too much when we deserved to gain it, instead. Fun avoids grief, delight contradicts it, and joy overwhelms it.

Great moments of joy are remembered years later, along with precisely what gave us the feeling. There was too much of ourselves invested in it then, to abandon its memory, now. Fun? We forget the thousands of times we had it.

Profound joy borders on the ecstatic and becomes a mystical, transcendental experience. It becomes a thing of the spirit and other-worldly, contacting the supernatural. One's senses, perceptions, and emotions are beyond neural connections. At its height, it is the experience of transcendence and oneness with realities outside one's own being, a trancelike, ecstatic state religious mystics, especially, know too well.

Between the opposite extremes of frivolous fun too easy to come by, and profound ecstasy seldom attained, the important values and symbols on which we build our individualities are instantly contacted to tell us, or remind us, who and what we really are. It is part of the universal drive to find our authentic selves stripped of social facades. Joy is always self-discovery and self recovery of the brighter side of who we are in constant battle with the darker side of who we ought not to be. Joy verifies our most beautiful desires and hopes. It leads us to the threshold of ecstasy, or being beside oneself on the vantage point of self-authentication. Joy is the affirmation of the most precious values we hold; it reveals and clarifies them buried in the mystery of our being. In joy, whether it is an element of surprise and discovery, or the successful outcome of great effort and yearning finally rewarded, there is a sense of triumph, of hope fulfilled. Fun entertains us; joy fulfills us and quenches the thirst of our deeper longings. Fun is escape from boredom; joy is gratitude for fulfillment.

Keats said, "A thing of beauty is a joy forever." This is a conditional truth, however, because beauty fades and dies. When it does, it no longer appeals to the senses and gives us sadness. The opposite is the real truth—a thing of joy is beautiful forevermore. Joy never fades. It is in the soul appealing to the spirit, and the spirit is with the eternal in the heavens, not in the temporal things of earth. In a sensate and degenerate culture like ours, we are always seeking fun—the wilder the better. We have too much spiritual pain we need to avoid because we are anchored in nothing substantial. Hence, anything will do; anything can be fun if it diverts our attention from anguish, no matter how briefly.

There are countless points of suffering in life. When suffering gets intense enough, it agonizes. There are those who make an art of trying to deny suffering and agony. It cannot be done. To risk living, is to risk suffering and agony. Sometimes, we can escape them, but only briefly. Usually, we cannot. Then, we must face them and fight. The one thing we cannot do is to deny them, for the more we deny, the more we agonize.

We have all wondered—why must there be pain, anguish, agony? The spiritual, emotional kind is worse than the physical kind. It is the great mystery of life, the question most often asked by innocent and guilty, by young and old, by theologian and scientist alike. I, too, do not have the real answer, but I have my own response to it. Without pain, suffering, or agony, we can never know of the courage necessary to fight that which degrades man. Without them, we can never learn compassion with which to sense the other's anguish. Without agony we can never know the God who raised humanity above the level of the dung beetle.

Fun avoids agony, if it can. Joy triumphs over agony because it must. Fun is something coming to us from the outside. Joy is the discovery of a wonder hidden inside.

I have a strong conviction that the greater the triumph of joy, the greater the agony and yearning that preceded it. It is easy for a hunter to lose sight of the difference between fun and joy, but the critic never had a grasp of the difference to begin with, which is why he always asks the stupid and insulting question, "What possible fun do you get out of hunting?" Immediately, the question lays claim to a superior humanity by one who is above that sort of barbarism. It is the central secret of modern liberalism that preaches the equality of all in order to be above the unequals without detection. Fun is Dionysius who wants revenge on suffering, but runs away from it as an act of heroism.

Many books I read on the subject were at loggerheads with each other, creating an abundant confusion. I tossed them aside. My philosophizing lacked professional profundity, I know, but it satisfied me, because it was born of my own experience in the reality of wilderness, not from armchair, cerebral doodling. I knew, while there was much pleasure in the wilderness experience, there was joy, sometimes ecstatic joy, in great moments of the hunt, depending on how well I had played the game. But there were moments of hardship and agony, too, of which the proponents of fun seemed to be blissfully unaware. The agony of hardship was more a part of my hunts, than fun. The fun was really the joy of satisfaction in having overcome great difficulties, not the superficial or frivolous. Joy was in knowing that excellence had been attained by one's great efforts; fun was easy come, easy go, even when one took it easy.

The central truth for me in all this is that we do not hunt for joy, fun, delight, or whatever. We hunt for the bloomin' trophy or the game. Fun, joy, delight, or whatever, do not make the hunt possible. It is the hunt that makes them possible. Truth is, we hunt though it may not be fun, joy, or anything else. We even hunt when we rightly suspect there will be nothing but hardship and agony. The ignorant charge that the hunter hunts or kills for fun is the revelation of prejudice. It is a projection of the mental state of affairs in the critic's mind, not the hunter's. When Teddy Roosevelt talked of the strenuous life, he must have scared the daylights out of the lazy and timorous.

The hunter is joyous, not because he has killed an animal, rather, he is joyous, because without the kill, he has not hunted successfully. Success is the key here, not the killing. No one does anything to fail. Neither does the hunter. There are a dozen grounds on which one can argue against hunting, but having fun is not one of them. Odd, is it not, that the hedonists most obsessed with the pursuit of fun, no matter how amoral or immoral, suddenly become moralists denouncing the hunter's "fun" for reasons which do not exist?

There is irony in the hunt. We go to it for a successful outcome that can give us the bonus of excitement, enjoyment, and joyous play, letting us escape the boredom, drudgery, and failures of life, only to embrace ordeal, hazard, agony—and sometimes death. The critic does not know that, in overcoming the ordeal, the hazardous, and the agonistic, there is joy, satisfaction, and achievement unlike any other.

It was the problem of agony, which always threatened joy on my hunts, I turned to next and found some interesting connections. They opened many doors into the philosophy of hunting—that mad quest to understand what had wrecked many a ship of inquiry on the shoals of why and because.

The hunting trail is where joy and agony slug it out in the hunter's soul. What could be more human than that? I believe it a valid generalization that all big-game hunters have known agony at least a few times during their hunting careers. I believe there is no such thing as a big-game hunt without the potential for agony happening anytime during the hunt, more than anywhere else in life in the same time span. If one is fortunate enough to live a joyous and carefree life, free from anguish, suffering, and agony, he will find it on the hunting trail sooner or later. There is no escaping this. If one wants to hunt badly enough, one must take that risk. It is part of the hunt. If one wants to live badly enough, one must take other risks. They are a part of life.

How did humanity endure its agonies, sufferings, and tragedies in centuries past, when life was "short, nasty, and brutish"? The business of living all too often becomes an agonizing contest in the competition of life against death, with its myriad forms and despite our best efforts to avoid pain. Those who detest this view of life, preferring utopian fantasies, are often the same ones who deify the Darwinian version of evolution without raising an eyebrow at the contest and agony of daily life in the survival of the fittest and natural selection.

Oddly enough, it is in the nature of sports, of which hunting is supposed to be a part, that the nature of agony is first studied. It is ritualized in the athletic contest, where play controls the uncontrollable in real life. It appears early in the process by which the primeval in man masquerades with the amenities of civilization. The ancients knew for some of life's exigencies, there are no escapes, only heroic resistance and wise forbearance. While the Roman arena provided orgiastic cruelty to divert the sufferings of its populace, the classical Greeks preached health, beauty, strength, and wisdom.

The Greek *palaestra*, or combined gymnasium and school, was largely a place for athletic training. Unlike the Roman citizen, who preferred spectator sports, the Greek citizen was a participant sportsman given individual training for athletic supremacy—it was pre-military training for the greatest agony of all—war. And the Greeks fought many wars, first with barbarian invaders, and then for empire. It required manly quality they called *arete*, after Ares, their god of war.

Liberals have been terrified at the dangerous connections between combat, athletics, and manliness ever since, which is why they are suspicious of contact sports or blood sports, as they love to call some of them, and, apparently, want to transfer the dangers to feminists in combat roles.

What began as private athletic contests in Greece became annual festival games witnessed by citizens traveling long distances from all over Hellas. Wrestling was perhaps the most popular of all sports. In fact the word *palaestra* came from the Greek word for wrestling. The pentathlon was highly regarded, and a champion athlete had to win three of five events in the standing broad jump (with weights in each hand), the discus throw, the javelin throw, the sprint, and wrestling. There were boxing, foot races, horse-and-chariot races; in one chariot race with 40 starters, only one finished the dangerous course. Honest, hard-fought competition and strife were honored. A Persian general witnessing one of the games wondered aloud, "What kind of men are these who contend not for money, but for honor."

Indeed, the prizes won at the games were little more than the laurel wreath, but what made up for it was public honor and prestige. Cities made generals of their most heroic athletes, or gifted them with large sums of money. They were subjects of poetry and prose. Some were given free food and shelter. Some were idolized in stone and bronze sculpture. By the end of the fifth century B.C., corruption altered much of this. But the athletic contest for prizes and honor at public games had become known as *agon*, which produced the agonist and the antagonist. The contesting athletes, whose maximum efforts to win, created heroic struggle, combative strife, ultimate athletic effort, suffering, intense emotions, pain and passion, "extreme pain of body or mind" (as one dictionary puts it), and from all this we get the word agony; to agonize is something every human being has experienced at one time or another, without even being an athlete.

From the ancient Greeks to the modern athlete, the risk of agony is a constant given in any sporting activity requiring utmost physical effort. Few athletes, especially today, are totally free from pain and suffering caused by athletic injury and accident, even as they play. We even have a new clinical category called sports medicine to care for countless such cases. Long after retirement from active participation, when an ex-athlete has become a senior citizen, he still suffers with pain from decades old agonizing, crippling injuries. That risk or probability goes with the turf. This is just as true in sport hunting where risks are no less hazardous and just as constant.

The firsthand observation of athletic triumph over great strife led to philosophical speculation about agony, its meaning, and emotions. This led to one of the many great art forms the Greeks invented—drama. It was *agon* again when the main characters on the stage played and acted out painful emotional contests reflecting the real struggles and agonies of life. Audiences flocked to the theaters to see in the actors' emotions what they all felt at one or another time.

The Greeks, who had a word for everything, had another one—catharsis, or the cleansing and purging of the soul of its anguish, which is prolonged agony. By identifying with the actors' agony, the audience could understand reasons for pain and suffering of the spirit and find relief from their own—or so went the theory. As a new art form, this drama led to other art forms, like music, painting, sculpture, architecture, and the rest. In a real sense, athletics played a crucial part in the development of institutional values in one of history's great civilizations. That lesson has not been lost on twentieth century totalitarians, who are notorious for the use of sports as a technique for political propaganda and control.

The *agon* of athletic contest and drama taught that one could not always escape agony or the destiny that brought it on. It had to be endured. That was life. Today, progress has made too many of us so soft, effete, and craven, we can no longer endure any stress without outside help from drugs, alcohol, or governmental assistance.

Physical pain is one thing, but emotional pain is something else. We have no inner capacity for handling it, and, surely, there ought to be a law against it. The slightest stress (how popular that word has become) plunges us into despair, because we cannot take the least strife or agony. Yet, we ridicule those who have survived it when we couldn't. If our pioneering forefathers saw the stress for which we take tranquilizers or freely associate with the psychiatrist, they would be stunned with incredulity. They might even laugh uproariously.

The curriculum of the *palaestra* had three parts: writing, including reading and arithmetic; music; and gymnastics, to which was later added drawing and painting. The purpose of the school, or schole, was not to prepare one for a career or vocation, as it does these days, or for living in a participatory democracy, whatever that means. The purpose, like a finishing school's, was to prepare the leisured class for gracious living. No male in that class could claim respectability had he not learned to wrestle, box, swim, hunt with bow and arrow, drive chariots, play the lyre, attend the theater, and read philosophers and poets—to lead the good life, wherein agony was held at bay. He had *arete*. Today, we ridicule such a man by calling him macho.

In Rome, outside the gladiatorial arena, manliness was based on *virtus*, or virtue, of which courage, endurance, and prowess were the key elements. The rest of it was very similar to the Greek *arete*. In both cases, hunting, physical prowess, athletic ability, and the martial arts were basic elements. The virtues, in both cases, inevitably lead to *agon*, and *agon* requires ultimate and agonizing physical and emotional effort between agonist and antagonist. Their relationship is based on struggle regulated by rules. It is what we call a contest; in this case, an athletic contest.

Ever since the Greek *agon*, the contests of real life that create agony in the human soul have been transformed into play, where they could be regulated by rules of fairness and reason to make up for the unfairness or absence of rules and reason in real life. Yet, the play contest, sometimes, is more real than life itself, and, in both cases, the essence of the contest is the same. The contest is an undertaking, the outcome of which is in doubt, and it is to resolve that doubt competitively, in one's favor, where the win or loss becomes the issue. In what sport or athletic event, or any other contest for that matter, do contestants struggle to lose or break even? The whole point of the agonizing contest is to win by the rules.

It is a very long way from the Greek *agon* to the courage and honesty of Vince Lombardi's statement that, "Winning isn't everything. It's the only thing." Our liberal effete elite hit Mach 5 going into orbit on wings of vituperation and calumny. They ripped what Lombardi said out of context and made him sound like the voice of the evil establishment, ready to sacrifice humanity for the sake of a dollar. That's because the critics didn't know sportsmanship or the rules of the game, having destroyed those virtues long since.

All Lombardi referred to was the sporting contest honorably won by the rules of the game in a football locker room pep-talk to a Green Bay Packers team who had lost the ambition to play hard, agonize, and win. They had become All-American with a lower case a. If winning a football game is not the only thing, then why play? To lose?

Americans had always prided themselves on being a nation of

winners, and that's the image the political left was trying to change, so a new, emasculated, wimpy, American social type would be more acceptable to the pacifists of the world, and more easily controlled by any centralized authority. The imagemakers tried to make Lombardi sound as though he advocated any unfairness, injustice, or foul play to win, which was the only thing. He knew better than anyone else that, with a dozen referees on the playing field, illicit play would destroy any chance to win in the end.

To win is to prevail, to succeed, to gain, to earn, to possess, to procure. Can the hungry man eat the crust of bread he has lost? Does the football giant, hammered into the ground by two-legged steamrollers, writhe in agony with an injured leg because he was trying to lose?

When Teddy Roosevelt, one of the founding fathers of conservation and one of our country's greatest hunters and outdoorsmen, sang the virtues of the "strenuous life" (his phrase), we understood what he meant. Today, we ridicule it, and the Vonneguts of our time boast that we must end all competitive sports and just play for fun without competition, without winning and losing—it sounds suspiciously like sexual foreplay without getting down to business. Those who believe only in fun without winning or losing, have won if their view prevails, while all those with the opposing view have lost.

The patterns of social action were called social process by the wiser sociologists before the discipline became Marxified. Three of these processes, which are central to our discussion here, are competition, conflict, and cooperation. These words are used by everyone in ordinary usage, but they also have a technical meaning, and much grief has resulted by misusing them.

The processes appear in all areas of life. At any moment, there are always more people who want the good things in life than there are good things to go around. Since the beginning of man, the question has been—who gets what and how does one get it? We either compete in the open marketplace, or it is allocated to us by some political power, in which case we are all at its mercy. Sometimes we can cooperate to acquire things, and sometimes things get ugly and we get caught in conflict or war.

Competition, by technical definition, is the attempt by two or more people striving for the same scarce good according to rules and regulations that govern the terms of competition, thus giving all contestants a fair chance to participate. "May the best man win," and if you lost, "better luck next time," as it used to be said. Ideally, this is the condition for sports. Conflict knows only one rule—the abolition of all other rules to obtain the coveted good by any means fair or foul. The best way to do that is to destroy or prevent competition, and the devil take the rules. This is the one condition in sports that is totally forbidden and that's why there are referees, umpires, or arbiters at all times. Cooperation in sports is required only among members of the same team to successfully compete with the opposing team.

Traditionally, our folklore has always emphasized success and achievement, which are other words for win. We have prided ourselves, until recently, on being a nation of winners. But our educational system has turned the tide. Today, the emphasis is on cooperation, which may be the code word for submission to central authority. Competition and winning have become code words for the enemy, or the traditionalists, or what remains of them, who still believe in personal initiative, responsibility, and hard work. It is these values and their concomitant attitudes that the left-wing intelligentsia is trying to control. Nowhere are these values and attitudes more prominent than in sports—especially hunting.

One way or another, everything important from life to death is a win or a loss—we just don't call it that, anymore. If we are to have fair competition, there must be rules binding on all competitors, and they must be enforced. But we hate rules and enforcement after a half century of permissive philosophy that says "do your own thing." We won't compete by the rules, so we sing the praises of nonconformity (when our prejudices do not prevail) until everything becomes lawless confrontation or conflict by force. Now we beg government to intervene on our behalf, which is what government wanted in the first place. This makes us the only nation in history whose people pay huge taxes for their own homicide. We do this by the other social process called cooperation. Notice, in athletic contests, we cannot cooperate with the opposing team and win.

Today, cooperation is the fad. Everyone extols it. Now, there is nothing wrong with cooperation, as such. Sometimes it is a good thing, sometimes it is the necessary thing, and sometimes it is the only thing, and nobody would have complained if Lombardi had said that instead of what he said about competition. But cooperation, too, has a technical meaning overlooked or unknown by those who use the word most often. It requires compromise and surrender of some sovereignty, some goal or desire between cooperators to accommodate each other's willingness to cooperate. It is a bargain hunt or bartering process. Everything is negotiable.

The "60s" activists were confrontational enough to state some demands as nonnegotiable, after vilifying everyone else for their refusal to cooperate. The trouble with bargaining in order to cooperate, is that one is never sure of what the real costs of the trade-offs are. Question is—who surrenders how much of what? Usually, when liberalism wants cooperation (its favorite word), it is fast-talking the other into submission. Subterfuge substitutes for the win of honest competition.

Let's not be naive. We know there are those who will try every trick in the book to get around the rules, to cheat outright, or otherwise take whatever advantages they can in violation of the rule or its spirit. In real life, it is not always easy to penalize those who infract the rules; the travesty we have made of our so-called justice system often guarantees that. But when it comes to sports, athletics, and games we enforce the rule and mete out penalties immediately or else the play cannot proceed. We enforce the rules in the playful game, but we won't enforce the law in serious life. Maybe that's why we are a nation of sports lovers. We can see justice done on the playing field far more often than we can in the legal system. We can know the joy of seeing our side win in the stadium when we are cheated elsewhere in real life.

When we have a headache, we remove the ache, not the head. The solution to the problem of bad winners and bad losers is not to decapitate competition, but to teach how to win with compassion and charity, and how to lose with grace and dignity. These are virtues grounded in morality. Cynics do not believe in either virtue or morals, and without these, no sense of honor can prevail. Without honor, integrity has no meaning. It may well be that the golden age of the ancient Olympiads is where the sense of honor was born. It was on all this that Western civilization created the idea of sportsmanship that was honored by those who gave it the name—sportsmen, of course, and especially the hunter.

Given human nature, obviously one will find those who violate the norms (including hunters), but tens of thousands more live up to them. Even the boys in a school yard fist fight lived up to the norm when the winner wanted to be a good sport, by extending his hand in respect for the loser who took that hand in gratitude for the show of gallantry. This is no longer necessary, of course, now that we have sex education. Gang rape and teenage pregnancy have replaced the black eye or the grin with a missing tooth.

Winning and losing are facts of life, and doing so fairly and honestly are based on natural law. Only in our radically egalitarian legalisms do we believe we can eliminate all losers by declaring anyone a winner.

Today, talent, ability, and effort are often nullified by those who are empowered through legal fictions that politicians devise for reelection. The urge to compete and win may well be a biologically determined drive and not culturally learned. That urge may not be a response to culture at all; rather, culture is a response to that urge in large measure. Culture only determines the norms and regulates the channels by which the drive is legitimated.

Since the number of possible outlets for the drive are limited in any social system, the surplus is stifled, frustrated, discouraged, or outlawed. That drive, however, is especially typical of male behavior, which may be one of the reasons why male-bashing is so common, these days—it makes for easier destruction of those attributes most naturally capable of winning. We may well be creating a process of unnatural selection which eventually extinguishes the genetic basis for a key biological drive that, thus far, has been indispensable in human development.

The political stigmatization of masculinity derided as the macho male, or machismo, as a social attribute of gender may falsify a biological reality of primary sexual characteristics. All this is one of the main reasons for the assault on the hunter's aggressive behavior. No matter how variable in form or content, that drive has been so all pervasive throughout history that, where it has been blocked in real life, it has emerged in social conflict or channeled into the more civilized imitation of it through athletics. We really compete and win or lose in play forms, personally or vicariously, when we cannot do it in real life. Sports, games, and athletic contests that lead to joy or agony are sophisticated forms of play providing the outlet for the surplus competitive drive to win, which society cannot absorb entirely.

We now reach the intriguing problem of play, which is at once a make believe of real life often becoming more real than life itself. No human society is known without play forms. Some scholars

(Huizinga, for example), have observed that the play element in *agon*, with its rules and regulations, was the origin of codified law in the institutional life of all civilizations. The rule, or enacted law, rather than arbitrary dictate, became the central element in the democratic experiment, and the ancient version of the rule of law spread to all institutions. It became the basis for Western parliamentary government rather than Oriental despotism.

If the play element, or the ludic function (Huizinga's phrase)[1] was so basic to culture and society, what is the nature of play? Oddly enough, this most vital question has no definitive answer and even today, it is very much up in the air with all kinds of speculation. It is this which forces my speculation here because it is too vital a part of hunting to ignore. Almost every opinion on the subject assumes that play is the opposite of work. But is it? In my judgement, the opposite of play is not work, but boredom because both work and play are interesting activity, the true opposite of which is the lack of it, or boredom. There are reputable experiments with boredom where all stimuli are cut off from sensory reception, which results, progressively, in frustration to aggression, then hostility to hallucination, to pre-psychotic behavior with measurable alpha wave alterations in the brain.

In a sense, the brain is the greatest sensory organ of them all, and, to stay alive, it is constantly receiving stimuli from the outside world, signals from the rest of the body that it controls, or provides its own symbolic stimuli in thought, imagination, or dreams. It may well be that the hunter's psychic structure has the ability to handle greater and more varied amounts of sensory input from wilderness surroundings than others for whom wilderness, and anything associated with it, becomes a disorienting trauma.

In any sport, the play element must be undertaken seriously with the risk of agony, if one is to win. Sometimes, the serious in anything must be done playfully to make the undertaking less agonizing. There's the paradox. We need to play to get away from the drudgery of hard work, but if we are going to play well, we need to work hard at it. Therefore, an amateur, weekend-ball-player who does it for neighborhood fun becomes a serious workaholic if he does the same thing professionally, with all its rigorous full-time training, practice, and agonizing play during a real game, even if it's not fun any longer, but plain, hard work to earn a living.

Then there are, or were, primitive tribesmen who work feverishly to the breaking point around the clock during an all too brief fishing run. Standing in a wide circle, they close in, each holding up his section of net. Their physically demanding, exhaustive work in waist-high water, is made more bearable with a play element. They sway in rhythm and chant; occasionally, the wiseguys among them will splash water on the next man, they will joke and make their work playful as they close in on their poor, defenseless fish.

In our own frontier days, the hard work of house raising was lightened with the playful participation of many neighbors who had a party or festive occasion to go along with the work, as did women who chatted and served tea and cookies when they plied their needles in a quilting bee. Today, in military training, the onerous drill-marching routine is punctuated with a singsong cadence; the tedium of the assembly line or office routine is lightened with the coffee break, chin-wagging, and the crossword puzzle.

In all areas of life, play becomes boredom or boredom becomes play with the flip of a subjective switch. It is difficult to define play with precision because the number of subjective responses to play and boredom, and the attitudes about them, are virtually unlimited. Enough has been said about it here to go on to the next point.

If the 19th century term, sporting holiday was a vacation or a recreational renewal, and the phrase sport hunting evolved in that context, we need to understand sports in general to understand sport hunting in particular. In perusing or studying dozens of books on sport and teaching its socio-psychology over many years, I have been struck by one singular fact. Since the counterculture revolution of the 1960s, one will look in vain to see hunting listed as a sport, or anything else for that matter, in serious sports literature.

One book referring to over 2,000 games and sports in various categories and cross-cultural references, does not see fit to include the world's oldest, most singularly cross-cultural, and universally pervasive of all sporting contests. To say all of this is an oversight, repeatedly, is like saying one goes to Gizeh and overlooks the Great Pyramids of Khufu, Kephren, and Mykerinos. However, one will see, or have shoved into his eyeballs, all sorts of studies with derogatory, defamatory, and degrading material about hunting which justifies the new attitude, the new look, and the new she-he unisex of the New Age and the New World Order, waiting around the corner to wipe out hunting forever.

Often, the very people who rail against censorship are the same ones who censor serious and honest study of hunting in the sporting literature. The very people who deny hunting as a sport, suddenly resurrect it as a defamatory "sport." We need to compare sport hunting with sports in general to see what is going on. The trick is to know what is worth the contest, and again, how to win with charity and how to lose with grace. That is sportsmanship based on a morality we have long since lost.

Today's All-American Unisexed Wimp who denounces violent body-contact sports senses that he doesn't have what it takes to agonize in winning anything, and stays out of the contest. So what's his problem? He doesn't want anyone else to win so he can win by forfeiture—without contest. Isn't that nice?

We can have fun and play where winning is not the point, in which case, we are talking about a hobby, entertainment, pastime, recreation, amusement or whatever—but not a game, sport, or contest. What better outlet for instinctive *agon* than sport regulated by the values and norms of what used to be Western morality? Were the ancient Mayans or Aztecs, who played their version of soccer by kicking human skulls across the arena, more praiseworthy? Were the Jivaros more genteel for shrinking the heads of their victims to orange size, and then sporting them about town as a symbol of the contests they won in skirmish or ambush as a sign of honorific status?

It is necessary to understand some broad generalities about sport which, admittedly, defy easy classification. But, without it, hunting will continually be misunderstood. There are many attempts to classify sports, and they all have problems, but three popular schemes divide them, inadequately, to be sure, into individual and group (or team) sports, or indoor and outdoor sports, or organized and unorganized sports. Some individualized sports are skiing, tobogganing, skating, fencing, boxing, wrestling, track, tennis, rock climbing, hang gliding, racing (stock car, speed boat, and horse,) equitation, tauromachy (bullfighting,) angling, billiards, and the like. What one does in these cases does not necessarily require simultaneous support from another team member at the moment of action or play.

The locale, site, or designated area for some of these sports began in the outdoors and were eventually modified and moved indoors where the big money was, especially if they became spectator sports like boxing, wrestling, organized football, base-ball, and so on. Others, like angling, hang gliding and hunting must obviously remain outdoors.

It is apparent at once that area or space for action is an important variable. Some sports mentioned can take place even in a densely populated metropolitan area in a gym, stadium, at home, or in the backyard.

Others must take place in wilderness areas. Obviously, the difference in the requisite space is that, in the first instance, such space is comparatively small, clearly delineated, and standard-ized. The boxing ring, fencing salon, tennis court, etc., are stan-dard sizes, ranging from a few feet to a hundred yards or more for outdoor team sports like the football gridiron, baseball diamond, cinder track, and so on. The playing area is the small manageable world that has an immediate, definite, and present boundary. At every moment of play, those boundaries must be accounted for and within which time has limits.

There are time limits in each round of boxing, with time limits on rest periods between rounds. The rounds themselves differ in number, according to title or preliminary bouts in amateur or professional classes, and so on. In tennis, there are fair and foul areas inside and outside the court where the ball may or may not be placed or hit. In team sports like football, there are 10-yard markers, end zones, 15-minute quarters, scrimmage lines, etc., while in baseball there are innings, foul ball areas, and the like.

All these restrictions are intrinsic to the nature of the game itself. Play, or action patterns, cannot proceed, or are discounted, or penalized outside delineated boundaries or when an established time limit is exceeded, or an illicit move is made. The moment that happens, the game stops and the play must start over. Otherwise, fair play is impossible.

The rules of conduct within a play are not made up as one goes along. They have long since been standardized, and competition for the prized goal must be regulated according to those standards. There is an objective reference point against which the fair and foul may be determined. Hence, we have order. Orderliness is the essence of the game allowing the play to occur, or else the competitive play deteriorates into disorder that creates conflict and chaos making further play impossible, as noted by Huizinga. Competition becomes conflict, play becomes chaos.

In organized team sports like football or baseball, the interaction is among the individual players of the team where one athlete or team tries to score against the opposite member or team, while the opposition tries to prevent the score. The cumulative total of these scores determines who wins or loses.

Agonist and antagonist both know, and play by, the same rules that determine not only the play, but the ethical conduct of players, especially in what are known today as contact sports. Too much contact turns channeled drive into illicit aggression, hostility, brutality, or all three where the play becomes real life again. Hence, the need for ethical restraint or sportsmanship.

In individual sports, which do not require bodily contact or interaction, the win or loss is determined not by a play against an opponent, but by meeting or surpassing some objective standard, like distance in a javelin throw, height in a pole vault, time in a hundred-yard dash, weight in a body press, form in equitation, and so on.

No matter how varied the sports, they have some things in common that can now be summarized to compare them with hunting. What is common to most sports are: (1) the playing sites or the boundaried areas (the court, ring, gridiron, etc.) which players must take into immediate account constantly while play is in progress, (2) the player or players have knowledge of the rules and regulations binding on all, and of the penalties for infractions, (3) the contest with its doubtful outcome between competing persons and teams, or against objective standards, like height, weight, distance, speed, and so on, and (4) the agonistic action requiring generalized athletic or physical ability and specialized skills by learning, training, and practice. How does hunting compare to all this?

The hunt as an agonistic contest contains elements of sport, game, and play without being any one of them entirely, but parts of all of them, together. Moreover, with life and death being involved, it is at once a spiritual and metaphysical issue of finalism. Hunting is unique, and whatever else it may be, it is unlike any other sport. Some critics will gleefully agree with this, but for totally different reasons, of course.

In hunting, at the very outset, the hunter's opponent is not a human athlete, obviously. It is an animal who knows nothing about the rules of the game. The interaction, or the game between hunter and quarry, is played out with no regard for time limits or boundary while the play is in progress. It can go for as long as a hunter wants, anywhere he wants, within a vast area several hundred, or even a thousand, square miles during several days, weeks, or months in duration.

The space or the playing field for hunting has boundaries that are largely administrative, political, or geographical. There are also time limits based on biological and seasonal factors—mating, birthing, etc. But these have nothing to do with the inherent nature of the play or game. In other sports, the play must always allow for the immediate boundary lines and time limits during its enactment.

However, the hunter may be in a boundaried area, but he does not have to take into immediate account the boundary lines, which cannot be seen, anyway, at the moment of play. They may be 100 miles and 10 hours away. They are irrelevant to the conduct of his play when the hunter makes his move. One can hunt even if all restrictions of space or rules of play are eliminated or nonexistent, as in the prehistoric past. But one cannot play soccer or tennis without boundaries and rules. For all practical purposes, the hunter's playing field is without immediate space or time limit.

The hunter hunts within a labyrinth of statutory law (and he'd better know it), but these are for the protection of wildlife, environment, and public or political interest—not for the integrity or orderliness of the play of the game. Law can limit the number of rounds one may have in the magazine of his rifle, usually three, with a fourth optional one in the chamber, but it has no interest in how many shots the hunter uses to down his bear. The sporting ethic, however, has a great deal to say about it.

In all other sports, games, or play, every player knows the rules, and the rules are binding on each and all the players. A foul play causes the referee's whistle to stop the game, the infraction is penalized, and the play is restored.

In sport hunting, the ethic is a set of premises, tenets, or norms that are known only to the hunter, not to his opposite. Infraction of the ethical norm based on morals, has nothing to do with the law and everything to do with a loss of self-esteem and feelings of guilt, shame, failure, sin, dishonor, and all the other torments of emotion, spirit, and soul.

Our Western, liberal culture scoffs at such internal mechanisms of self regulation. Cynics don't believe the other guy can feel a loss of moral integrity because cynics themselves do not believe in either morality or integrity in human behavior. Hence, they think it a sham when one feels the spiritual pain of redemptive self censure. Cynics or liberals, often they are one and the same, believe in external support for man's inner state of being. They go to psychoanalysts, sensitivity sessions, and group therapy to learn why they suffer when their significant other's infidelity is discovered, and forget they never believed in fidelity to begin with.

For the player in any sport, the contest with doubtful outcome is resolved by some kind of scoring system against an opponent, or against some objective standard. For the sport hunter generally, the outcome is evaluated, or scored, by two standards. The objective standard is the carcass of his kill. He either has it or he doesn't. As Ortega long since pointed out, "one does not hunt in order to kill; one kills in order to have hunted." The kill is only a part of the total hunting experience.

The other standard of the total experience is a purely subjective one, especially for the trophy hunter—quality. The excellence or mediocrity of the hunt; the quality of the trophy's size; symmetry of antlers, horns, and other esthetic qualities; and the subtleties of the spirit that were involved in the entire experience of wilderness.

Big game hunting is the only game where play becomes reality in an instant, and the reality becomes play in the next moment. It is never one or the other, but always a dialectic between the two, where the resulting play has real and final consequences for one of the contestants who may never play again—win, lose, or draw.

Another crucial difference between hunting and other sports is the agonistic strife between two opponents is a one-sided affair with the odds against the hunter, much to the surprise of critics who think it the other way around. Athletes in their sporting games are roughly equal to each other in physical conditioning with approximately similar reflexes, stamina, strength, speed, and so on. They have all learned their skills based on high aptitudinal potentials, which are largely genetically determined, their apprenticeship periods have weeded out less stellar performers, rigorous seasonal training has put them into top-notch condition, and years of experience have made them formidable competitors. A sudden moment of play that instantly demands ultimate physical and mental response will probably get it.

The analogous counterpart to the top-notch athlete is not the hunter, but the animal. If it is a trophy animal, especially, it has been around a long time to develop the size of body, horns, antlers, etc. If it has been around that long, it is a highly specialized killing or surviving machine who has earned his Ph.D. in the wilderness university of hardknocks. His genetic endowment has enabled his kind to win survival for millennia so he doesn't need seasonal training to reach top-notch condition. He's already there and stays there.

Given a stable food supply, he is always in top-notch condition. Every day he runs, jumps, fords, swims, and otherwise does maximal and ultimate things with his body, reflexes, and instincts. While the hunter is not in the same class as a top-notch athlete, who is not in the same class as the average big-game animal, the hunter outclasses his average fellow human beings when it comes to the physical. He is not a highly developed athlete with specialized skills, but he may be the best all-around athlete there is with generalized ability and expertise.

Often, the hunter is a physically large man, though he doesn't have to be. But large or small, he must have enough toughness, stamina, and strength to traverse difficult terrain under conditions that may require utmost exertion and agony. It is an effort the hunter makes for a few days out of the year. During the rest of that year he sat at his desk or used his power tools without using much muscular effort and energy. Even when he vowed to exercise himself into adequate physical condition for the hunt, he ran out of time to do it. Yet that hunter must be able, at any given moment, to run, walk, crawl, jump, or climb, and be able to paddle, row, pole, snowshoe, ski, shoot, lift, carry, skin, and backpack real weight. In addition, he ought to know horsemanship, enough mechanics for emergency repair to vehicles, and be adept at campcraft and wilderness lore to survive an emergency.

There is no structure in the game of hunting, or orderly progress in its play, because the quarry does not know the rules. This allows for the free-flowing creativity of an unlimited number of plays that are not formal and standardized, but informal, innovative, and spontaneous. Since the hunter's main objective is to kill his quarry under ethical tenets of sportsmanship, the interactive plays or moves between both, constantly alternate between the contest of a game and real life.

The only thing coming close to it is bullfighting, but that is played out in an enclosed arena, according to established procedure, for the appreciation of spectators. Hence, it is a pageant in its entirety, but the action between bull and matador has been correctly identified as the "art" of bullfighting, and the phrase has general and preferable acceptance. The generic term "sport" as applied to hunting may be a gross misnomer because hunting is unique and unlike any other sport.

Why then is the phrase "blood sports" so often used in a negative context against hunters? Because the phrase is a cover-up for the real enemy: maleness, competition, and winning. Much of Western culture or civilization rest on these attributes. As long as hunting is a "sport', it can be denounced as a travesty on all sports where "fun" is more legitimate. The white male hunter is now an ideal target, because he is the representative for all those values hated by the anti-Western mentality.

In Medieval Europe, which gave rise to the foundations of the hunting ethic in our Western culture, hunting was known as the venatic art or the art of venery. The first known handbook on hunting was written by Xeneophon (430-335 BC), and entitled, *Cynegeticus*, which meant hunting in the original Greek (from the cognate "kynegeticos'), and referred to hunting with dogs. Was he also the same Xenephon who authored the more famous work, *Anabasis*, which described "The Retreat of Ten Thousand" in one of history's greatest military withdrawals from Babylonia to the Black Sea?

Flavius Arrian, who renamed himself Xenophon the Younger out of admiration for the former, wrote his book, also entitled *Cynegeticus*, sometime in the beginning of the second century AD. It is heavily based on the earlier Xenophon's work, but it added crucial descriptions of hunting in Central Europe for the first time. Perhaps that is how the word got its start in Medieval references. At any rate, it became well known in popular usage and is still used today in sophisticated quarters. Hunting, venery and cynegetics were known as an art form from its earliest literary accounts. But the word "sport" has hung on since the democratization of the art as already noted, and is so well entrenched, it is not my intention to contrive a neologism to replace it.

However, to use the word "art" in popular discourse about hunting has serious consequences. Artists of modern art schools, who themselves are part of the counterculture revolution, would be the first to object. They would throw Jacksonian seizures at the thought of being associated with Paleolithic practitioners of the blood sports.

The feelings are mutual for too many hunters who feel discomfort when artists flaunt images of the left-bank Bohemian (as they were labelled not too long ago) with radical ideas and life-styles that make them look like weirdos emerging from the blotches of color and abstract forms—painted, sculpted, or photographed. Neither side seems to be aware that some great big-game hunters of recent times have been great artists of wildlife. Carl Akeley, J.G. Millais, R.H. Rockwell, A.R. Dugmore, C.G. Schillings, and James Clark are some who come to mind, instantly.

The term "hunting" is too generic; it includes everything from poaching to market hunting, subsistence hunting to big-game hunting, or trophy hunting. Critics lump them all together and arbitrarily conclude that they are all the same thing because killing is killing. When used connotatively, one must be careful. One can be hunting for his misplaced cufflinks without intending to kill them. Cynegetics can only mean hunting animals and, while the point may be pedantic or the word too highfalutin, one can rest assured no one will be cynegeticking the same set of cufflinks.

In cynegetics or sport hunting (especially trophy hunting) there are two main tenets of the ethic. The first one (again), is the hunter must allow the quarry its chance to fight back or escape. From this, there follows the unnecessary restrictions and difficulties the hunter imposes on himself to create the fair play between the quarry and himself. His objective is not killing in any old way that happens to be the most expedient or foolproof method—as in other kinds of hunting. A chance for the animal to escape or fight back, to deserve fair play, mercy, and the other moral attributes already discussed, are not the only bases for the hunting ethic, however. The other basis is in the nature of the contest and its *agon*.

The hunt, like many other kinds of play, sports, or games, is characterized by patterns of sequential actions where one naturally follows the other by its own logic. Each action is a part leading to a total pattern. Psychologically, the person in such a situation does not have to ponder and cogitate on what to do next. Intuitively, with a kind of supraconscious awareness, which has often been called a sixth sense, he knows in advance what each sequence will require. He then does what needs doing without being consciously aware he is doing it. He is so much a part of what is being done, he loses self awareness and becomes one with his action and the immediate world outside himself in which the action occurs.

Everything—self, other, action, and world—become unified, and each loses its separate identity. Those who go to the Orient to learn of Zen, sartori, yoga, nirvana, or spiritual transcendence could have stayed home and got all of them during the supreme moments of one great bang-up hunt.

The hunter's behavior, at any moment, is trying to bring about certain future goals, 5 minutes or 5 hours away, which he has intended all along. All of this is autotelic behavior,[2] or behavior in which the person himself is the real cause producing the desired result. Here, we reach a critical point. The key factor that must make the difference in the action patterns that win or lose at the critical moment is the person himself. If the conditions of action are so difficult that the win is due to chance or accident, or if the win is so easy it is the predictable result of infallible routine, then there are no final ends because of the individual's abilities. The ends resulted despite the individual who made no difference in this outcome. How does the person know he is making the difference? Because he gets constant feedback from what he is doing.

When one wrestler's back is pinned to the mat, the other wrestler knows he and no one else did the pinning. That's autotelic feedback. While almost any kind of action can be autotelic, it is in hunting where the most supreme instances of it can be found. This is one of the chief reasons why the hunter hunts—and where agonistic supremacy reigns in deciding the doubtful outcome of the contest.

The sport hunter, it must be remembered, imposes unnecessary difficulties and restrictions on himself, but not so severe he nullifies his own efforts, thereby leaving a successful outcome to sheer chance, but severe enough to remove routine certainty so that he is the deciding factor in the outcome, win or lose. He must make the difference. Without that difference, there is not much point in achievement, winning, losing, or contesting anything. The hunter knows how much of a difference he is making because of the constant feedback he gets from the quarry. They are interacting—each influences the behavior of the other; each anticipates the possible actions of the other and adjusts his own accordingly. For the hunter, therein lies the excitement and thrill of making the correct and decisive adjustment or choice because the consequences are so great.

In any fair, competitive contest, an action is played out according to rules between the contestants. In sport hunting, ethical mores determine fair play. Since the quarry does not know anything about the ethics of fair play, there are no restrictions on his behavior, but the hunter is bound by fairness at all times and at all costs. Respect for the quarry and the rules of the game deserve that much, at least, or there is no game or contest. In an athletic contest or ball game, for example, a referee whistles the foul play, or the broken rule, to halt the play, and he reinstates the conditions of fairness and regulation, without which the play cannot proceed or act itself out. Often, there are penalties for the infraction. There is always a fair or foul, a right or wrong. Like it or not, all contests or games are codified morality plays by any other name. That includes hunting.

Most people in a modern democracy do not like morality; it requires too much from us. What results is the chicane of law and the corruption of culture that sooner or later permeates sports. One needs only to look at the corruption of professionally organized football, baseball, basketball, and boxing these days, or any place else, where big money is involved. Those who ridiculed honor and morality the loudest, now denounce loudly the corruption they helped create.

The hunter is his own referee. His whistle is his conscience that prevents foul play, based on his knowledge of the rules, from occurring in the first place. Hence, the hunter is not only in a contest with the quarry, matching skills, intuition, intelligence, prowess, and stamina, but he is in a contest with himself on two levels. He must not only meet the physical, emotional, and skill requirements of the chase. He must also live up to moral standards often difficult to attain, even in less challenging circumstances.

That is the other kind of contest within the hunter's soul. He, more than most, knows human nature is capable of reaching noble heights of sublimity and degrading depths of ignominy. He is committed to an ethic which confronts temptation, in every single moment of the encounter with his quarry, to cut a corner, no matter how slight. To bag that trophy unethically, when so much has been sacrificed to get it, is what he must resist. Does he rise above human weakness or does he embrace it? After all, he is an imperfect human being, and easily forgiven his transgressions in a good permissivist society on its way to perfection, even if it takes another 10,000 years.

In nine out of ten hunts the hunter does not even get to see his animal, let alone get within shooting distance of a trophy. And when he does, nothing guarantees his success in bagging it. For every success, there have been a dozen failures and when he finally sees his trophy, there can be a strong temptation to do whatever is necessary to score and make up for past failures. But to do that immediately subverts the hunting ethic. The authentic trophy hunter has the integrity to overcome that temptation. The integrity of the hunt is its own reward surpassing the success or failure in obtaining the trophy. In fact, the trophy wrongly attained is no trophy by definition. If the hunter commits a deliberate foul, he knows it is not some mysterious subconscious force, or a faulty social system that made him do it, but willful choice or what we called evil in the old days.

His commitment is not to relativistic ethics. Right is not whatever pleases him. What pleases him is whatever is right, and that is not necessarily what he says it is. Admittedly, this is difficult to understand for those who believe there are no objective standards of right and wrong, but that right is whatever one says it is. This makes any besotted opinion in the local pub take on the validity of a universal truth attained by centuries of tested wisdom.

The mature hunter has long since settled the conflict in his soul between virtue and vice, right and wrong, good and bad when on the hunting trail. He knows the quality of the hunt in his search for the unique and the excellent can only rest on his sporting sense, hunting ethic, and honor.

Of course honest mistakes are possible, but when they occur they cannot be graded on a curve based on a group average as in some popular freshman class where the A student would have flunked the course, otherwise. One either passes honorably, or fails based on an absolute standard. The ethic is the standard of the sport hunter that decides the grade, not the moral relativism of modern society. Without quality in the hunt, which is the key element in the pursuit of excellence in any endeavor, any sport becomes a "sport'—a mockery.

Excellence is simply the best quality attainable. But there are countless sports in which autotelic challenge and the pursuit of excellence may be attained. Why devote oneself to a sport in which killing a poor animal is necessary? Why not be a sporter in something less barbaric and bloodthirsty?

It is difficult to imagine any contest with doubtful outcome that does not require some amount of risk to win. Sometimes, one loses no matter how little the risk or wins no matter how great the risk. It's one thing to risk the loss of a friendly badminton game on the greensward some Sunday afternoon, or a couple dollars in a bingo game. These are trifling, or at least nonlethal, risks. It's another thing to confront an infuriated Cape buffalo or grizzly bear, or the treacherous mountain slope to get within shooting distance of a shy Dall sheep at a 6,000-foot altitude at any time. The risk in these instances is maximal—the loss can be one's life.

In any high-risk sporting activity, no agonist intends to kill his antagonist, except in a gladiatorial game. If death occurs in the sporting arena, and it occasionally does, it is accidental or unintentional. Excepting bullfighting, it is only in hunting that the high risk endeavor takes on a different quality. It is only in hunting that either agonist or antagonist gets killed intentionally and deliberately. No high risk autotelic undertaking can have a higher risk factor than that, because the risk is ultimately the highest when one's life is deliberately placed at stake. Resolving the doubtful outcome of a contest has no riskier autotelic feed back, hence no greater psychic reward in one's favor. That is one of the central attractions, obsessions, or mysteries that motivates the hunter. It is an ultimate that exists in no other sporting activity.

Naturally, the greater the risk, the more joyous and ecstatic the win, or the more disappointing and despondent the loss. One's emotional and spiritual responses, one's relatedness to the result, is in direct proportion to the degree and quality of the risk that went into the autotelic undertaking.

To know great joy resulting from personal effort and agony requires the readiness to take great risks if and when necessary. This is one of the chief reasons the hunter chooses his adventure where the risks are highest, but the psychological rewards are greatest. The problem is the difficulty in knowing in advance how great the risk is, which succeeds in winning, or fails in losing. And then, all too often, sheer chance, accident, or the unexpected upsets all the careful calculations of risk and planning of strategy.

Some people are good judges in anything. Some are poor judges in everything. Others come in between with the luck of the Irish. That's life.

High risk action is not sustainable for long periods of time—

the nervous system, under split-second timing, has limits, or the odds finally turn the tables. Therefore, such action tends to be of relatively short duration, because speed is involved, demanding utmost coordination and balance to see it through. Hence, surf boarding, sky diving, skiing, and tobogganing, tend to be exciting, exhilarating, and innervating. Golfing, boxing, football, and hunting tend to be tiring, exhaustive, and enervative, leading to agony. Each of these categories has elements of the other, at certain moments in the activity or play, but the main characteristics remain.

All too often, hunting is plain hard work, and sometimes prolonged, Herculean labor. It requires a variety of skills and abilities. The hunter is met by constant challenges from wilderness, elements, and wily, alert animals—some of which are dangerous with lethal abilities. Often, the hunting activity continues over many consecutive days of sustained effort. And at all times, the hunter is in harm's way from either a dangerous animal or wilderness calamities.

The thrill—the challenge—is to survive these odds, some of which require low-level risk, and some of which require high-level risk. These must be calculated carefully. One cannot take reckless risks that are suicidal, but one cannot play it safe, either, with foolproof guarantees that contradict the very nature of the hunt. To hunt is to risk and only experience can tell the good risk from the bad one. Then comes the day when the good risk was too bad, after all. A good hunt is one of the most demanding enterprises one can undertake. Let it be known to all and sundry—there are easier ways to have fun.

The joy of hunting cannot be separated from an entire philosophy of life, philosophy at odds with an effete modernism that reaches for the heavens without knowing that one slip is all it takes and hell is at the other end. Between those polarities lies the treasure we all talk about and rarely achieve—the true freedom of the spirit released from the confines of trivia.

Perhaps no other human being in any other situation of life has such total and real freedom to create what he can, to do what he truly wants, to accept nature's challenges and rewards, to reach the limits of his being, to win or lose on his own, to choose the right from the wrong. There is nothing to pass judgement on him except his own conscience and his god.

Hunting is not for those who can commit themselves to anything, but only if the cost, effort, and daring are negligible. It is not for those who dislike competing fairly against great challenges. It is not for those who lack the nobility of spirit to win with compassion and lose with grace. It is not for those who believe the triumph of spirit is unreal. It is not for those who believe killing an animal is a greater crime than the sin of killing an innocent person before or after it's born. It is not for those who believe they are God with accountability to nothing. It is not for those who put love of self before reverence for the animal. It is not for those who love life but have no respect for death. It is not for those who demand humanity for themselves but deny it to others. In a true democracy, all others qualify.

1 Johan Huizinga, *Homo Ludens* (New York, N.Y.: Harper and Sons, 1975) I express my great indebtedness to Huizinga whose germinal work goes far beyond my use of his work in this chapter.
2 Mihaly Csizkszentmihaly, *Beyond Boredom and Anxiety* (San Francisco: Jossey-Bass Publishing, 1975) I express my indebtedness and gratitude to the author and book for his concept of *autotelics* on which I have relied in this chapter.

Sheep Never Come Cheap

The more Rick made it sound like it would be the greatest sheep hunt in Alaska history, the more I felt it would be like a New England clambake. This was his first sheep hunt, we were hardly acquainted, and he wanted to learn from me (he said) as though I knew all about it. However, he wanted me to meet Burlson, who was organizing the hunt, who had heard about me, and wanted my acquaintance. He was inviting me through Rick. Well, I'd heard about Burlson, and felt honored that he would invite me, sight unseen. He was a sober, responsible family man who taught school in Big Delta, because it gave him summers off so he could do what he really loved—ranching and hunting. He had a good spread near Big Delta a couple hundred miles from Fairbanks and enjoyed a good reputation as a hunter.

Two of his friends were also invited—Jack, who was an army veterinarian stationed at nearby Fort Greely, and Gary, who was today's answer to yesterday's mountain man who opened up the west. Mostly, Gary trapped for a living, worked for Bureau of Land Management, fought forest fires on occasion, and went to school part time. He and Jack were total strangers to me.

The real reason I didn't want to go was I had dug out the crib-walled, dirt cellar to my house to enlarge and upgrade it. The house now sat wide open on pilings with furnace and plumbing exposed. Winter would drop in cold sober in two or three weeks and completion of the project was vital. On the other hand, powdery glacial silt, which had stuccoed my lungs almost immovable while digging out the basement, had left me more breathless than a popular vodka ad. I was meeting the challenge of the North again, fed up with it, and feeling too much like a sourdough, which old timers characterized as one who was sour on the country, but without dough to leave. Maybe the real reason for accepting the invitation was just to get away from it for a few days. I showed up at Burlson's ranch, with Rick rarin' to go, resolved to fight the fast-approaching winter on my return and do or die—the hunt came first.

Burlson and I hit it off immediately. We shared the same views on the state of the union, the coming self-destruction of the American educational system, and drank to its ill-health until Jack and Gary showed up. Promise for a rollicking good time was overwhelming whether we got sheep or not. It rarely happens on a hunt that five guys who hunt together for the first time and barely know each other hit it off as well, but we did. There were too many of us for any to take the hunt seriously—there couldn't be that many sheep in sight on the mountain range hugging the Johnson River and its glacier.

Burlson was an easygoing, good-tempered fellow, but the occasional glint in his steely blue eyes or the flick of his hands, when he stabbed a thought into submission, hinted what later proved to be true—he could reach a decision quickly and stand by it at all costs.

He showed us the corral, horses, mule, and entire operation he and his wife ran with obvious efficiency. We slept soundly that night in the bunkhouse, as happy as kids let out on a school holiday.

By the time three trucks reached our takeoff site some 50 miles from the ranch, a slight drizzle had started. We off-loaded six horses and a mule, diamond-hitched two of the horses with already packed and balanced panniers and other gear, cinched saddles, and by 7 AM, we were on the trail.

Although no expert, I knew something about horses, but nothing about mules. When it was suggested I might ride Sally, the mule, I accepted gladly, anticipating a new experience. Burlson made the suggestion facetiously, since Sally was about 14 years old and was equivalent to a man aged 60. I wasn't quite that old yet, and Burlson, the next oldest in the party, was 15 years my junior, but I agreed. The match between man and mule was compatible in more ways than age. I came to love that cantankerous critter before some moments of terror in this hunt were safely put behind.

Since one horse, the splayfooted one, was used as a pack animal, that left Gary to walk and trade places with the others when he got tired, but it seemed certain he could walk halfway around the world if he put his mind to it.

The dirt road soon deteriorated into a muddy trail through thick, filmy fern and foxtail growth and made the lush forest look like a South Sea island paradise. It thinned out to scraggly spruce soon enough, as we climbed up the steep face of a pass leading to McComb Plateau. One glance showed it should be great caribou country, which it was, and a few years later it, too, became bedeviled with laws and regulations curtailing much of the hunting there.

We crossed the plateau already seared and bleak. It dropped precipitously. Halfway down a steep trail, we reached a heavily wooded glen which protected a halfway camp site with a primitive corral and a wooden frame for the tent, which was cached in trees.

Other gear was cached in trees beyond reach of bears—both black and grizzly. We hobbled our animals, set up camp, had dinner, and turned in early, exhausted from cold rain and a long day of hard riding and walking.

By noon the next day, we dropped down to the Johnson River confluence, with the river in the distance. We enjoyed a few hours of sunshine, and forded several streams, creeks, and rivulets meandering their way to the silty glacial waters of the mighty Johnson. A rock and gravel stretch along the river pushed into a lush patch of fodder for the animals, and we pitched a primitive camp.

A large tarp, with altogether too many holes in it, was strung between trees to cover our gear and double as a living room, around which we staked our two-man tents. I dubbed the exquisite architectural triumph, Hotel Taj Mahal.

It was about 4 PM when we heard the buzzing of aircraft overhead. We had arrived just in time. Burlson had arranged in advance for the plane; we had already crisscrossed several roles of pink-colored toilet paper into a large X on the tundra, and the pilot found it easily enough. He air-dropped a half dozen chop boxes of grub and gear. We were ready for the morrow, which we met early, packed saddle bags, but only lightly, and hit the trail full of hope.

Sally would nudge the horses out of the way, take the lead and break trail. I enjoyed the wild vistas, as long as they were visible beneath the grey and soggy skies. Johnson River surged around the skirts of the range. Whenever I dismounted to photograph the beauty of that rugged grandeur, Sally would come over, nudge me, and demand a handful of lush grass, which I wouldn't let her dally over when making trail. Then, she would stall getting back onto the trail, until a dash of inspiration led me to lean over and softly sing to her a song I had learned more than 40 years earlier in grade school:

I had a mule her name was Sal,
15 miles on the Erie Canal.
She's a good ol' worker
And a good ol' pal,
15 miles on the Erie Canal.

We've hauled some barges in our day,
Filled with lumber, coal, and hay,
A-n-d we know every inch of the way
From Albany to Buffalo-o-o-o . . .

She picked up her pace again. The female sex always wants something, except Sally wanted nothing more than a handful of grass when we stopped where there was none. To get her going, I substituted a slice of apple from my saddle bag. She conditioned me into giving her a slice every time we stopped, which taught her to stop more times than I had a handy apple slice, but my singing about my gal Sal on the Erie Canal conditioned her into a response that was to be a minor miracle later on. It was to become an unexpected blessing when my life depended on it.

We traversed the basin we were in, which tapered to an end, and ran out where stood an enormous two-story boulder we had been referring to as the big rock, until I saw how bleak and isolated it looked with the river swirling madly around its right side, blocking all escape. I quickly renamed it Alcatraz.

We hobbled our animals at the base of it and cached our excess gear (which was precious little). Beyond this point, we would have to climb to the left of it, cutting through roughly bouldered terrain, beyond which were the inevitable and miserably thick alder hedgerows on the bank. It was a struggle through the scrub, but we got out and looked down on the river far below.

Ahead, about 4 or 5 miles, a mighty, snow-clad massif rose to an edge dead-center to our line of approach, but between us lay a deep ravine. On either side of the massif, the gorges were spectacular, though treacherous. On the left, a wild river dropped swiftly to join another tributary on the right of a knife-edged slope. Deeply gouged ravines halfway up, and gray shale washes above them indicated this ought to be prime sheep country.

We were bone weary by the time we reached the edge of the escarpment on our side of the ravine. Beyond, the mighty mountain shielded the wild river in a rift between its skirts and our slope. We flopped down in a row behind a rocky barricade and set up two spotting scopes.

Just as we had guessed, there were rams on the far slope across the ravine—six or seven of them and all legal. One had what looked like superbly full-curled horns. We had lunch and meticulously studied the rams and their terrain. I thought it would be a full day of very hard work getting to them and back.

The more we studied, the more the problems multiplied. First, some of us would have to climb down the ravine, ford the river, and climb the opposite slope, but the knife ridge which provided cover on the right side ran out below the sheep. This would require a wide arc to get around and above them.

The second problem was that time was playing out. It was already 3 in the afternoon. Even if we got our prizes, we could barely make it back to Alcatraz in time, and then, stumbling through the dark, it would be madness getting the animals back to the Hotel Taj, so we'd have to camp overnight, except that we had deliberately left our sleeping gear and shelter back at the Hotel. It would be miserable trying to survive the night in that weather.

Third, and most importantly, the problem, which none of us had wanted to face, was shaping up rapidly right before our eyes, and it wasn't going away. Dark clouds were moving steadily and rapidly toward us. Undoubtedly, they were already covering the higher slopes ahead, shrouded in mist, with heavy snow, and it was only a question of time before it reached us.

Obviously, we had underestimated the logistics. It was best to get out on the double and come back on the morrow with tents, equipment, and food. We simply needed to pitch our fly camp further than the Taj, and Alcatraz would be the better roost. In all probability, the sheep would still be there on the morrow.

It started to drizzle again as we descended and reached Alcatraz. Temperature was dropping rapidly and even though we were at lower altitudes, it could snow all the way in. We were already exhausted when we saddled up, strung out single file, and Sally and I took the lead heading back to the Taj, double time.

We took a bend in the trail and some vague sense of apprehension engulfed me. I stopped short because the creek we needed to cross for the other side of the trail was no longer there. Had I made a mistake in my turn? Impossible. The terrain permitted only one turn—the one I had made. What, then, was this in front of me?

All I could see was a raging, roiling, torrential river right in my way where the trail used to be. In a few moments the others caught up and there we were, mounts and men, jammed up against one another refusing to believe the evidence.

Slowly, it dawned on us that this was the earlier creek, which had paralleled the Johnson at this point. The Johnson had risen, overflowed, and our former creek was now a roaring, furious tributary more than a 150 feet wide! There was water, water, everywhere.

We finally admitted the truth. In the 6 to 8 hours we had been gone, the water had risen perhaps 5 feet where we were now standing! Not a single gravel bed we had used for crossing was visible. To our right, blocking our trail, was a towering mountain slope which tapered down into a precipitous rocky wall, sharp as a knife-edge, cutting out into the tributary. The muddy, glacial water, now infuriated, swept around in a huge arc.

The mountain had not moved to the water; water had moved to the mountain by at least a quarter mile! Earlier, the creek had skirted that wall with plenty of room to spare. Now, it was a river so high it pushed right up against the precipitous slope, blocking the way with the trail submerged under 5 or more feet of water.

The entire landscape had changed. It was impossible to climb over that obstacle with horses. We had to get around and past that point, but the raging torrent swept right before us, and there was no other way.

In the middle of that watery nightmare, there was a small gravel bar maybe 200 yards to our right, almost awash, tapering to a point and just long enough for a landing. It formed an island around which our tributary swept and emptied into the Johnson on the other side. Earlier, the far side of that gravel bar had been a steep bank which contained the Johnson, now gone completely berserk.

We were in very serious trouble. All hell must have broken loose with the weather back in the heights of the Alaska Range to generate rain or snow which had produced all this water. It wasn't until several days later when we learned that many square miles surrounding the flats around Big Delta, 70 to 100 miles back, had experienced a devastating flood, fed by the very wild waters which we were now confronting. As I say, it was even more serious than we imagined.

We powwowed, grimly and briefly. My thinking was that we had two choices. We could retreat to Alcatraz and get ourselves and the animals a little way up on high ground just before the steep incline with its alders. It would be high enough to get above the water, which would soon reach the Big Rock, but we'd be pinned down without food and shelter for at least a couple days, maybe more. Survival could be a real toughie, especially if it snowed.

The other alternative was right before us. If we could cross these raging waters and get to the island in the middle of it, we could walk to its tip, which seemed to go just a bit past the rocky wall blocking the way on our side. Then we could recross the tributary back to our side past the rock wall obstacle. Then we'd be back on course with plenty of maneuverable ground. I was sure there were no other rocky abutments between here and camp.

There were two problems, however. Did the tip of that island go far enough to ensure clearance of the rocky abutment? We could not see clearly with the abutment in the way and the curve of the tributary. The other problem was, of course, could we cross the tributary?

To understate the case, it was an overly high-level risk. So intently was I thinking this through, that what the others were saying had completely gone past me. When one of them asked me what I thought, I kept quiet, for a change, shrugging my shoulders.

Burlson was the trail boss of this dude outfit. Horses and mule were his, and they cost a small fortune. Only he could make the decision. When no sound came out of me, and they all stared in silence, he asked me point blank what I thought.

"It's your decision," I said. His steely blue eyes drilled right into mine.

"I know that," he said, "but I want your opinion, which is why I'm asking."

Okay, I thought to myself, you did ask for it. "Straight ahead," I said, "and right now before it's too late."

I didn't know what he'd say in the silence of the others. A broad grin spread across his face and he said, "Hot Dawg! That's just what I wanted to hear."

Before any of us realized what was happening, he whirled his roan around, told us to hold on until he checked things out, spurred his mount into the water, and yanked the reins of the two pack-horses. His mount took two steps, faltered and balked, as the icy glacial water with creamy-mud foam hurled itself against the poor beast. His eyes widened into two large orbs of fear, but there was no turning back now. Burlson yelled, kicked, and quirted with the loose end of the reins.

The packhorses were already in too deep and aswirl in the vicious current trying to tear them loose from Burlson's grip. He was being dragged off his recalcitrant mount, and either his arm would tear out of its socket, or he'd have to let go of the reins, or follow the others into the swirl.

He instantly followed the others into the swirl as the roan was swept onto its side. We yelled, shouted, and swore to get the roan to go. Somehow, Burlson got it rolled right side up again and things began to happen with lightning speed. Only the heads of the pack animals were now above water. They fought helplessly, hurled by the current, while Burlson was dragged with them, now completely broadside to the rushing water. Again, the roan rolled on its side and Burlson disappeared under it for a moment, only to come up spewing water and struggling to keep from being torn loose, but the pack animals were helplessly tossed and buffeted. In a few moments, they were in a hellish midstream.

Our hearts sank as they gathered momentum, occasionally blotting out of sight under exploding crests of water. In another 50 yards or so, they would be swept past the island's end and hurtled into the raging Johnson, which roared past the far side of the island, meeting our tributary past the island's tip.

Once in the larger waters, nothing would stop them from certain doom. There was a sudden silence among us as we realized the end to which one man and three horses were being propelled. Man and horses were almost past that tip of land when a miracle occurred.

A sand or gravel bar, just submerged beneath the roiling, booming surface, stopped all of them almost at once, as they smashed and piled atop each other. Man and horses became a mangled mass for a few moments, kicking and thrashing, half submerged. Burlson looked as though he crawled out from underneath, uncrushed, undrowned, and undaunted. He tugged, yanked, and pummeled at horseflesh until he got the animals staggering to their feet in knee-deep water, and no sooner had they gained footing on that submerged gravel strip, than they were back in the water on the other side of it scampering through a quieter and narrower span to the safety of the island.

How Burlson survived and did all that, we'll never know. Later, we couldn't believe the deep lacerations around his wrist, like bracelets from where the reins of the pack horses had cut them. I'm still amazed his wrist wasn't traumatically amputated or his metacarpals pulverized to mush.

We couldn't hear him across the water's roar, but we saw his needless gesticulations. He was trying to tell us that he was standing directly across the point of that submerged bar where he had found footing. We all knew what could and couldn't be done— now that he had shown us.

We didn't know how long that submerged gravel bar was, but we knew no matter which way it extended, Burlson's position was our reference point. The thing to do, now, was to get far enough across our tributary, upstream, so that when we got swept into the current we, too, would slam into that submerged bar. We would have to aim our mounts at 10 o'clock and move as far forward as possible until the current drove us down and into the bar at 3 o'clock. It was our only chance, but that's all we needed. Burlson had done it with his mount and two half-crazed packhorses. Surely, we could do it with only our mounts.

Rick and Gary were in the water in a moment. They held tight rein obliquely to their left and went several paces, struggling to keep their mounts on even keel until the current swirled them around, too, in a circle, flipped them on their sides, and hurled them adrift. The horses smashed against the bar, rolled around, and scampered out safely, dragging their water-spewing riders ashore.

The men were strung out on the island's bank, undoubtedly soaked and chilled to the bone with ice-cold rain pelting them, and under the blustering wind which now raged freely in the open channel. They had so positioned themselves in a line along the bank that each might get to us quickly if Jack and I did not get grounded with conviction. We were special cases and were reserved until the end.

I was to precede Jack because of poor, sweet, Sally. She was short-legged compared to the horses, and if any of the animals could be tossed over, belly up, and hurled down that current, the guys had all guessed that Sally would be one of them. Could she make that swirling, roiling current?

I tugged gently at the reins, then yanked, then kicked, and then cussed. Why that bloomin' female jackass! She got right to the edge of the water and stopped and I was not going to rummage for a slice of apple. Nor was she going to move, period, if you please! Of all the moments in eternity, this was the one she picked for her mule-headed stubbornness. In a flash of inspiration, I leaned over and, desperately trying to keep my voice calm and even, I began to sing softly:

"I had a mule, her name was Sal,
15 miles on the Erie Canal."

She moved! I'll be hornswoggled if she didn't move! I kept singing more boldly. Two mincing steps further into the fluid mix and the poor thing was up to her nostrils.

Icy water went over the saddle and stabbed at my sensitive parts, reflexively skyrocketing me out of the saddle and ending my song abruptly on a surprisingly good high C sharp. It was the wrong thing to do, even reflexively. I had learned that mules, lacking withers and being so round bellied, hold a saddle poorly. My sudden shifting of weight downward in the right stirrup spun the saddle hard, down, and around.

I managed to kick my left foot loose and, half afloat with my left leg across Sally's back, my right foot out of its stirrup, I wrapped my arms around her neck hugging her for dear life while water savagely tried to tear me loose. Several exploding cascades of muddy water broke over our heads.

I gagged and spewed a lot of it out, as my head emerged gasping for air. I was no longer in control of Sally's direction toward 10 o'clock, and I knew from here on out, it was up to her. I was helpless, barely clinging on, half submerged, trying to keep my head up. All I remember was telling her a couple of times, what a good girl she was, and I knew she would make it, doubting my prophecy all the while.

Well, she did make it! The next thing I knew, her mincing steps were scraping on the gravelled bottom and she clambered out.

From 10 o'clock, where I had pointed her, she emerged at 1 o'clock, or almost directly opposite the point of entry, instead of much further downstream at 3 o'clock where the sand bar was. She had not flipped or rolled over once! She had gone steady, beautiful, no panic, right on course without batting an eyelash, even with that displaced saddle interfering with her movements! I had the best crossing of all. They thought my Sally might not have made it, did they?

I will never know how that gorgeous, adorable, lovely creature did it! When I struggled off her, bone-chilled, soaking wet, and frigid-rigid, like a Fairbanks's icicle, she nudged me with her muzzle, wanting some lush grass. Grass? I would have given her 10 bushels of apples right then and there if I could have, so, instead, I planted a big smack on her muzzle and ambled to the men for Jack's reception. It was now his turn.

He had been riding the splayfoot nag (its panniers now in camp) with an hip impairment, causing it to walk with a limp. If we were to lose any of the horses, this one was most likely—the poor critter. We had left Jack until last so that all of us could be on the island, spread out in a line, just in case there might be something we could do if he washed past.

Jack was an instructor in water safety and a powerful swimmer. He urged the poor animal into the drink. She was totally helpless from the very first, immediately swept into the current, and hammered over to her side, throwing Jack free. He hung onto her mane trying to guide her and keep her from being swept away. They weren't even halfway across, yet.

He seemed reluctant to abandon the animal, even though Burlson kept yelling again and again, to let the beast go. Maybe Jack couldn't hear over the water's roar. We all started to yell and wave to let go of the animal, having accepted the inevitability of sacrificing her.

Jack finally let go, or the current tore them apart, and he attempted to swim the rest of that raging current without the animal's flotation. His mount, now completely helpless, flailed and thrashed in the water, then went belly up, her legs sticking stiffly skyward, and zoomed past me.

Scores of times, I had read about horses in similar circumstances, with their eyes rolling in terror, and now I was seeing such eyes, and I shall never forget them and the awful feeling of guilt for not being able to help her in the slightest.

The current swept Jack around a couple times and as his head emerged intermittently, trying desperately to stay aright, he hurtled toward the sand bar. As we watched him in fear, we had forgotten about the poor horse that had, moments earlier, submerged and disappeared from view. When we shifted attention to the bar hoping that Jack would smash into it, there was the horse flailing furiously, trying to right itself and scramble aground! Jack swept right into her, grabbed on to her mane, and both scrambled out. When they reentered the water heading for us on the island, we grabbed both, pulling them ashore before something else happened.

All of us made it and none of us were seriously injured. We were soaking wet and freezing rapidly. Rain and bitterly cold wind whistled and moaned over the gravel island like Halloween banshees. We were aware the worst was still ahead. In an hour or so the gravel island itself would be submerged if the Johnson rose just a bit higher, and it was certain that it would.

We stumbled to the tip of the island which stabbed into the juncture of our tributary and the Johnson. We saw the only bright spot, if it can be called that, in the throes of this ordeal. We had not hoped in vain. The tip of our island barely went past the rock wall on the opposite side that had blocked our way. Now we had our chance. From our present vantage point, the tributary was narrower and much less turbulent than before, but it was much deeper and twice as swift!

After it rushed past the rock wall, it hugged a gravel strip about 100 feet long and wide enough for a landing. It was instantly obvious to us, if that current did not dump us on the landing strip, it would sweep us into the juncture of the Johnson, which was Hell's own insane asylum at this point.

A million words would beggar description of the river gone into a maniacal rage. It rushed along at frightful speed, with roiling crests that looked mountainous, flecked with muddy foam whipped up by submerged obstacles. Above its roar, we could hear the booming cannonade of large, submerged boulders smashing into each other from the tremendous force of the current. Now and then, a crazily tossing tree trunk or bole careened by, and who knows how far inland it had been ripped out of the earth or swept off a bank.

We were numb and even terrified at Mamma Nature gone berserk. Our bodies shivered from cold and rain, reluctant to obey our wills, and our wills were on the verge of paralysis.

The channel may have looked like a sheet of glass compared to the river, but we agreed that Sally and the lame horse might not make it again—they would have to be roped across. This time, Burlson left the packhorses behind, headed up the bank a ways, then spurred his roan in, diagonally, slapping its withers and yahooing it, but the second the current got them, they were swept ahead like lightning. They stayed upright, however, and on course. I'll bet no group of sinners at a revival meeting prayed harder than we did. The current carried and dumped them on the gravel parking lot with barely a few yards to spare, beating the Johnson out of victory!

We couldn't hold back our shouts of wild joy. Rick and Gary grabbed a packhorse each and diagonally spurred their mounts into the current, which instantly whipped them to the channel's center and tumbled them out in a few moments where Burlson was waiting for them. Jack and I waited, shivering blue with cold, until the guys finally fished out a coil of nylon rope.

They tied a rock to it and Gary whirled it overhead, in larger and larger circles, and then heaved it across. It took some effort to get it aloft, but it fell several feet short. They knotted a length of clothesline to it and again it flew overhead. Jack and I were waiting for it, but we still couldn't reach it only inches from our grasp. We had gingerly tested the water's depth scarcely one foot in front of us, but it felt bottomless, and the current threatened to lift me off my feet, and probably would have, if Jack had not been holding me by my belt. Nor would the line stay put. No sooner did it hit the water, than the current ripped it out of reach and sight.

In the midst of the futile frenzy, a fickle muse heaped some high comedy on us. A couple of the horses on the other side panicked and raced to the river's edge, prancing, and whinnying with fear only to turn and stampede, throwing loose their saddle bags and packs, scattering their contents. We had to wait until they were retrieved and finally calmed down. Again the rope came at us, and again we couldn't connect.

I looked across in exasperation and couldn't believe my eyes. Of all times! Poor Burlson, with his trousers down, simply had to take time out. It looked so funny—I mean the improper timing and reckless procedure, I dare say. I wanted to laugh but couldn't because I was too cold and miserable. (I asked him later whether it was reflexive or volitional and when he said it was volitional just before the reflexes took over, we all laughed.)

The rope came whirling overhead again, and again we missed. This time, it was sweet Sally's turn to throw a nervous fit and head for land's end. It was my turn to chase her around, retrieve, and calm her down. Again the rope came sailing overhead and halfway across the men behind it let out a cry of dismay. In the excitement and mounting tension someone forgot to hold down the rope. It plummeted into the water and swept out of sight in an instant. Jack and I looked at each other silently asking, "Now what?"

Fanaticism is the redoubling of effort when the original goal is lost sight of, as Santayana said. It is also the redoubling of profanity, when it is known in advance it will not improve matters one bit. The boys on the other side, now a little warmer with the trees to their backs, were screaming lots of it, and loudly.

I lost my faith in the opposite shore and decided to take matters into my own hands. I waved to them that I was going to risk swimming for it, the water probably being warmer than the blustering wind and rain, anyway. But they waved their opposition frantically. They pointed to Sally, and I suddenly realized I'd forgotten all about little sweetheart. How could I even think of such a thing? How would she get across? Jack would have his hands full with his own problems.

Ah, yes, Jack. I'd forgotten him, too, in my freezing shivers. He was less than half my age, had three children, and the rest of his life ahead of him, if he survived. I thought of giving him the rope, if and when we got it, so he'd have first chance to cross. But if that rope did not hold, there went that brief young life full of promise. I would have to test it for myself, first.

There was nothing to do but wait, and when I looked at Sally I felt absolutely wretched for having forgotten her. Freezing, drowning, dying, or whatever, if we went, Sally and I would go together. No, I didn't feel like a noble martyr. I was just totally dubious about the manufacture of the new rope. How would it be made? With what?

I watched the frenzy on the shore across and started walking around in a circle trying to warm up. Those glorious guys were trying so hard for us by buckling their belts together, and hitching them to bridles, and to shorter pieces of rope, or whatever else they could find. Wet, cold leather was stiff in its flight pattern as it got airborne and came squiggling across like a shot duck and plummeted into the water like one. They tied a different rock to it and heaved, again. Jack barely snagged it, and I snagged him from the near over-lunge.

We were so cold and exhausted, we couldn't shout with joy, even if our hearts skipped a beat. My stiff, clumsy fingers would barely move, but I finally got one end of the rope tied to Sally's bridle. I was so clumsy trying to get into the saddle that Jack had to help me get up. Now, Sally just stood there. My heart wasn't in it, but I began to sing the Erie Canal again in a frozen, wavering voice. She stepped in without a tremor, and I think she knew better than I what was about to happen.

We zoomed out into mid-current, which squeezed us tightly together, and I saw Sally's head turned to the taut rope. I expected it to snap with its dozen lengths and knots when they pulled it against the full force of the current. I prepared myself for the worst and looked up to see the guys and blessed them for doing the right thing—they were running diagonally to prevent the full strain on the rope against the current and yet provide enough direction to Sally. No sooner had we started, then it was over, or so it seemed, due to the swiftness of the current. Incredibly, the rope held and we were out! I almost exploded with relief as the guys hugged and thumped me with congratulations, as though I had anything to do with it. Yep, it was warmer on this side of the channel.

We undid Sally's reins and hitched them to the rope for a safety margin. One of the guys tied on a stone and the rope sailed across, landing ashore on the first launch! We worried, watching Jack moving in slow motion to secure the rope to his animal.

It was understood the poor nag would go it alone since Jack would be more endangered on this trip with her than without. He finally got her hitched, slapped her flank a few times, then began to push. She balked. We yanked our rope, and she was finally dragged and pushed in. The current grabbed her immediately. Steadied with the rope, she was all right, kept her head up, then swirled sharply into her landing pad, and we tugged her scrambling hulk to safety.

The rope with its many makeshifts sections of freezing leather was losing its limber. It took another three heaves before we finally got it to land. A strange silence befell us. Good ol' Jack. He looked so forlorn and helpless as he fumbled again to wrap a loop of rein under his arms and then grab on to the lead end. He seemed paralyzed not wanting to do what he had to and not one of us failed to feel his agony; yet we seemed stupefied with the sense of awesome responsibility for his life. Then he bowed his head in what looked like prayer. I heard a muffled sob from one or two of the guys, and it brought me out of my paralysis. We were losing our nerve and Jack needed that like a hole in the heart.

I yelled at the top of my lungs, "Jack, you old horse thief—if you make this, you will live forever!" It was a calculated risk, no matter how tasteless or macabre it may have sounded, but as I had hoped, it worked! He lifted his head, and we could see his grin which gave us the feedback we needed. We yelled, we cussed, we cheered: "Are you ready, Jack? Do you really swim? What do you want, a heated swimming pool? Where do you think you are, in Hawaii?" and all sorts of nonsense. Maybe we cheered ourselves on more than Jack. It did the trick, and he waved he was coming in. We sobered instantly and braced ourselves. He took one step and disappeared from view.

In a split second, we were double-timing diagonally down that bank easing the tension on our rope. Our eyes were riveted on the spot where we guessed him to be so we could adjust accordingly. I thought I saw his head bob up twice, but it turned out to be the shadowy underside of waves. Jack did not surface one single time during that eternity when we were watching the end of the rope. I shall never forget the image of it tapering to a pinpointed end far away in that gray-brown swiftness, held taut, which is all that told us there was a submerged weight below.

We were hampered by the loss of his presence to our sight, and the feel of his weight did not tell us whether he was still alive or whether to speed up or slow down in our movements. No, I was too busy to look at how close he was to the edge of the insane Johnson, but the talk, later, settled down to 15 or 20 feet. Whatever it was, I know we all instinctively sensed the moment of heightened danger when we could have lost him.

Suddenly, his form emerged from the water in a fetal curl, looking like a Creature From the Black Lagoon movie. Was he alive? He sure was. He spluttered, gasped, choked, gagged, and gulped gallons of air as we dragged him ashore. Not one of us could have done what he did under water. He must have had lungs like a whale!

Our pent-up emotions exploded instantly. We hugged him, we hugged each other, we wept, we laughed, we yelled, we danced! For the past many minutes our talk was mostly profanity. Suddenly, quietly, one way or another, the word "God" became audible from each of us, no matter that none of us went to church and some of us had never gone. We just sensed a new invisible Presence. None of us were seriously injured, and we had survived against enormous odds, somehow, and "somehow" and Presence became one. I heard it often said during the war that there are no atheists in foxholes. Let it be said that there are none on the banks of demonic rivers, either.

We now became aware of our total exhaustion, the prolonged freezing cold and wet, and the frayed, unraveled nerves. We struggled into our saddles and headed home. Sally pushed ahead finding the trails. I was almost frozen solid to the saddle, deep in numbed thought, when Sally sidled through some stunted spruce to the edge of a long, narrow clearing and almost stepped on a rooting grizzly bear. It was a beauty, nearly 8 feet tall as it reared on its hind legs with sudden amazement.

I don't know which of us was more surprised, but I creaked upward in my saddle and said one word, "Scat!" I was too weary to tangle with him. He dropped instantly on all fours and took off like a shot, more scared out of his wits than I. Only when it was out of sight did my fear start to circulate between toes and scalp. What irony! I had already taken a grizzly bear long since, but it was nowhere near as big. I'd have given my eyeteeth for that bear at any other time, but not now, even if it were in season. Now, however, I was so cold and exhausted that I had no willpower for anything but sitting frozen to the saddle, waiting for Sally to get me to the Taj.

Somewhere along the line, Sally began to pick up her pace, and the pack horses broke into a trot. I knew we were almost there. No sight that I remembered in a long time was so welcome as that miserable, perforated tarp. Our first duty was to the animals. We got them off-saddled, hobbled, and fed. Too tired to make a good dinner, though we were hungry, a few tidbits sufficed. We took off our wet, cold, miserable clothes at long last, crawled into the cold sleeping bags, and before our bodies warmed them up, we were fast asleep. It was one of the soundest sleeps I've ever had.

When we awakened, it was still drizzling. It was tough to keep the fire going because everything was so wet, but we built a rack around it to dry out clothes and boots. We cleaned and oiled rifles, and I gave my brand new movie camera, I had bought just for this trip, a decent burial. It was hopelessly waterlogged. For the next 2 days, we nursed our bruises and recuperated, waiting for the drizzle to end. For 2 days the river roared past, but the booming of the submerged boulders became less frequent and more muted.

On the third day, the drizzle finally changed to light snow. Though the skies were still gray and soggy, we saddled up and packed enough grub and our tents to take a last stab at it. The river and all other waterways were receding. The deepest ones were now fordable. We could see the high-water marks, and yes, they had been 5 feet or more in some places. We cached everything at Alcatraz and took to the heights for skyline treasure.

Our sheep were still there and our three youngsters were so eager to go, that Burlson and I sent them off, after lecturing them on the absolute need to get above the critters on the opposite slope. Maybe we might get a shot at them from our side if they rushed down that slope. We watched for a couple hours as the guys forded the river and climbed the mountain, but it was obvious that impatience would defeat them, and it did. They cut across just below the sheep who got up and calmly walked away unseen. Burlson and I had wagered that this would happen and when it did, we roared with laughter.

We scouted our side of the slope and found a herd of 50 or more sheep, but they were all ewes and lambs. By the time we descended our slope, it was nearly dark, but somehow we made it to Alcatraz to find our stalwarts fast asleep; bless their hearts, they had set up a tent for us so we didn't have to fumble around in the dark.

Our time had run out and we dismantled the Taj in 5 minutes, packed, and headed back double time. We dropped down the slope of the plateau single file through patches of snow, but not before we each took a caribou for the table. When we reached the bottom, a wide but shallow stream, crystal clear and icy cold, invited us to drink. Dismounting, I joined the others lying prone with my face buried in the exhilaration of pure water and drank deeply. Then something lovely happened. Sally's hooves clattered on the gravel, and she sidled up to me, gave me a nudge to let me know she was there, shoved her muzzle into the water right beside me, and drank deeply. We had grown so close to each other in the misadventure which befell us that I'll never forget her.

When I got home, I threw myself into my basement project with nonstop frenzy and got the dirt bulldozed around the finished walls just in time. Shortly after, I had a professional society conference to attend. My flight was delayed, as usual, getting out of the airport in Fairbanks. Walking past the cocktail lounge, I saw someone waving at me. It was one of the top-level administrators at the university inviting me to join him for a drink.

We knew each other casually, and it seemed rude not to accept, though I had some doubts. He was reported to be another intellectual with contempt for "blood" sports and their devotees, but I joined him anyway. Surely, he was gentleman enough to be courteous about it. That hope turned out to be futile.

Soon enough, he steered the conversation to his kind of hunting, when he asked if I had gone for sheep this season. I knew what he was looking for and immediately went on full alert.

"Sure did," I said with a sudden interest in the ice cubes tinkling in my glass.

He came at me from a different angle. "I know," he said, "that hunting is supposed to be dangerous, but is it really—I mean, a sheep is such a shy, defenseless creature. Where's the danger"?

Well, here we go, I thought to myself. "The danger is in getting to that shy, defenseless creature," I said, as the magic mirror of my mind reflected men and horses fighting for their lives in savage currents.

"Well, I suppose it could be dangerous climbing up a mountain," he said.

"Well," I said, taking another sip of my highball, "the real danger is crossing rivers even before you get to the mountain. Sometimes, you worry about the mountain only after you fall off," I said, as the magic mirrors projected on the mind-screen a sheep hunt of a few years back when the forces of gravity nearly did me in on Mt. Sillyashin. At that point, I said, more to my drink than in answer to him, "We must separate the men from the boys on the preliminaries." It was just a routine idiom which had a meaning different in those days than it does now.

Of course, he had to hear it and put his own finger prints on it. He blushed (that was the first psychological complex triggered off which invited examination). It was his turn, and I knew what was coming.

"Does that really prove one's manhood," he asked?

Now, he gloated. He had me, he was sure. It was the most frequent, ridiculing, gratuitous insult that smug, urbane liberals used to increase the social distance between them and us Neanderthals, with whom they had to share society.

That's not what irked me, however. I was irked because it was

241

a retort lacking all originality, and what's worse, it belonged to left-wing urbane women intellectuals who used the cliche all the time. My host (he had invited me) was a clod at heart. Under pretext of cordiality, he had set up an ambush which I had hoped against. What's worse, he was a thief for stealing feminist women's verbal belongings, even as he hid behind their behavioral skirts.

He blanched, as my eyes bore through him. Just this once, this simpering cockroach needs his soul to be skewered, I thought. He had his Ph.D., but he had no savvy.

"May I assume," I asked, "that you urinate from a standing position? If so, shall that be construed as proving your manhood? Does a woman prove her womanhood by having a baby"? He blushed pomegranate red. "I trust you'll forgive me," I said, "but I'm not trying to be vulgar. Merely illustrative, if you catch my meaning," borrowing one of his favorite catchall expressions. It escaped him that what is done naturally as a function of the male sex needs no proving, merely doing what needs to be done.

While he was still trying to think of a clever comeback, I asked, "By the way, can you shoot?"

I knew I would now be accused of trying to prove my manhood again, with such a high-powered, macho, reference to the "violence" of firearms, but mercifully enough, the loudspeakers announced the boarding for our flight.

"I insist," I said, pushing his money back and paying for the drinks. Maybe he would not think that too macho a gesture. All the way to my seat, I berated myself. A contest won too easily has no honor in it. I felt degraded. Besides, it had spoiled my enjoyment of a fine drink.

A year later, almost to the day, Burlson phoned me from Big Delta. Would I like to hunt, at the same place again for the sheep that got away last year? Only Mountain Man Gary would go with us, and a young man named Richard, who would not hunt, but was to be our wrangler and the camp's major domo. How could I refuse, with such improved odds to boot?

When I got to the ranch, I headed for the corral and there was sweet Sally. When she saw me, she came over immediately. I gave her a hug of gratitude for all she had brought me through last year.

I think the look in her eyes was asking, "Have you brought me a present?" I had, so I gave her two apples.

We finally got to the campsite where the Hotel Taj had been, pitched a large sheet of heavy plastic for the new Taj, cached our main supplies, and headed for Alcatraz. All along the way were signs of last year's flood. Some landmarks had completely disappeared, and new ones had been made.

From Alcatraz, Richard returned to the Taj with the horses and Sally. We stuffed our packs with everything we would need for 4 or 5 days, hunting each day and proceeding the following day from where we had stopped. There would be no returning each nightfall to the same fly camp. Now, we could really cover territory.

We took a slightly different route and came to a huge ice cavern at the base of the glacier with an opening that looked like fractured Ming jade, from which there spewed thick, muddy, icy water. From the top of the cavern, there oozed out a slow trickle of gravel with an eerie, grating sound plunging down into the muck. It was the labor pains giving birth to the waters of the Johnson.

We were surrounded by glacier, moraine, expanses of orange-colored snow (from the soil's iron oxide), and huge, grotesquely eroded boulders. Mamma Nature had long since thrown a temper tantrum here. Vistas were unequaled in their beauty and grandeur.

We went further and climbed up a steep slope to our first camp, and found our rams on the far slope. The following day, we scouted our side of the mountain to make sure there were no sheep closer to home. There were, but the wrong kind—nothing but ewes and lambs.

Next day took us through some of the most glorious country I'd seen in Alaska, and what's more, the sun came out. We climbed down our slope and crossed the valley with its creeks carving their escape routes through blue-striated ice banks. We rested at a glistening, tumultuous waterfall and climbed the steep slope along its side. There was good cover behind a long barricade of rocks, but soon it ran out, and we still had a couple thousand feet to climb. Trouble was, the sheep were resting on a cantilevered ledge jutting into space, with better than a 180° visibility from 4,000 feet. Smart sheep, they were; they could have seen a mosquito in our camp 2 miles away. My bet was they had been watching us since early morning.

There was now a lively discussion as to the best way to go. I insisted on climbing above them for a descent from the back, even though it was a much more treacherous and difficult climb. In fact, this hunt would succeed or fail in the next 15 minutes—no matter how far or near we got to them. The guys finally agreed.

We had climbed above, crawled down, and reached a grassy knoll. The rams were below us and could not be seen under a ledge. Soon, they would start to feed and move upward toward us, so we took our positions behind large boulders to wait. Two young rams, heretofore unseen, appeared and began grazing and moving upward.

I saw my comrades could not see them, due to their positions. One of the young rams heard something and froze in his tracks. I was well hidden. I waved my buddies down. In a few minutes, the ram went back to his grazing without sounding the alarm to his kin on the ledge below, but he was wary without doubt.

I crawled to my buddies and told them about the bad luck. Now, we could not wait out the big rams to get into our view, because the young rams would get to us first and blow the whistle. We had not seen them until just a few moments ago. I had spotted them with great good luck.

There were gullies on either side of us and, if our trophies broke from their watch tower, they would run up either gully to higher ground. The strategy was clear, so we drew lots. Burlson got the left, Gary the right. They would climb down to the level of the sheep and wait. I drew the middle slot and didn't know what I'd do, because the ledge ran out in front of me, still hiding our prizes from my view.

We synchronized watches. I was to give them a 5-minute head start to let them find their positions on either side, so I wouldn't spook the young feeders directly below us. I was on my own after the first shot. It didn't make much difference where I moved, because the odds were the greatest against me in any direction.

Two minutes hadn't gone by when, to my left a rifle boomed. Burlson, in the throes of total euphoria, began yelling, "I got him, I got him, a beautiful ram!"

Well, there went our strategy. It turned out the rams had either spotted Gary or got spooked by the little rams and bolted right into Burlson. There was nothing else for him to do but fire and right handsomely, at that.

As for me, oh, goody gum-balls! My guess was the other two rams would have spun around abruptly and charged back into Gary's direction, so I took off full speed for the gully, not seeing Gary anywhere. I hadn't gone 50 feet when, from down below, Burlson shouted, "This way, for Pete's sake, hurry, this way!"

I spun around adroitly, and for Pete's sake, I hurried. What a comedy on that 45° treacherous slope! I moved full-speed ahead, but tilted all the way like Pisa's Leaning Tower. A later consensus showed it to be a 150-yard sprint, but somewhere along the line, I felt a sharp ping on my lower left leg, but paid it no attention. Then, I saw the two rams ahead and below me, running uphill behind the sloping edge of the gully.

I don't know whether I had reflexively chosen the huge flat slab of rock, or if it had stopped me cold in my tracks, but I became aware of lying around it with my body twisted at a right angle, my lungs heaving desperately, while I tried to hold the rifle steady to find them in my scope.

I found the two rams about 300 yards away, charging up that gully, full-speed ahead, side by side. All that was visible were their heads and necks above the rocky rim and empty skyline behind them.

Actually, it was an easy decision, no matter how tough the shot. A hit anywhere on the neck was an instant kill, or it was a clean and total miss. I was trying out a new Weatherby .300, zeroed in at 300 yards, over-gunned, perhaps, but trajectoried flat enough. So, I elevated the sights and squeezed. Of course, it was a clean miss. Since I saw no puff of dust, nor heard the sound of rock being hit, I assumed I had overshot. Well, I had almost grasped my moment of glory, but lost. So, what else is new with the hunter's roulette wheel?

Then, the unexpected happened, as it always does on any hunt. Instead of dropping below the rim and into the slope of the gully to disappear forever, as I expected, they leaped to the top of the stony rim on hard ground for better footing than the loose shale in the gully.

They were one of the most gorgeous sights I have ever seen—now in full view, neck and neck, their shoulders bunching, legs pumping with powerful thrusts, racing neatly, swiftly, eternally. For an instant, there flashed through my mind's eye the stately rows of sacred stone rams I had seen on a half dozen trips at the main entrance to the Temple of Karnak in Egypt, . I fully expected to see my sacred rams with a burnished golden chariot behind them carrying some resplendent pharaoh to his moment of glory. What followed may leave the reader with a big dose of skepticism, and I can't blame him. I would disbelieve it, if I hadn't experienced it myself. How can I deny it with a couple of witnesses to boot?

Those rams were somewhere between 300 and 400 hundred yards away at a somewhat higher elevation, but so clearly outlined against the skyline that every instinct in me said to go for it. I held a little lower this time and squeezed, the rifle boomed, and the one on the near side stopped. When I got the scope back on, the other ram seemed to be leaning against him, with both their rear ends pointing at me, standing motionless, but ready to plunge into the gully.

Through my mind flashed an image of elephants, which seemed so odd. I was pretty sure I had scored, but frankly it didn't look like it. I should have fired again, but didn't want to risk forcing them over the rim, feeling sure I could get closer for the telling shot in case I had scored a hit.

By the time I got to my feet, or tried to, whatever breath I had was knocked out of me, and the rams disappeared down the slope. A sharp jolt of pain stabbed through my lower leg, but this was no time for a clinical examination.

I limped as far forward as I could and rued my earlier decision not to shoot for fear of scaring them away. Scared or not, they were down and out of sight, anyway. I hobbled some more, until I got to a point where I could see lower down the gully and had to flop down to relieve the pressure on my leg, which was now quite painful.

A couple minutes or so seemed like hours, until a ram appeared, staggering slowly down the wash of shale, rocks, and boulders. When I got my scope on him again, my heart nearly burst with exultation. My shot had gone true! A splash of crimson was visible below his left shoulder. But then the anguish set in. With a hit like that in the boiler room, how come he hadn't gone down, and stayed down? Where was his buddy? He must have gotten away to the top of the slope.

It was a long shot, maybe 500 yards or better, and if the ram was not wounded, requiring the needed mercy-shot, the traditional misericordia, nothing could have justified it with those odds, but I squeezed trigger and missed. Watching that ram struggle so valiantly to keep going tore my heart to shreds. Was he starting to feel his pain, which I could not end for him? Compulsively, I took another quick shot and hit him, poorly, and still he didn't drop. Now I hated myself for botching the job, as I hurriedly reloaded and then, to my total surprise, I heard a rifle boom higher and further ahead on the slope.

It was Gary who had finally gotten there, now lying prone on a ledge. He quickly fired a couple more shots. Why is he shooting at my ram, I asked myself? It was my responsibility to finish what

I had started. I took another shot, missed, and Gary took several shots rapidly, obviously reloading in between. I was irked at his interference, but maybe he was trying to put that poor animal out of its misery to help me. Now, I started hoping that he would do what I couldn't. I took another shot and gave up, when he fired again. Finally, that poor ram staggered down some more, his legs buckled, he fought gravity for a moment, fell to his side, and rolled down a few feet until a large boulder stopped him. I heaved a sigh of relief and sadness.

Soon, Gary joined me asking me what in blazes I was doing shooting at his ram. I asked him why he was shooting at my ram. Burlson joined us. He insisted he had seen me hit the ram first, before Gary ever showed up and asked him if he had seen the other ram. There was no other ram, Gary insisted. The first and only one he had seen was right down there, with at least two bullet holes in his rear end. He got to the bottom of things, of course, by refusing to believe I had scored a probable heart shot. I needed a little more rest before I went down that slope to check things out.

In the meanwhile, Burlson had gone up a little higher, and back to where he'd been when he saw my first connecting shot. In a few moments, he shouted, "Hey, fellas, there's a ram up here."

Gary leaped forward, while I dragged myself along using my rifle as a crutch. When we got there, sure enough, there was a beautiful ram with decent horns at about 38 inches, and a hair better than full curls. He was slumped against a boulder, laying on his left side with a bullet hole below his right shoulder.

"Gary, you hit him right in the pump. Congratulations on a beautiful shot and a fine ram," I said, wishing it were mine.

He held firm and insisted that he wanted only his sheep, which he knew he'd hit in the hind end, and it was dead down below. But the sheep at our feet was not mine because I knew mine was hit on the left side, and that was the one down below. Gary said we'd settle this right now, bet me $10 I was wrong, and took off, leaving me to limp behind.   When we got to the other ram down in the shale, Gary proudly pointed to two bullet holes in the butt end. "Just like I told you," he said, gloating.

"Yeah, you're right," I said, "now turn him over, will you?" He did, and I said, "Just like I told you." There was a bullet hole on the left side, right in the boiler room, and another one further back, to the left of the spine. Now, I gloated. In fact, I was almost ready to brag about my better-than-500-yard shot, when suddenly it hit me looking at that ram, turned over.

"Hey, wait a minute," I shouted, and started to limp double time back to the first ram. Why hadn't any of us thought of it before, I asked myself and my heart was pounding with wild anticipation. It took some doing with my leg refusing to bear my weight and movement. I managed to turn that ram over. There it was, as I had suspected and hoped! There was a neat hole on the left side, right through the pump station. Burlson showed up, and in a few minutes so did Gary. We pieced it together.

The wound on the right side, which we first saw, was not the entrance hole, but the exit hole. I had hit my ram beautifully, right in the pump, and he had toppled over dead instantly. The Nozzler bullet had plowed through and entered the left side of the other ram, mortally wounding him.

The wounded ram ran and staggered down slope, and when he emerged into view, naturally I thought it was the first ram, since the splatter of blood was on the left side, appearing just about where I had aimed. I remembered the instant image though my scope when I thought of elephants. For a second, it had appeared as though the second ram was trying to hold up my ram. The image of elephants had flashed in my mind because one of my boyhood heroes, Carl Akeley, the great hunter-naturalist and artist who sculpted elephants helping a wounded comrade, had made the association. I had heard of caribou doing this, too.

I wrongly thought the ram was propping up his comrade when, in fact, I had seen my ram toppling against his comrade in his death fall during that split second. I had killed two rams with a single bullet. They died minutes apart. I had anguished and berated myself for bad shooting on the second ram when, in fact, I had made one of the most sensational shots of my hunting career in bringing down the first ram!

Gary felt badly about the second ram, since he had not drawn first blood, but both of us had shot needlessly. We did not know how fatally the ram had been wounded at the outset. He would have died, shortly. Hopefully, we had lessened his suffering even a little.

We consoled Gary with the fact that he had shot well, indeed, and had a beautiful trophy. We caped the hides, boned the meat, and tied them to our packboards. The guys took off ahead of me, and I barely limped, in great pain, using my rifle as a crutch. Halfway down the slope, there they were sprawled out for a rest, waiting for me. They gave me my orders. I was to leave my pack there and they would come for it in the morning. They would carry their packs to the base of our slope across the valley and cache them there.

"I'll take your rifle," Burlson said, grabbing it out my of my hand. I objected vehemently. "Do it our way, or we carry you down, if we have to knock you out to do it," Gary said.

There were two of them, and either one was more than enough just now. I lost my usual zest for a challenge and said the worst dishonor for any disabled hunter was to walk out and have someone else carry his rifle. They smiled at each other, and Burlson handed my rifle back. Next, I would carry their jackets, rifles, extra ammo, and canteens, since they were carrying real weight. They handed me their gear, and I lashed it to my pack-board, leaving meat, cape, and horns. Tomorrow was another day.

When we got to the base of our slope, they made me climb up first. By the time I reached our tent, I was long since finished. A little way from the tent there was a bank of slush and rotting snow. I went there and examined my leg. There was an asteroidal tear in the flesh right over the tibia, around which was a sickening swell of hematoma already turned black and blue. I didn't think there was a fracture, although it hurt like one, so I packed handfuls of slush around the wound, now swollen like a balloon. It helped. So did the emergency codeine in my medical kit. I slept fitfully despite it.

We were up early in the morning, and the guys returned for the rest of the meat, horns, and capes we'd left behind. When they got back, they halloed from below, and I tossed them all the food we had left, except for a couple packets of dehydrated stuff for myself. Although they had a long, tough haul before them, they took much of the meat, and covered the rest with a tarp. I crawled up the slope in back of our tent for a better look and waved them good-bye when they reached a bend in the trail.

The sky was overcast, and a good wind was blowing across the slope. Marmots would suddenly appear, stand up rigidly, looking like tenpins in a bowling alley, whistle, and disappear as quickly as they had come. The opposite slope sprawled out with exquisite grandeur, and I could barely make out the ledge where we had spotted our sheep. The entire scene looked like what I hoped to be eternity.

Then, what captured my attention, were the tiny yellow flow-ers at my feet where the snow had melted. They looked like little butter cups, their heads bowed, stalks vibrating tautly, roots clinging to dear life against the onslaught of the winds. They were beautiful, reminding me of my wife, and I knew how much I missed her. I plucked a few of them, folded them gently in tissue, and put them in my wallet. It wasn't much, but it would be my gift to her saying that she had been with me in spirit this day, that I never forget her no matter what, and that I loved her more than anything else in this world—even more than my own life.

When I awoke shortly after midnight, the winds had picked up to a raging storm. One of the tent poles had snapped. The nylon was flapping and lurching furiously, trying to tear loose from its moorings like an ancient pterodactyl. I tried to mend the broken pole to stabilize the tent before it blew off the mountain, but to no avail. I removed the other pole, flattened the nylon, placed rocks around the edges, and crawled underneath. Soon, the rain started pelting me in the face and soaking through the nylon. I dragged my sleeping bag up against the bank, which provided a little shelter, and slept fitfully 'til early morning.

When dawn tried to break through the overcast clouds, the rain had stopped. First things first. I went to the snow bank and again wrapped my leg in ice-cold slush. Several heated canteen cups full of snow were needed for enough water in which to boil the last packet of soup mix, but I ate it half cooked—the cannister of fuel ran out. Then I read a western the guys had left behind, and by 12 noon, I finished it and began to fidget. If I went down the slope for some meat and firewood, I'd never climb up again on my bad leg, now. The tent was useless. Weather toward the Taj had looked bad since yesterday. Maybe the guys didn't make it to camp. Maybe I'd better get down and fend for myself.

I waited until 3 o'clock and went nuts just sitting and gazing at the pile of meat down below. Maybe with roast lamb in me, I might even make it to Alcatraz; who knows? I struck camp, packed everything, and was ready for my journey down the slope. I was giving my leg one last dose of ice therapy when a halloo sounded from below. How my spirits soared! Far down the trail were Gary and Richard, the wrangler.

Gary, bless his soul, had brought a fine, newly-cut staff to help me walk. They had also brought grub and their sleeping bags. We would stay overnight for an early start for Alcatraz in the morning, where the horses were waiting. Larry related the happenings on their trek back, yesterday. Past Alcatraz, they walked away from the storm, reached the Hotel Taj, roasted delicious sheep, and thought of me often. This part of the story he repeated several times and kept asking, "What did you have for dinner?" He thought it was really funny.

First, the tent. We toiled like tigers, tearing big rocks out of the ground, stacking them atop each other to the height of the tent's peak, and tied it to the top rock in lieu of the pole. I ate heartily that night. Early next morning, we struck camp, climbed down the slope, and made two big loads of meat, capes, and horns for Gary and Richard. My pack was as high as a skyscraper with all the sleeping bags, tent, and gear, but compared to the weight of the other packs, it put me in the bantamweight division. What saved me was the ice-cold creek I walked in for much of the way. It numbed the pain in my leg, and the staff Gary had cut for me was a great help. I caught up to them at Alcatraz, and there was dear sweet Sally! As they say in the old country, I had finally reached my father's house; from here on out, it was easy going.

No hunt ever ends, and it was little more than a year later when it came alive again in the midst of tragedy. Our marriage fell apart and ended in divorce. It was in the midst of a grief nearly destroying my sanity, when I chanced on the little flowers I had gathered on the mountain. They were tossed into a box of odds and ends she'd left behind. Like my shattered love, they, too, were faded and crumpled—nothing in this world is forever. They seemed as irrelevant as my life. They taunted me in my agony, as I wandered lost in the wilderness of my soul where the medieval mystic said was God's abode. I finally understood why the real pearl of great price is not of this world.

My ram was proudly displayed, but it always brought back painful memories of that hunt's aftermath. My antidote for a heart broken by a marriage ending in agony, was another hunt. I took another ram a few years later, a much better one, which finally dampened the bad memories. But nothing went wrong in that hunt, so there's nothing to write about.

It occurred to me that I could not be a hunter and husband at the same time , so I swore off marriage, or so I thought. Only then did the woman come into my life who is the promise fulfilled that true love is forever, but only if angels lead the way. What's more, she knows that I would give up hunting for her, but she has never asked.

Reflections

Oddly enough, the thing loitering my mind from that first sheep hunt was the irony of its aftermath. We nearly lost our lives, yet my airport encountered colleague, who knew nothing about the hunt, classified it as an ego trip or, as he put it, an exercise in manhood proving. Was that what we had chosen to do in the maelstrom of the raging Johnson? I had heard that accusation often by many, and always chuckled at its absurdity, dismissing it. As the antihunting movement gathered steam, the charge was heard more frequently, and I realized it became a standard technique in stigmatizing hunters. That was the preview of coming attractions.

I could find nothing in current periodical literature to rebut the serious implications of that charge. Though it came up often in bull sessions among fellow hunters, we all teased each other with its nonsense. Truth is, we had no answers to combat the obvious intent. Ridicule is one of several techniques to build negative stereotypes for informal social control. When public opinion is created, then controls become more formal and on their way to legalization. I needed to get serious in understanding what lay ahead, so back to the drawing board I went to tie loose ends.

In polite conversation, the main charge leveled against the

hunter is that his ego is trying to prove his manhood. To prove something is to justify it. Except for an insane tyrant, to whom on this earth does any man have to justify himself for being a man? Or a woman, a woman? Does any one hear the charge, "She's trying to prove her womanhood because she had a baby?" If the hunter is trying to prove his manhood, because he hunts, then why?

Subconsciously, it is asserted, he is supposed to have serious doubts and inferiority feelings about his masculinity, and he compensates for them by acting in the most masculine or macho manner that has been around for millennia—sport hunting. Hence, killing for "sport" or "fun" is a sadistic, hostile, aggressive, compensatory behavior for mental causes that are not corrected, but merely disguised by hunting. The cause persists, which is why it is "neurotic, psychotic, or abnormal" behavior. A characteristic attribute of liberal intellect is its skepticism, and then its cynicism, resulting from a suspicious and untrusting nature, even as it always boasts of trusting people. Since it assumes a superior intelligence, it always knows an honest answer is not to be taken at face value. Hence, it must be analyzed for its real, secret, unconscious meaning, since people (especially hunters) have intellects arrested by outmoded tradition. Therefore, they are too ignorant to know real truth, or are liars for hiding it.

At heart, liberals are amateur psychologists and antihunters are Freudian psychoanalysts. They "know" what's really going on in the hunter's mind and in his macho charade. They ask a hunter why he hunts, and they get the honest answer, "Because I want a trophy that symbolizes one of the greatest of human experiences." The interrogators do not want the meaning of his answer. They want to discover the subconscious motives and find it instantly: "Ah, I see. What you really mean is that . . ." and a diagnosis follows and displaces intelligent dialogue.

An obvious question arises—to whom is the hunter trying to prove his manhood? To himself? But he is not a man because he hunts; he hunts because he is a man and already knows what needs no proof. If one compensates for something absent, why should one compensate for that thing when it is present? Since he is a man, and not a woman or a pygmy elephant, anything he does is an automatic and needless justification of his manhood. Therefore, he enjoys his full-course, 16-ounce steak dinner (medium rare), not because he loves steak, but because he is "proving his manhood."

Or compensating for his neurotic guilt because, subconsciously, he is a vegetarian.

Does the hunter prove his manhood to antihunters who are on the lookout for his scalp? If anything, he stays as far away from their voracity as he can, because his hunter's instinct tells him he will never get fair chase from them. Does the stranger think he is so important that the hunter finds him worth the effort to justify his manhood—to a stranger? The stranger is responding to the projection of his own vanities and prejudices, not the hunter's intent. What the hunter says and writes are for the hunting fraternity.

Is he, then, trying to impress them when he knows he wouldn't last 5 minutes before experienced and seasoned confreres who see through his "macho charade?" Sport hunting has been around for some 4,000 years in all kinds of civilizations and cultures with a widely diverse male royalty on the hunting trail. Was it all neurosis showing off its manhood? If so, what did they not have in power, wealth, status, or anything else which needed compensation?

From the beginning of sport hunting, there have been its critics, but never with a social or political antihunting movement. There is such a movement today, and moral objections of yesteryear have been transferred to psychological and political ones today. Ancient right or wrong about hunting is now about the "flawed" human nature of the hunter, who has become a symbol of evil and villainy.

The average citizen, who makes the charge of manhood proving, probably hasn't the slightest idea of how and why that charge came into being. He simply picks it up from social wreckage left in the wake of the 1960s counterculture activism and the sexual revolution it spawned that is wrecking the nation today.

As a hunter, caught in this wreckage, I sensed how my humanity had become an evil target, when traditionally my avocation had been so time-honored. I knew many hunters who felt the same way. While there are many articles today indicating the hunter's awareness that he is under fire, I see no systematic explanation of some critical aspects of the problem.

Undoubtedly, there will be many answers to come, but here I give my own. What follows, in the rest of this chapter, tries tying together many loose ends that are part of a complex puzzle. It cannot be understood with superficial skimming. It needs digging into.

Moral collapse and cultural decline of our nation today has many causes, but it is largely the result of liberal sexual revolution based on theories of its intellectual pioneer, Sigmund Freud. Objection to hunting as an aggressive, hostile, and sadistic manhood-proving scenario is based on his theories which antihunters, particularly, and liberals, generally, resort to because they, like Freud, see the world as a cosmic orgasm. No fooling. Wilhelm Reich, of the psychoanalytic school (about whom more later), sees the Milky Way, with its two comma-like galaxies juxtaposed one atop the other as a "natural" law of energy-release duplicated in human oral sex! After that, nothing said about the hunter is outrageous.

In all fairness to Freud, he said nothing, that I know of, about hunting as a form of human behavior or about the hunter as a personality type. But his psychosexual theories about human nature, masculinity, and femininity, culture and civilization, are so far-ranging they easily provided America's liberal intelligentsia with the pseudo-scientific basis for labeling the hunter as a manhood-proving, compensating psycho. There are no other psychodynamic theories, systematic enough to explain it.

Nowadays, it is easy to point out fallacies and errors in Freud's theories with new, factual discoveries of molecular biology and neuroendocrinology. At the same time, there are emerging some key works showing that Dr. Freud doctored his famous case histories, and he deliberately lied about some facts. A good deal of his scientific theorizing was concocted fantasies from his cocaine addiction and illicit sexual behavior.

In my view, however, the most crucial fact of all is a tiny scrap of evidence, the significance of which has yet to be researched. He said to a colleague, "Do you know that I am the Devil? All my life, I have had to play the Devil in order that others would be able to build the most beautiful cathedral with the materials I produced."[1]

He was an atheist who turned against the faith of his Jewish fathers and blamed Christian doctrine for anti-Semitism. His doctrines of anti-Christianism remained disguised as scientific investigation of human sexuality. The Devil, in both Judaism and Christianity, was the supreme tempter leading the faithful astray, starting with the Garden of Eden. The "most beautiful cathedral" will obviously replace the Christian one that exists and the "materials" he "produced for others" (like Reich) were his psychosexual theories that others would use for their deviltry. The results are all around us today.

Among others who helped him get started were six of his

colleagues, known as the Secret Six, who came complete with secret signet rings, passwords, and a revolutionary philosophy secretly aiming to destroy the moral basis for the value system of Western civilization. No great scientist like Darwin, to whom Freud has been compared, ever used his scientific theories with such deliberate intent. But Freud did, when he systematically asserted that religion, with its search for the sacred and assertion of God's existence and authority, was a neurotic projection of "infantile illusions" that repressed the sexual drive. Ultimately to him, all neurosis and mental illness was the result of sexual repression.

However, if religion is a neurosis, how do we explain its persistence in every known culture, from primitive to civilized, without damning all humanity? If culture is the result of sexual repression (as he claimed), how do we explain religious practices that sanctified the most libertine and perverse sexual excesses Freud himself thought were natural instead of sinful, like bisexuality, for example, in which he had more than a scientific interest? The trouble is many of Freud's critical concepts cannot be proven scientifically, although he speaks in the name of science. Therefore, he believes in their truth or correctness as an act of faith. The blasphemer makes a religion of his blasphemy.

The devil in Freud's convoluted theories rests on one single keystone. Remove that and the whole arch comes tumbling down. It is the Oedipal complex, named after the Greek mythological figure who killed his father and married his mother, unwittingly, in both cases. According to Freud's theory, the male child develops his first sexual urges toward his mother, who was his first source of physical contact and pleasurable sensations. But he is afraid his secret will be discovered by the father.

Jealous at the father's possession of his mother as a sex object and afraid of being castrated by him if found out, the boy develops a secret desire to murder his father. This is, supposedly, the unconscious origin of all hatred, aggression, guilt, and anxiety in the boy. The cause of neurosis is unresolved sexual repression enforced by the authority of the father sanctioned by his religious code of morality. If sexual or libidinal drive is not transferred to a different sex object (made difficult by moral inhibitions), it carries into adulthood and produces certain abnormal behaviors.

Satanic Sigmund's chief accomplishment was not his theoretical fantasies, but the subtle transfer he made from moral basis of right and wrong behavior to a clinical basis of normal and abnormal behavior. Of course, only he and his followers could determine what that was. An obscure fantastic dogma, known to a handful of nihilists, became the revolutionary program in this country by equating lust with love, depravity with delight, and salacity with sex. It was received with open arms by secular humanists and liberals who found just the weapon they needed for their ongoing battle against the normative status quo. Even Christian theologians, at odds with each other's orthodoxies, joined the enemy for their own suicide.

Who would argue against free sex with its promise to wipe out all human unhappiness, misery, and neuroses? There had been free-sex advocates for centuries, but none had provided a "scientific" basis for it as the grounds of "mental health." There were fully intended consequences to all this across the entire social system by the 1930s when the cognoscenti began to popularize Freud. I will give only two necessary examples.

Wilhelm Reich was a renegade Freudian, but in 1936, his German edition of what was translated as *The Sexual Revolution* put Freudian theory in the service of Marx and Engels, who some half century earlier had tagged capitalism, Christianity, and the traditional family as enemies of the collectivist state. Reich lambasted all three and made an amazing "discovery." The dominating father in control of the traditional family's sexual morality was the origin of Fascism, which, politically structured, was the basis for all social inequality. He refused to see the Russian Communist *nomenklatura*.

He urged destruction of the husband's status over his wife and the sexual liberation of his daughters. With earlier and earlier childhood sex education today, not one teacher of it in 10,000 knows where his or her ideas came from. Reich got what he wanted—millions of younger and younger teenage mothers with illegitimate births costing government (the taxpayer) astronomical sums for welfare. The family has been devastated as the basic social unit, and myriad social problems of drugs, crime, and depravity plague our society. The new nihilism destabilizing our society, gained respectability before Reich died insane from ravages of tertiary syphilis.

By 1944, Theodore Adorno, another Freudian and a Marxist, fled to this country, after Hitler threw him out of Germany. He masterminded what is really a spurious bit of left wing propaganda under the guise of a 1950 scientific study, *The Authoritarian Personality*. His California "F" scale ("F" for Fascist) allegedly measured potential Fascist attitudes resulting from "emotionally disturbed personalities" to begin with. What caused the emotional disturbances? Sexual neurosis, and here Adorno parades Freud's theories all over the political landscape.

Who is the Authoritarian personality? He is essentially Christian, patriotic, domineering, sexually repressed, paranoid, cold-blooded, unfriendly, and traditionalist who is a nativist American (which in those days meant the descendent of the original, white European Anglo-Saxon immigrants), and was anti-Semitic and racist to boot. This covered a lot of ground. Adorno then sneaks in his left hook. Based on his paradigm, he then concludes, without any scientific verification, that all political conservatives are neurotic pre-Fascists ready to become jack-booted, storm trooping *Sturm Abteilungen*. These are, of course, the bad guys, designated as Authoritarian Personalities who are all those critical of American liberalism. (Hang on, please. We are getting close to the hunter.)

Were there any good guys? Of course. He establishes this by implication—they are liberal Democratic Personalities. In his book of 970 pages, he devotes only 2½ pages to the "genuine liberal" and the rest is chock full of goodies about the authoritarians. But he does not scientifically establish the differences between genuine liberals and artificial ones, or between them and the authoritarians. He confidently assumes that those opposed to the political right are the good guys on the political left who are free from religious, patriotic, and sexual neuroses; they are full of compassion, humanity and goodness. (Hang on please, we are getting close to the antihunters.)

He overlooks two serious considerations which I do not think are simple errors in methodology. They are deliberate ideological distortions. First, the true opposite of authoritarian is permissive, not liberal or democratic. One of the worst authoritarianisms in human history came from the political left wing of Lenin and Stalin, both of whom boasted they had the "true" democracy. Every tyrannical horror that Adorno finds in right wing authoritarianism has its equivalence in the political left wing. It is not the exclusive property of either side, but a commonality of both.

Secondly, if such a thing as his "Genuine Liberal" or Democratic Personality existed as the opposite to the "F" Scale Authoritarian, then he was obligated to develop a California "L" or "D" Scale to test for Liberal or Democratic Personality traits and demonstrate differences between them and the authoritarians. He was not entitled to assume this difference and create his political fiction that political conservatives are pre-Fascists, but political liberals are not pre-Communists. But that "scientific" conclusion is why the liberal left assumes a danger to American "democracy" will come from the political right. Five minutes after President Kennedy's assassination, every telecasting pundit jumped to the conclusion that it had to be the work of a right wing Fascist. Surprise! Surprise! The assassin, Lee Harvey Oswald, turned out to be a dyed in the wool Communist to the chagrin of the liberal left wing telecasters long since indoctrinated by Adorno's theories.

Those theories did two things: they covered up the antidemocratic, totalitarian tyranny from the left and for 40 years, they created a paranoid fear that right-wing Nazis are behind every antiliberal criticism which is equated with anti-Semitism. That alone was enough to stifle all legitimate discussion for fear of being labeled anti-Semitic. The liberal left could continue its Marxist-Freudian domination of higher education from whence all the rest derived.

Permissiveness, the widely touted philosophy of new child-rearing theories, was already in vogue and drawing sharp criticism for its real anti-family message. Had Adorno used that concept in its obvious political context (anti-familism was a cornerstone of Marxist philosophy), he would have immediately invited the question: what is it you political permissivists want permitted—other than the counter-cultural overthrow of American society? Then Adorno's incredible secret would have been revealed to which I shall get in a moment.

He used the words "democratic" and "liberal" because of their respectable aura which is not questioned too closely lest the many sins they cover be discovered. What average American in reverential awe of democracy would suspect what Adorno was really up to? Most of the population does not even know that the Founding Fathers of this nation had their own revulsion of democracy. The word does not even appear in the original documents on which our nation was founded because what the founders gave us was not democracy but a constitutional republic—a concept which political scientists avoid like the plague.

Adorno, one way or another, became required reading in most of required social science courses for captive undergraduates. We have had two or three generations of young students exposed to this who are today's adult voters and liberal intelligentsia in charge of the nation's affairs.

Students are not really given a choice. They are seduced, coerced, or brain washed into identifying with the Democratic Personality, whatever that is, because it's easily done. That's the popular and sexually rewarding thing to do on campus and forever after. Who, then wants to be a conservative if that really means being a crypto-Fascist, emotionally disturbed right wing kook? Even too many "conservatives" are closer to the radical left than they are to the moderate right—they have been exposed to the same class room prejudices. They, then share the same liberal left conceit that they are truly intelligent compared to the uneducated slobs who cannot answer back.

It has never occurred to liberals that almost nothing, conservative or otherwise, opposing their views, is allowed a hearing in the mainstream curricula. They research, publish, and distribute sophistication based on one-sided foundation and federal grants. Who then can learn anything to contradict the intelligent left in the absence of a conservative subculture with its own research and knowledge? The real reason why liberals feel smug is the absence of vocal opposition. In the deafening silence, they naturally believe their's is the only sound in the cosmos.

There were two studies in the early 1970s that researched Adorno's *tour de force*, but if there were right wing, pre-fascist misanthropes and sex-repressed kooks among political conservatives, randomly sampled, there was no indication of it. "Are right wingers really the kooky, tennis-shoed misanthropes that liberal intellectuals like to believe? . . . Surprisingly . . . to the possible dismay of liberals, two recent studies suggest that the rabid right winger is as psychologically normal as anybody else . . . 'they were not generally psychotic, irrational, or severely disturbed . . . most of them seem to be pleasant, considerate and law-abiding'" This finding was barely mentioned in an article in Newsweek magazine, hardly noted as a right wing publication, dated March 2, 1970 on page 54, some 20 years after Adorno's "scientific" propaganda. Big whoopee! The studies never got equal time in academe if, in fact, they were noticed at all. Adorno's theories still prevail.

For 20 years I let the textbooks speak their piece and demanded equal time to rip into them as the "fair play for the other side." I knew exactly where Adorno's ideology was coming from, but could not prove personal political involvements.

He, and his colleagues, had successfully kept hidden the secret of his own personal psychology, which explained a great deal of his "science." It was not until 1981 that the cat finally slipped out of the bag. He who denounced the conservative in America as a pre-Fascist authoritarian had collaborated with the Nazis in Germany! He had written propaganda tracts praising Baldur von Shirach, the Nazi Reich Youth Leader and later Gauleiter of Vienna; supported Joseph Goebels' philosophy of "romantic realism" and wrote articles favorable to the Third Reich. Why then would Hitler have Theodore W, Adorno thrown out of Germany before the full genocide of the Jews took its monstrous course? This is where the plot thickens.

Despite my best efforts, I have not been able to find documentation positively identifying another Theodore W. Adorno who suddenly shows up in London under the auspices of the Tavistock Institute of Human Relations (the lynch-pin "think-tank" in the New World Order), and shifts his ideological loyalties to the Marxist radical left. My guess is the two Adornos are one and the same. How many Theodore W. Adornos could have participated in the project directed by Max Horkheimer, or how many of them could have come to the United States in a "cultural exchange program," with Herbert Marcuse, another Marxist-Freudian third rate philosopher, whose books became the sacred writ of the campus counterculture activists during Vietnam? How many Adornos could have returned to Berlin after World War II? How many could have been forced out of Germany for writing a new revolutionary theory of music for youth in an *Introduction To The Sociology Of Music* identified with the Cult of Dionysius in Germany which infuriated Adolf Hitler? How many books with the same title by the same author's name dealt with the 12 atonal system of modern music and then experimented with it in London? Today, we know such music as Rock and Roll, Punk Rock, and Heavy Metal which enhances the "fun" of drug and sex orgies to the present. This had to be one and the same man who apparently wrote at least one of the first songs for the group known as The Beatles, named after the sacred scarab beetle (Scarabeus sacer) of the ancient Egyptian Cults of Isis, which had their imitators among London's disgruntled youth. Where else but in America could there be more fertile proving grounds for pitting youth against the traditional, conservative, "pre-fascist," and "F" Scale institutions of the country? The Beatles were sent here and took the nation's youth by storm, which began the process of social upheaval. It was a short 10 years between this and the college campus culture wars.

This is a free country (or what remains of it), and if Adorno wanted to write the kind of music with which to steer the nation's youth toward the camp of the radical left, so be it. If I have correctly identified the musicologist and the sociologist as one and the same, then he cannot be faulted for his success with the new music for doing what he intended. The fault belongs to the "guardians of the nation" who not only failed to stop him, but knowingly supported him. But, he must be faulted as a sociologist for the professional duplicity of pretending an objective "scientific" study of right wing political "kooks," while committed to the political objectives of the Marxist American left. No fox in academe more cunningly guarded the chicken coop.

Under the guise of "science," he created the shadow of suspicion over the respectability of political conservatism totally unprepared to cope with the new nightmare. He established the fictions on which the political monopoly of the liberal left wing has survived for so long in our nation.

The few voices raised in academe against Adorno's sleight of hand science went unheeded. Why not, when 97.3% America's professoriate in the social sciences and humanities or liberal arts were from liberal to radical left in their personal, political beliefs. The university as a meeting place for the free inquiry of opposing views in the social sciences is a very large myth. It, on the contrary, is practically a closed system, which purveys a one sided view of its indoctrination program, produces an oversupply of one-sided recruits, and then selects a one-sided faculty to perpetuate its monopoly. Non-liberals are the "paranoid kooks" who have the door slammed shut on them. Today, some academics are wondering out loud what went wrong with our country. We academics went wrong with our country with our sorry choices in theory.

Today, our educational, funding and governmental institutions are manned by intellectuals programmed to subvert the nation, even if some don't know it and most know it very well. This is not paranoia. This is cold, empirical fact, like it or not. What they are doing had its start long ago in the history of tyranny. It was best enunciated, perhaps, by Rabaut de Saint-Etienne, the President of the Assembly of the French Revolution: "All the established institutions of France only crown the misery of the people. To make the people happy, it is necessary to renovate, change the ideas, the laws, the morals . . . to change the men, the things, the words . . . to destroy everything. For everything must be started anew.[2]

It has always been thus—the destruction of everything to start anew based on a different whim or passion of the destroyers in the name of the people's happiness, and never mind the centuries of humanity's travail and achievement which have brought us thus far. Always, things would be better tomorrow. Always, tomorrow has brought its own share of grief and agony worse than yesterday's. Still, everything old, no matter how precious, priceless or sacred must be destroyed for it is the only way the revolution can feed upon itself. It too will become part of everything old the moment the new malcontents conjure a new utopian image in the name of progress.

Few things are older as a tradition than hunting. Few words in any human language is older than the words for hunting and hunter. What human behavior has been more necessary for survival or more impassioned for spirit? No American history or nation could have been real without the pioneer hunter whose Westward odyssey made it all possible. Hunter and American are virtually synonymous for those who created this nation. It is still a deeply ingrained part of the national character, the American personality.

Today, there are 20 million American hunters. They are part of the "men, the things, the words," that must be destroyed. Today's malcontents realize this better than even Saint-Etienne, and they have more effective means for that destruction. And, they will destroy, not because hunting is the evil they imagine, but because it is part of "everything" that needs destruction for the sake of destruction to bring forth another utopian new world—not because it will be necessarily better, but because it will soothe the malcontention of the malcontents. There is the delusion of grandeur, the basis for all paranoia.

The power to manipulate the symbols that work the change are not in the hands of the hunters; it is in the hands of those who have been programmed to instantly loathe everything associated with the hunter. The mere sight or sound of the hunter will give any nice democratic or liberal personality an instant Freudian angst, or anxiety neurosis, since they understand these things, being as intelligent as they are, and more compassionate and tolerant than anyone else alive.

I once had a highly intelligent, older graduate student taking one of my courses as an elective, who told me at the end of the first lecture that she was a liberal who knew I was a hunter and my ideas, style, and "hunter's appearance" . . . made her "knees tremble." I thought, "What, at only the first lecture?" and immediately understood her problem, but there was nothing I could do about it.

She stayed the course, never missed a class and never said a word, but at the end she seemed less wan and haggard, even smiling once or twice. I had to record her "A" because there was no way out of it—she had earned it. To this day, I regret not having had the bad manners to ask her if her knees had stopped trembling. But I know how the hunter's appearance, even when he's shaven, in a suit, white shirt, and tie, impacts some people.

The hunter is not only seen as a politically threatening symbol. More importantly, he is seen as a kind of twisted psychopath, thanks to Freud's Oedipal complex nonsense that is always present in the major assumptions about the male sex. Freud's (and Adorno's) theorizing is obsessed with the idea of aggression, which he insists is triggered by hostility—a polite word for hatred. He knows the kind of intellectual aggression with which he is assaulting aggressive bastions of Western European culture. Fearing his real motives might be discovered inevitably leads him to discredit all aggression except his own. He sought basis for it in psychosexual theorizing, and a half century later, it was still a problem unsolved.

The 27th Congress of the International Psychoanalytic Association convening in Vienna (Freud's hometown) in 1971, with 2,500 psychoanalysts gathered from all over the world, was occupied with ". . . the major theme of the congress—aggression—a subject deemed exquisitely appropriate for discussion in the land that gave birth to Adolph Hitler." (Newsweek; August 9, 1971, p. 62) The hunter is seen (thanks to Adorno) as a right-wing political threat, but even more, he is seen as the quintessential aggression machine of Freud. That combination is deadly, if I may. On it is built the symbol of the Jack booted, Nazi storm trooper. Is it possible to imagine a non-aggressive hunter or hunt? Just to walk a quarter mile on the tundra under a 150-pound pack is one of the world's most aggressive acts without firing a shot. But it's not the kind of aggression Freud is talking about.

Let us go back to his cathedral to see how his followers see the hunter's aggression. Finally, we get to the question they have answered their way and filtered it down to the average citizen already conditioned to jump out of his skin with anxiety and fear. He is only too glad to charge the hunter with manhood proving to extinguish his anxieties. We go back to the Oedipus complex.

Why do boys who grow up to be men develop so much aggression, which is a hostile and murderous attitude erupting into violence and danger at any moment? Because the attitude is there from boyhood as a repressed neurotic hatred against a possessive, domineering father who so traumatized the son that the poor kid never developed his sexual drive beyond that fixed level of normal father hatred.

Moreover, a sexually repressed society will not let him seek orgasmic release whenever and whichever way he wants. If and when he finds an outlet, often a compensation for sexual repression, he is cruel and sadistic with all the catching up he must do to finally get even with the old man and society. The Marquis de Sade opposed capital punishment because fear of it prevented him from killing whomever he wanted to, including women whom he sodomized with de Sadean glee. His feelings toward his father are unknown.

Why does the hunter hunt according to Freudian theory? Because he has found a substitute sexual outlet through which to vent his repressed sexual aggression and hatred. The moment he kills that animal, he has killed a symbolic substitute for his father, and finally gets even again and again. He justifies his manhood, by proving he has no castration complex. He has taken his revenge and liberated himself from the old man's domination, or society's, or God's. He can no longer be punished for once having sexually craved his mother in secret. He has gotten rid of his guilt complex, finally, and the greater the sadism and cruelty inflicted on the helpless, victimized animal, the greater the orgasmic glee in sublimated form. The hunter is now seen as a sexually repressed neurotic killer who takes his hatred out on animals, but hatred is a constant menace that can be turned against a person or humanity in an instant. Hence, the antihunters or animal-rightist's heroic defense of animals and opposition to the political right. But is this the way things really are?

If hunters really get their jollies from slaughtering animals, there ought to be some indication of this in their writings, and that's where we must seek evidence, not in antihunting, animal-rights prejudices. To the best of my knowledge, there is not one hunting book anywhere with the slightest hint of any hunter who says he gloated with sadistic joy in the suffering or dying of any animal.

If there is such a clue, why have antihunters and animal-lovers failed to document a single source in their voluminous attacks on the hunter? Perhaps contemporary hunters are too clever to admit such a thing in today's antihunting milieu. How, then, can we explain the hunting literature of 100 years ago when hunters were idolized, could do no wrong by the public opinion of the times, and were under no restraint to boast of their sadism, if that is what they felt?

Animal-lovers and hunter-haters cannot document such episodes. Why? Because it is not there in the hunting literature. Why? Because the hunter did not experience it. Why? Because he was not looking for it. Why? Because he was looking for something else— the integrity of the experience within bounds, fair chase, and honor of the hunting ethic.

Charges of the hunter's alleged lust for wanton cruelty is a result of psychological projections, and not a result of objective fact. Projections, ostensibly on behalf of helpless animals, actually demonize the hunter with irrational hatreds that, supposedly, can become violent and murderous behavior against fellow human beings. This is the Freud-Reich-Adorno context in which such projections originate. Actually, it is the animal-lover and hunter-hater who have murderous hatred against humanity and assuage or deny the subconscious guilt by loving animals on a conscious level loudly proclaimed. This technique, after all, is the standard Freudian notion of defense mechanisms known as reaction formation and displacement, and since all human beings are capable of it, there is every reason to use the theory, especially in analyzing Freudians themselves. (By the way, Freud borrowed these concepts of defense mechanisms from Nietzsche without crediting him.) They are all too often the least aware of it in their own behavior. All this psychosexual theorizing is not bad for a fictional detective mystery by a cocaine addict. A good anthropologist can tell you what's wrong with the Oedipal complex, from whence all male aggression and hatred emerges, supposedly typical of the vicious hunter.

In matrilineal societies, where lineage is traced from the

mother's side of the family, the son lives in his mother's home, not his father's. Hence, the boy's uncle (his mother's brother) is the disciplinarian, not the father. The growing boy is ticked off, not at his father, but at his uncle who disciplines and controls him, and he doesn't give a second secret sexy look at Mom.

When discipline is brutal and severe enough in any culture, any red-blooded kid will hate his old man, and if he runs to Mamma and hugs her, he wants protection, not seduction. Freud, of course, held his father in contempt by his own guarded admissions (it is now believed that as a child, he may have been victimized by the father's sexual abuse), and the nanny who raised him may have gone too far in her tender love and care, or so it has been suggested in both instances. Then, there was his suspected bisexuality and incestuous affair with his sister-in-law. Without doubt, all of this must have influenced his sexual theories.

At any rate, there is no scientific support for a lot of these theories, and much to controvert them. But that is not important. What is important is that his genius succeeded in subverting Western morality. He should be chuckling in his grave as our nation, having bought more of his stock than any other, is now morally bankrupt and would be the envy of Sodom and Gomorrah. Freud's followers, who concoct their manhood-proving theories so readily picked up by the average person, overlook one thing, since they don't dare hunt. May I respectfully suggest that any man who can take care of himself on the hunting trail will not have any difficulties in the bedroom? But there is a more serious and important reason.

What about those cultures where there is no guilt, fear, or hatred to compensate for sexual repression because sex is not repressed? The Indian brave, Masai *el moran*, Hindu maharajah, medieval liege lord, Moslem warrior, Chinese warlord and so on, who did not suffer from sexual repression—were they all neurotic, and did they hunt to compensate for a lack of manhood or fear of castration? In those cultures, especially in days of yore when women were virtually chattel, all any man who wanted a sexually attractive woman had to do was to tell her to disrobe and submit. Which poor woman would have dared refuse? Isn't this the sexual domination and brutality that today's feminists complain about? How, then, did these macho males develop a sexual insecurity needing compensatory behavior?

The Freudian view of masculinity was never valid. In fact, it was one of the biggest hoaxes of the twentieth century. Men have always hunted, they have always been aggressive, some have always been brutal, but Oedipus, repressed sexuality, mother possession, and father hatred had nothing to do with it, not even for wimps.

To understand the problem, we need to look not to Freud, but to the Big T—testosterone. Before doing that, we must respectfully understand why animals are as important to some non-hunters as they are to hunters, but for different reasons. These non-hunters have a genuine love for animals, and are in a different class than antihunters, who love power more than anything else.

The concrete-molded, politically motivated antihunter is one thing. But there must be legions of sincere people, with no political axe to grind, who have a genuine love for animals just because animals are wild, beautiful, and beleaguered with the progress of civilization. These are the hunter's feelings too. I knew some people like this who timidly used the manhood-proving argument, but their hearts were not in it. It sounded like the last straw they could grasp, and they seemed too pained, not at the thought of someone killing animals, but of animals dying. The death of the animal was caused by the hunter who killed it as though the animal would never have died if there were no hunters about.

Where was the real resentment—against hunter or against death? "Well, we all gotta die, sometime," was said to accommodate the other fellow. We didn't believe in it for ourselves. Death and its finality (contrary to Freud) is the reality we fear and suppress, not sex. There is no finality in sex, only "freedom from that tyrant, desire," as Plato's old and doddering Glaucon said, if I recall correctly, to young Thrasymachus, who apparently had no faith in going past 25 and tried to make up for it. I went back to the drawing board to do some more thinking.

Not only has the large extended family disappeared, but even the nuclear family is in trouble. There was a time, however, when death of loved ones was a personal loss experienced often, since there were grandparents, parents, relatives, and neighbors in close contact with each other. Growing up with those families in such neighborhoods and farms painfully, slowly, and repeatedly taught the young to accept reality, grief, and tragedy of death, no matter how one rebelled against it. Of course, religious faith softened grief a good deal, and so did surviving kin and neighbors who gave comfort and support.

These days, however, the family is disappearing in the nightmare of divorce, where children are separated from one or both parents and from each other. Grandparents are too often neglected and forgotten, so they're not around, and spatial mobility moves families, or their remnants, thousands of miles apart so they're not around, either. There may be a rare holiday visitation, but then again there may not. Grief of personal loss is rarely felt, since we intimately know few kin who die and people next door are lifelong strangers. We bereave more for celebrities, whose deaths are eulogized in the media, than we often do for those we grew up with and left behind as strangers in time, space, and spirit.

This leaves us with a surrealistic death by violence in television, and most who die there do so too constantly and too horribly. To keep the audience interest from jading, more and more bizarre, perverse, and grisly methods of killing and dying are devised by producers. Death becomes a depersonalized, abstract caricature; its anguish, terror, grief, or sadness becomes an illusion or a sensory impression with no deep emotional involvement. It's just another abstraction in a meaningless world.

Then, there is the worst abstraction of all—bureaucratically conjured death and dying courses in public schools that needlessly and prematurely program children with routinized terror that becomes insensibility in due time. In adulthood, those repressed lessons come out of hiding to force an unreal perception of death. Its mystery and spirituality have been politicized, and no one needs the family or religion for support, only supportive services of an impersonal governmental agency. Instead of fighting for life, we easily accept surrender to death that our education taught us and is now part of the bureaucratic process for population control. When the governmental Pied Piper plays the tune for "reasons of state," we, the aged especially, will imitate lemmings parading over cliffs. There will be no resistance. There will only be the duty to die on command. That docility was the programmed objective in school.

Depending on sources of demographic data, our nation has an illegitimate birth rate anywhere from 25% to 35%. In some ethnic and racial enclaves and regions, this rate may be as high as 70%. In any event, at least a quarter of our population grew up during childhood with a single parent, not knowing who the biological father or mother was. Some of this group did not know both parents; some were raised in foster homes, government care centers, or by resentful relatives, when located. Many of these children have been tossed from pillar to post in strange environments, where it has been extremely difficult to develop authentic loving and supportive relationships. What has happened to their emotions and the way they relate to people?

A lot of these children for years have felt alienated, lonely, anxious, and anomic, even in the presence of guardians or surrogate parents or professional caretakers. Then, there are single parents forced to support themselves who need the services of catch-as-catch-can baby-sitters. One cannot fake a genuine and sincere love for children based on substitute parenting for wages or salaries. What do lonely children, often unwanted, do to form normal, stable, emotional attachment when there are no siblings or adult relatives they can truly love, trust, and depend on in makeshift or institutionalized care? There are terribly lonely people in our nation these days surrounded by mobs of strangers. And loneliness of this sort, which remains from childhood, is one of the most debilitating ailments of human condition.

We cannot be truly human without reliable, intimate others. Under these conditions, animals become surrogate intimate others. They are not additions to a normal family, they are substitutes for absent or malfunctioning family and friends. True, children ought to be taught early to respect wildlife, but a tremendous identification and psychological complex is developed which, in later life, can easily be triggered for political manipulation against guns, hunters, and right-wing authoritarians.

Even children, in comfortable family surroundings develop special relationships to animals. Lonely children deprived of such surroundings, develop even more intense relationships with animals, real or imaginative. There is a great emotional need to love and want and to be loved and wanted in return. This is where pets come in.

Of the senses of touch, smell, taste, sight, and hearing, undoubtedly the first and major one is touch or tactility. Babies will explore the outside world so different from Mamma's uterine, inside world, through a wide range of touch sensations even before the eyes can focus without double vision. The mouth and fingers become important exploratory tools learning the differences between comforting and discomforting surfaces. The warm, soft, smooth contact with Mother is soon extended to anything else that can be substituted for the feelings of comfort, safety, and security. Witness the sleeping baby clinging to her blanket.

Human beings, more than all other living things, require constant stimuli and sensory input for growth and avoidance of boredom. Play activity is not merely incidental. It is life sustaining and Mamma, or other family members, do not always have time to play and provide stimulation of activity on demand. Toys enter the world of play, but soon become boring, because their stimulation is too predictable and lacks spontaneity of self-generating action. If the child lucks out, the ideal toy is an interacting, self-perpetuating motion-machine that responds to the living with its own life. The ideal is an animal—enter the pet.

Next to mother, nothing better establishes contact with the outer world, or provides more stimulation, than a warm, soft, furry pet. Babies have to be taught not to depilate a kitten or puppy, and naked, on a bearskin rug, the tot is equal to a Mongol horde following Genghis Khan.

The peripheral nervous system sends all kinds of pleasant sensations to the brain. In the crawling or toddling stage, nearly everything looks tall or large to the infant from ground level. The first of these are parents, who always tower over him like skyscrapers. Scientific evidence suggests infants relate with larger animals first, probably because of size. Tallness and bulk are parental familiarities that are dominating and intimidating or protective and supportive at different times. Right off the bat, the poor kid has to figure out when to submit or retaliate. Horses, cows, elephants, lions, or anything bigger than he or she, absorb attention on the farm, in zoos, or in pictures.

By the end of puberty and beginning of early adolescence, the preference now shifts to smaller animals who can be better dominated and controlled. This is when conscious personal identification with pets and other animals takes place. In broken homes, those animals can become far more important than people.

Children instinctively gravitate toward animals. Pets are animated and full of life. They have facial movements and expressions that are similar to parental or adult expressions of love, irritation, anger, acceptance, and rejection—or so the child thinks. Most of all, pets are soft and cuddly, and the child's brain registers pleasant sensations of comfort, security, and pleasure when they hug, caress, pet, and fondle them. Sometimes, this is the only joy some children get to know.

Children preponderantly favor mammals most, and amphibians or reptiles least, because skin and scales just do not produce the comforting, pleasurable sensation of fur or hair. Soft, cuddly pets enable the recall of familiar moments when the infant was curled or fondled in Mamma's arms or clung to Papa's knees before Mom and Pop went their separate ways, leaving the kids with a gaping void in their hearts they could not understand.

Children and their pets give and take lots of love and support. Before long, the pet or animal becomes the child's alter ego—a companion, friend, playmate, or significant other that is almost human. Emotional attachment is deep and forms so important a part of the child's self-image that it often lasts a lifetime. All of this is an asset for lonely children, but there are some liabilities.

Many domestic pets are old, at 10 to 12 years of age. Surely one of the more tragic things to witness is a child in tears who cannot understand why his dog does not answer with its familiar bark when its name is called, but just lies there in stillness of death. The first severe experience with death that many children have is when their pet dies, and pets will die after a comparatively shorter life span than human beings, when the child still has a long way to go—without his or her alter ego. But the trauma of separation from a loved one early in life is stored in the memory bank. It will come back with agonizing remembrance later, under certain conditions.

The other liability is what has become known as anthropomorphism—attribution of human characteristics to an animal that no animal can ever really have. Because we love pets or animals, we identify and bond with them. Love, among other things, is the trading of imaginal identities. It is trying to be like the loved one. We know pets are a part of us, and we think or hope we are a part of them. This is how it is with our human relationships, and we assume this is how it is with our animal relationships.

The next step is easy—we attribute or assign to them characteristics which are human and which they can never really have. Logically, we may know this. Emotionally we falsify it, anyway, because our feelings are much stronger than our ephemeral ideas.

Our pets cannot realize a single word can have many different meanings, and a single meaning can have many different words. For animals, words are not symbols referring to an infinity of meanings. They are signals with specific nontransferable responses. It is not the meaning of the word, but its sound, tonality, intensity, and the body language accompanying it that elicits a fixed response.

We ascribe to animals human emotions, behavior, qualities, and characteristics they can never have. We project our own onto them and respond to the mirrored reflection as though it is the animal's, when it is our own. We think we know what the animal thinks of us, and see ourselves through thoughts we imagine to be the animal's. This, after all, is exactly how we respond to other people. We think we know what they think of us, but we can never be sure. Hence, we see ourselves through the eyes of the other as we imagined he saw us. That is how we see ourselves. That is what determines our responses. That is how we develop a self-image.

When I say my grizzly bear fought magnificently, I know that reflects my projected evaluation of magnificence. I know the grizzly doesn't have the foggiest notion of what magnificence is, let alone how to fight that way. He just fought his way, whichever way that was. Or I could have said that he cringed with cowardice because he didn't complete his charge. I anthropomorphize in both instances by attributing human qualities to him that are not his. Because I know I am doing this, I do not mistake my projections and thoughts with the animal's, since I do not know what he really thinks, if he can think at all. True, the bear fights with animal ferocity, but even that is in comparison to my lack of it. If I really believe qualities of magnificence or cowardice belong to an animal, I falsify its real nature and rob him of what constitutes his animal integrity.

Of course, I am entitled to say the animal fought with magnificence, because that is how it impressed me. But I am not entitled to mistake my impression for the true feelings of the animal, because I do not know what they are beyond the roughest guesses. Because I do not anthropomorphize an animal, I do not dehumanize or animalize a human being. I must discriminate between the two and evaluate them differently, even though I love some animals more than some human beings, but there are moral priorities, fortunately, and I must hold human beings to be more important, despite my own feelings.

There are countless persons who pretend to love animals, and those who really do. There are antihunters who hate hunters with a purple passion, and non-hunters who simply don't like hunting. Both anthropomorphize animals. The diehard antihunting activist is aggressive, hostile, and even virulent, which is common in political power striving. His love for animals is an important recruiting device for political control, and he demonizes the humanity of the hunter. He is opposed to every value hunters stand for, and has ulterior motives that have little genuine regard for animals.

But what about non-hunting critics, who just don't like hunting and hunters and couldn't care less about politics? Although they know they are separate and distinct creatures from animals, they nullify the real differences by attributing human qualities to the animal and falsify its integrity by transforming it into a substitute human being. This is the result of human emotional and spiritual needs unmet in childhood that led to humanizing animals to begin with. One can understand this with compassion. But then such children grow into an adult world and lo and behold! That world is replicating childhood emotions, needs, and lovable alien animals with an anthropomorphizing vengeance.

It is a world of strange creatures in movies and television that speak our language, express our emotions, and understand us better than we understand ourselves. They give us emotional support we never got in childhood, and win our love and friendship. They are not always horrifying monsters out to destroy us. Though they are composites of distorted animals and humans resembling outer space creatures, they are more pleasant, amusing, compassionate, and people friendly. They are abstractions of human beings, with a human nature far better than our own. They are not only our equals, sometimes they are even more equal. They invite our identification with them, because we have become aliens to ourselves and to what is human. We can more easily displace an entire community of mere people than move snail-darters, spotted owls, or kangaroo rats to other habitats. We have come to humanize their caricatured counterparts, as we dehumanize the hunter or humanity.

Then there is the evolutionary theory these children bring into their adulthood. They were taught we are so much like monkeys, orangutans, and chimpanzees. Apes differ from us by only one gene or chromosome—which will be even less with the next promised discovery. Is it fair that we act their superiors for such a small difference? It rubs our sense of equality, which we have attributed to animals, the wrong way. It is we human beings who are alien intruders in their world that was once dominated by Pre-Cambrian cockroaches, and we already know how unimportant we are in the scheme of things.

Obviously, non-hunting animal lovers do not espouse such

extreme conclusions programmed by professional animal lovers or hunter haters. But equally obviously, they do not oppose them, either. It is not logic of adult understanding that counts. It is emotions and memories of substitute intimate others, buried in the soul from childhood, which anthropomorphize adult perception of animals. People who have no firm religious feelings, but are closely attached to animals, often object to hunting because they want to know there is just something out there in the wilderness beyond human defilement. That something is the spiritual, sacred, and reverential. It is a vague searching for the divine or supernatural through an animal symbol.

Primitive religions and animisms are loaded with such spiritual symbols and feelings. That tendency is also present in the modern sophisticate who is not yet aware of that psychic impulse leading to spiritual symbols.

Suddenly, that subconscious impulse is rudely jolted by the hunter, who is seen as an indiscriminate killer, a dealer in death, and death is not only the great fear about ourselves we repress in our subconscious, it is also the finality that threatens our beloved anthropomorphized animal images and profanes the sacred impulse. The result is anger and hatred of the sacrilegious hunter, the defiler of the psychic temple, the murderer of the poor animal alterego part of us. Tell such a person he is at the beginning of a religious search, and he will probably resort to ferocity, himself. Ironically, by different routes, non-hunting animal lovers and hunters are in search of the same icons for the same ultimately spiritual goals.

I have often been asked by non-hunters why I do not take photographs or movies of animals, who are alive, over and over again instead of killing them for trophies. But I do take photos and movies. The trouble with it is that they lie unviewed, buried in their albums or stored in video tape racks. They are not visible in my immediate outer world without my taking an hour to sit and turn pages or gaze into the boob-tube, when I don't always have time to coincide with my desire to visit with them.

My trophies? There they are, always, constantly available, waiting patiently to catch my grateful eyes in an instant, when I don't have that hour. They never leave my presence or hide away in some corner shelf when I'm at home. Others cover their walls with photographs and paintings for the same reasons.

The male brain contacts reality mainly by sight, in a way

different than female brains do, and it is the reality behind the trophy symbol the hunter is looking for, or at. The ease and immediacy of that look at a trophy instead of a picture is why I respectfully say, although the Chinese proverb is correct that one picture is worth 10,000 words, it is more correct to say that a "real," live three-dimensional trophy is worth 20,000 pictures. It is as close to reality as reality permits.

The hunter loves, enjoys and respects animals. He often uses them as transcendental symbols on his way to spiritual maturity, though he may never get there. But he relates to them as animals as he grows older, not as anthropomorphized substitutes for human beings. He has learned the difference between reality and imagination. For people who do anthropomorphize animals, the animal-creature-humanoid types represent a far more likeable human being than human beings. Any assault on an animal is an assault on the anthropomorphized reflection of that self-image.

To kill an animal is to kill that self. The response is sorrow, pity, and anger, which triggers the natural desire to retaliate in self defense. One of the safest forms of retaliation underwritten by free speech is verbal.

We humanize animals even as we dehumanize people, of which class the hunter is the worst part. By ridiculing manhood, critics neutralize the evil hunter's supposed threat as a danger to the self in the name of genuine sorrow for the cuddly animal inside projected to anything four legged on the outside.

One clue to all this was dramatically illustrated to me one afternoon when I guest-lectured to a wildlife management class. A mature female student in her 50s explained why she feared hunters. If they could kill animals, they can hunt and kill people. I asked if she knew of any factual cases where this was true, and she said there was a retired general she'd heard about who captured human beings, turned them loose on an island and then hunted them to death.

I asked if she referred to General Zaroff, and she blurted, "Yes, yes, that's the one," in total triumph.

I had to point out that the story about the General was a work of fiction, *The Most Dangerous Game*, a prize-winning short story by Richard Connel. The irony was that the General had tested his mettle against Rainsford, world-famous, big-game hunter, who turned the tables on the madman by out-hunting and killing him, first. So there were good hunters and bad hunters. The episode gave me food for more thought. Since trophy hunters know death firsthand and adhere to a hunting ethic based on Western moral values, they make a moral distinction between animals and humans. Ideally, at least, hunters who may kill animals may never strike, let alone kill, a human being, except in self defense.

Having a moral or ethical sense about the value and integrity of animals, they have even a higher moral sense about the sanctity of human life. This, of course, is an age-old, traditional mandate with its religious roots in Christianity. That rootedness is the Authoritarian enemy to democratic liberals and radicals of the pragmatic left, liberated from such outmoded moralisms and now free to confuse all objective distinctions.

Human and animal, traditional and modern, right and wrong, sanity and insanity, normal and abnormal become blurred. Choices are made without care for consequences. When there are no distinctions, irrational is just as good as rational, and we lose common sense. By the 1960s Freudianism was well established in our country, and man was regarded as a neurotic animal whose only salvation was in never-ending orgasm, which left neither time, room, nor energy for much else.

Sexually beautiful became erotically disgusting. In television these days, lovers do not kiss each other's lips with romantic adoration. They slurp each other's oral cavities with the sucking action of bilge pumps. Man had been a little lower than angels, but soon animals became a lot higher than man. By chance, I read a newly published book in 1964 that clarified the problem for me in a way the author never intended.

Harlow Shapley, Dean of American Astronomers at Harvard and well known publicly, had published his *Beyond the Observatory*, which seemed reputably scientific and farsighted, all right. I needed some light reading during those days of campus anguish in my life. Between pages 111 and 129 (in the paperback edition) the noted astronomer wrote like a third-rate theologian in cahoots with the Freudian Devil.

He said, "Because of the confused meaning, perhaps we should abandon the deity concept altogether . . . it is quite satisfying to equate Nature and God . . . a shorter version is 'Nature is God and God is Nature.' Still shorter, and deeply meaningful is 'Nature is All.'"[3]

Instead of clarifying the confusion in his own mind concerning the nature of deity, he found it deeply meaningful to throw the baby out with the bath water for the rest of us and then bestow that confused meaning of deity upon Nature, anyway, with the name of God obliterated, who did the confusing in the first place. Shapley's view was nothing but pantheism, which has its own deified confusions, where everything alive contains God and vice versa.

It had seen its heyday during pagan antiquity before Western civilization lifted the triumphant cross. In pantheism, it is difficult to separate good and evil, since Nature is God and Nature knows no morality. In fact, the Devil claims to be God and demands equal time for worship—witness his surrogates who invented the Colosseum or the concentration camps and today's Satan worshipping cults. Morality is a hindrance. God is not the necessity who creates the world from nothing. Creation is unnecessary. The world had no beginning or end. It always was, is, and shall be.

What baffled me was how Shapley, a renowned scientist, could abandon the very basis of science and logic—the search for cause and effect relationships in everything except the most important thing of all—cause behind the effect known as the universe. We may never get final answers for it, and there are several conflicting theories, but at least the West kept searching, and often things changed for the better and we called it progress.

The West didn't abandon the problem and pretend it didn't exist. That is intellectual cowardice. But Shapley opted for the tried-and-failed pantheism of a universe that never had a cause, since Mamma Nature was also Papa God, who disappeared in the equation, while she emerged supreme in Shapley's All, which is everything, everywhere requiring worship. All distinctions are blurred, liberally. Shapley can generalize, but he cannot particularize. I confess to having a tough time with this one, since Nature knows no morality, no right or wrong.

It produces, by human standards, good living things like *Bos primigenius taurus*, or domestic cattle, and bad ones like *Trepanoma pallidum*, the syphilis bug, and Homo sapiens, a combination of both good and bad (in the West, anyway), who must make a choice between steaks and venereal disease. In pantheism, one venerates everything that lives in Nature so that in India, where it is the basis for religious faith, all life (except human life) is venerated or worshiped in one form or another.

Some sub-castes, even today, have such high regard for the divinity of the rat they will move the entire village when rats take over rather than exterminate them, and then it starts all over. This makes it tough to know whether rats are good or evil (since there is neither in Nature), when they eat nearly 35% of the stored grains and cereals with rodential gusto, while people go hungry or starve.

It is an adjustment to Nature, so touted these days. I am obliged to respect that faith (though I disagree with many of its tenets) because it is sacred for too many people. For centuries it has given them hope, and for that alone it deserves respect. We have different imperfections. I just get mad at those who blame their starvation on Western free-enterprise capitalism, which is not to be confused with state monopoly capitalism of Communism or Fascism now being emulated in the United States.

Nature couldn't give a twit about who lives and dies. She applies the survival of the fittest with full democratic equality to all living things. Inevitably, Shapley reaches the tragic conclusion—he cannot make up his mind concerning the value of man on this earth. He says man has nothing to strut about on this planet as a superior being to Pre-Cambrian cockroaches, oysters, spiders, and other forms of life which is ". . . an assumption based on our religious creeds and preliminary scientific analysis . . . (which is) an incompetent cosmic outlook . . ."[4] Almost as an afterthought, he begrudgingly admits that man's forebrain ". . . is of high consequence in the animate world and perhaps justifies a separate classification (of man from other life forms) . . . I have almost brought myself to the point of believing that man is important in the universe."[5] This is the pantheistic basis for today's animal-rights movement that goes all the way. It deifies animal life by annihilating human worth bestowed by God.

The stargazer does not say he believes or disbelieves; he says he "almost" brings himself to the "point of believing" and reaches a safe haven between tweedle-dum and tweedle-dee—the ubiquitous gray area, or middle ground so beloved in liberal thinking. If it were not for man's outmoded creeds about deity, he would see himself in a true light—no more important than descendants of "Pre-Cambrian cockroaches important in their own time." We have lip service to full equality at last. Shapley had to be a liberal.

If Shapley plays with words, Comte Donatien Alphonse Francois le Marquis de Sade doesn't. A contemporary of the French Revolution (after whom sadism was named), the Marquis had the guts to reach the inevitable and unequivocal conclusion, no matter how perverse, which Shapley avoids. De Sade asks, "What is man? And what difference is there between him and plants, between him and all other animals of the world? None obviously . . ."[6] There we have it. De Sade was of the forgotten past, remembered by only those who read his books. But Shapley was of the constant present surrounding us with ubiquitous publicity. If Nature equalizes man and cockroaches, and there is no difference between them, then we can dispense with the importance of either, and some will surely make the wrong dispensation.

Couldn't Shapley see this? I would have guessed the excellence of his vision if I had known then what I discovered 30 years later. He had loaned his prestigious name and office to at least 25 Communist front organizations. Why would he do this? He was a dedicated liberal doing what many prestigious liberals did in those days, but the better question was—why would he not do this? Didn't it follow from his premises that man and cockroaches were the same thing, and it made no difference to a Nature that was All? What was more natural than gas-ovens or Gulags, to reduce human beings into cockroaches or worse? What was more natural than to cry about man's inhumanity to man and plead for the humanist heaven on earth—even though hell preceded it?

"If there is no God, then anything goes," Dostoyevsky's genius had observed. There is no if about it, Nietzsche thought later. God must be dead because, he asked, "If He exists, and I am not He, how can I bear the thought of it?" That was the secret envy of all liberal intellectuals. How well I knew the aberration I had flirted with in my own student days. That is the trouble with total equality; it's no good unless we are equal to God, which is why no one wants equality with his inferiors.

Liberalism's great oratorio sings the perfectibility of human nature, because it can be changed for the better—hopefully. We always served humanity for the new utopia, with the guillotine, gas ovens, machine guns, or barbed wire. These were more efficient than stone axes. What could sustain the myth of freedom for the global village and a New World Order except naked force or diabolical cunning by a few over all the rest? No one would be able to resist the panel of experts who could decide which of us would be treated like so many of Nature's Pre-Cambrian cockroaches in the name of humanity.

When some animal-rights activists, who are an extension of the

1960s counterculture activism, openly declare that animals with prior existence on this planet have rights before human beings, I know global human perfectibility is right around the corner. At any other time in history, such a contention would be considered madness. Now, it is touted as mental health. Some of us should die so cockroaches, or their equivalents, can live. All distinctions are turned topsy-turvy with implications that we laugh at to deny their terror. Contrary to media con artistry, it is not hunters who are emotionally disturbed kooks presenting a secret danger to society. There are others, more highly qualified who do that better.

The good-intentioned public does not see the threat when it contributes $10,000,000 yearly to the ever-popular People for the Ethical Treatment of Animals (PETA). To treat animals ethically is a desired and laudable goal, but the program goes considerably beyond that. Its director, Ingrid Newkirk, says, "Mankind (sic!) is the biggest blight on earth . . . I don't believe human beings have the "right to life." That's a supremacist position." Will she do more than talk about it? She doesn't realize her own supremacist position when she indicts all of mankind as a blight. (This, and the following asterisked references are from The New American, pp. 31-32, March 7, 1994.) She has also said that if animal tests produce a cure for AIDS, she'd be against it. On the Dennis Praeger show, she compared the slaughter of broiler chickens to the treatment of Jews and others in concentration camps, knowing that Praeger is Jewish, who asked her the obvious question—how could she slander the dignity of Jews and other humans by comparing them to broiler chickens?

Another animal-rights activist, Tom Snyder, says that if destroying medical research, ". . . means there are some things we cannot learn, then so be it. We have no basic right not to be harmed by those natural diseases we are heir to."* But the real question is—do we have a basic duty to be harmed by natural diseases? If so, then may I respectfully suggest that this is not animal love but self-destructive masochism. Had that belief prevailed years ago, with a wide variety of prenatal and postnatal diseases, Snyder might not have made it through the birth canal to sentence others to the same fate now. One cannot help wonder if such animal enthusiasts would subject themselves to dangerous medical experiments for the sake of curing animal diseases.

When a Paul Singer wrote a book entitled, *A Declaration of*

War: Killing People To Save Animals, wherein he wants his followers to ". . . hunt hunters, trap trappers and butcher butchers . . .," * one wonders how he would react to a hunter who advocates hunting antihunters who threaten hunters. These activists love their animals because they suffer alienation from their own, and others' humanity. This is a psychiatric problem, not an ecological one.

ALF (Animal Liberation Front) openly uses violence and terror. The FBI wants its perpetrators, who are responsible for 270 attacks, break-ins, arsons, fire bombings, vandalism, and death threats. By 1990, some 176 medical schools reported losses of more than $4.5 million and 33,000 hours of effort to correct the damages of such nihilism. Now, medical schools spend $15,000,000 and 100,000 hours of work to defend and secure research centers. Laboratories, zoos, and animal dealers have spent $2 billion complying with animal-rights Federal regulations, which amounts to 15% of the total amount spent on medical research. A spokesman for the Fund for Animals says, "We have no problems with the extinction of domestic animals. They are creations of human selective breeding." * Another animal-rights author, ". . . has compared the keeping of pets to human slavery and written, 'The cat, like the dog, must disappear . . . We should cut the domestic cat free from our dominance by neutering . . .'" *

These groups collected more than $190 million from donations of their followers of whom 87% are pet owners themselves and do not know they are targeted by the very groups they contribute to, nor do they know that 90% of their contributions are used to generate more funds and salaries for administrators, who plan animal-loving programs.

Even domestic animals and pets, if they are products of human selective breeding (cattle, milk cows, draft and transport animals?), are targeted because the real target is the human being. Putting animals before human beings and then destroying selectively bred domestic ones, with its negative consequences to people is not so much love for animals as it is impassioned contempt for humanity—misanthropy's finest hour. Yet, these are the darlings of Adorno's Democratic Personality types, full of love and compassion, who are opposed to Authoritarians. They are also the same people who have stereotyped the hunter as a vicious killer of animals and a potentially vicious killer of human beings. Do these same people protest half as loudly about the vicious killing of unborn, innocent human babies in the name of legalized abortion? Have these people ever identified a single hunting group that advocates any harm to antihunters or animal lovers, destruction of their properties, or abridgement of their lawful rights?

When mankind is seen as a blight, it cannot be dismissed as crackpot rhetoric. There are other animal rightists with equally alarming statements like: (1) "We are the only people in the world who have a decent attitude toward animals; we will also assume a decent attitude toward these human animals . . ." (2) "It is necessary to show sympathy with the animal's pain. (There should) be an immediate prohibition of vivisection and have that practice made into a punishable offense." (3) "I am an ardent opponent of any torture of animals, in particular of vivisection, which means the scientifically disguised torture of animals, that disgusting product of the Jewish materialistic school of medicine . . ." *

It may surprise current animal-rights malcontents to know these statements were made long before their time—the first by Heinrich Himmler, head of the Nazi SS; the second by Herman Goering, Reichsmarshal of the Third Reich, who officially approved high pressure and high altitude experiments with human beings that killed unknown numbers of them; and the third is the statement of Adolph Hitler, himself.

There, the basic ideas between our contemporary animal-loving misanthropes and those of the Third Reich who, oddly enough, believed in the compassionate caring for animals without granting them constitutional rights or blighting the supremacists. Somehow, current "pre-Fascist emotional kooks" are hardly the conservative types Adorno talks about.

Human beings with normal inhibitions against heinous crimes and mass murder do not develop such attitudes overnight and put them into practice at random. Such people who do, have a well rationalized, systematic personal philosophy that justifies breaking down those inhibitions. Then, it requires lots of dress rehearsals where thoughts, actions, deeds, and responses are repeatedly acted out in imagination. Only then is there sufficient emotional preparation to activate thoughts into overt action with a degree of confidence. Today, we call this getting psyched up. To reach the pathological phase where large masses of human "blight" can be liquidated, one begins with hatred for small groups at a time. Today's militant animal activist does not hate hunters because he loves animals. He loves animals because he hates hunters.

Human life has become cheap. We already have the cadres for future blight removal at work. Today, it is the unborn. Tomorrow, it will be the aged. Who knows who will be next, and when it will be the turn of 20 million American hunters?

The Neo-Nazi and Neo-Communist cleansing of human blight will not come from the ranks of traditionalist hunters. It will come from the miasma of liberal-humanist modernism that has no moral moorings. We all have a stake in protecting and preserving the beleaguered environment and wildlife, but must it be done by transmuting human worth to the dignity of Pre-Cambrian cockroaches? Let's see the social problems involved with the foregoing contentions of democratic personalities.

Our fixation with social and political equality is at the bottom of a very great confusion between roles and statuses that are often closely linked and inseparable, although they are distinguishable as two different things. Roles refer to what we do or perform or the functions we enact, as in carpentry, stenography, motherhood, or fatherhood. It is based on social expectation to make human interaction rational and purposeful instead of chaotic and irrational. It would be awful if my plumber insisted on representing me as my attorney in a court of law, and most assuredly, vice versa.

A status is a social position we occupy in relation to someone else, like a son to his father, a wife to her husband, a corporal to his general, the rich to the poor, engineers to laborers and so on—and vice versa. These are vertical statuses with obvious role differences. Society assigns or ascribes different values of importance to status with different rewards and prestige. This is based on the bottom line of reality that genetically (not environmentally) determined aptitudes, abilities, and temperament impact training and education that are mandatory for the performance of certain roles attached to status.

A neurosurgeon's role is different from a shoe shiner's, and, while both have equal value as human beings, they have different value as functionaries because their skills, training, and abilities are different and their statuses will be different. Society rewards this differentially. A good Marxist will argue both should be paid the same amount to prevent status and class distinctions and inequalities. Who, then, wants to undergo the arduous training of years to become a neurosurgeon? This is why liberal professors become revolutionaries when they see truck drivers making twice the money in the name of social equality the professor lectured about in the first place. How is any social status attained? There are only two ways: By personal achievement like becoming a physician; or by social ascription like a senior citizen where sex and age occur regardless of personal effort. Because we confuse role and status, it is then easy to manipulate gender and sex. This central issue we cannot avoid.

Hence, one of the great fictions of our time is that boys act like boys, not because of hormonal or sexual differences, but because of socially gendered role assignments and evaluations. Ditto for girls. Boys are supposedly encouraged to be tough and aggressive, while girls are coerced into being dainty and ladylike, and then are easy to dominate and control in adulthood by chauvinist males. This is pure malarkey. Gender is used as a substitute word for sex more and more under the pressure of feminist rhetoric to disguise basic and unalterable sexual differences. One can manipulate the meanings of gender, but not of sex. Originally, gender had nothing to do with people. It related to language and grammar.

The painful truth is, parents have no choice but to accept the reality that boys will be boys and assign social (gender) differences accordingly because they cannot control the sexual hormone that predisposes them to certain kinds of behavior, but not the reverse. For millennia, parents have known boys are aggressive, energetic, and vigorous, growing into manhood with those qualities intact, without ever having heard about testosterone. It was androgenic hormones and the Big T—testosterone—that forced the fiction of gender accommodation to falsify the reality of sex, and not the other way around. The same for females, due to estrogenic hormones.

It was only in our times a democratized remedy was found for this "imbalance" of Mother Nature. If testosterone could not be neutralized (there have been suggestions of prenatal anti-androgenic injections, or the proper chemicals in the water supply), then legislation could "compensate" with the abuse of the word "gender." Legal standards for entrance into traditionally all-male fields could be lowered for females, while they remained the same, or even raised, for males to get weighted equality—another oxymoron if there ever was one.

In the male, the Big T enables certain behavioral functions that have nothing to do with genderization. Gender doesn't cause the hormone. The hormone causes "gender." While genderization can modify hormonal tendencies, there is a limit to how far this can be done without severe negative results. At present, not much can be done about hormonal manipulation, but given the radical feminist agenda, drastic changes in the entire sexuality of the male will become a political target before long under the guise of gender.

Modern science is telling us what any cave-woman grandma knew all along. Men have traditionally been warriors, hunters, providers, and protectors, and did a more effective job than women for survival of the species, not because women are inferior, but because they are naturally different. Long live the difference!

Unfortunately, feminists today do not ask for the development of new scientific discoveries to create undreamed-of opportunities for the innate aptitudes and talents where women can excel. They choose to compete with legislation against men in traditional male fields by handicapping men. Men do not see this as striving for equality, but striving for revenge and humiliating, gratuitous one-upmanship. Radical feminists who justify this as a response to what they have suffered for millennia, now complain of a male backlash, as though men should gratefully and passively accept the destruction of their identities. The real backlash has not yet begun, and, hopefully, it can be prevented before it does.

Now, we get to the bottom line concerning what the Big T does to the male, and why it has made men into natural hunters for millennia with no gender nonsense.

From infancy to old age, androgens enable males to have larger lungs and hearts, with higher basal metabolism rates. This gives them a longer diastolic heart rest and higher systolic blood pressure. This allows them greater latitude for tolerating stress and physical exertion, to the point of agony. The hormone will be one of the main reasons why males have greater vigor, and vitality capable of generating more energy, power, and stamina. Males also have more hemoglobin, resulting directly from male hormones that enable more vigorous, active, and strenuous behavior that require massive, gross muscular activity. Males have a much greater tolerance for muscular stress and pain, allowing them to better withstand the agonistic effort. None of this is an imagined socially assigned gender difference.

Nature has simply made the male sex with more power,

strength, and stamina. In an increasingly effeminated society, males will appear more dangerous, as moral inhibitions, which regulated excessive behavior, are destroyed by permissivists. The merely aggressive male will become the brutal male. This is how hunters are stereotyped by feminists, and even by male antihunters.

Many men detest the strenuous requirements of the hunting trail because they cannot do it themselves, and the inequality rubs them the wrong way. Why can they not do it? Because testosterone is not equally distributed to the male sex. Some men have 20 times more of it than others! What's more, the male brain is masculinized with testosterone by the seventh week of uterine life! From then on, the male brain thinks differently and functions differently in many regards. This will predispose some males to be more masculine, and no role behavior is more masculine than the hunter's. If the radical feminist's agenda is to be realized, it must get rid of the male sex, which is already seen as superfluous, given sperm banks and the welfare state.

Right and left hemispheres of the brain control different functions. In the male, the right hemisphere is dominant and the source of control for perceptual-motor and nonverbal functions, especially spatial perception. This is the ability to visualize three-dimensional objects in depth and the relationship of parts to the whole, even when diagramed bi-dimensionally on a flat plane. This ability is constantly demonstrated in the male who will outscore the female nine out of ten times in any test designed to measure it.

Without a marked degree of this spatial and depth perception aptitude that is related to neuromuscular coordination, no one will be a competent hunter. When men and women tell me they wouldn't hunt an animal for anything, I point out that their choice of refusal is invalid if they cannot do it in the first place because of inadequate hormonal preconditions over which none of us have any control—we either have enough of it or we don't. It is a fact of genetic sexuality, not gender assignments.

Do some women have more testosterone than males? Do some males have more estrogen than females? Of course. They are the few exceptions, which still do not invalidate the general rule. Men and women are what they are because each has more genetic and hormonal determinants of his or her own sex than those of the other sex. Yes, some behavior can be modified between the sexes, but no, they cannot be modified beyond genetic limits, which is why we have weighted norms to create a phoney "equality" between men and women. But this is political subterfuge, not biological reality.

There is yet another inescapable fact about this hormonal difference and its associated aptitudes which is "disturbing." It will forever gall the radical egalitarian who does not want a social accommodation to this reality, but its elimination. The aptitude is easily one of the most important variables in intelligence, some aspects of which are so crucial to hunting that without them, no hunting is possible.

Intelligence does not have a clearcut definition even today, except for the operational one that intelligence is whatever an intelligence test measures, which is a popular piece of positivistic puerility, but the best we can do. If and when science can measure wisdom, only then will we have a reference point against which intelligence can be defined with precision. The point is that psychology has many tests for intelligence and consensus accepts the fact that intelligence is not a single function or attribute, but a complex synthesis of several different factors or aptitudes. One of its most obvious and constant variables is, precisely, spatial perception.

It is this factor that enables the right half of the male brain to visualize and manipulate the imagery of three-dimensional objects. When weighted and factored with arithmetical reasoning (at which males score predominantly and consistently higher), and verbal ability (at which women score predominantly and consistently higher) we get a measurement of intelligence which is successfully measured by several different tests that correlate surprisingly well with each other. Today, such tests and measurements are in disrepute because, allegedly, they are culture biased, which is pure baloney.

We hear with sickening regularity the fallacious argument that such tests are unfair and discriminatory against women, minorities, and the rest of the eternally woeful ones. In the case of one test (the General Aptitude Test Battery), it was geared for anyone with an educational level as low as the sixth grade. Even a Sasquatch could do it if he understood the directions in simple English, which is why the taxpayers sent children to school. The spatial perception part had nothing to do with culture-bound language or arithmetic. The test items were all expanded diagrams of forms to be matched with the original intact pattern, no words or numbers needed.

Its problem was in being foolproof. It immediately separated those who did not have the genetically determined aptitude from those who did. It became a political bone of contention because it told the truth we didn't want to hear. It was eventually discontinued and made illegal because, allegedly, it was culture biased. In a day and age of standard, bureaucratized education and televised diffusion, which subculture is so isolated from the other ones, it makes a real biased difference? The differences are not in the tests, but in the brains that respond to them differently, which is why we test to begin with. Tests were not faulty. Our prejudices were.

Until further evidence changes the picture, we are stuck with the fact that the results of such tests are really unequivocal. They show there is no difference in the average intelligence for males or females because some variables cancel others out, but their distribution is different. Female scores will cluster around an average, but male scores will have a greater spread and range. There will be more male genius at one end of the distribution and more idiocy at the other end. In fact, most characteristics that can be measured indicate such a spread. Only way to get full equality here is to kill off, or sterilize, such males to prevent distribution of genetic components.

Male cognitive mode of intelligence will better see the relationship of parts to the whole and vice versa. It will be more object and thing oriented and better understand and create ideas and theories. Males have dominated the intellectual field since time began, and it had nothing to do with gender chauvinism or sexual neuroses. Fortunately or unfortunately, males have dominated literature, science, theory, art, music, engineering, architecture, philosophy, religion, and just about everything else. Even in typically female activities like cosmetology, cooking, hairdressing, dress designing, esthetics, interior decorating, and so on, males have been dominant as creators, inventors, and innovators. What does all this have to do with hunting?

All this is not discussed in a hunting book to show off male vanities or downgrade women. It is discussed to show that whatever definition applies to creativity, the phenomenon by which things, including art, come into being, it is primarily a male function related to the brain's spatial perception and the Big T. Why is the great art of world civilizations throughout history a dominantly male creation? Because males think, imagine, and intellectualize differently than females. This fact is bound to fly in the face of our radical egalitarian theories. Because, among other things, male intellection depends on spatial perception not chauvinism—the latter a precise word, by the way, which was never meant to mean what it does today.

Why is the male a natural hunter? First, because of physical abilities and aptitudes; second, because a high degree of creativity and originality is required in the unstructured situation of wilderness and animals, who have their own reactions, instincts, and intelligence. Dozens of variables have to be put together just so. The male does it better because of hormones influencing a masculinized brain, which has a particular spatial perception/intelligence connection, enabling necessary creativity, which is the art of hunting, which does not have to be proved—all of it based on the biology of sex, not the politics of gender.

There is another male attribute involved in hunting to which reference has already been made. Novel and new situations normally arouse curiosity and invite investigation and exploratory behavior. This includes vast unknown territories that challenged adventurous adult men as well as toys, sights, and sounds which arouse childhood curiosity in a playpen. All children respond the same way in all cultures to such stimuli because it is biologically determined and not a product of Western sexist culture or gender. All scientific cross-cultural evidence we have demonstrates that girls are also curious and exploratory at the beginning, but soon change. Girls master verbal proficiency, at which they excel, earlier and with different modes of cognition and perception; also, they mature earlier; emotionally, they are far more intuitive, sensitive, and skillful in human interaction. A good woman knows her man in 5 minutes, intuitively. He requires belabored cogitation and logical analysis for 5 years before he gets to understand her, and then he's apt to be wrong.

With earlier verbal maturity, girls do not require exploratory behavior, thereafter, for three probable reasons: first, with greater linguistic proficiency, they lose interest in physical and sensory exploration; second, they are not as creative in problem solving, especially in unfamiliar wilderness terrain or contexts; third, they are more apprehensive, anxious, fearful, less vigorous, and more sensitive to stress and pain they control less capably.

Males, for opposite reasons, carry the exploratory urge through most of life because they handle it better emotionally, mentally, and physically, whether on the forest trail or in outer space. What adaptive function did this serve? The best deduction is, it enabled species survival during evolution long before gender politics. Nowhere was exploratory behavior more constant and crucial for survival than in hunting. The hunter, prehistoric or modern, explores dozens of square miles for signs of game, sometimes every square foot for days on end. To hunt is to explore with all its risks.

I have contended earlier, hunting is involved with a great deal of esthetics, and that it is an art requiring the creative, innovative, and exploratory. It will be argued, of course, that all kinds of male non-hunting activities include some or all of these characteristics, so how does hunting differ? All of these attributes amount to nothing if they are not put into high-risk action. Hunting has a final element that makes it different from all other equivalent activities. It is (dare I say it?) authentic aggression—minus any Freudian claptrap.

If testosterone is related to anything in mammalian species, and especially the human male, it is related to aggression most of all. Unfortunately, aggression has been getting rotten press lately. There are a host of books about aggression, constant experimental research and total social preoccupation with it. Unfortunately, there is little, if any, consensus about what it is, and that is because life cannot exist with too little of it or too much of it. Using the right amount is itself an art. Its consequences, no matter what they are, have important political implications and catch democracy and equality between tweedle-dum and tweedle-dee.

Let us admit two things: (1) there have been many regrettable things done by aggression, and (2) nothing worthwhile in the human drama has been achieved without aggression. The negative side of aggression has been largely a Freudian *cause célèbre*. To combat anti-Semitism of his Vienna, he needed to understand its roots of aggression he found in repressed sex, as already mentioned. In my view, he then made another serious mistake, assuming that aggression was virtually identical with hostility or hatred, which is the way most intellectuals see it, today.

But these two or three words do not mean the same thing. Some hostility can lead to aggression, but not all aggression is hostile or hateful. Aggression is vigorous, assertive, attacking action by definition, while hatred or hostility is an emotional state which may or may not be present during the behavior. It is difficult to imagine a back-alley thug knocking his victim over the head for his wallet and doing it out of hatred for a stranger, but it sure is an aggressive act. Conversely, it is difficult to imagine a Victorian lady as being aggressive who hates every man she sees, but maintains a timid, discreet silence—unless motive and behavior are considered identical, which reduces both words and meanings useless. This common assumption and teaching that both are the same, or necessarily related to each other, is exactly why antihunters, who are most hostile and aggressive, think the hunter's aggressive act is identical with hatred, cruelty, and sadism toward some "poor animal." A hunter can fight back with frenzied aggression at an attacking grizzly bear with no hatred for what he recognizes as a normal response of grizzly behavior, which he, the hunter, may have incited. In fact, he is too busy to feel any emotion except fear and the love for survival—his own.

Daddy splitting logs for an evening before the fireplace is engaged in a very vigorous and aggressive act, but this does not mean he hates logs or the chopping of them. If every human being who feels hostility and hatred translated it into aggressive attack, or vice versa, human history would have self-destructed shortly after it began.

I have often thought of this problem and the possibility I am a hostile, hateful fiend for routinely and aggressively swatting Alaska mosquitoes, which are awesomely big, plentiful, and viciously aggressive themselves, though I don't know how much hatred they feel in a routine feeding frenzy. I just feel pestered with a fact of life, not anopheline hostility, which requires swatting behavior now that aerosol sprays are outlawed. It's hard to see what this has to do with a repressed Oedipal complex.

Evolutionary theory says aggression has many advantages, chief among which is survival value, itself. Those who swear by the evolutionary theory of struggle for survival of the fittest, find it difficult to accept aggression as the dynamo behind the struggle. Why is the male more aggressive than the female in any culture, any time, in almost all behavior? Because Mamma Nature put lots of Big T in him and only a little in her. Castrate a male mammal, including the human, early enough and there goes all his aggression. Virilize a female with male hormones early enough, and the promise of a passive clinging vine grows into an infuriated brutess. (My dictionary does not show the equal female label for brute, but I want to be fair and so created the word just now.)

Later in life, while the added hormone may increase the aggressive vigor of a male, it will have no effect on the female.

Experiments show that, while androgenized females may develop greater strength and muscle power to become champion weight lifters or swimmers, this lasts for only as long as the hormones are taken, which is not too long before the liver starts to rot—in both men and women. In women, it does not add an iota to their aggressiveness, or lack of it.

There is a surprising twist to all this. While females will imitate the aggressive actions of males without the same degree of efficacy, males will not imitate the actions of females. Excepting verbal aggression in females, the male is at least twice as aggressive in all other modes. He not only initiates his own aggressive behavior, he incites it in other males. Normally, boys do not show aggressive behavior toward girls, but invariably direct such behavior to other boys. Constraint of aggression in boys or men against girls or women is in part due to moral precepts initiated by religion or culture, and in part by innate inhibiting mechanisms not yet well understood, but it appears in all cultures at all times. More males seem to be beating up more females these days—an unfortunate, but predictable, consequence to unisex and feminization of males who treat women equally and not with deference.

Aggression is not an isolated factor, however. Around it revolve two other major human characteristics—ambition and drive. Most of our behavior results from motivation, which gives us reasons and drive to do what we do. If motivation is to be strong enough to energize or generate our behavior, then it must be vigorous enough. This is what determines the duration and strength of ambition and drive. Without sufficient ambition or drive, motive becomes a useless wish, which, by itself, accomplishes nothing. Eliminate aggression, if possible, and we eliminate ambition to go to work Monday morning, strive to get promotions, and struggle to stay on top against those who only want upward equality. Nothing can be achieved without ambition and drive, which are part and parcel of aggression without which no worthwhile achievement is possible. And there lies the rub.

Without moral guidelines, aggression cannot be controlled or guided into socially acceptable channels accounting for the rights of others. For a half century, we have emphasized a permissiveness that has all too often invited a destructive and hostile aggression we now aggressively complain about with equal hostility. Despite freewheeling sex, neurosis has not dissipated and neither has aggression or hostility, Freud, notwithstanding. In many ways, it has become worse. We have tried to destroy regulated competition which channeled aggression and drive, only to see it turned into chaos, violence, and brutality.

America's manhood, today, is in great difficulty. The Delilahs of the feminist revolution have shorn the hair of ersatz political Samsons betraying America's manhood stumbling around whimpering about lost identities. Males with an identity crisis, are not going to find themselves by imitating Indian braves in sweathouse rituals playing tom-toms and looking for male mothers. Indian braves went out the day after the ritual and cracked enemy skulls with tomahawks. They never substituted tapioca for testosterone, nor whimphood for manhood. The modern male will find it more and more difficult to fulfill the hunter's role as his rifles, then his archery tackle, then his slingshots, and then his androgens are taken away.

Why does the hunter hunt? Because his maleness gave him the kind of body, hormones, physiology, and emotionality that enable him to do so in response to profound biological, psychic and spiritual impulses. The genetic factors that make this true are not equally distributed, however. While most men can be good hunters, some cannot. While genetics make it difficult for most women to hunt, it enables some women to be good, or great, huntresses, and there have been notable instances of it. Since women respond better than men to the tonality and directionality of sounds, this is a great asset in locating and tracking game. Also, women have greater finger dexterity because of greater control over refined neuromuscular coordination, which is why I believe so many of them are great in target shooting tournaments. Rifle scopes compensate to good measure for the handicap of poor depth perception.

Modern technological improvements enable women (and men, for that matter) to function well in many tasks on the trail not requiring maximal strength, speed, or stamina. Ballistics are more efficient in lighter weight and more powerful rifles. Dehydrated foods and lightweight camping and hiking gear enable women to perform tasks that could not be done in earlier times. Guides and outfitters provide more services, engine powered conveyances, and accommodations which eliminate or reduce many hardships or hazards.

If women truly desire to experience the glory of the hunt, they will avoid the negative attitude of trying to "prove their manhood," and there should be a great future in store for them as authentic huntresses in their own right. More women are joining the ranks of the hunter than other male dominated statuses. Men can only applaud and welcome their increased numbers into the ranks. More women are glad to accompany their husbands on the trail instead of feeling left out and complaining about unfulfilled relationships. Single mothers take their sons along on the hunting trail and teach them how to be men as their fathers should have had, if they had been around. Maybe a new breed of huntresses can teach us men how to be better hunters. Maybe enough women will fight beside us men to protect hunting rights for both of us. Maybe. Maybe. What else can male hunters do in such an event except stand up in awe, wonder and gratitude singing the praises of such womanhood?

In the meantime, political and social forces crowd in the male hunter. What these forces become in the future is anyone guess. Despite our best plans and efforts rarely have we seen a future that went according to plan. Futures have their own way with man who tries to evade the present which is the promise of past futures gone awry.

We search the past to find in humanity's collective experience the meaning of life and what clues it holds to guess the future. That is the province of mythology, which has recorded its own meanings felt in the soul by an unending line of humanity. But we reject such fantasy and resort to intellectualisms that create their own fantasies nearer to the heart's desire. We must turn to mythology to see what maleness was when men were men and women were proud of it.

There is surprising similarity among mythologies that are as different as Eskimo from Roman, or Egyptian from Chinese, or Aztec from Hindu. These different cultures can only create different symbols indigenous to their collective experiences, but they all try to understand the universal constant—the human spirit common to us all. This understanding has been the task of history's great philosophers, poets, and religious teachers, whose geniuses lie buried beneath layers of modern forgetfulness.

We know in advance what an acorn in the ground will grow up to be. It already contains its future, its destiny writ microscopically small within its shell. Acorns may have different characteristics that unfold, if they have enough soil, water, and sunshine. They may all grow to be one or another kind of oak tree, but an oak tree nevertheless, and not an elm, maple, spruce, cactus, or celery.

Likewise, structure of the brain and function of psyche is

potentially already there at conception, requiring only the right conditions for maturity. For the human being who belongs to one genus and species, there is one psychic system, with its archetypal tendencies or prototypes waiting to be released at various levels of maturation. Those tendencies give us universal meanings common to mankind everywhere.

Symbols and their expressions may differ but meanings are the same. Whether it's a naked, ancient Greek hoplite with shield and sword or a mounted Medieval knight clad in armor holding high his mace, the symbols differ, but both mean the same—warrior, contest, combat, or battle—or three or four mounted, painted Sioux Indians leaning over their horses, bows drawn taut, sending arrows into the midst of crazed, stampeding bison, or the American male in a broad-brimmed safari hat, clad in bush-jacket and cargo-pocket trousers, leaning into the anticipated kick of his .458 with *Loxodonta africanus*, trunk curled high, ivory tusks gleaming, coming straight on. Symbols differ, but meaning is the same—the hunters taking their committed stands, making their play against the primordial, both caught in spiritual drama and pageant of cynegetic art, man against beast, where only one will live to remember the instant of glory.

Patterned instincts of creativity and aggression wait for the right time to express themselves from birth. They express themselves with vigor, one way or another, on the hunting trail, battlefield, sporting arena, playground, stock-market, coal mine, or halls of political power. If the tendency is suppressed, so that it finds no socially approved constructive channels, it will express itself otherwise, perhaps in the brutality of the back-alley thug, sexual pervert, young bully in the school yard, older bully in the bedroom, or rioter and looter in the streets. If he internalizes his aggressions, because it is easier to pick on himself instead of others, then the symbols may change to drugs, alcohol, debasement of self, and psychopathy. Today, society does not try to invent or discover proper channels for the flow of natural aggression; it tries to wipe out the hormone and end masculinity.

Manhood gets its start in what C.G. Jung called the "child-hero archetype". It is there in the mythologies of all cultures and civilizations. It is the male infant who is born in the midst of dangerous and perilous conditions. He is abandoned or hidden away for safety, and, somehow, he survives miraculously.

King Amulius' daughter, a vestal virgin, is raped by Mars, and she bears his twin sons. Amulius orders the babies drowned. They are placed on a raft and set adrift, but, miraculously, storm-tossed waves dash them ashore where a wolf finds them. Another miracle; instead of sitting down to dinner, she suckles and protects them. Thus, Romulus and Remus grow to manhood and create the future might of Rome.

Jocasta, wife of King Laius, bears him a son, Oedipus, and when the old man introduces sodomy as an alternative life-style, the oracles tell him the son will kill him for betrayal of his mother. He orders the infant boy abandoned in the wilderness. But, miraculously, a shepherd finds the child and gives him as a gift to the King and Queen of Corinth. When he grows to manhood, Oedipus leaves his parents, because an oracle tells him he is destined to kill his father and marry his mother (which is where Freud got his idea).

Years later, Oedipus kills a man, a wild outcast in the wilderness, and never learns it was his father. The city of Thebes is held in terrified bondage by the Sphinx, whose riddle Oedipus solves. He is given the city as a reward, with all its treasures, including a lovely woman that Oedipus marries. The woman is his mother. Oracles finally tell him the secrets. Oedipus, horrified at what he has done, blinds himself with a flaming faggot and runs off screaming into the night. The gods are appeased.

Then, there was the infant, Moses, who was set adrift in the bulrushes on the orders of an angry pharaoh, but the child is rescued, miraculously, and when he grows up, he leads his people to the promised land, after the Red Sea parts to allow a passage, and he gives them the moral code which has influenced three major world religions to this day.

In our times, there appears one of the greatest child heroes of all time, whose mother dies of fever in the west coast of Africa shortly after giving birth to a son. The poor father writes the last lines in his diary, "My little son cries for nourishment—Oh Alice, Alice, what shall I do?" He drops his head in despair, and, at that split second, the cabin door bursts open, and the vicious Kerchak snaps the neck of the father—John Clayton.

Kala, the she-ape, whose own baby has died, throws its lifeless form into the cradle, grabs the hungry infant lying there, and raises the son of John Clayton, Lord Greystoke, to become the mighty killer of beasts, King and Lord of the Jungle, aka Tarzan of the Apes.

Miraculous male survival was a mythological explanation of a biological fact. The reality for human infants on this earth until the 1600s was that, although a mother had an average of 20 children, half of them died before birth or infancy. Male infants have had about a 25% higher mortality rate by miscarriage or neonatal morbidity than female infants. Mother Nature's unequal treatment of males continues to this day, causes unknown. Random legal abortions today kill off more males, because there are 20% more of them at conception. Somehow, the constitution does not push the equal protection clause in this case. Today, male infants need miraculous survival more than ever.

Old mythology showed the fate to which gods subjected the male in order to find his identity. He must find the ". . . treasure most hard to find . . ."—Jung's transformed phrase for what Christ called the ". . . pearl of great price . . ." which symbolizes the true identity of who we are. This required a perilous search through strange foreign lands, both in and beyond this world. Gods assign challenges and tasks that make heroes of those who can overcome in dangerous contests with doubtful outcomes. All these contests are what being human and male is all about—the eternal battle between forces of good and evil in the soul of man. Animals don't have this problem, and neither do those of us who are less than animals.

In Greek mythology, the gods assign Hercules 12 labors which include, among other things, cleaning the immense Augean stables, killing a lion bare handed, and killing dragons guarding the Garden of the Hesperides so he can steal the treasured golden apples most hard to find, all in order to find who and what he really is. Perseus must travel to the underworld, behead the snake-haired gorgon, Medusa, and bring back the grisly trophy as proof of his obedience to the goddess Athena, who had assigned the task, so she can wear the head on her breastplate. Theseus battles the minotaur, a half man, half bull creature who devours innocent youth, and he hunts and kills the evil monster.

Ulysses, the Roman version of the Greek Odysseus, is gone for 25 years hunting for his treasure, slaying dragons, Cyclops, and other monsters. He ties himself to the ship's mast so he will not steer himself to doom bewitched by the sirens' songs, and finally comes home to realize that his real treasure, all along, was his beloved wife, Penelope, who waited patiently and faithfully for his return. Jason and his famed Argonauts escape death, battle monsters, and finally find the priceless Golden Fleece.

Gilgamesh, of epic Assyrian fame, slays evil lions and bulls for his challenges. In Persian lore, Mirin and Gushtasp vanquish the karag or unicorn. Marduk slays Tiamat, the terrifying monster-mother, and her brood of 11 dragon children. There is Sinbad, of Arabic fame, whose seven voyages give him death-defying adventures and lots of priceless treasures.

Tristan, the Germanic knight, is sent to Ireland to woo and bring back his beloved Isolde, but only after he kills the dragon and removes its tongue as a trophy. (Men worked real hard in those days for their women.) Mighty Siegfried battles and slays Fafner, the dragon, who is guarding the entrance of the cave where lay the treasured helmet that makes one invisible, and the ring hammered from gold at the bottom of the Rhine, bestowing the power of gods.

In Arthurian legends of Angles and Saxons, Galahad and Percival succeed, where so many knights have failed, to find the Holy Grail, the symbol of Christ's perfection, the treasure hardest of all to find, but only after vanquishing the demons of evil. St. George slays the dragon of evil in many mythologies. Hopefully, this is sufficient to make the points that follow.

Every culture has its pantheon of heroes, starting with those who created the culture to begin with. They share several things in common, no matter the other differences. They must all have the courage to face the danger and difficult challenges. Our world has always been, and always will be, a very dangerous place, whether danger comes from saber-toothed tigers, maniacal dictators, back-alley hoodlums, overly ambitious politicians, next door neighbors, or atomic bombs. We need courage to search for the symbolic treasures that bring tranquility to the troubled human soul. Copulating our way out of the human agony will not do it, Freud notwithstanding.

So we are always searching for something, for some soothing balm or elixir, some treasure, some sacred icon to balance the scales. Happiness, that great delusion of effete and rotting cultures, is just around the corner, and the corner gets further and further away. Always there is a treasure to pursue, to hunt for, which requires the utmost effort, agony, daring, and heroism to find it. Few and fortunate are those who do, and many are those who fall short of the demands made on us by treasures that do not pry loose with ease.

To do so, our mythological heroes traveled in strange lands, over the oceans and into worlds beneath, they crossed seas of fury, lands of flame, desert wastelands, mountains of evil, underworlds of mist and shade, or what we call wilderness, today. Wilderness is where the unknown and dangerous lurk, challenging man's courage and survival. This is where heroes seek and kill demons, monsters, and fabled animals. One way or another, these heroes are hunters. It is surprising how much of this folklore and mythology is replete with heroes doing heroic things in the wilderness.

The hero is a social type who is superior to the average, while the villain is inferior to the average. The function of the hero is to uphold and defend the time-honored values and traditions that have given a society its identity and survival. Heroes do this even at the risk of death on the battlefield. Modernism, which often chooses change for its own sake, never asks why traditions have been around for so long. It's because they have worked successfully in protecting those cherished values that have given continuity to a culture and its people.

The villain is a traitorous danger to that culture and its value system. His rebellion does not necessarily offer a better solution; it merely opposes the established heroes who enjoy the prestige and status because he, the villain, wants what he calls sour grapes. He is often the spoilsport in the sporting game.

There is a cyclicity here where yesterday's heroes are today's villains and vice versa. When this happens, we know a society is in a stage of tumultuous transition, often for the worse. Its values are undergoing radical change. Democracy, which tries to avoid extremes and extols the average, is always hard on its heroes, who are better than average in all walks of life, and recruits villains, who are worse than average, so they can climb up the social ladder to the vaunted average where all are finally equal. Heroes are already at the top and will only fall off if they don't hang tough. Mythology and fable saw this fact of life long ago. Today, the hunter is the villain, and the antihunter is the new hero, both symbolizing radically opposed views of life.

While the modern trophy hunter does many heroic things on the trail, he does not do it to be a hero, or think of himself heroic, and in fact, he shuns the popular conception of heroism. This is because the deeds accomplished by him are routine requirements if he is to gain his icons. He does the heroic in routine fashion to suit himself, not to earn society's awards of status and prestige, when the exact opposite is modern society's reward. The best way

301

to gain more ridicule and opprobrium with variations on the major theme of proving manhood, is to claim heroism. It is those cosmopolitans, liberated from traditional mentalities, who cannot, or will not, venture into the hunting arena to make the effort and take the risk, who see the heroism of the better than average, involved in many a hunt and resent it. It is easy for critics to make the proof of manhood charge to maintain their own on lesser grounds.

Often, the hero hunters of mythological vintage die or are killed, and they are resurrected, coming back to life more resplendent, more wise, more good, humble, and noble. They have embraced the transcendent and are born again to tell us about life and death. The rebirth ritual is always a part of the hero hunter's quest for his renewal and spiritual rejuvenation. "Except ye be born again," said the first psychotherapist of human history. This spiritual or religious theme should not be difficult to understand in a society that believes there is no being, but only becoming.

The reborn hero hunters show us mortals what lies ahead on paths which they have crossed, which beckon us, too, so life will not have been lived in vain. They teach us there are no short cuts, no free lunches, no instant successes or rewards, the U.S. Congress notwithstanding. Each of us, in his own way, can find a path on a less agonizing level, because legendary giants who went before us, have shown us the way. We only need to find courage to walk. The trails are blazed for us.

Today, there are many who do not, or cannot, take the trail. There are a few who do. Some find one trail, some another, at the end of which are the treasures as each sees and values them in a world that has never destroyed value as recklessly as this one does today. The hunter has found his own trail leading to his treasures.

As molecular biology discovers, with painstaking care, that genes and their formative mysteries are at the bottom of psychic influences on our behavior, then it well may be that the soul never loses the original images, instincts, and spiritual urges of mankind, which form his cultures and civilizations and not the other way around. It may be the hunter, as modern man, is an authentic extension of an unchangeable prototype. But today, it is virtually a liability to be born a male and become a man in America. If feminists, politicians, and wimps don't obliterate real manhood, their concocted wars or homespun brutality and violence will.

No matter how handsomely behavior modification is packaged

these days, it is still the manipulated product of some other modifier's standards at variance with our own. Orwell's Big Brother still shouts that slavery is freedom. How much can we modify man and still have men, and how can we know those who want his modification do not have something worse in mind?

What happens to the human when that linkage is destroyed with sophisticated Frankensteins genetically engineered to suit the whims of gods who have become the demons of the new mythology, when the past becomes prologue, indeed?

Often, I have been asked, "What and why is today's hunter? What makes him tick?"

My answer evokes quizzical looks, when I say in him is a Sinbad, Siegfried, Hercules, Perseus, Tristan, Gilgamesh, Galahad, and the others all rolled into one, no matter how toned down, and our cultures and gender have little to do with it. The American hunter, too, crosses his own oceans, deserts, jungles, mountains, and hostile territories, all with their perils and dangers.

The hero of myth hunted for his treasures in the form of a magic lamp, Medusa's head, Golden Fleece, *prima materia*, philosopher's stone, unicorn horn, divine fire, gems in the bellies of fish, fountains of youth, tongues of dragons, jewelled eyes of fabled beasts, and other treasures most hard to find. They were symbols of what we today call trophies symbolizing the meaning of the spirit in the soul of man.

Today, the trophy hunter is still searching for treasured symbols, only now they are the trophies of the 10-foot black-maned lion, 100-pound ivory tusks, 42-inch Dall ram horns, 60-inch greater kudu horns, and 70-inch moose antlers. Search for these trophies as ultimates is still the search for the icons made sacred by the gods. Symbols change, but the basic archetypes and spiritual urges of the soul remain universally the same.

In a democracy, where the common man can enjoy the privileges of yesteryear's royalty, we all strive for trophies for contentment of the soul and fulfillment of one's creative urges. Trophies appear in many forms in different contexts: The first place blue ribbon for the homemaker's winning entry of her blueberry pie in the State Fair; golden Oscar for the outstanding Hollywood actor or actress in a box-office smash hit (even though the winner is probably an antihunter); Heisman trophies for the outstanding football players, Wimbledon trophy for tennis; platinum platter for the million music records sold; gold and silver belt buckle for the world's heavyweight boxing title; soldier's Medal of Honor; high school scholarship or valedictorian award; gold watch for 30 years of faithful service to one's employer; hunter's trophy; and so on ad infinitum. Why not? It's beautiful to see merit and talent rewarded, when fairly won against the odds. What they all have in common is the attainment of excellence, which required effort and achievement beyond the ordinary. Take that away, and the soul of man is no more.

The hunter's trophies, too, are symbols referring to the quality of life, to creative effort, to agonal contest telling us what life is all about, of who we are, of what hunting has meant all through the ages to make life possible. When we colonize other planets, the same spirit will be there unless genetic engineers improve mankind and destroy man in the process.

Few who are born in sanitized hospitals today, deliberately risk their matured manhood to the hunting hazards, dangers, and perils so eagerly. Few incite the challenges and meet them head-on so gladly. Few lust for the thrill of contest, staking all they have on their own abilities to reach a victorious outcome so repeatedly. Few so defiantly search and risk their lives for treasures so many others denounce. Few travel as far and wide, searching and exploring so diligently. Few deserve their triumphs and trophies more.

Which artist creates so much magnificence in such a wondrous studio? Who in our modern times has the touch of madness and daring to do all this and find the sacredness of his humanity that began when he and the ape parted company? Who else except the hunter?

Time is running out for him. Let others who have lost the way find it soon and join the hunter's campfire at the end of the trail. That is where life begins and ends, and begins anew.

1 David Bakan, *Sigmund Freud and the Jewish Mystical Tradition* (New York, N.Y.: Shocken Books, 1965) p. 181

2 Thomas Molnar, *The Counter Revolution* (New York, N.Y.: Funk and Wagnalls, 1969) p. 56

3 Harlow Shapley, *Beyond The Observatory* (New York, N.Y.: Charles Scribners Sons, 1967) p. 111

4 Ibid, p. 121

5 Ibid, p. 125-126

6 Marquis de Sade, *The Marqui de Sade* (New York, N.Y.: Grove Press, Inc., 1965) p. 329

The Bears Of Manley

The hot summer of 1964 caused a swelter for the little village of Manley Hot Springs in Alaska's Interior. Several cock-and-bull theories sprang up to explain why black bears in the area went berserk. Some said the unusual heat produced feverish ursine hallucinations. Others said windblown toxic spores produced the same mind-poisoning results. Some said berries on which bears fed were contaminated. Still others said the area had become overpopulated with bears, who needed more *lebensraum*, so they just moved into the village in the absence of zoning restrictions. Nobody had a real, convincing answer. My own guess (as good as any) was the ornery bears decided to hold their annual convention just for the fun of raising mayhem. At any rate, they mauled several villagers and killed one man. When a couple more men were reportedly killed in the general vicinity, people retaliated by killing 27 bears in about 30 days. All this slowed things down, but the menace did not altogether evaporate.

It was about this time, Carolina Bob, whose thoughts paralleled mine, got hold of me. He was spoiling for a fight no less than I was, so we threw some gear into his truck and barreled 200 miles from Fairbanks, along the dusty, choking, bone-jolting, unpaved road to Manley and asked to see the site where the bear killed a man the day before. They showed us. We found what looked like a good stakeout near the trail, unrolled our sleeping bags, and spent a fitful night waiting for the return of the monster. We waited all night and all the next day. The bear didn't show, and we knew our long-shot odds would not pay off. We went to the trading post, made small talk with the natives, and returned home, disappointed.

The papers carried on for several days about the killing. No matter where you went, the only talk was about man-killing bears, and how temperamental and vicious they had become without apparent reason. Everyone swore there were still more of them in the area, and odds were there would yet be more fatal bloodlettings.

My brief visit to Manley, and all the bear talk at home, were minor episodes, except for one thing. The experience created a mental set that was to have a major impact later. It turned out to be a delayed, emotional time bomb. In a totally unexpected way, it was to bring me much grief.

Shortly afterward, an urgent message asked me to get hold of a man named Don. (Obviously, this is not his real name.) He wanted to go hunting with me in Manley. He had a Piper Cub on floats, and we had hunted together twice, earlier in the spring, but some problems had arisen between us. We were not exactly the best of friends—business acquaintances might be a better term, if used in the loosest sense. We had met casually, and learned we knew each other by reputation, which wasn't difficult in those days. Fairbanks was small, fairly primitive, and unspoiled before the oil-pipeline boom debauched everything.

He was professionally affiliated with the local hospital and knew I taught at the main Fairbanks campus of the University of Alaska. Over our cups, he had made me an offer I couldn't refuse. He knew of my passion for the hunt. His passion was flying an airplane, I later wished I'd never seen. He had to meet some kind of requirement to keep his pilot's license current and had to log all the flight time he could before some deadline. This was expensive, given the price of aviation gasoline. If my finances could stand the costs of the gas, any trophy we got would be mine. He would log his flight time.

Before the end of the first trip, it became obvious he was different on the trail than at a cocktail party. He had proved to be unpredictable, secretive, and indecisive. Which of my faults (there were many) had rubbed him the wrong way was anyone's guess.

By the end of the second trip, each of us knew our personalities clashed. This didn't seem important when I returned his phone call and accepted his invitation to fly to the Manley area to hunt for berserk bears.

It was early fall and an ideal time for such a hunt, and those bears were still around. He still wanted gas money, and I still wanted one of those bears. Since our relationship was purely pragmatic, all other factors were incidental. Experience had not yet taught me that when two men hunt together, nothing can be incidental. I was so eager for that bear, I put the past aside hoping things would be different this time.

All discomforting thoughts receded from my mind shortly after takeoff. We were drawing closer to Manley, following the tortuous contours of the mighty Tanana River—a silty, wild, glacial-fed river, second in size only to the mightier Yukon. The peaceful world far below was bathed in sunlight and beauty. The river glinted like a ribbon of burnished steel. In serpentine twists, it curved in tattered loops, sometimes doubling back on itself, until it found its main direction again. In the foamy whorls and swirls, many sand bars had long since emerged.

At one innumerable turn, a long sand bar fingered out, separating the river from a long strip of stagnant backwater. It pushed against a longer strip of high ground covered with withered, windblown brush. Somewhere in the middle of that ridge, a bit further up, a black dot grew larger and larger as we flew lower and lower. It was a black bear, a magnificent fellow. He looked like he was feeding on berries. I hoped they weren't contaminated with poisonous spores, or whatever it was troubling the Manley bears.

Don circled back about a mile over some quiet backwater and landed. In those days, hunting from an airplane immediately on landing was legal.

Securing the plane, we ran as fast as our legs would carry us. I didn't notice Don had fallen quite a ways behind. My mind was obsessed with one thing—catching sight of the bear as quickly as possible, while the wind was holding in my favor. Soon, the ridge of dried grass and brush loomed ahead to my left. The bear had to be only a couple hundred yards ahead in the midst of it.

As anyone knows, hipboots are awfully clumsy things to run in, and to run quickly and quietly was vital, no matter how the terrain had changed. Underfoot, it had become a silty, ice-cold, gray muck hugging the river rushing along to my right. It was not a sand bar, as it had appeared from 1,000 feet up. At the moment this did not seem important.

Running on sloppy silt banks along a river's edge had happened to me a few times before. You learn to move quickly and lift your feet before the sucking, sticky softness grabs you. Sinking 3 or 4 inches is not serious in such circumstances, although it wears you out if it goes on too long. My brain registered that my pace was slackening, and my ankles felt more deeply embedded than usual, but I paid little attention.

My mind was bent on two things: was the wind holding, and where was the nearest and likeliest break to cut through and climb the ridge? A few yards ahead, there it was—the water squeezed together like an hourglass between the ridge and silty bank. Back of that spot, the ridge dropped a little. This would have to do. The bear could not be much further ahead. To run any further might take me upwind of him, he'd scent me, and the game would be over for sure. I started to cut across.

Don's voice screeched like a buzz saw above the river's growl. "Sark! Get out—get the hell out. You're in quicksand!"

His shouting brought me to an instant halt. At any other time, yes—it would have been delightful to leap out immediately. But surely, his shout must have spooked the bear. It rattled me.

It is well known that, more often than not, a black bear—or any bear, for that matter—will flee at the sound of the human voice, especially if he has not had previous experience with humans.

It is also well known that, not infrequently, a bear will investigate out of anger, curiosity, or surprise, especially if he has had experience with humans and has lost his fear of them. We were close to Manley now. Suppose this was one of those berserk bears contemptuous of mere man? Even a non-berserk bear (a nice, gentle, timid fellow) would have no trouble charging down the ridge right on top of a man stuck in that mire! If I had known then what I know now, it would have occurred to me that no bear was as stupid as I. He would have sensed instinctively the quagmire was there and surely left me alone. If we knew every "if" in advance, life would be different, as it is often said. But the Manley bears had molded my mindset. My split-second decision was to cover myself from a berserk bear. He simply took priority over the bog.

Instead of scrambling out, I bolted a shell into the rifle chamber and riveted my concentration on the length of the ridge. It couldn't have been long, but after what seemed like ages—in which no bear showed—the tension left me just enough for me to become aware of my immediate world. In those few lost moments, my legs had become more deeply immersed, and my knees clamped together by the muck. It was past the time for getting out.

My surprise was at the rapidity with which this had happened. One moment I had been up to my ankles in this muck, and the next moment I was in up to my knees. I must be in a hole, I thought, and the next question was obvious—how deep?

It squeezed all the effort out of me to squirm and twist my body around to face Don. He was on the edge of a spit of solid ground scarcely 10 paces away. Stuck fast, and winded, it struck me with amazement how unreal all this felt. There wasn't supposed to be quicksand along the Tanana. This was part of the lore of every hunter who hunted along its banks. Yet, here it was. It felt real enough to take seriously.

Don's behavior caught my attention. He was running back and forth erratically, obviously trying to figure out what to do. He'd lurch around in a circle, shift from one foot to the next, stand still for a moment, then stagger again like a drunkard, all the while moaning. All he could do was to shout, "Hang on! Hang on!"

It seemed comical to me. I wanted to laugh, and I believe I did. Hang on, indeed! What else was there to do? Then it occurred to me. Don was really giving those directions to himself, which betrayed his state of mind. A pang of doubt shot through me. He might not see the obvious answer in his panic. All he had to do was dash up the bank and find a branch, log, or dead fall. There should have been plenty up there. I shouted his name, and he looked at me for a moment, standing still. It was a ruse, of course, but a smile forced itself onto my face, and my hand slowly waved toward the bank. Now, he would think, hopefully, that things were okay and my calmness would calm him down.

"A branch! Find a branch—a log!" I bellowed. It didn't work. It made things worse. He sank to his knees, buried his face in his hands, and began to sob loudly enough to be heard over the river's growl.

Suddenly, it struck me what had vaguely disturbed me ever since we met. Ambiguous, subtle nuances of behavior, seemingly trivial, fell into place. I suddenly realized that he was prone to hysteria. The deadly situation of the moment was bringing it out of him, making clear what my vague feelings had tried to tell me.

Fear shot through me. It occurred to me for the first time in my adult memory, my life depended on someone else, and he was totally useless to either of us. My precarious predicament was not the most immediate problem, however. Don was. Only he could help me, and I needed help desperately. Fighting my own anxiety, which was mounting by the minute, it occurred to me how utterly ludicrous it was for me to miss the comfortable surroundings of my office. I tried to analyze Don's behavior and figure out my next move in an absolutely immovable situation. However, there was an incredible irony to it. It was only much later, in a totally different setting, I learned Don was already under psychiatric care.

Again, Don looked up at the sound of my voice. It might be better not to tell him what to do, but just to wave toward the bank. He ignored my motions and stepped closer to the edge of the bog. He unbuckled his belt, whirled it around and tried to toss it over to me. It should have been obvious to anyone that he would never make it. He might as well have been 10 miles short. It was better to pretend reaching out to grasp the belt and demonstrate it couldn't be done. He flipped the belt out a couple more times, and it seemed to finally dawn on him it wouldn't work. He was responding to reality, anyway. That was an improvement. Maybe now would be the right time to shout for the branch or log. Before my voice reached him, his reached me. "I'm coming in!" he yelled.

Something inside me groaned with despair, "Oh, no you idiot! There isn't the least good you can do either of us in here." What stuck in my mind, however, was an instant and profound sense of gratitude that he would even consider it. It was not only irrational, it was suicidal. His heart may have been in the right place, but his head wasn't. What could justify both of us in the same fix? If he could not help me from where he was, why would I want him to risk his life from where I was? I never believed in that kind of equality—not even now in quicksand. He stopped as though poleaxed when I bellowed with all the power I could deliver. "No!" He seemed stunned. It was a good sign—maybe he was reconsidering.

Meanwhile, I had been flexing my feet, or trying to, hoping they would find solid ground. They didn't. We had lost precious minutes (which seemed like hours), and the chill of glacial muck was paralyzing me. It seemed neither body nor mind wanted to work anymore. At nearly arms reach, there lay safety and life, yet there was nothing either of us could do about it. It was maddening—the thought of how to breach those few feet.

My mind was laboring to figure out how to get Don up the bank, but nothing came through the freezing, numbing cold. I had just enough sense left to keep my arms above the muck so they, at least, would be free to embrace some miracle. It broke on my awareness that the icy chill now reached my arm pits. World War II and the Alaska hunting trail had occasionally forced the strange sensation in my guts that death could be waiting just around the corner. But those were times when things were happening fast, and there was life and movement within me to do something, anything to fight back. But this! How bloody unfair it was, just waiting while my whole world stopped, leaving me helpless and hopeless. Time had stopped still. I could not recognize anything around me except a shadowy blur that had to be Don.

Just seeing him was the only comfort left in a rapidly disappearing world all around, being pulled down into some kind of oblivion, I knew not where. As long as my eyes could see him like some spectre, there was a tie to the world out there, no matter how far, how hazy, and how unreal it felt.

So, it was, his mere presence, standing there like a shadowy phantom, became the only thing and everything to me. That shadow told me, when it was no longer there, then I could no longer be here, deprived of everything except a terrifying aloneness only he had kept away, thus far. We were transfixed, gazing at each other. Each in his own world. Each paralyzed in his own way. Each mutely trying to read the other's thoughts.

I don't know how many minutes I slowly sank during that eternity, but I learned the infinite meaning of aloneness—it is feeling totally separated from fellow man when in his very presence. That must be the basis for all despair and the loss of all hope. I wanted to say "good-bye" to him, but nothing would come out, yet my eyes must have said it for me, because, for a moment, I swore I could see his eyes trying to say "good-bye" to me. Between drifting in and out of awareness, I sensed vaguely what I was feeling toward him—sorrow, nay, pity. Here was a man of his stature in our community reduced to a pathetic bungler, and, somehow, I felt responsible. Of all things to come to mind, and at that moment!

Was Don coming out of it, at last—or was he running away?

311

His voice stabbed through my numbness, returning me to full awareness. "I'm going to the plane to get some rope," he yelled.

Again, something groaned inside me, and a thought flashed that, even if he were an Olympic runner, he'd never make a nearly 2-mile round trip in time. More, he was taking away the only thing I had left to cling to—the image of something human I could recognize. He turned to go, and my voice didn't sound like it belonged to me, but to some total stranger I never knew, when I gasped one word, "No!"

Did my voice sound so grotesque it frightened him? Or else, why did he seem so terrified when he stopped, turned around, looked at me so oddly and fell to his knees again? A feeling of surprise tried to stagger into my mind at the sound of my voice. It was a gasp, instead of the shout I intended, because the deep breath needed for it could not be sucked in. Another surprise. The icy muck, now almost at my throat, had compressed my rib cage, imperceptibly, like a steel band. Instead of the expected shout, only a gasp barely trickled out, and it was eerie how the surprise and new sensation skewered itself into awareness.

Hearing myself utter such a helpless, almost plaintive, whimpering sound, is undoubtedly what did it. I sounded like some alien being. I had given up all hope Don could do anything for me and accepted my aloneness. I had resolved to wait for death with the only thing left to me—my sense of dignity.

When I heard the sound of that feeble gasp I barely uttered, I realized there was nothing dignified, or even human, about it. I was not going to my death with calm dignity. I was going like a squeaking, trapped rat, and I knew I could never go that way.

It's funny what happens to a man's ego not yet broken—even in such a moment. That thought did it, filling me with a raging fury, refusing to accept the reality my mind had resigned itself to only moments earlier. I wanted to see death face to face so I could at least throw one punch at that thief who wanted what was mine.

I will never know what made me do it, and resorting to the subconscious mind was an academic cop out. Something seized my very being, and I felt a flow of strength I had never known before. In my earlier exhaustion, my arms must have dropped, for they were immersed in the muck—my left hand still holding my rifle now almost completely submerged. With all the might my body could muster, born of strength and fury, I tore my arms loose from that mire, raised them high, and brought them down full force on that hateful expanse of silent terror claiming my life. It was my last act of defiance against the final humiliation, or so I thought.

I glared at an alien world in front of me that had become a cold foggy mist of surrealistic shadows without depth and substance. My fingers had loosened around a solidness that must have been my rifle. The last sensation I remember was a gritty grinding between my clenched teeth of muck that had gotten into my mouth. There was a flicker of a memory-trace recalling similar teeth grinding grit in rain-filled mud-holes in World War II. I don't know how long my mind went blank after that.

What made Don do it? Who knows? The high-pitched tension of his voice broke through—or was it just imagination? His words seemed to come from another planet. "Spread eagle! Spread eagle!" That's all he screamed, hysterically, but it was enough to rattle me loose from oblivion.

I'd heard of drowning men clutching at straws, but no one clutched more desperately than I to the vanishing sounds of those words. A glimmer of hope and the urge to finish the fight came back. My right hand clawed into the ooze and my left hand, still clutching my rifle, accidentally buried the butt of it into that muck. It stuck upright like an oar giving me some purchase against which to pull. It took all the effort I could regain to pull with my arm, and paddle after a fashion, with the other. The signal wasn't strong, but did the sensations below suggest my legs were angling upward?

The thought struck me, there must be a ton of silt and water in my nearly waist-high boots weighing me down. Mechanically, my chest pushed itself into the muck, and I tried raising my legs. It seemed, maybe, the sinking motion stopped and I felt a slow upward flotation. Suddenly, like a cork popping out of a bottle of champagne announcing some wild celebration, I was squeezed out of the muck until I was laying flat on that undulating surface. A uterus of death was giving me a second birth.

I don't know how long I lay there, exhausted, barely panting for air, my rib cage coming back to life. My mind tried to function, but all I could feel was the now icy wind blowing off the river freezing my brain. An overwhelming urge coaxed me into an uncontrollable desire to sleep, and how delicious it felt. I remember thinking how pleasant it would be to have a warm blanket over me for a little sleep—just a short nap to awaken refreshed.

I didn't have the faintest inkling, of course, that hypothermia was freezing me into a lethal, hypnotic state. I was floating on a cushion of dazzling light that I could see all around me. How seductive it was to hear soft musical chords from afar sounding like a Debussy tone-poem. Oddly enough, I had lost total contact with Don. I saw only splashes of pastel colors where I thought he had been standing. He seemed to have vanished forever.

I have no idea how long I was insensate, but something connected, somehow, somewhere deep inside. Something clicked (I really heard the sound), and I was jolted awake as though I had been drugged for a week. Had I really fallen asleep, or was there something more to it? I felt consciousness taking over. It felt utterly strange and unfamiliar, until I became aware of what I had fastened onto—the vague idea life still wanted me. I must have wanted it more than I knew.

I can't remember when I started to swim out of that nightmare, but became aware I was wiggling, thrashing, flailing, and squirming a tiny bit at a time trying to break free from a million fingers of viscous ooze tugging me back. Every momentary stop for air between movements pulled me downward with that tonnage in my boots. I was dimly aware some misshapen bulk in my side pocket acted like an anchor stopping forward movement (it turned out to be my camera, useless thereafter forevermore). I ran out of the little breath I had and stopped for a rest until my legs began to sink.

When I turned to my side again, there was Don, on his knees, right where I'd seen him last. He hadn't vanished anywhere. He had been there all along, only I had looked right at him and seen only pastel colors. I thought my musical tone-poem was his distorted voice, but he said, later, he was speechless with terror, thinking my feeble thrashing would suddenly stop. I don't know what gave me that burst of strength and those strange sensations in my nearly frozen state. Either I had had my own game of tag with a psychotic episode, otherwise known as going bananas, or had briefly experienced paranormal, transcendental realities I cannot explain rationally to this day. Neither one of us had the slightest idea how long this entire episode lasted.

I don't know when the endless mechanical motions stopped and when the nightmare ended, but I finally felt the rocky skirts of that great and elegant lady, Mother Earth, and lay exhausted. Don was deathly silent. I uttered his name a few times. Some while later, I felt his hands trying to pull me to my feet.

I cannot recall when I had last so welcomed the warm handclasp of another human being. No matter our past grudges, we embraced and I managed to gasp that I didn't know how to thank him for what he had done for me. I was looking right into his eyes, so I couldn't miss the way his gaze wavered and fell. His face seemed pale and his hands trembled. I was still half frozen, so was it I, or did he really seem as though I'd hurt him just by expressing my most sincere gratitude?

He must have read my thoughts. "Oh, yeah? After the way I panicked just kneeling there watching you?" he stammered.

Of course! He didn't know—how could he—what his mere presence, his just kneeling there, had really meant to me when I thought it was all over. He deserved better than his shame and self-reproach, and only an unregenerate scoundrel would have refused to help him. I had started walking to get some warmth moving through me and trying to figure out how best to handle it.

Never mind what the past had done to us. There was only one decent thing to do now, so I stopped, turned him around and said, "Look, you really came through for me when you yelled for me to spread eagle. I didn't think of that myself, you did."

Given some of our past dislikes for each other, it was not exactly easy for me to say. He seemed finally to appreciate what he'd done and how I felt. One more thing needed saying, because it was just the way I felt and if he wanted to laugh at me, let him. "There's no way I can ever repay you for this, but I am in your debt—I owe you," I said. It got through to him.

"You know," he said, "I thought of spread eagle only when you smashed your arms into the muck. Why didn't you do it sooner— that's what made me think of it."

I told him the absolute truth. "I don't know. Maybe I should have gotten madder, sooner," I said, but knew the ice-cold muck had frozen my otherwise fiery temper. I said nothing about my futile efforts at trying to be dignified, or my strange, semiconscious episodes. We broke into laughter realizing how each had unwittingly contributed to the solution. It is truly said two heads are better than one. For the first time in our pragmatic relationship, real warmth seemed to glimmer.

As we got aloft, heading back home, Don said, "I'll take you to the hospital as soon as we land—just for a checkup."

My opposition was immediate. It was already too close to 1 o'clock—the time for my introductory psychology lecture at the university. He began remonstrating, but reluctantly agreed. When we landed, he broke all speed laws driving the 12 miles to my home.

My appearance in the mirror aped the Glob from Outer Space encapsulated with drying muck. Stripping off my clothes broke off chunks of mud. Where it had dried, it cascaded off me in a powdery spray. There was time only for me to get into clean, dry underwear and trousers, grab the rest of my clothing, and finish dressing as the car sped toward the campus.

A dash across the quadrangle got me to Schaible Auditorium, where the clock on the wall showed 7 minutes past the hour. The students had only 3 more minutes before their 10-minute courtesy wait for tardy professors was up. They gawked at me charging to the lectern. My appearance must have been something, indeed.

By odd coincidence, my scheduled lecture was on the reticulated activation system, the hypothalamus, and the medulla of the brain. These are the areas of the brain involved in the emotional and involuntary workings of the rest of the nervous system. Diagraming them on the board, it occurred to me that my theoretical discussion had been an agonizing reality barely an hour earlier. Nothing could have had a more uncanny timing.

Suddenly, my body began to shake and my teeth started to chatter. Stress, ice baths, close calls, or whatever. It was impossible to continue speaking, so violent did my shivering become. My brain was doing precisely what theory said it would under such conditions. Stumbling to the back of the hall, I waved at the warm parka on the chair next to its student owner, who caught my meaning and lent it to me.

Returning to the blackboard, it became obvious what the front rows of students were murmuring about. Every time my hands wrote or erased on the blackboard, the overhead lights were caught in shimmering reflections on tiny particles of mica glistening wherever the hateful mud had dried on my skin.

A student asked if anything was wrong, and that prompted me to give a brief and guarded explanation of what had happened. Later, several of them said it was one of my best lectures! Experience is a great teacher for the mind, body, and soul of a man who has seen the end in quicksand, but by some miracle, survives it.

There was yet another odd coincidence. Three days later, the morning mail crossed my desk—including a scientific journal carrying an article on quicksand. I devoured it, never having read anything like it before.

The fellow who wrote it said no one could drown in quicksand, and if one kept his head high enough above the surface, eventually he would float. I wanted so much to believe that and think my nightmare in the ooze had been some kind of joke. It was hard to believe, because, like all theory, it was torn out of a real context. It said nothing about how the silt and water in one's hip boots would weigh one down to upset the flotation theory. Nor did the article say how long one could stay alive in temperatures just above freezing, even if flotation worked. My conclusion was the theory might work, but only if one fell into quicksand in the tropics, stark naked.

The afternoon found me with my rifle at the local gunsmith. "This rifle has been doused in quicksand. Would you please clean, oil, and check it"?

"Quicksand"?

"Yeah. On the banks of the Tanana."

"The Tanana? You're crazy!"

"You wanna bet"?

He didn't say anything more, but watched me walk out of his shop. He wore a peculiar expression on his face.

Within the next few days, two important things occurred. First, my rifle was retrieved. It looked clean, beautiful, and shiny, like my good old bear-killing rifle again. This overjoyed me.

The second thing shocked me. By accident, it was revealed to me Don was charging me three times the actual cost for his gasoline. Given my feelings of gratitude toward him, this discovery stirred mixed feelings. It really wasn't the money. It would still have been worth it. It was the deception on top of all else. It hurt perhaps more.

My first resolve was to tell him I knew about his secret, but my sense of gratitude helped me decide the honorable thing was to end our relationship and forget the whole thing.

A few weeks later, Don called again reporting lots of bears were being seen again in the Manley area. Ah—my wretched passion for the bears of Manley! Hunting fever was rekindled so intensely my earlier resolve was thrown aside. So was my caution and resentment. In ancient language, this must be what was known as selling one's soul to the devil.

No man should want anything as badly as I wanted a Manley bear. If I had only listened to those who had told me often about the consequences to idolatry. My compromise would exact a high cost, eventually.

No sooner did I hang up the phone (after my acceptance) than second thoughts assailed me. They weren't about Don. They grew out of a vague, undefinable feeling, a foreboding unfamiliar to me. Experience had yet to teach me such feelings should not be dismissed. They must be heeded and grappled with until one's intuition makes their meaning clear. The soul can understand what the mind, with its reason and logic, cannot know. My professional education was of modern prejudice that rejected the mystical. It took a long time for me to become reeducated.

Again, the thrill of anticipation lulled all this into the back of my mind, as we cruised along in a bright sky. Far below, everything was bathed in sunshine, peaceful and verdant. The terrain looked like a giant, fuzzy blanket, quilted with a hundred different shades of green. Master artist, Autumn, was already dabbing spots of gold, yellow, and brown on the unlimited canvas man calls the Alaska wilderness.

The drone of the plane's engine had lulled me into a delicious drowsiness, when a jolt jarred me wide awake. Don banked sharply, bouncing the plane briefly in a bit of turbulence. He was heading back home. Out of the corner of my eye and the corner of the window something appeared a moment. It was a pinpoint of black in the middle of a sand patch, surrounded by evergreens at the edge of a lake. It would have meant nothing, except it just didn't belong there. It was decidedly out of context. Was it a bear or a weathered stump? Why was Don turning back so suddenly?

My hand shot out and squeezed his shoulder, but he shouted immediately over the engine's drone, "It's a stump!" There was a difference between what it could be and what it was and that's what needed resolution in my mind. If Don knew for sure it was a stump, then he had phenomenal visual acuity for any man at that altitude. Besides, his answer had been too immediate to sound cogitative; moreover, how did he know to what my signal referred?

My mind took a decidedly nasty turn, but if I were wrong, there was plenty of time to feel guilty, later. Right now, I wanted to be as sure as he was about the stump down there. There was a simple way to find out. At my insistence for a closer look, he grew more resistant, then evasive, then visibly irritated, but finally gave in when he saw I would not. We descended.

From 500 feet, circling back, the blackened stump glistened. The lower we got, the bigger it seemed—bigger than any stump could possibly be on tundra where only spruce, no bigger than a man's forearm could grow.

Suddenly, my eyes locked into the movement of the stump, and my adrenaline shot into high gear. "It's a bear!" I shouted, trembling with excitement.

Don shouted back, "Nope, it can't be," and started pulling away after a halfhearted tipping of his wing—he didn't even bank.

Now my suspicions became certitude, and I insisted (with some profanity thrown in for good measure) he circle lower. This time, he admitted it was a bear, but now he shouted back quite cavalierly, "It's dead." Like a splash of ice-cold water, it finally struck me beyond a reasonable doubt. My good ol' hunting buddy, about whom I had changed my mind, now changed back to his good ol' self. We were back in business.

"Dead my eye!" was my instant retort. The expanse of jet black fur glistened and rippled with movement. It was impossible to mistake that, even if one had only half an eye. It was a large, magnificent animal clawing dirt and leaves over the remains of a moose kill (just as clearly visible). It was trying to hide tidbits for tomorrow's luncheon.

What did Don say about all this? He repeated the incredible claim that it was dead and began to climb again, heading for home. This was not reality denial; this was a damnable lie.

My suspicions had not been based on some nasty paranoia, but on sound intuition. It required no crystal ball to see Don's intent. Without doubt, he would return tomorrow, and so would the bear to claim his chow; it would not be a coincidental luncheon engagement. Any prior agreement that the bear would be mine was being abrogated. Don wanted my money and the bear, who was too magnificent to ignore.

Another nasty thought occurred to me. I had assumed the bear had killed the moose—he was big enough. It seemed more plausible Don had shot the moose previously and left it there for bait, precisely to attract a giant like the bear we now saw. Had we been flying around only to find out if a bear had discovered the bait? That being done, no wonder Don was so anxious to leave the area before I could see what I had seen. Of course, this was speculation, but it was not idle, and there were enough facts to warrant it. I would confront him later, because for now I was angry with myself looking for trouble.

Don was testing me—calling my bluff by changing the ground rules at 3,000 feet aloft and gaining altitude rapidly. I was disgusted for having tolerated my pragmatics leading to this deception. There was no need for reality-denial—the fault was mine from A to Z.

Who says there is no justice? If Don was calling my bluff, then it could no longer be ignored. Leaning forward so my words would not be drowned in the engine's roar, my ultimatum was delivered—turn the plane back to the lake, stay out of my way while I go in to get my bear, and stay out of my way henceforth and forever after on our return to Fairbanks—the charade was over.

The color drained from his face, but he banked the plane and headed back, circling over the lake. Mixed emotions raced through me. There was some satisfaction in having made him submit to my will. I had a feeling elemental justice had been done. Contempt for the man and what he tried to get away with, however, shook my feelings of gratitude, leaving me with too much anger at my earlier compromise. My thoughts were interrupted as the pontoons split the water into twin jets of spray. He cut the motor and taxied the plane around, heading toward the shore straight ahead. Don let himself out and nimbly cat walked the narrow pontoon to its leading edge, then slipped into the water.

Easing out of the cabin, still angry, I peered into the water, but the bottom was not visible. A quick glance forward revealed Don pushing the plane around to squarely face the shore, skirting a good-sized clearing straight ahead. He was in about 3 feet of water, the top of his hip boots barely above water line. My brain registered the fact we were about 15 feet from the water's edge. That seemed odd. The plane should have been pulled up ahead until the forward tips of the pontoons rested on the gravel—the usual procedure for anchoring a floatplane. My brain registered the fact, but it made no sense. To enter the water where I was standing would have gotten me in too deep. Swinging past the struts, I too, got to the leading edge to let myself into the water.

Don's fingers gripped tightly around my ankle. "Where are you going?" he stammered.

"You know where I'm going—to get the bear," I growled, kicking his hand loose. He grabbed me again, just as I knelt to slip into the water.

"What happens if you don't get him first, and he comes tearing into this plane? He can wreck the plane," he said, his voice rising to a sharp, hysterical pitch.

So, that was it! That's why we were anchored so far from the shore. While the water between us might not stop a determined bear, it would surely reduce his odds at close quarters. A wave of revulsion seized me at the shabbiness of the trick. It was nothing compared to what followed.

"You've got to stay here," he insisted, "and if that bear comes into the clearing, we can both get a shot from the plane." It was legal, but hardly ethical or sporting.

My cool instantly evaporated. As he scrambled back onto the pontoon, my only thought was to hammer him into oblivion. Is this what we had become—hunters shooting from the safety of the plane? Maybe Don thought black bear were vermin not worthy of our respect. My thought was, were we worthy of the bear's respect! It was bad enough using a plane to land in his back yard; now he was to be shot from it! How much more could we debase the sportsman's code and still claim we were sportsmen—or even men?

My blow never landed. It was Don who knocked the wind out of my sails. Never before had his voice sounded so calm and deliberate, "Have you forgotten the quicksand?" What a moment to demand his due! It was perfect timing. I'd have preferred he punch me out and leave me there to rot than to strike that way. He stopped me cold. There was nothing spontaneous about his delivery—he had obviously prepared his strategy well and played his trump card without batting an eye.

It took several moments before recovery set in. Don watched my every move, and knew he had me. There was nothing for me to do but catwalk back to the cabin, my brain whirling with a hundred conflicting thoughts. If he thought my debt of gratitude could be paid off so cheaply, then very well—pay him off and cancel the debt. But something inside me snapped. Something beautiful in my dreams of the noble confrontation between man and animal became something dirty and ugly. Somehow, the follies and deceptions between men profaned the dignity of that glorious animal by making him part of a sordid bargain. Suddenly, every desire for that bear disappeared. The only thing mattering now was to protect him from being hunted as Don understood the term.

A couple of shots overhead might chase him away, but then he would return tomorrow and dally near his kill—and Don would be there. If the bear could be frightened away now, it would be possible to go in and drag the moose kill into the water and scatter the offal pile. When he returned tomorrow, he might not hang around too long, no matter how angry he would be. That would reduce Don's odds and increase the bear's. That would require leaving the plane, and my resolve to discharge my debt of honor was now compulsive. To be freed from the hold Don had on me, it would be better to refuse a dozen bears—so strong had my contempt for all this become.

I was boxed in, trapped, stalemated by the dilemma. If the bear did not show, Don would be here tomorrow. If the bear did show in the clearing ahead, and made any move toward the plane, Don would fire, without any doubt, on the real or fancied premise his plane needed protection. If it was wrecked, his insurance would cover it. If we survived the bear and the plane didn't, rescue crews would have found us. Our flight plans were filed. These worries were the farthest things from my mind just then, no matter what Don thought.

The only thing left was to admit I had lost, demand he get me home and let chance do whatever it would on the morrow. The only thing more shameful than betraying that bear was betraying my self-respect to Don again. The bear had a chance—I didn't.

Don did not go so far as to gloat openly, but neither did he hesitate at my request to get me home. Quickly, he unscrewed the cover off the first compartment in the pontoon and began pumping out water that always seeps in on landing. He was kneeling on the pontoon, bent over, and didn't see it, but looking over his shoulder my eyes could not miss it. It was the bear!

He was absolutely gorgeous, as he strode rapidly and stiff-legged into the clearing. It was the unmistakable shuffle of an enraged bear who knew no fear. His huge shaggy head swung side to side as he sniffed the trail—and then he saw us. The berserk Manley bear at the quicksand may have bolted at the human presence, but not this one. He spun adroitly to his left and came straight on. Obviously, not the water nor anything else was going to stop him.

It took a moment for me to recover. That bear should have left the area long since, or taken a lot longer to get to us. A hoarse whisper escaped me, though it might as well have been a roar.

"The bear, Don, the bear!"

He raised his head and saw it in an instant, and, in his haste to stand up and get back to the cabin, he nearly slipped and fell in.

"My gun, my gun," he demanded, his voice betraying panic. His crouched stance, restricted by the narrowness of the pontoon, placed him exactly in the way of my sight.

Brusquely waving my hand, I ordered, "Get out of the way!" He would never have enough time to get his rifle—the bear was moving too fast.

Don froze. We were close enough for me to see the look of release in his eyes, as though he had just let go of the world. Again, he ignored the wave of my hand, and it was obvious he wasn't going to move aside, just like he wouldn't climb the bank at the quicksand. For a wild moment, it occurred to me to jump into the water, but luckily some instinct stayed the impulse. The depth of the water, the uncertain footing below, and the time lost in readjusting my position would make it a foolish risk. The problem was my unshakable habit of not pointing a loaded gun at anyone. It took a certain amount of conscious and deliberate effort to do so—even over his shoulder. It did the trick, however, and there wasn't a moment to lose. Babbling something that sounded like, "No, no, no, don't hit the plane," he finally ducked.

In those few moments, distracted by Don's antics, I'd lost eye-contact with the bear, and when next I zoomed in on him again, he had covered a lot of territory. His sudden nearness rattled me. My body leaned into the anticipated kick of my .338 and the shot, though hasty, went true—over Don's head, past the struts, under the wing, and right into the bear's shoulder. Down he went in a heap, as they say. The narrow footing on the slippery pontoon didn't hold me too well, and the recoil nearly flipped me over.

Maybe now was the time to do the fair thing—get into the water, wade ashore, and deliver the telling shot from ground level. He looked like he would stay down under the impact of that 300-grain slug. But he didn't. He was up in a moment. He was a fighter, all right. He shuddered for an instant, trying to fix whatever it was that wouldn't support his leg, and started coming for us again, without slowing.

In an instant, I froze the image on my brain. My memory has clung to the thought that the distance, cautiously guessed, could not have been more than 30 yards, and there was time to do nothing else but shoot fast. Wading ashore was impossible.

Slamming home another shell and bracing myself for better footing on that miserable pontoon, my aim was careful and my trigger squeeze calm and deliberate. His slightly elevated head offered a beautiful chest target. Rarely have I been so stunned as in that next second. All I felt was the hollow click of the trigger, the total lack of recoil. A misfire! With modern, factory loaded shells? Impossible! Something must be wrong with the rifle—the thought raced through my mind—but there was no time to find out now. There wasn't even enough time to lower the stock from my cheek. My fingers flew to the bolt, yanked it back, and shoved it forward again. What if it doesn't fire was the last thought in my mind as my finger squeezed the trigger, hoping against hope. Sheer exuberance hammered through me as the rifle boomed and the recoil delivered its usual jolt. Even better, the bear collapsed without a quiver as he came down hard, with a perfect heart shot, almost at the water's edge.

Don, who had stayed put, fully aware, apparently, of what was going on, became jubilant and profuse about my shooting. Guilt has nagged me ever since for my petty retort, "Why, because he didn't wreck your bloody plane?"

Nothing but disgust filled me with the way everything had happened. The bear had not given me a real chance to go in after him on his own terms. Neither had Don. There was nothing more to say or do except fight back my disappointment. As I lowered myself into the water, my legs began to shake—my mind obsessed with the misfire and the closeness of that call. What if the first shot had misfired instead of the second? It was simply impossible to have stopped that bear, even if my calm had not been rattled. It was equally obvious that if the third shot had failed, there would have been no time for another chance. Chills went up and down my spine. The cold water had nothing to do with it. My lucky star had shone on me again—Don and I would have been helpless in the water and could have been seriously mauled or even killed—to say nothing of Don's wretched plane.

Don joined me in a few moments, helping me to skin the bear. He was voluble, friendly, and cajoling—only too much so. It was an act to cover up his foiled plans to get that bear for himself and to mollify me. If he couldn't beat me, he'd join me, was my guess. Again, he complimented me for my shooting, expressed admiration for my bear, and stammered the phoniest of apologies for having honestly made a mistake about the stump. I was trying hard to repress my fury. Did he really think I was so dumb? Apparently. When he met my icy stare of contempt, he got placatory. With a breezy smile, he assured me I would get over hurt feelings and we would go again soon and have even a better hunt; maybe we could even try for grizzly!

All I said in reply was, "Please give me the bill for what I owe you," and silently vowed I would never hunt with him again, even if he put me on the trail of the world's number one record. I could not barter my pride again for another deal like this one.

The bear went 1 inch under 7 feet, and my guess was he could have easily weighed 500 pounds, maybe more. He was a big black bear for Alaska, or anywhere else for that matter. I should have been delirious with joy, but all I felt was bitter disappointment. He just didn't feel like a trophy. Yet nothing in the world would have forced me to abandon him to become carrion—that would have mocked the tragedy of this day and robbed the animal of deserved honor. I would have faced a firing squad before I admitted that Don, given the attitudes he revealed, deserved that bear one tenth of an iota. To let him have the bear I no longer wanted, would have been blasphemy. I was stuck with the bear.

Flying home, my feelings were of disgust with myself and sorrow for a magnificent bear. I had not really hunted him because there was no stalk on his own turf. I had merely killed him in a strange encounter, unwanted and unexpected. How my very being wished the circumstances had been different! However, there had been no other way—that's what reality had compelled; that's what the gods of the chase had decreed. When I got home, I brooded all night.

What bothered me again was the misfire and what could have resulted. Suddenly, it hit me. Just after my acceptance of Don's invitation on the phone, second thoughts and a vague premonition had bedeviled me. Was this what it was all about? Had I gotten close to the bear on his own turf, with a malfunctioning rifle, he may very well have won! Was it possible Don's wretched behavior had saved me from greater grief? I would never know.

It was impossible to sleep that night. In the wee hours of the morning, it became apparent my confidence in the rifle was gone. That is more deadly in its consequences than to lose confidence in a wife who has betrayed you.

Suddenly an inkling of things past wracked my brain. Then a wild guess flashed through my mind. Out came the rifle and my fingers flew over the bolt, taking it apart. There it was! The spring was imbedded in solid silt. The firing pin orifice also was packed with silt, leaving a needle-sized opening through which the firing pin was barely able to emerge. My fist slammed the table top so hard, the coffee cup bounced clean off the saucer and broke. There was no use trying to go back to sleep.

It was still early, and the gunsmith had not yet opened for business when I pounded on his door. He let me in and stood sheepishly at my denunciation of his assistant's work. He had cut corners for a paltry $5 and could have cost two lives and, oh yes, an airplane.

He seemed genuinely appalled as my story unfolded, and he promised to make amends. He was told what to do with that offer. It might not have been fair to say more since his fly-by-night assistant had already left his employment, and the state.

Not long after, Don, true to form, had the gall to call, again. He needed to log more time before the fast-approaching winter set in, and he wanted to "make it up to me with a super hunt."

Contrary to his earlier prophecy that I would get over hurt feelings and change my mind, I refused. I couldn't recall when I had been so polite in refusing, so firmly and finally, anything to anyone.

The last time we saw each other was about 4 years later. A flood devastated much of Fairbanks, and our paths crossed briefly. A barricade had been erected at the water's edge on what had been a main intersection now congested with traffic. We were driving in opposite directions, and he saw me first. He shouted my name and a big hello. When I looked out, he was waving his hand wildly out the window. My reaction surprised me, for my heart jumped with a gladness I did not think possible. Time had healed most of the bad memories and introduced some good ones. My salutation rang out to him, but we could not stop to chat in the jumble of traffic the policeman was directing.

Shortly thereafter, mutual friends told me Don had left the state. Sometime later, I learned he had died of a drug overdose. It was a bit of news that left me with a deep sorrow that has never left me entirely.

Reflections

Memory is a blessing and a curse—it is also imperative because without it life has no continuity. Without continuity, meaning is impossible. Without meaning, there is no purpose. Without purpose, there is no desire to go on. Without desire to go on, reason sneaks in to ask us why should we go on despite the odds.

It is a truism that life is a collection of memories, but it is not true you can't take it with you, because it depends on what "it" refers to. "It" does not mean only material things. It also means our memories that I believe to be our ultimate possessions—the only things we really own, uniquely ours—we take to whatever final destination because no one has yet figured out how to steal them from us in advance. (This does not rule out, of course, the possibility some governmental agency will not do so when it figures out how.)

Whether memories delight us, or torture us, depends on which unique events in our life we have experienced. One of the unique experiences in the memory bank of my life was the bears of Manley. Subsequent experiences, even routine ones, have, on occasion, pushed the buttons that activate memory and connect it to so many other things with meaning in my life. The great

Armenian poet, M. Beshiktashlian has asked, "What sound beneath the stars aflame, so lovely as a brother's name?" The question always torments me when I think of Don in the episodes at Manley. In spite of having lived through some of life's most intense moments bringing us to the edge of death, Don and I could not become friends—let alone brothers. Often, I was rankled by the question—what more was needed to make friendship or brotherhood possible?

It is the hunting trail, forever brutally honest, that tears off the social masks and reveals the real self within, which men wear when they hunt together. If the finest of men can fall apart on the hunting trail, and even become enemies, then may not the worst of men find the best friendship traits on the same trail? Surely, the hunting trail of the primitive past is where the sense of brotherhood was born—or how could man have survived the brutal ordeals of mere existence on pragmatic arrangements alone? Without trust in his partner, which hunter would have risked the onslaught of the saber-toothed tiger?

The immortal, Omar Khayyam, said of life, "We come into it like water willy-nilly flowing, and like the wind go out of it, willy-nilly blowing without knowing why nor where." It just happens. It seemed true of the relationship between Don and me, like water willy-nilly flowing. The real symbols were all there to characterize it—the Tanana River, the quagmire, the lakes—and waters of the flood when we saw each other for the last time. Yet, the man who caused me so much anguish, grief, and ill-will on the trail, saved my life, nevertheless—didn't he? And he left me with a debt of gratitude I can never repay. What I would give after all these years to embrace him for just a moment and tell him of my sorrow for all the ugliness and wrongs that no longer matter, for the true friendship never born, for reverence to his memory the years built up within me, so contrary to whatever I imagined then.

Whenever memory taps on the window of my mind to quietly peek in, I feel sadness at his passing, so untimely because he had so much more to give to our community. That's what counted, not our failings on the trail. Then, I become angry because, of all things, it had to be despicable drugs that claimed him, when he better deserved a more honorable and longer life. What a tragic waste! Then, I say to myself the only thing I can—may your restless soul rest in peace, forever, my friend.

There lives in my memory another piece of this mosaic I inherited from Manley—that glorious, magnificent bear so undeservedly taken. Given my reasons to prevent Don from killing that bear in the penultimate moment, it would have been impossible for me to squeeze the trigger and take that bear's life if he had not charged and changed the situation so dangerously in the twinkling of an eye. True, he gave me a few exciting moments, duplicated only twice in my hunting career with close calls in Africa: once by a lion a split second before he sprang, and once by an elephant who was well on his way toward me, with murder in his eyes.

However, I shall always be sorry I could not take that bear on his own ground, on his own terms, worthily stalked and confronted with a fairer chance to escape or fight back. Secretly, however, I have always been glad he charged and almost made it—it reduced the odds against him, if only a little, and if it's any satisfaction to him in bear heaven or the Happy Hunting Grounds, I'm prouder of him for the way he died than I am of myself for the way I lived on that fateful day. Yet, I know if he had taken me first (hunters have lost in the contest), it would have made no difference to him either way.

I resolved from that day forward to pursue the ideal of a perfect black bear hunt. Aside from other desires, I felt such a hunt would make it up to my Manley bear, who fell so quietly at the water's edge, by giving one of his cousins the odds he never had. That came to pass 2 or 3 years later with a scrawny, undersized bear who gave me the greatest thrill of my life, and changed it spiritually.

The hunts for black bears of Manley taught me more than most books about the spirit of the hunt and the motivations of hunters. They just provided raw experiences later related to other events and became important parts of my philosophy on hunting—an intellectual hunt for the real meaning of hunting, which has occupied so many thinkers on the subject.

That glorious bear, cherished to this day as a rug I rarely step on, radically altered my attitude toward all black bears. I had always respected the black bear, because I respect all animals, but I did not think of him as something special. This was hard to do, given his public image with things like the caricature of Smokey the Bear in his forest ranger's uniform, things like movies and magazine photos showing a docile, dumb-dumb animal begging for food from the tourists in our national parks, and the clever political propaganda concealed in television serials showing how gently bears, even grizzlies, played with children and romped with real he-men (who, somehow, were not stigmatized as being macho) who really "understood" these "cute" animals. How I came to detest the creation of that public image.

The black bear is neither cute, nor vermin. He is one of nature's most noble creations. He may look like a funny, adorable clown, and maybe he is, on occasion (and I imagine so was Tyrannosaurus rex—on occasion). He is also formidable, with plenty of killing power, and he can move with the speed of lightning. He is not as ferocious, powerful, or efficient as the grizzly, but he is plenty dangerous, especially if wounded, and the records indicate a fair share of hunters have lost the encounter. My respect for him changed to admiration after my own encounter. He is something special. Only a fool, or those making movies with trained animals, will caricature him and falsify the reality of what he is.

Almost no hunt for big game animals is really ever finished with the kill. The more unique the hunt, the more perilous the exigencies, and more dramatic the adventures, the more likely it is such hunts will not only stay alive in the hunter's memory, but are apt to be shared with others. Nor does one have to rely solely on memory. There are cameras, camcorders, video tapes—and best of all, the mounted trophy in one's home.

This—the mounted trophy—is the objective, the treasure most difficult to find. It symbolizes two of the most dominant values in our culture: achievement and success, which are often denounced by those who fail to attain them, or by those who have more than their fair share, will not relinquish it, and cover their guilt by protesting too much.

If that trophy was obtained with honor, according to the tenets of fair chase, it will always give the hunter a sense of pride or self-respect. If obtained dishonorably, then the code was violated and, no matter how much a hunter may deceive others with his exploits, he cannot lie to himself. He will feel the shame and guilt. It is better not to have a trophy, because it will goad memory with what should never have been, and that can only produce pain. It is respect and reverence for that animal that produces the code, and it is the code that separates the men from the boys in the field. Every true hunter must kill his animal (if he is to have hunted successfully), but not every killer of animals is a true hunter.

Another attitude developed in me was born at Manley. The

next three or four hunting episodes I experienced strengthened my beliefs into a firm conviction. It has gotten me into trouble with antihunters and fellow hunters alike. There is a totally erroneous and even perverse notion abroad in the popular wisdom that hunting is fun, or should be, and this is why hunters hunt—for the fun of it.

When a hunt lasts anywhere from 3 or 4 days to 3 or 4 weeks, and it is fun every day in every way, it must be taking place in the lunatic asylum. Things can, and do, go wrong on a hunt and can be so mortally unfunny that fun becomes a cruel joke. There is a difference between the ecstatic joy of having achieved some challenging goal and having fun for the routine killing of an animal. In that simple fact is all the difference in the world. Killing is the most regrettable part of the entire affair, but it is the necessary thing if one is to have hunted successfully or no trophy is possible.

There was no fun, or anything funny, about my ordeal in the quicksand. Nor did I think it fun to kill a noble black bear I would have given anything to avoid under the circumstances. Nor will I use the pretext of fun to deny the constant sadness mixed with joy, the occasional guilt and shame, the pride in what was well done, and one's humanity that paid the price for it all.

As I've already said, it took three or four more hunts to teach me what I was really hunting for, and it was not fun, as I found out the hard way. Yet, I, like so many others who have known the excitement of the chase, increased my commitment to the calculated risk. What I sought and hunted for could be had in no other way, fun or no fun.

There was something else from Manley. Why did I return the second time, when there was enough grief the first time to have kept me away from the hunting trail forever? When they asked Willie "the Actor" Sutton why he kept robbing banks, his answer was, "That's where the money is." I am often asked, especially by opponents to hunting, why I go on the hunting trail if it's so risky, and I can only say, "That's where the trophies are."

I know, of course, the question is not concerned with my well being. It is concerned with the equanimity of the questioner—he would just feel better if he knew I had not gotten something I really wanted. He just doesn't want me out there to begin with, for his own peace of mind—never mind the animal he will probably never see or know anything about. As long as it stays out there, safe and unharmed in the mystery of wilderness, then there is something to revere, to hope for. It is the promise of heaven arriving in due time. And then the hunter steps in to screw it all up.

I learned another lesson that day, and it became an immutable rule of thumb for me—no matter how skilled a hunting companion may be, his skills are no substitute for character traits of mutual respect, trust, loyalty, and responsibility. There is too much at stake on the hunting trail, too much that can go seriously wrong, and if tragedy is to be avoided, it may require the kind of commitment and integrity only the best of friendships can provide. In this day and age of the pragmatic, those are rare qualities to find, and maybe this is why true friendships are so hard to come by. Even if nothing seriously wrong occurs, the companion who does not know of what companionship consists will produce unpleasant and ugly moments to mar or spoil what would have otherwise been precious and beautiful.

Some technical lessons I learned that day—never fail to personally check any repair done by a gunsmith. Most of them are superb craftsmen, but at least one I know did not oversee faulty work. It forced me to transport silt in my rifle from one place to another, causing a malfunction that could have had disastrous results.

In a more humorous vein, I learned another lesson that may not matter to others, but it surely did to me. Sometime after that hunt, I had occasion to sleep, or try to, on a waterbed. The moment that undulating, rolling surface moved beneath me, I leaped off. I have never slept on one, and never shall.

Then, there is the matter of hip boots. I wore them around water one more time with dire consequences. I swore off them after that. I would rather risk trench foot than wear those deathtraps.

There was another lesson learned from that hunt, and it is the most important. It can be learned and relearned on almost every hunt, but the right kind of hunt teaches the unforgettable lesson once and for all. The attitudes developed from such a hunt are present in every other hunt. With me, the basic ambience in many of my hunts carried over from the attitudes learned from the quicksand near Manley.

All of us, at one time or another, have engaged in overly serious philosophical discourse, better known these days as a bull session. We start with genuinely intelligent questions, and end with genuinely stupid retorts masquerading as answers, creating even more disagreement than before the question was raised.

One of these philosophical discussions, which often trapped me, had to do with death and religion that any hunter can hardly avoid, these days. The retort (mine to others and others to me, depending on who was losing the argument or his ego, which amount to the same thing) was we turn to the comforts of religion because we fear the unknown after death. This was a nice way of saying those who feared the unknown were cowards and needed help and I, too, shared this attitude. Perhaps this is so, but if so, then it is for reasons having little to do with the unknown. I have come to believe it is not death we fear so much as the manner of dying, which we cannot know until it is upon us. Inevitably, any serious hunter of dangerous game faces this problem.

The world's major religious faiths tell the believer what lies in the hereafter, sometimes with stark, detailed clarity. The faithful, who have lived up to the standards of the faith, hope for the better world to go to. Those who rebelled against their faith, without disbelieving it altogether, know the worse world they go to. Even here, their faith leaves a way out—their own atonement or the entreaties of others on their behalf. For the skeptic or total unbeliever, of course, the problem is even more simple. If the grave is the end, then there is nothing further to be known, or unknown, about the other side, since there is only one side—the one he is in now for keeps. It turns out the unknown has been only too well known in advance.

Yet, there is a dread of dying, even when we welcome it to end the dread, but the reasons for it have nothing to do with the unknown. It is just the opposite. My own nightmare in the quicksand gave me answers and imponderables to my own questions about the problem. It turned my thinking around, in due time. What follows, from a real, life-threatening situation, are my own answers from my own experience in a single, highly specific context where death was imminent.

I do not imply one can generalize from one specific instance to all others where life is threatened by similar circumstances. I do know in similar circumstances, someone else would probably experience it differently. I am not making a contribution to the death-and-dying literature. I merely share my interpretation of an experience, for whatever it's worth, to illustrate two crucial points: Some of the greatest dangers facing the hunter have nothing to do with dangerous animals; they have to do with routine wilderness hazards. And a little faith, bordering on the religious, is involved in every wilderness adventure—no matter how it is labeled—especially by those of us who have proudly boasted, with some disdain, that we don't need religion—we worship wilderness. I learned a great deal about wilderness worship from that quicksand episode.

If death comes swiftly, hopefully in an instant, then the victim is dead before he even knows what it was that came. There is no next moment in which to contemplate knowns and unknowns. It no longer matters. This is why we say, "Poor Joe, how lucky he was. He went just like that (snap fingers, please), so fast he didn't suffer at all. Thank God," or Lucky Stars, or whatever, depending on the kind of guys Joe hung around with.

Since there was not a single appropriate response I could make to extricate myself from that quagmire, and since it seemed nothing, or no one, could get me out either, then death seemed inevitable. If it was on its way, what delayed its arrival? It was not coming fast enough to get it over with and end the agony.

The human being, from the mother's womb before birth, to the very last moments of life, is never totally separated or alone from others—be they relatives, friends, or strangers. Even in his loneliest moments, his memory tells him who is absent or present in his consciousness. In amnesia or coma, we do not know how much awareness of self is present, which often cannot be remembered even if full consciousness is regained. It may be, there is no total loss of self to our awareness (even in sleep, our dreams let us see ourselves or others), except in death that no participant has been able to report in a manner observable and measurable by others.

While trapped in the quicksand I had time on my hands for my mind to meander under freezing duress. One moment, I knew who and where I was. The next moment, I was only aware of hazy, formless, lifeless, one-dimensional surroundings, so strangely barren. Something was missing, and it was more than Don, the person, I was trying to see. It was the humanity he represented. That's when I felt strange, devoid of my own humanness. There was nothing human out there with which to contrast the rest of a surrealistic world. Hence, there was no way I could gauge the world outside of me. Nearly frozen into an icicle, I had even a tougher time gauging the world inside me, in contrast.

The gyroscope to my space/time orientation had jumped its

pivot. Out there and in here were kind of mixed up, and I had no sense contact with anything except a self already unrecognizable. I don't know how often I ping-ponged between here and there—between two mirages. It was like the carnival shill daring you to guess which cup held the marble. It was always in the one you had not guessed, until he turned that cup over, and the marble wasn't there either. It was back in the first cup! Don, or any other human being, was that marble. Until I could find that marble, I couldn't find myself or know where I was, or even who I was. Without that connecting linkage, there was no reference point.

Later, I put those thoughts together. In those final moments of awareness when we go from this life, we know we go alone. My thought is—if we fear death, it is not because of some unknown we are going to find. It is because of the known we are losing, the sense of self in relation to some other person, from which emerges the reality of being human. The self grows with so much time and effort on the love of those who have helped us, or despite the hatred of those who have spurned us, which is the most precious constancy of our lives. The self is always there, even if we are unaware of its presence. When we need its presence to respond to a sudden demand of the world and it has vanished beyond the grasp of memory, we are left with the stranger inside us.

The self, with which we were more familiar than anything else in this world, is suddenly gone, to be found nowhere, and a consciousness is left without the thing of which it was most conscious. We grow frantic trying to find, in the next few moments, what took a lifetime to build, and are stunned with the awful truth—we are lost to ourselves and that is where dread stampedes us into terror. The lost self searching for itself, knowing it cannot be found. It is the known that terrorizes us, not the unknown. It is truly said that death is merciful.

This feeling of separation is not between person and another. It is between person and self; the connecting linkage between the two is a fragile thing of the spirit so easily torn asunder. The fear of death may be of the unknown—but routine courage will take care of that. The real fear is in losing the humanity that gave us our own. We do not know what it is to be without it. This is where the animal has it all over us. It was those final moments in the quicksand that taught me what genuine aloneness is.

Some 20 years later, I understood the archetypal aloneness of all time, and it made mine pale into absolute zero. Confronted with a courage I could never have, for a cause far more worthy than any I could ever pursue, I finally understood, for the first time, what the Man of long ago meant when his voice rent the heavens with the cry—"Why have You forsaken Me?" Modernism sweeps the problem under the rug with a single narcotic injection that dupes us all. We think we have escaped the problem by mistaking hell for heaven under the spell of narcosis.

I learned one final and crucial lesson in the Manley quicksand. Never assume life is finished until it's finished, because there is always the possibility of the unexpected—the purely chance factor.

Then, there was the possibility of miracles, if one believed in the miraculous. I toyed with the idea, but dismissed it as fanciful imagination, because there are no miracles in nature. If they exist, whatever causes them must be supernatural, and I just didn't believe in miracles during this stage of my life. I rejected my supernatural light and music episode as inconclusive and hallucinatory. What saved me in quicksand was Don's sudden insight to yell "spread eagle," which resulted from chance or coincidence, but most likely from association of ideas based on sensory data— after all, he said he got the idea from seeing my arms come down on the quicksand, making the connection in his mind.

This entire quicksand episode was a unique experience. It was too arresting and too exceptional to experience routinely. Such experiences result in two things: a definition of it by the mind to give it meaning, and corresponding emotions that predispose behavioral standards. All the genetic and environmental determinants on our behavior mean nothing independently of the way we experience them. The self is a product of our unique experiences. All the theories about innate mechanisms of behavior and personality typologies miss the point that do not account for the way in which one experiences reality. It is a vitalistic approach to the problem of human nature, and denies a mechanistic view of it.

To me, the most important part of any hunting story is how the hunter experienced his hunt and what it meant to him. That, after all, is the unique reality of his hunt and made it different from all others. That is the part most absent from the stories I've read.

The point is, I was to remember all this later, when other events on hunting trails forced these thoughts back into recall. In the meantime, De Unamuno came to mind. He had observed, "All that is rational is anti-vital, and all that is vital is anti-rational." I wondered. Would he have classified the miraculous as vital, since the rational resisted it so easily? With all due respect to my professors of philosophy and all else so many years ago, the freezing quicksand where I nearly perished was one of the greatest teachers I ever had. It taught me much in a big hurry. It surely taught me philosophy. Or was it theology? I'm not sure, but in either case, it was vital for me, no matter which way De Unamuno might have answered the question. I've forgotten much of what he said, anyway, but I still like the sound of his name.

It is sheer music.

Death In Miscellaneous Ways

It was barely 5 months after the Manley incident, when Ted, flushed with excitement, burst into my office. He was an older student, and one of the best we had in our graduate program. One of his friends, a young army lieutenant and superb pilot at nearby Ft. Wainwright, had some time off, his private plane, and a yen to visit the Eskimo village of Anaktuvuk, scarcely a hundred miles from the Arctic Circle and still fairly primitive. It was providential. That's exactly the one place I desperately needed to visit.

Ever since my arrival in Alaska, my attention had been drawn to native masks, made of caribou skin, on sale in all the tourist-trap curio and gift shops. Though primitive in handcrafting and appearance, they were attractive and unique to Alaska. To me, they had a stylistic influence more Caucasian than aboriginal. I was doing research on cultural change theory. The masks totally intrigued me, and had implications in my theory.

I needed firsthand interviews with the principle sources of the masks to get answers for my research. Eventually, I completed my work, wrote a monograph, read it at a science conference, and published it as a lead article in the March 1966 issue of Science, the Journal of the American Association for the Advancement of Science. I am deeply indebted to Ted for all he did to make the study possible. Nearly 30 years later, it is still a popular publication, judging by the coverage it gets, and is a standard item for the public in the recently founded museum at Anaktuvuk. The point is, those who read it do not really know what it took out of me to get it, and that is what this story is all about.

When Ted's friend, Phil, volunteered to take us to Anaktuvuk so I could get my research data, I instantly grabbed the opportunity—it was better than the long-winded process of filing an application for the research grant I probably wouldn't get anyway, unless I lied for a sum of money big enough to make it worth while for the federal government's effort. They wouldn't settle for just an airplane fare and a two-man team. All this had a totally unexpected consequence and a totally unexpected hunt. It was to be another unique experience nearly claiming my life, and others, including Stan, a colleague, who had just arrived in Alaska and had come along for the ride.

We got safely to Anaktuvuk. I successfully met all the principle informants involved in the story, taped the interviews, clarified odds and ends, and got answers to all the necessary questions. We were staying at the home of Mike Lockwood, the school teacher. He and his wife were true Alaskans, and meeting them was a privilege for anyone. We were finishing our coffee while the airplane was warming up on the runway, almost ready to take us home. Casually looking out the window at the surrounding acres of windswept snow, we sensed the bitter cold, although spring was supposed to be just around the corner at the Arctic Circle. Things stayed colder and more dangerous here, longer.

Suddenly, we heard muffled shouts in the distance, and then we saw several natives brandishing rifles and running full blast after a red fox, who was a blast more fast by maybe 200 or 300 yards than his pursuers. Imagine the scene—desolation, snow-covered mountains looming up in the back ground, and this mad chase by seemingly miniaturized men and a red dot. The whole thing looked so out of place and funny, I laughed uproariously. The thought struck me that, at any moment, one of the pursuers might shout, "Tallyho! The fox!" and I wondered if it would help matters any. I couldn't help the laughter, although the others looked at me with reproach, because they all knew what was going on, and it was serious business.

The fox population had proliferated as part of its growth cycle, and most of them were rabid. Many got into the sled dog compound, infecting some huskies, who were immediately destroyed. Villagers were keeping a sharp lookout to shoot any fox on sight. Of course, it was an awful waste of what could have otherwise been lovely fur coats for lovely ladies, but it was the best way to protect the dogs that, naturally, came first in this case.

Several natives were in hot pursuit of the fox. Its cuteness notwithstanding, it had to be destroyed. Mike opened a window and quickly emptied his rifle with no success. The fox was now a quarter mile away, moving like lightning, greased with synthetic, non-viscous, space-age lubrication, good for 300 degrees below zero.

Sitting near the fireplace, I had not yet fully dressed, but I did have on my thermal underwear, which was too hot, and my unlaced shoe-pacs. Here was a chance to cool off quickly and do something worthwhile at the same time. I grabbed the 12-gauge shotgun leaning against the wall near the doorway, and, I knew I had to get closer to the fox; not even a cannon would reach him from the window. I made my charge out the door.

The snow was deeper than I thought. It was crusted enough to make it easygoing for the fox way out there, but it was not firm enough to hold my weight, and each step sank in maybe a foot deep. My long running stride I had developed years ago on the track team had become a habit. I was now running automatically, or trying to, but sinking into the snow required me to pull my knees up high. The spectators back in the house later said none of them had ever laughed so hard. I looked like a mutation between a sprinter and a right tackle.

The effort, however, made me feel like a caterpillar humping along, in spite of which I must have made good time. I headed straight ahead, and the fox's trajectory would bring him directly in front of me at right angles, if I could intercept his path. He had almost reached the imaginary intersection, about 30 yards in front of me. It was obvious he would zoom past in a split second. I was too winded to stand up, let alone shoot. Besides, I am not as good with a shotgun as with a rifle, and I thought it was a great effort, all in vain. At that split moment, the critter suddenly saw me, did a double take, spun to his right, and charged straight away from me, full tilt.

It was my lucky break. Shooting at him straight ahead with his full stern to view rapidly disappearing, it was much easier than trying to lead him if he were going straight past. I elevated the barrel a bit and squeezed for what we Alaskans call a Texas heart-shot right in the bun-buns. He somersaulted and came down dead. It was simply a lucky shot, but when I reached the house, holding the fox by his tail, half the village was already there, and the crowd was delirious with joy, heaping accolades on my prowess and, of course, I did not disabuse them concerning my great shot.

They had already decided to have a potlatch—a wild celebration indeed. I had not only killed a probably rabid fox, but what is more important, I had provided a legitimate reason for the party. Anything for an excuse, I thought, and it seemed like a skookum idea to me, too.

The plane had been loaded with our gear, the engine was warmed up and ready to go. We had to go with it; there was no choice. I know we missed one of the great parties of all times in Northern climes. (Months later, I learned a new mask had been created, bearing my features, to commemorate the deed.) We waved good-bye to these hardy people, who held so firmly to their traditions. (Who would have suspected how things would change for them with the coming of the oil pipeline?) The plane taxied down the primitive runway and was aloft without any trouble.

Our flight plan took us to Bettles, another village halfway to Fairbanks, where we could gas up, eat a quick lunch, check the reports at the weather station, and head for home before darkness set in. The agent told us what we wanted to hear. The weather was good all the way to our destination. The report banished our anxiety, because the plane was not equipped with instrumentation for blind flying. All it had was a radio, which we thought would do nicely.

We were far enough out of Bettles so we couldn't turn back when we realized the weather report given to us by that nice agent was grossly in error. The sapphire blue sky quickly became a sodden gray, and it delivered almost immediately what it promised—a snow storm. Since it worsened with every minute of flying time, we knew we were in for it. We also knew somewhere ahead of us the mountain range would soon get in the way. We had to fly over the mountains to stay on course. We could not fly high enough to clear them without getting lost. If we increased altitude, it, would be impossible to see down through the deepened layers of swirling snow obliterating all landmarks. It was already difficult enough to make out landmarks at lower altitudes. Moreover, each added foot of elevation increased the danger of ice formation on the wings.

We had to fly low enough to get under the snow canopy to see any landmarks. Through the blowing haze, we checked them against our charts. To fly low, without seeing far enough ahead, risked our crashing into the mountain flanks, whose peaks loomed above us.

Phil let out a groan. The radio he had been talking into, trying to establish contact with anyone who might pick us up, quit cold. It was the worst possible thing that could have happened to us, at the worst possible moment, and now we knew we were in for it. Two of us whistled, the other sang, and I hummed. They were four different tunes, all at the same time, all off key, each signaling the other there was nothing to worry about, while trying to cover up his own mounting fear.

After several minutes of circling to ascertain what we suspected—we were lost—Phil and Ted, sitting up front, held a seminar on what to do next.

The proceedings were interrupted a couple of times, as we veered quickly away from a mountain wall. Up front, the seminar bogged down. The guys couldn't agree. One wanted to go straight ahead and risk the mountains. The other wanted to crash land and risk whatever happened. One abstained. I got a little irritated when they asked me to break the tie and this required coming up with an answer sooner than I preferred. I urged a few moments more of circling, only wider and lower. There was something down there needing closer inspection.

Phil had been computing out loud how far we must have come from Bettles, given the airspeed and elapsed time aloft. We should have been over Stevens Village by this time, but there was no way of determining that now. We weren't sure, but we thought we had caught glimpses of flat stretches of what could be ice wedged between the mountain bases. The blowing snow and heavy, gray pall hid the one answer we needed. Were these small, flat, severed sections merely random patterns, or were they part of a continuous stretch? If they were the latter, we could be over the frozen Yukon River. Far or near, Stevens Village had to be on that icebound shore, somewhere.

There seemed to be snow covered humps barely visible to the right, and wisp-like smoke floating over them. We couldn't be sure. They looked too much like everything else covered with shifting, moving flurries of snow. If only, that wildly weaving snow shroud below would stay still for just one moment! That's all we desperately needed. Just one moment, but we couldn't have it. We had to resist our imaginations. Spurred on by desperate hope, we were tempted to see what wasn't there. Was it imagination or could it really be Stevens Village?

Something inside me said if we landed with a crash and survived, we might have a way out. The thought scared me. It was winter in one of the most isolated spots in Alaska. Survival would require superhuman effort until rescue parties discovered us, without radio signals, assuming we could stay alive that long. On the other hand, if we kept flying and hoping for a better break, the chances were very good we would be splattered against some mountain side.

I leaned forward and shouted to Phil, "How many days of survival gear do we have?"

He shouted back, "Three days."

My time at the ballot box had run out. I voted to crash land.

Phil responded quickly. He circled another half dozen times, dropping lower and lower over a flat stretch of ice and snow. I looked out the side window at what now began to take shape—a washboard of corrugated, snowy hummocks, windblown drifts, and icy patches. We were flying a Piper Tri-Pacer, not on skis, which would have been bad enough, but on wheels with rubber tires, and a third wheel, forward of the main landing wheels, just under the engine cowling. To land that craft in one piece was out of the question. The question was—how many pieces? We hadn't figured on landing or taking off on anything but the snow-plowed, gravel strip at Anaktuvuk and the blacktop at Ft. Wainwright. Now, we were going to land on what looked like the landscape in Casino during World War II after our guys had finished bombing.

The die was cast, however, and now we needed two miracles: one to keep us alive when we crashed, and the other to keep us alive for 3 days. We had done all we could. The rest was up to Papa God, if he existed, which I strongly doubted, or denied, to suit the occasion. Phil urged us to tighten safety belts and grab onto anything for support. Then, he said, "Here we go." He angled down, then leveled off, and just before the tires hit, he switched off the ignition to hopefully prevent fire or explosion.

The wheels hit something with a thud sending violent vibrations through the cabin, and sprays of slushy snow plastered all the windows in an instant. The already dim light in the cabin became a sudden darkness, and I couldn't see a thing outside, but it made no difference. The plane went into a crazy, zigzag, shuddering skid, while its forward momentum plunged it recklessly ahead. In the dim interior, our bodies hurled one way with the zig, and back again with the zag. The seat belts tried to cut us in two, while clamping us in our seats. It seemed like eternity, as I rattled like a claustrophobic skeleton shaking apart in that catapulting coffin. I was still gripping tightly to the top of the front seat and silently yelling, "Stop! Stop!" when the craft finally reached the end of eternity and lurched into a sudden, smashing, halt as its nose rammed into the ice and snow.

I flew forward and down, doubled over my safety belt, and joined Ted and Phil in sledgehammering our skulls into the windshield that was now the floor, while Stan piled on top of me. The seat belts held, but everything we had piled behind our back seats flew forward. The swishing, crunching noises had stopped, and in the twilight of the cabin, there was absolute silence. For a moment or two I must have lost consciousness and I guessed the others had, too, although I didn't ask, because we all were coming out of it slowly to the sound of groans and moans.

I became aware of Ted, underneath me, trying to wiggle. He managed to unlatch the door. We finally succeeded in pushing and pounding it open. One by one we tumbled out like twisted gnomes. We stood there, groggy, no one saying a word. I took several deep breaths; nothing hurt inside. I moved my limbs. They were okay, too. I spat; no blood. What more did I want? I was alive, and so were the others! There were bruises and a few lacerations, but unbelievably, no serious injuries.

We gawked at the plane. It was finished. It had preserved our lives at the cost of its own. The propeller was wrapped around the nose cone that was screwed into the ice. The front wheel assembly under the forward fuselage was rammed up into the engine. The tip of one wing was shorn. A strut was buckled, as were the main wheel assemblies. What had been a plane now looked like some modern, abstract piece of junk sculpture, sticking into the air at a 45-degree angle. It would have won first prize over any million-dollar, tax-funded art sitting in front of many a city hall. We could have wept at it, if we weren't so glad we miraculously missed being part of the esthetics.

In the funereal gloom beneath that overcast sky, I must have looked as pale to my companions as they looked to me. Ted never let me forget it. He says I broke the silence with a chuckle and said, "Well, now, that was a unique experience, wasn't it?" Slowly, our shock began to wear off, and we were exuberant to be alive. We congratulated Phil on his superb handling of the plane. He was as good as Ted said he was. No compliment was more sincere or better deserved. He had brought us through by the seat of our pants, as pilots are wont to say.

As for the unique experience Ted referred to, I had been lecturing on that concept as the mechanism by which we establish attitudes as a basic part of personality structure. The experience we had just lived through was unique, indeed, not only because none of us had cracked up in an airplane before, but also because we had become part of that select group of Alaskans who can say, "We walked away from the crash—unhurt and alive." Crashes under similar conditions have claimed the lives of dozens of Alaskans, whose unmarked and unknown graves are scattered throughout the wilderness of Alaska. If one does enough flying, his turn is only a question of when. We were lucky this time, or was there more to it than that?

Our bubbling enthusiasm quickly fizzled out. On ground level, the snow seemed to be falling much more softly, in large Christmas-sized flakes, and I could have easily imagined Yule logs, jingle bells, and all the rest of it, but an ugly, harsh question bugged me and the rest of us, I'm sure. In this forbidding and desolate wilderness, what would we do after 3 days, when our survival gear ran out? Until then, we had a fighting chance, and much would depend on how soon the storm ended. A week or more of unrelenting weather like this was not uncommon. The swirling canopy of snow would have to clear before a pilot could see anything on the ground.

We dragged out all the duffel bags, sleeping bags, and other gear, dumped them into a pile, and asked each other where the coffee, the pot, and the primus stove were. We needed a hot drink to warm us up before we could innovate some kind of shelter. Sometime during our rummaging, the wind gusts stopped for a few moments, and the calm coincided with a brief cessation of our activity. The silence was deafening. We all heard the barely audible sounds, like branches moving or creaking under too much snow, and then another gust of wind drowned it out.

Another moment of silence, and then we were sure we were hearing sounds, and every nerve stretched taut. In a few moments, those sounds grew louder, and suddenly we could tell they were human voices! Out here? We stood aghast. It had to be a cruel joke; some kind of wild dream. Through the gray, foggy fuzz of swirling snow, there emerged, in a kind of slow motion, a single line of human figures, swaying and weaving through the haze, coming straight at us like spectral Viking warriors. No, it was not a cruel mirage. The Unseen Powers had looked on us with mercy. We had crashed within a mile of Stevens Village on the frozen Yukon. Our gamble had paid off.

The entire village had turned out to watch our circling plane through the blinding snow. We were granted the second miracle we needed. Our pent-up emotions exploded. Delirious with joy, we embraced our rescuers!

Our native stalwarts each picked up a piece of gear from the pile and led us to the river's bank, less than 100 feet away from our plane, and yet, we had not been able to see it through the gray haze. We were led through the trees to a trail, and then to the home of the school teachers, Mr. and Mrs. Henderson.

What can anyone say of people like them? They welcomed us with open arms and hearts. Their quiet dignity and genuine kindness would make anyone proud of the human race. They fed us, put us up, and put up with us for 3 days, while we waited for the weather to clear enough to establish contact with the outside world through their short wave-radio. On the morning of the fourth day, they were able to reach one of the villages up or down river which, in turn, relayed the message to Fairbanks.

Later that afternoon, and out of the gray, dismal skies, we heard the duk-duk-duk chopping sound of a helicopter. It turned out to be one of the giant Army rigs out of Ft. Wainwright. We said good-bye to these gracious people, who had befriended us in our hour of need, and climbed aboard the helicopter. It rose like a giant spider, dangling our victimized plane at the end of a long, steel cable. That's how we flew to the tarmac at Ft. Wainwright.

We felt like celebrities the moment we emerged from the chopper. Our families, friends, students, and press were there. Unknown to us, of course, the local newspaper had carried the front page story of "the professor and his student missing in light aircraft," and so forth. When I arrived on campus the following day, students had posted Welcome Home signs all over. Moreover, a dozen or so groups of five or six volunteers each, many of them my students, had formed rescue squads, already equipped, ready to take off the following day on a rescue mission of mercy. We had arrived just in time to spare them the toil of searching needlessly. There was a big place in my heart for these generous people. I would have swept them up in my arms and hugged them unabashedly. If it were possible to get away with it, I would have given those students straight As for effort.

Shortly afterwards, Ted, Phil, and I had a celebration dinner with our wives. We reminisced about our close call. My friends knew nothing about my Manley episode, and I said nothing about it now. But I pondered on it. This was the second close call for me in less than 6 months making me wonder why, over and over again. No answers came. Not yet, anyway.

About 6 months after the plane crash, and after much correspondence during the interim between Mike Lockwood (whom I had dubbed Little Mike) and me, he invited me to a sheep hunt with him and his friend, another Mike I shall call Big Mike for this story. We chartered a plane that took us to a lake at the base of Mt. Sillyasheen, about 6,000 feet high, in the fabled Brooks Range, not too far from Anaktuvuk. Little Mike had it on good advice there were Dall sheep on that mountain, and so it turned out, as we flew around it. Dall sheep are one of the world's prized trophies, because they are a truly magnificent animal, and very difficult to get. I was elated at the chance.

We landed on a lake at the base of the mountain. The pilot swore on his mother's and grandmother's graves he would return for us as scheduled. We waved him good-bye, and hauled our gear a little way from the shore to a very old, abandoned trapper's cabin with half the roof missing and logs rotted out here and there. Two contiguous sides and the section of roof above them seemed sound, however, and it would make a good windbreak in case the weather got ornery. We pitched our tents inside and set up housekeeping to make ourselves comfortable for the night.

The following morning, we had a heavy breakfast, made our packs as light as possible, and got an early start to conquer the mountain. The first obstacle was the Hunts Fork River, wide enough with swirling, waist-deep, whitewater moving at a fast clip, to make it exciting. We held on to each other at arm's length, got soaked fighting the current, but made it across without mishap. We got to the skirt of the mountain, climbed up a steep, rocky incline, without difficult obstacles, to about 4,000 or 5,000 feet. It was a good, rugged climb, given the terrain all around and the kind of trophy we were after. Besides, it was a lovely, sunny day, and we made it in great shape, our hearts full of hope now that we could get down to serious business.

After very cautious scouting about, we realized the sheep we had spotted yesterday were gone. Somewhat dismayed, we climbed a little higher, and belly-crawled around some rim rock, and spotted them on the opposing slope about a half mile away. Yesterday, we had spotted seven of them. Now, there were only four, even though Little Mike could see only three. The plot thickened, as they say. Why had they moved there, and where were the others?

We glassed for a half hour, without an answer. The critters across the way just loafed around. The slope they were on did not look too formidable, so we decided to really hunt—climb down, cross the ravine, and climb up the other slope from the back, and get on top of them. It meant a lot of work, and we got started pronto.

We eased down the slope quite a way and took a break. Big Mike was a little too anxious to draw first blood. I suggested he hike around the rim to the left and curve into the slope across from us. Then, he could have first choice. Hopefully, when he shot his sheep, the others would dash down the slope, cross the ravine, and head up our slope, and we might get a shot if we were lucky. Big Mike should get there in a couple hours at the most. It was a deal he couldn't refuse. Little Mike and I lounged on a mossy rock slab, and I did heavy thinking about where the other three sheep were.

Big Mike hadn't been gone 5 minutes, when the four sheep began to get skittish. In a few moments they quietly moved on without much alarm, but obviously something was wrong. It could not have been us, or they would have taken off long since.

"Well, there goes our sheep," said Little Mike, wistfully.

I felt that way, too, but I was still pondering why they had moved away and where the other three were. Little Mike, who was a very reasonable man, got very unreasonable with a half dozen hypotheses to explain these questions. He wouldn't listen to the single reason I carefully presented to him. The missing sheep had to be right beneath us, on a lower ledge, which we couldn't see because of overhangs, and Big Mike must have spooked them with his movements, not suspecting their whereabouts. If that were so, I argued, then they telegraphed the danger signal to their cohorts on the opposing slope. That made them skittish. Little Mike got more obstinate.

"It's elementary deduction, my dear Watson," I said and made a wager he couldn't refuse, but he did. He agreed, however, to climb down just a bit "to see what would happen," but I knew he was hoping to disprove my hypothesis. The problem was, he had successfully hunted sheep a couple of times before, while this was my first shot at it in his Brooks Range stomping grounds. It didn't look too good—my theorizing against his experience.

I didn't blame him for feeling the way he did, but we had to do something. We had only climbed down a short way, when pounding hooves broke the silence, and then, three beautiful rams broke into view, heading down grade to a lower ledge, and they were going full tilt.

"There they go," I yelled to Little Mike and dropped to one knee at the same time. It was a hurried, snap shot at the leader, but luckily, it connected at the base of the neck, about 5 inches higher than I intended it, but it did the trick right handsomely. He crumpled instantly.

I heard four rapid shots from Little Mike, then a moment of silence. He must be reloading, I thought, but I was already on my way, full tilt, to my prize. Frankly, I felt a little twinge of disappointment, because my trophy had come a little too easily, and then, I heard another shot.

Then, came Little Mike's voice, yelling in the throes of total ecstasy, "I got him! I got him!"

Try as I might, I could not see him or his sheep. He must have been around the promontory to my left. By this time, I had reached my ram.

He had dropped to a lower ledge, about 10 feet down, and rolled or slid to within a couple feet of the very edge of a drop, perhaps 100 feet going almost straight down, though it was tough to judge, and our estimates differed. I thought lady luck had smiled on me again. The ram lay on a steep incline, head pointed downward, his hind quarters bunched up, and quivering slowly. The only thing stopping him from going over was his horn twisted under his neck and embedded in a rocky fissure covered with moss.

Unwittingly, I had gotten there just in time. A few more seconds, and the quivering weight of his body would move all of him to the edge, and he would plummet down, express delivery all the way. There was not a moment to lose. I made a dive for his hind hooves, grabbed them tight for dear life, and tried to pull him back. It was a mistake.

With the slight lifting of his feet and legs, his weight suddenly lurched forward, the embedded tip of his horn slid out of the rocky fissure, and his head and shoulders spilled over the ridge dragging the rest of him down, along with a big patch of sphagnum moss. His weight and momentum, which I had grossly underestimated, began to drag me with it.

My hands let go as if those hooves had become molten iron flowing out of a crucible. There was just a split second left, and it was enough to let me see the carcass plummet out of sight, but it had done its work. It had pulled me off balance just enough so my feet slid off the moist rocky patch covered by sphagnum moss just a moment ago. Now, it felt like a petrified banana peel. My feet shot out from under me and stabbed into empty space. "Oh, no, not again," I groaned to myself, silently, but I knew nothing was going to hold me, and I was on my way down.

It wasn't quite the way Little Mike wrote it in his story for *Alaska Sportsman*. From his vantage point, he had seen the entire caper, and in describing how my trophy and I tumbled down, he used such gymnastic phrases as "man over sheep, and sheep over man." That may have been true for one or two tumbles, but not all the way down. Little Mike didn't see it, or feel it, more accurately, as I did. I went past that sheep, because every time his carcass bounced off one boulder, he landed on another, almost draping around it with his four legs. This slowed him down long enough for me to shoot past before he slithered off again. I know. I was right behind him on his first hang-up. After that, I was on my own.

A boulder would break my fall before it bounced me off and down to the next one, slowing me down just a smidgen while I tried frantically to claw into something, anything; but the incline and momentum would become operational again. Alas, if only I had two more legs like the sheep! I know I bounced and groaned off at least six large boulders, or ledges, slid through shale strands between, and finally hit rock bottom. So, it was not quite a free fall, or Little Mike would have had two dead sheep and one dead man to carry out. Luckily, the fall was not like "Ooo-whee-ee-ee," but more like a "bump-thump-bumpety bump" sort of thing.

When I landed, I slid right into rushing water and stopped cold against a large, flat table of rock, finally on the level (no pun). I climbed onto it, soaking wet, with an aching mass of pain. Around it swirled a cold, clear, shallow creek. I heard the sound of tearing leaves on the bank, and my sheep rolled into view, landing a few feet away in the water. "You're late," I said. "What held you up?" I wanted to reach over and give him a big, brotherly hug, but it hurt too much to move.

I had no broken bones, but lots of bruises, cuts, and gashes. The ice-cold stream had great analgesic powers, and after washing grit, sand, and a pebble or two out of my wounds, I packed them with the best antiseptic around, a quid of chewing tobacco, and bound them with strips of my bandana.

What really hurt was my well-pounded bottom, and there was little to be done about it except to sit in the icy creek. It gave me much comfort at first. Then, it got too much for the rest of my anatomy.

Soon, Little Mike broke through the underbrush. He had climbed down a more time-consuming and cowardly trail and looked very glum. Little Mike had pulled a Little Bo Peep and lost his sheep. He knew it had rolled out of sight over the precipice at 150 feet or so to the left of where I had dropped mine. He headed back to look for it, and I knew he'd find it, because there was no place else for it to go once it reached the creek.

To save time, I skinned, caped, and boned the meat while he was gone. I soon had it done, despite my difficulty in moving around. I wrapped it up in plastic and lashed it to my packboard. With the meat, wet cape, skull and horns, and rifle, it weighed about 125 pounds, I guessed, and would require a few rest stops. Little did I guess how many those few stops would be. I finished the remainder of my lunch, and before a little catnap, Little Mike showed up.

He had found his prize, skinned, boned, and packed it, and was now beaming with joy at the curled horns perched on the top of his pack. He was solicitous about my condition, suggesting a little more rest, but it was time to start for camp. It was already getting late. Then, we made the sorriest mistake of our lives.

Admittedly, it would have taken a Herculean effort to try to climb up the wall with our packs to get back to our trail, but later how I wished we had tried. Instead, we chose to walk through the creek I'd landed in, hoping it would curve around and into the Hunts Fork River a few miles down. It would then be easy to follow the river's confluence to camp.

The creek flowed through a gorge, with walls as high as the precipice I'd fallen down, and hugged the creek tightly, allowing no escape to the sides of it. We were in a chasm, and who knew how long it was? We walked in ice-cold water for the better part of 2 hours. The creek was filled with rocks, dead falls, and sweepers. If we went 10 paces without being blocked by any of them, we were lucky.

Then it got dark, and with no starlight reaching into the chasm, we couldn't see what we were doing, so we tripped, stumbled, and sprawled time after time. Our heavy packs smashed their full weight on top of us. Trying to squirm into position to push ourselves up to our feet and stand in the fast, flowing water was an ordeal.

Somehow, we reached a point where the brooding shadowy walls of the gorge dropped low enough so we could see the slightly lighter darkness of the sky above it. For the first time in a couple of hours we could make out the top of the rocky rim about 50 feet above our heads. It was worth the try.

We made the climb, which was child's play, in spite of packs, compared to what we had been through. Reaching the top, we flopped down on a patch of tundra grass, soaking wet and cold. We had left our parkas in camp. It was late September, and winter was just around the corner in the Brooks Range—a place always colder than most places in Alaska. We scavenged for wood in the dark, but all we found were a few skimpy bushes.

The fire was a wretched thing, but poor Little Mike was so hungry we tried broiling some sheep. He was hungry, all right, from the way he smacked his chops on barely cooked meat. I was hungry, too, but I could barely get it down. It was such a long way from the traditional barbecued lamb, of my ancestors, I made at home whenever we had a party. This was no party, and I was too tired to eat. I wouldn't spoil it for Mike by saying the service was excellent, though the food was lousy, so I lied a little and said "It was great, delicious, superb." I'll be hanged if he didn't quote my relative falsehood as an absolute truth in the article he later wrote.

We tried to sleep. It was too cold. We got up and walked around to stay warm, but were too exhausted. Then, we laid down again to freeze. We were miserable until a ribbon of faint light began to emerge, revealing ground covered with frost. We had just enough light to see, so we took off. Finally, we reached the Hunts Fork River. Hopefully, we could follow its confluence in a fairly routine walk. It was not to be. Yesterday, we had walked up on the other side of the mountain in a long, steep incline. Now, on this side, we were in a different world. The slope splintered into jagged wedges cutting far out into the river and curved in a wide arc. The distance to camp was three times longer than if we had returned the way we climbed yesterday.

To follow the river's merciful course, we were forced to climb up and over the unmerciful rocky abutments and descend again to the other side. This meant tearing through alder clumps on top of those rocks. It exhausted us, trying to unhook our packs caught in the branches. A half dozen such climbs, and we admitted it couldn't be done. At this rate, we'd be long dead before we got anywhere near camp. We had already covered barely 5 miles and had roughly some 15 more miles to go, and we couldn't do it—not with our packs.

There was only one alternative. We had frequently looked to the top of the mountain and shuddered at the thought. The price was too steep like the jagged slopes. But now we paid it. We had to climb back up that slope, full pack loads and rifles, and find the trail to the incline we were on yesterday. Getting there nearly finished us. We staggered 15 paces by the count, and flopped down for a rest of not more than 2 minutes. We didn't get out of our packs, for fear we could not get back into them. Then, the pacing would start all over.

Of course, we considered the possibility of leaving the packs behind. The dead weight each of us carried was behind this nightmare. We could come back for them later, but we both knew this was an excuse. Who would have the willpower or insanity to begin this ordeal again? How could conscience censure us for having reached the limits of human endurance? If we left our packs there and never returned, how could conscience ever let us think we were sportsmen living by the ethics of the hunting code?

The moment we squeezed the trigger, we had committed

ourselves to seeing this through—or we had no business wasting an animal on contingencies. I wanted to give in to Mike's sane suggestion of leaving the packs behind, but some stubborn madness opposed the idea. I told him to leave his pack, for I couldn't blame him, and go on without me. I would try to catch up later. Mike, bless his heart, said he would not leave without me, no matter what. I said I would not leave without my pack, no matter what.

"What do you want to do—die?" Mike asked.

"Only if I have to," I said. This sounded like flippant rhetoric at the moment, but much later, it raised some really profound issues for me. We were too tired to talk, and the clouds overhead were gathering for what promised to be a storm—either rain or even snow.

Right now, there was only one thing to do—the thing we had been doing—get on our feet and keep going. It was 15 paces, rest 2 minutes; keep going 15 paces without thinking beyond two paces, or we would lose our mind trying to figure out why we were doing this. Something inside said, "Just because."

We finally found the trail and the incline, and tried to take a short cut at the bottom. Another mistake. We fell into a swamp and got lost. Before we found our way out, we had lost our sanity to the endless clouds of flying, stinging insects. We didn't know where we were now, so we fired SOS shots, and to our relief, we heard Big Mike's answering signal. We headed in that direction and shortly found the cabin before it got dark again.

Big Mike asked which of us needed help with his pack. I pointed to Little Mike, stumbled through the door, barely slipped out of my pack, dropped on my sleeping pad, and fell asleep on contact.

When I awoke it was afternoon of the next day. It had rained. The boys were hungry. I was famished. While we prepared some grub, we talked and I learned that one of the shots I thought was Little Mike's had belonged to Big Mike. At my shot, one of the sheep had bolted to our left and had practically rushed into Big Mike's arms. Big Mike had a treat. He caped his sheep and simply walked down the same trail we had climbed up, nice and easy, and had gotten to the cabin long before nightfall.

I ruminated some more after dinner. What had started out as a lead-pipe cinch turned out to be the most gruelling hunt I have ever been on. I have hunted for 30 years and have had some toughies, but never had I experienced such a savage ordeal as this one.

There was something ironically amusing about it. I remembered that no sooner had I dropped my ram, than I felt a twinge of disappointment that it had been too easy. It was premature, of course, and destiny gave me more than I bargained for when that hunt became an agonizing nightmare pushing me to my limits. I had wanted an ultimate experience and I got it, though in a way I never imagined.

My appreciation for that ram could not be greater than if it were the world's number one trophy, now that I had paid the price for it that I did. It was not even superior trophy, let alone a magnificent one. In fact, it was barely average. Though mine was the biggest of the three taken, they were all within an inch of each other, with barely three-quarter curls, the legal minimum in those days.

We had been a grueling 30 consecutive hours or so on the trail. The last 15 of 20 miles had been under a heavy load over very difficult terrain. Then there was my unbelievable fall I luckily survived, which left me in great agony every inch of the way. All for a barely average trophy. There are those who have made, and others who will yet make, that ultimately stupid remark, "But it's just another pair of horns." Those who have said that to me, I have rebuffed as being just another primate.

I would fight to the death any person or any army who tried to take it away from me. It is a nonnegotiable symbol of my life. I will protect it at any cost. Why not? I was willing to risk death for it, if I had to, and nearly did.

I know, shamefully enough, I thought I might have to abandon my ram on the trail, when it seemed I couldn't go on. It was only a thought, to be sure, but I felt my resolve should have never wavered. It made me feel I had disappointed the ram with my doubts. He deserved unflinching loyalty.

A year later it was September again, the hunting season nearing its end. Two hunts for moose had not been successful—bulls were not where I hunted for them. This time, there was some urgency about it because I was not hunting for trophies, but just meat for the table. It went a long way to meet the outrageous cost of everything required to face the challenge of the North. Moose meat is good eating, but I would not go so far as to equate it with beef. A good-sized animal, all dressed out, will provide about 800 to 1,000 pounds of meat. It will feed an average Alaska family for a long while, at a cost below supermarket prices. Those who are well off in the South-48, and want to wipe out hunting because they love animals, forget human beings ought to be loved also—at least enough not to endanger the wrong species.

The next thing to do was to hunt for caribou, which I think is better tasting, anyway, but there's a catch. While moose are good eating all the time in season, caribou's taste can go from excellent to downright awful. That's because when they are in superb eating condition, they are high up in the mountain ranges and difficult to reach, while moose are generally in the valleys. Later in the season, when caribou are down low in migratory patterns, winter has really begun, and caribou flesh is not as good. When I first moved to Alaska, politics had not yet deprived the white, urban Alaskans from most of their hunting areas, and they were allowed four caribou each season.

I had just purchased a new four-wheel-drive pickup truck with a power-driven winch. It was still possible, back then, to reach good caribou country from gravel roads and trails, then hike the rest of the way. Dean got hold of me and said he wanted to go, especially to try out my new truck. He was a good hunter, a fine gentleman, and a good friend.

We headed for the Cantwell area, at the edge of Mt. McKinley National Park. The caribou would be on the move now, coming down from the heights with the season's first snow. Soon, groups of them would bunch together in larger herds, and then thousands of them would start their annual migration. I had seen that breathtaking sight, twice.

The tops of the mountain slopes were already covered with a light mantle of snow when we got to the hunting area. We were driving on a stretch of gravel road that began a sharp slope downward. On the left side, the embankment swept far away and leveled out into a large plateau 1,000 feet down, now being dusted with light, falling snow. Wind gusts kept sweeping the surface of the road.

We saw what looked like a caribou track, parked the truck on the left side of the road, and carefully searched for tracks. Dean started off to look for more sign. I was peering intently through my binoculars studying the valley far below, hoping to see moving animals.

Dean suddenly gave a loud shout of alarm, "Sarkis, the truck is rolling!"

I snapped my head to the right, and sure enough, my brand new truck was slowly rolling. In a few seconds, it would reach the sharp decline of the road, and its whimsically meandering roll would pick up speed and become an infuriated juggernaut. There were still some kinks the mechanics had been working out, and obviously, the emergency brake was one of them. It had not held, and I'd forgotten to park it in reverse gear.

I raced off full tilt, in what felt like my high school 40-yard dashes, and caught up with the truck. I shall never forget the dull gleam of the chrome button on the door handle. I started to push it in to yank the door open, jump in, and steer the truck away from the edge of the embankment before it really took off. I will never know what caused a sharp tug at my elbow that jerked my hand back, and I heard something inside sharply say, "No!" I have no explanation for this, but it saved my life. Instead of jumping into the truck, I ran beside it, reached through the open window, and tried turning the steering wheel.

I know I didn't run that way for too long, because I suddenly became aware I had lost contact with the wheel. My arm was high above me, and the running board was brushing past at shoulder level. For a second, I didn't know what had happened, but a furtive glance downward explained it. The truck had nudged me off the road and onto the embankment, where I had been running lower and lower while trying to hang on to the steering wheel, that was feeling higher and higher. It was an odd sensation, indeed, to become aware of tires rolling past me suddenly above my head. That's when I knew the awful truth and saw everything in perspective. The truck was rolling off the road, teetering on the edge of the embankment, and ready to topple over me.

At such moments, one does nothing consciously or deliberately. All I remember is pivoting about face and seeing a narrow plateau several hundred feet below me. Oddly, I imagined a gigantic swimming pool down there, felt I was on a diving board, bent my knees and sprang up and out into space, hoping I would clear that truck behind me. (Later, Dean said I had swung my arms back and then forward in a swan dive that had perfect Olympic form except that my knees had bent in midair robbing me of a graceful execution. Indeed!)

I had a strange sensation of the ground turning over me. The somersault my swan dive had thrown me into had landed me flat on my back. The light snow acted like grease on the loose gravel, stones, and steep decline. The momentum threw me into a lightning skid on my back, for about 100-foot descending angle. I stopped with a smash, when gravity hurled me against what I thought was a huge boulder. It almost knocked the wind out of me. I looked up for just a second, wondering where the truck was, and, of course, it was just where I feared it would be.

It was totally airborne, on its side, and coming down right over me. Reflexively, I flattened against the side of whatever had stopped me, and crouched so low my head went between my legs. For an instant, the light overhead dimmed, and then I felt a sickening thud, followed by the sound of shattering glass as the truck bounced off the top of my protective shelter and disappeared.

A small avalanche of rocks, gravel, and pebbles clattered down, and a few pelted me without mercy. I covered my head with my arms, cowering in anticipation of a larger slide that might be gathering above me. To my immense relief, nothing more came.

The clattering diminished into stony silence. It was then I heard Dean's voice calling my name several times, his voice choked with emotion. He later said he feared I had been smashed into pulp. I got to my feet on that precarious perch and looked up. To my surprise, there was an automobile up there that had apparently pulled up just in time for three or four of its passengers to witness what had happened. Gawking in disbelief, they stood motionless and silent.

Poor Dean. He was terrified, and still hollering if I were okay.

I yelled back, "Yes," it was I, not Banquo's ghost. It was impossible to climb up that steep grade with its sliding shale and rocks, so I yelled for some rope. While they started looking for it, I took a survey of my surroundings. It was not a boulder my body had been hurled against, but a heavy-gauge metal, 8- or 10-foot diameter culvert with only the tip sticking out of the ground. I squatted next to the culvert and looked up. The arc at its highest point above me was hardly 4 feet tall, with a foot of it dented flat where the truck had bounced. There couldn't have been much more than a foot of space between the top of my head and the truck when it hit. The truck had bounced up, righted itself in midair and plunged down about 20 feet, smashing its front end through the ice and into the water beneath, fed earlier in summer by the culvert.

There was enough water in the cab to have drowned anyone in it, if he had not already ricocheted to death when the truck hit the culvert. Moreover, had I slid another 3 or 4 feet, I would have gone over the ledge beneath the culvert and sliced through that ice right into the pool. The truck could not have missed pinning me under it when it crashed through the ice a moment later. I thought of the last time when I had nearly frozen —in quicksand.

Whatever the impulse, it had stopped me from getting inside the cab. It had saved my life without a shadow of a doubt, no matter what else had happened in the few following moments.

I just stood there dumbfounded, sensory cues coming at me through a daze. It was too much to take in, looking at all the things involved which I had again survived miraculously. How else could I explain it?

Finally, the crew above found a rope, tossed it down, and helped me scramble out. Dalton, the gentleman who owned the car, was about my age, and we hit it off immediately. He drove us to the Susitna Lodge. He and I became friends, and our paths crossed often in the ensuing years. It was my privilege to know him. He was the stuff of which old Fairbanks was made.

That night, the local inhabitants from Cantwell emerged from nowhere to dance and socialize. Dean telephoned his wife to come and get us, since we were not sure the truck would run even if it could be retrieved. She arrived in record time, 4 hours later.

Ah, Dean, my esteemed friend! How you enjoyed life, how you danced with your lovely wife to the music of the juke box into the late hours of the night. I sat there next to the fireplace, watching its leaping flames, deeply buried in my thoughts. So many thoughts crossed my mind, except the thought that could have told me this would be our last hunt together.

For the better part of 2 hours, the thoughts plagued me. In barely 2 years, I had brushed death four times and, discounting the black bear charge at Manley, there was nothing I could do about the other episodes, once the unfolding of the action sequences began. There was nothing I did, or could have done, to alter how those actions ended. They took their own course and ended their way—not mine. Never, in all my adult life, had I lost all control and felt so helpless when I was on my way to what should have been certain death. Yet, I had survived when, each time, progressively, death seemed closer in time and distance—in seconds and inches—when life or death could have gone either way.

All this raised questions I had pushed out of my mind for years.

They were too metaphysical, as we used to say, and metaphysics had lost respectability in the halls of academe. I reached no conclusions that evening, gazing into the fire, but gazing into my soul, I felt tremendous turmoil of intellect, reaching the verge of the unknown, where I began to doubt my former doubts. I concluded that the evening had been far more memorable in ways than the day had been.

The following day, we drove to Cantwell, and, what passed for a service station had what passed for a wrecker, an old Jerry-rigged World War II wreck. But it did the job. It took 3 hours to finally winch out my truck. Out of the water in full view, it was enough to make a heartless man cry. The left side of the body was smashed, the door caved in, glass gone, and the hood crumpled. (Later, the insurance company declared it "totaled out.") After the oil was changed, the second try with the ignition key started the engine. It had not been damaged by the cold, clear water it had sat in overnight. Some cardboard attached to the window opening, and the left front fender hammered out for just enough clearance from the tire it had gouged into, and I was all set, and drove home with no further mishap.

Back home, there were those who, with cocked eyebrows, asked, "What, again?" By now, it was the question of the hour among my friends, and there was cause to believe it was also the talk of much of the town. When would my charmed life lose its charm, or when would my lucky star finally fall on me, was their question. It was my question too.

Shortly after that, Dean and I had a celebration party with our wives. How we laughed at the incredibility of it all. The women looked at each other with that look which says if this is a man's world, then men can have it.

We talked about going on another hunt several times, but circumstances prevented it. Life got in the way, and we could not synchronize schedules. I have known few men as good as Dean. He was always considerate, wise, generous, and a great hunter. We cherished each other's friendship, no matter that life took us in different directions. Four years after that episode, he was killed in an airplane crash while hunting.

Business often takes me to the place where he worked. I see the desk where he often sat, and the chair next to it, on which he invited me to rest a few minutes for a chat. His work is now done by others sitting at that desk, others who obviously have not the slightest idea of the kind of man they have replaced. One or two old timers are still there. When we look at each other in passing, we know the emptiness of Dean's absence.

I despise death; it has no decency. All too often, it grabs with impatient greed what we must give it sooner or later, anyway. After all the years, I still think of Dean and how we embraced life shortly after my narrow escape. How we laughed when it was all over, at the miracle of it all, and how we vowed to hunt forever. I think of him often and celebrate his memory. That is the way Dean would want me to remember him, and I'll bet he's hunting now, wherever he is.

Reflections

Time, from the plane crash at Anaktuvuk, to the sheep hunt on Mt. Sillyasheen, to the truck calamity near Cantwell, was a kind of spiritual boot camp for me. It was a time when I seriously began to question vexing problems I had been aware of for a long time, but merely filed in deep cerebral storage until the right time. The time was now.

The plane and truck crashes preoccupied me, of course. I knew intuitively, to the marrow of my bones, that something profound was going on in my life—not just accidents or happenings—the likes of which I never experienced before. I asked myself the obvious questions—had I developed subconscious suicidal tendencies or accident proneness? Since these were new experiences, I had to examine them in the context of my hunts.

If Don had been ahead of me by a few paces at the quicksands, he, too, would have fallen in. The terrain and direction to the bear gave us no choice. When the black bear charged, the choice was his, not mine, and I did not let him assist me in my suicide. When the airplane crashed, I had nothing to do with the flying of it, or the weather, anymore than the others. Just before the truck rolled over, I had felt restrained from leaping into the cab, and if there was anything subconscious, it was precisely antisuicidal.

I dismissed a suicide hypothesis, since it could not be supported by fact or irrational motivation. As for accident proneness, the nearest I could come was my impulsive grab for the ram before he slipped over the edge, but then why did I let go at the last second when I realized what was happening? Poor judgement? Maybe. Lack of specific experience? Undoubtedly. I dismissed the accident-prone hypothesis on grounds of inconclusive evidence.

With no causal determinants for an explanation, the only thing left was probability theory. That made things worse. To explain what happened to me within the time span, and the narrow escapes from death each time on the basis of chance, would require a life expectancy exceeding Methusaleh's. I admit, I had no rational answers, but I couldn't be too far off with my sneaking suspicion something was going on. It would take one more "accident" to throw light on the subject. Meanwhile, aspects of that sheep hunt had already begun to fascinate me.

I thought a good deal about the "forced march," with its agonizing ordeal that I saw through to the end, although I had been tempted to do otherwise. Why? Why did I want that trophy so badly? What difference had its absence in my life made in my past? What difference would its presence in my life make in my future? In my present "now," it symbolized an enormous achievement all the more satisfying because of enormous challenges against which I had won. Yet, neither achievement nor challenge were the end of it. Rather, it was their promise of something better to come. All this was a means to some greater end I could not clearly sense, and yet for which the "all" had been worth it.

What I knew for sure was, all rational human action is purposive. It intends to attain some goal or objective. What one does in the present intends to cause certain results in the future, whether that future is minutes, hours, years, or lifetimes away. That is one of the differences between man and animals, and that is where my inquiries began. During every one of those agonizing steps for 20 torturous miles, I carried more than the remains of some dead weight that had been an animal. I carried a dream of my future. I carried the raw material, the basic elements, out of which there would emerge a trophy—a thing symbolizing the grandeur of wilderness; a thing whose value and worth would never change or diminish, in spite of costs and prices that spasm like grand mal seizures to the insane tunes of the marketplace; a thing of beauty that would not go out of style with tomorrow's change in fashions; a verity that yesterday was not lived in vain. Something of value was accomplished, and not all our ". . . yesterdays lead the fool his way to dusty death."

I know there are supposed to be no absolutes in this world, but I cannot deny the throbbing presence of it in my soul. When I deny it does exist (which is the delusion of flaneurs too tired or afraid to search), then I shall have traded my humanity for the robotical.

The hunter cannot live in the wilderness with his beloved animals. They must live with him, as mounted trophies in his home, where both find sanctuary. To find symbolic expression of the spirit of the successful hunt, what began as a dream is now overwhelmed by a routine and mundane reality. Not counting full-body-mount trophies, which are even more problematical, the shoulder-mount trophies will require on the average, 3 cubic feet of space projecting from the wall. It is a simple fact overlooked, even by the novice hunter himself. The trophy, for which all that effort, expense, and risk of life and limb have occurred, needs as much secure support, protection, and constant care as a Hellenic marble statue in a fine art museum.

Like all treasures, the trophy too needs its vault, gallery, sacristy, or place for safekeeping, where it becomes part of a treasure-trove to be rediscovered again and again. Its joy and beauty never fades. Among other things, the trophy hunter is a collector of a special kind of rare art. Sooner or later, he needs an enclosed space for the magical treasure-trove, the shrine protecting his cherished masterpieces.

One of the great spiritual urges in mankind, making our nature human, is the quest and struggle for sacred space, the enclosed area, the personalized and intimate private world that is ours and ours alone, to give us peace, respite, and renewal. It is here we find sanctuary from the outside world constantly assaulting our senses, making us strangers to ourselves. It is here we enshrine our symbolic treasures and icons, verifying the clues to the mystery of our identities—our very beings. It is here we have the reference points for self-continuity after the disjunctions of the day's trials, in no-man's land, in the outside world. It is here we find location in the infinity of the space-time continuum where these stand fixed and become one with us and our symbols. It is here we know where our absolutes are buried, beneath all the trivia of relativisms we mistook for our realities.

In every civilization, there have been childhood games that created the magic circle where one tot follows the other and plays on certain conditions. That sanctified space becomes special, out of the ordinary, a world of make-believe more real than the real world. It is made with little more than childish ingenuity and imagination. A piece of chalk or a stick of wood scratches the lines on the ground that becomes the enchanted forest, into which no one may enter without the secret password. Cardboard boxes turn into the castle where play transforms us into kings and queens, cops and robbers, or whatever our imaginations seduce us into being.

That spacing is a preparatory phase. When we become adults, we transpose the space for real magic circles and enchanted worlds to give us relief, for brief interludes, from the outside world of alienation and fellow man gone awry, or when wanderlust exhausts itself. That psychic urge for sacred space, for sanctuary, for protective bailey, enchanted to our own liking, is common to all mankind in search for home. The meaning is universal, no matter how its symbols differ. There are those who have found their Garden of Eden; those who still search for it, be it known as Shangri-La, El Dorado, Lost Atlantis, the City of Opar, Land of Oz, 30-year mortgaged home, the swank condominium, log cabin, moveable tepee, moated castle, mobile trailer home, soldier's pup tent, child's doll house, rumpus room, and whatever else that symbolizes magic, spiritual space. It is the world of make-believe come true where, today, one returns to find the real self that was left behind from 9 to 5.

A home is a man's castle, as it is so often said, his redoubt, and his sanctuary. He used to reign there like a king with his queen. Home, however, is not only where you hang your hat. As the old song used to say, "Be it ever so humble, there's no place like home," because it is the shrine where you keep your treasures making sacred your castle, and enchanting your land of make-believe. Hence, it is much more than a place of shelter and protection from the elements—one can find that, if it comes down to it, in a large packing crate (I know a fine, old gentleman who lived a couple of Alaska winters in one of them), or in a spartan efficiency apartment.

Our nation's suburbia, with its reasonably luxurious homes, has the envy of much of the world that doesn't even have adequate protection and safety in its shanty-town hovels. Our modern

houses are transferred into homes by virtue of a spiritual quality—
intimacy of relationships, emotional sharing, and communion of
its members with each other, or with objects, memories, and
experiences giving us fulfillment when no place else can.

One's children are born and grow up there. And before the little
elves grow into giants and leave to start their own magic circles,
your space is already filled with treasures and trinkets, souvenirs,
memorabilia from favorite books, to knickknack cabinets. High
school award for first prize in the poetry contest, clothespin doll
grandpa made, pennant of the college you attended, photos of dear
ones now departed, a multimillion dollar collection of Renaissance paintings—all have their places. Ming vases, a reproduction
of the Winged Victory, several display cabinets of porcelain flowers;
or trophies of the hunt, for which you had to add a new room to the
house (or build a new one). They ask for the enchanted space. The
hunter, like everyone else, will spend the rest of his life growing
up with things—not merely things, but extensions and reference
points of the spirit; this is why they are treasures and heirlooms.

These things are all icons, images, and symbols of one's life,
of one's joys and sorrows, wins and losses, of the efforts spent in
finding or earning them. These remind one that there have been
things in life worthwhile, which stayed faithful and give meaning
and continuity. They remind us how much gratitude we owe to all
that made good things in life possible. I know of people who have
few, if any, such possessions, though they could easily have had
them. Do their silent glances say they never had a good day that
gave them something worth remembering? Or are they of the
modern breed wanting no reminders of the gratitude they owe to
the past making their present possible?

Anyway, that world of dreams-come-true has required effort,
toil, expense, and even danger, in order to find those treasures.
Sometimes, treasure is in distant lands, requiring long journeys
filled with exciting adventures. Every tourist brings back a part of
the foreign lands he visits. He makes them a part of his home, with
souvenirs and trinkets, so he can recall happier moments when life
was better filled with renewal and joy. There are treasures worth
any price, to be had at any cost when they have a unique meaning
that adds worth and value to our lives.

Those treasures renew the spirit, making it possible to forget
briefly, to endure constantly, the anguish of life or the persistence

of ugliness that cannot be avoided, even by chasing after orgies of "fun." Who today, can delight in the society that yesterday's false promises created? No wonder we all crave the future and hope it will wipe out today's futility—"... yesterday's folly that this day's madness did prepare." It has always been thus.

That sheep hunt put me to one kind of test on the trail, and to another kind for weeks after, as I pondered that nearly fatal plunge and the agony of carrying back that trophy, the symbol of a treasure so difficult to find and claim. What plagued me was my retort to Mike—yes, I would die before I abandoned that sheep. It seemed so absurd to say a thing like that, let alone think it. A thousand world-record trophy sheep were not worth my life, or any human life, let alone the poor, barely average thing I had taken.

Was my retort just a figure of speech? I suspected it was more. The look in Mike's eyes, when I said so, told me he had suspicions, too. Of course, the sheep was a symbol of other things, profound and subtle inner feelings in my soul transformed into outer, observable action. I had committed myself to whatever consequences followed the shot, even before I squeezed the trigger. That shot, and what followed, gave me proof, in a totally unexpected way, to one of my pet assumptions about values.

Often, my students had asked me: if there is not a scientific way by which the correctness of a value can be proved, how, then, can we rationally determine which value is better than another? Did the whole thing remain a purely subjective affair and always a relative matter, solved by arguments only too clever?

Logic and theory always boiled down to what we liked, or didn't like, in this affair between heart and mind begging the question. I had my own rule of thumb based on praxis—the practical application of action, through custom and usage, of which values took priority over others. How did one do this practically? By resorting to what centuries of tradition had nurtured, so antagonistic to the modern mentality—the only practical and observable way by which the value of any value could be established was the action taken in defense of that value, including the willingness to fight and die for it.

What other actual test was supreme by virtue of the absence of any other possible test? Countless Christian martyrs had proven the value of their faith-values by dying for them in the Roman arenas (emperor worship could have saved them). Countless patriots died fighting for their countries (conscientious objection or surrender to the enemy could have saved them). Parents died for their children (they could have abandoned them), and so forth. Were they all fools? Are we so much wiser, or just arrogant? Let alone the importance of any value, how else could one determine even what importance really is, except by actions that have irreversible consequences to the decisions or choices we make—for better or worse? The more important some things are, the greater the consequences. Some consequences are absolutely irreversible—like death, for example. Has there ever been a relative death? When?

If the kind of rational action taken is the key to testing the value of value, then there are only two broad categories. One of these is based on contingencies, or what we call today, cost effectiveness. We calculate and logically analyze the cost of the means by which those ends are to be attained. If the means for achieving those goals are too costly in terms of risk, time, effort, or money, we either adopt other means less costly, in those terms, or we adopt different goals altogether. What we do is relative to other things, where morality itself becomes relative. We do what we want to do, not what we ought to do.

The other kind of action is at all costs, or at any cost. Such action is not contingent on anything else. Any effort, time, money, or risk is worth it, as long as it is possible. The goal is absolute and nonnegotiable, because it is of supreme importance and based on conflict between desire and right or wrong, not whether it is cost effective. What is at work here is principle taking on the quality of the sacred. It is beyond price and calculation.

In reality, both action patterns often overlap, and we engage in both at times. When we reach a crisis, however, in human affairs where there is no escape from either/or, one or the other action pattern prevails, depending on who, or what, we are. This is why I concluded the only test for the value of value was one's willingness to fight for it and die for it, if necessary. An honorable man ready to protect hallowed values will say, "Damn the torpedoes, full speed ahead!" A dishonorable man, who changes values every night, will say, "Quick, let me hide under the bed!" It is not the outcome of the crisis that determines the man. It is the man who determines the outcome of the crisis.

During my childhood, I had only a brief and shallow exposure to the idea that somehow human life was sacred. I did not understand what sacred meant. How could I, seeing what had happened to my people? When answers to my questions left me hopelessly confused, always my parents' last answer was, "You will understand when you grow up."

The other thing that had to do with growing up was when I hurt myself with cuts and bruises, and when I wailed and moaned in pain or fright. The futuristic crutch during these times was, "It will go away, and you will forget all about it when you grow up." I really looked forward to growing up. It was obvious all the good things were yet to be. (My dearest, sweetest parents—if only you were here to see I have grown up, long since, and now I can tell you what you didn't want me to know—there are some pains that do not go away, and some new ones that are worse.)

If I did not have the vaguest idea of what sacred was, I had a very real feeling about it. It was not learned or developed because of cultural influences. It was just there all along, in the psyche, a part of what we call human nature, just waiting for something to breathe life into it, or to smother it. It got the breath of birth as soon as I saw those pictures of wild animals. The feeling was one of fascination, wonder, awe, respect, and affection, mixed in a kind of spiritual dough, to rise later.

The bread, which became the staff of life and what it nourished years later, was the feeling I recognized as reverence, reserved only for the sacred. For decades, that feeling rattled around loose in an empty soul, like a marble rolling around in a large, round empty box, unable to find a place to stop. It resulted from the mundane endlessly surrounding us and blunting our fascination with life. Yet we know there are things out there beyond the ordinary. They are in a special class—rare and priceless—when found, we set them apart and protect them lest they be profaned by the ordinary. Hence, the sense of the sacred is born and saves us from the depreciation of the vulgar to which we so easily fall prey. There is always something better, higher, and more precious to intrigue and beguile us for ultimate realities. That which delights our limited senses can also jade them in due time. That which delights our soul is forever fascinated by the infinity of spirit. That is where authentic freedom finds its true fulfillment.

Years later, when I engaged in the action behavior known as hunting, to search for treasures or trophies to enshrine in the sanctuary I called my home, it was easy to transfer to them the feelings of sacredness I had sensed long since. Meanwhile, I had done more than my share of required reading in the usual college courses in anthropology. There were all sorts of explanations, from the cultural to the psychoanalytical, about primitive peoples (the euphemistic or politically correct phrase, pre-literate, was just emerging), about magic, ritual, animism, totemism, and the rest. It had to do with things of the spirit, though modern anthropologists had no use for things spiritual in their own lives.

The upshot was, exotic aborigines had a special relationship, a mystical kinship, with animals whom they revered as part of their animistic beliefs. Even those they killed were treated with veneration as part of the sacredness that filled the spiritual life. The audiovisual departments in every university, as well as ordinary television programs, glorified the spiritual significance in the hunting methods, ceremonies, and rituals before and after killing of animals, by these people who always had a nobility, wisdom, and simple dignity, in harmony with nature.

The commentators and scientists who made these statements, certainly worthy of applause, did not miss a single opportunity, however. They made invidious comparisons with the theological rationalizations, and religious superstitions of Western man, who raped Mother Nature and whose Father God led him to do other terrible things to this planet he plundered. Parenthetically, while Father God was denounced as a male sexist term, the female sexist term Mother Nature was used without batting a single eyelash heavy with mascara. The agony was not in hearing these subtle, defamatory insinuations, or outright propagandistic distortions, undermining our civilization and culture. It was in watching these scholars bring home beautiful films, made and shown with the space-age technological marvels, created and produced by the very Western culture they denounced.

I knew long since that my ancestry had been primitive (later, being realists, they used the word primitive to describe their own origins without moral indignation) and animistic. Some 3,000 years or so ago (give or take a few centuries), they developed sophisticated religious systems and a noteworthy civilization, for the next 2,000 years or so (give or take a few centuries). However, nothing since my birth had given me direct personal experience with anything remotely resembling totemic kinship systems, ani-

371

mism, or nature worship. Yet I, too, felt the reverence, the spiritual sense of the sacred, and the feelings of respect for animals long before I hunted them and got tangled up with anthropology. Those early feelings did not diminish when I killed my animals. They intensified.

There was a difference, however, between the romanticized native hunters and me. Fellow academicians and other cognoscenti said that after much laborious study of native languages, they could finally understand symbolic and spiritual reasons why aboriginals hunted, when it was not for food. Though my command of the King's English was no worse than the cognoscenti's who spoke the same language, they looked upon me as an animal-murdering savage. I told them repeatedly, I too, experienced the identical symbolic and spiritual feelings and emotions when I hunted (and still do). If man is of the same biological species everywhere, then why are men different when it comes to the archetypal, spiritual strivings of the soul? When would the Western intelligentsia realize not every civilized man who hunts is necessarily doing it for "sadistic sport" to enjoy the "fun" of cruelty. There are more honorable and moral reasons why some of us hunt, even though, admittedly, honor and morality are out of fashion among too many intelligentsia in Western culture these days.

No one can deny culture influences, in different ways, the reasons why men hunt. Neither can anyone deny those reasons are firmly rooted in the same instinctive, archetypal, and spiritual impulses common to the soul of man, no matter where or when. All aborigines have one way or another of expressing their sense of reverence for some of the animals they kill. Relics from parts of such animals abound, symbolizing the sacred or the mystical. Some natives wear lion manes or leopard mantles, while others use the plumage of rare tropical birds in headdresses as symbolic responses to special needs of the spirit. Claws, beaks, bones, horns, antlers, and other specialized animal parts become amulets, talismans, scepters, magic wands, and other sacred objects that connect warrior and medicine man, motherhood and sorcery, to the spiritual world.

What if these peoples had some miraculous, primitive technology with which to preserve animal parts, like a trophy shoulder mount or even a full-bodied mount they could enshrine in appropriately proportioned and lighted trophy rooms? Would their feelings of awe and reverence be any less? Would their identification with the spiritual be any weaker? My guess is, these would be far greater and much stronger. Witness the ancient Egyptians, whose polytheistic systems were far more sophisticated, complex, and rational than preliterate animisms. Their science and technology were breathtaking (consider the pyramids), enabling sophisticated methods of embalming not only dead pharaohs, but deified animals who were worshiped from the sacred Apis bulls of Sakkara to the Sebek crocodiles of Kom Ombo.

My early feelings of reverence for the sanctity of animal life naturally spilled over into a spiritual dimension that related me to big-game animals in my adulthood, because, during that phase of my life, I realized how fortunate I was to live in this country at this time. This was the country that not only gave my parents refuge, but allowed me to move from the lower class of my birth to the reviled bourgeois middle class. That is where I had access to a "decadent capitalistic" life-style safe from massacre and starvation. That is where I found the treasure of kings that created a miracle for me. It allowed for my trophy mounts, that were three-dimensional art symbols, which vibrated with the spiritual tremors in my soul—tremors also known to pharaohs of Egypt, kings of Assyria, Bushmen of Africa, Indians of North America, Eskimos of the North, nobility of Europe, and frontiersmen of my own country. No matter what the other differences were, the spirit that tied all of us together into one honorable and ancient fraternity was the same.

It is commonplace these days to say we all search for a sense of communion or community with those of like mind, interest, and spirit—especially since modernism produces so much alienation from the common roots of humanity. Well, there are countless attempts to find a sense of community, a special belonging to kindred spirits, throughout history. The hunting fraternity has had it all along, from cave to skyscraper.

I was proud of identifying with that fraternity of hunters that started around the campfires of prehistory, but I felt more blessed and fortunate than they and all those who followed them. There are few redeeming features in this modernism that destroys the human spirit, in the name of humanity, but one thing must be admitted— never before has there been a science, technology, craftsmanship, and art like today's taxidermy, creating exquisite trophies doing full justice to the majesty of those animals we hunt today. Therein lies the good fortune I share with contemporary trophy hunters.

Nothing in hunting of the past can equal the beauty and magnificence of those trophies come to life in our trophy rooms today. For me, my modest number of trophies are not only the best of their kinds simply to tickle my vanity. They were my gallant, noble rivals in nature's scheme of things, and are now my distinguished guests of honor, my soul brothers in spirit. They were the sacredness I had found without knowing it.

On occasion, I even wear my elephant-hair bracelet, or lion-claw choker, or ram-horn belt buckle, or grizzly bear-claw key-chain pendant. I reserve wearing them for special occasions, including professional conferences and such. Fellow academics who write with such high regard for the symbolism of accouterments, worn by primitive hunters, look at me with frozen smiles and icy glares when they see the similar symbolic things I wear in contemporary style.

The style may be different, but the soul of the hunter and the symbols of the hunting spirit are the same. Ancient and modern hunter alike, we share the same traditions. We have walked the same trails, known the same joys and sorrows, survived the same dangers, shared the same adventures, and have the same respect for each other's humanity, without the fanfare of modern "visionaries" who must kill off hunters to save mankind for some New World Order outmoded ere it begins.

From the pictures of my boyhood books, I had come to love, admire, and respect those animals that came to life for me and became the spirit by which things of beauty and sanctity were made that I cherished and respected. All this, without an "educational influence" about things sacred, spiritual, reverential, or venerable. I adored the creatures and never paid any attention to the more profound reality of the Creator who put them there in the first place. Those pictures were the mirrored images of the realities they reflected. I pursued the realities on the hunting trail—where else? The sense of respect those pictures created in me became the reverence for the sacred I hunted for in the real animals, until I found them in my trophies. This is why I believe that so-called sport hunting is essentially a spiritual search, and in its greatest dimensions, the big-game trophy hunt, a search for the sacred experience. No male can become a man without the sacred sense, no matter how the symbols differ, unisex notwithstanding.

There's the rub. The sacred is not sacred, the priceless is not priceless, the unique is not unique, if it can be compromised, modified, altered, or substituted. It is an absolute that creates, inevitably, its own morality to be attained at all costs. Even before I squeeze the trigger on any trophy animal, I know that no matter what consequences follow, I am responsible for seeing it through to the honorable end. That's why I am morally bound by the code that says once the decision is made to squeeze the trigger for that trophy, any trophy, then it has to be pursued, taken, and retrieved at all costs. And since it was intended finally to be cherished and enshrined in the enchanted space, the sanctuary of my home, then it must come to rest there—at all costs. That includes the risk of my life in crisis, insane though it sounded to Mike, and even to myself, when we were on the trail. If I am not ready for that risk, I have no business initiating its consequences. This attitude, obviously spills over into other areas of life for which I am willing to fight or die or else life is an unrelenting burden without the values important to me.

Of course, the thought astounded me. I didn't think there was anything in this world, aside from family, for whom I would take such a risk. But for animals? On second thought, however, I realized I was not so unique in this regard. There was not a professional hunter worth his salt, I'd read about, who was not committed to risking his life to save his client, or to end the suffering of a wounded animal, no matter how dangerous and how great the odds when tracked into closed quarters. The professional hunter does not do this because he is paid. No amount of pay could justify that. Yet the records are replete with such hunters who took the risk and paid with their lives, because the moral code, and the duty, is what did the justifying. Two other words for this are honor and integrity.

Professional hunters, however, are a mere handful compared to the rest who hunt on their own, for themselves. These, too, are obligated to the same moral code, to the same duty, to the same honor and integrity without which there is no sport hunting or trophy hunting or anything else of real and lasting value. That's why the true hunter is a moralist. That's why some die or are killed on the trail—not because of accident or incompetence, but because they lived up to that moral code at all costs. If the hunter is not prepared to submit to that code, then he is not a true hunter, but a pretentious disgrace to his fraternity. All authentic trophy hunters kill animals, but not all killers of trophy animals are authentic hunters.

What the ordeal of that sheep hunt taught me was, the true hunt must be true at all costs. There is plenty of room for calculated risks. There must be, and they must be taken, by the very nature of the hunt. If and when one commits himself to that calculated risk, there is not the slightest room for calculating cost, price, or bargaining with one's conscience to justify selling out one iota of that code and that commitment once the decision has been made to squeeze the trigger. Here is another version of the Big Bang theory creating a brand, new spiritual cosmos in the soul of the hunter. He is irreversibly responsible, thereafter.

Under no condition do I imply I am holier than thou, or present myself as a paragon of hunting virtue. I do not merit that, and never will. Moreover, I know too many hunters far better than I can ever hope to be. Many of them are my friends who know I could never get away with such an outrageous pretense, the skeptics notwithstanding. I say all this because there is a point to be made. Someone has to say it, because it must be said.

I say all this because, nearly 30 years after the fact, I still feel a twinge of shame that the thought of compromise even occurred to me on the trail of that sheep hunt—ordeal or no ordeal. It is the prerogative of youth not to care a whit about the long run. There's lots of "long run" for me, too, I thought, even when I was past my youth. But the "long run" has caught up, and what I didn't care about then, suddenly appears from nowhere to tell me I forgot to think about how short the "long run" really is. Its time has come sooner than I wanted. I say this now, so if one young trophy hunter understands me, he will avoid the anguish that, inevitably, is sure to catch up. Never let the code down, for when time catches up, you will know how you were weighed in the scales and found wanting when you gaze into the eyes of your trophy who does not speak, but who knows better than you what you are worth. Never let the code down, or you let yourself down, for you are the code.

Of course, I didn't abandon my ram and saw my duty through to the end. It is, therefore, so tempting to say, "Oh well, it wasn't that bad," and perhaps that is true. It is less tempting to say, "Oh, yes, but it wasn't that good, either." And that is certainly true. Often, during my routine activity, the look in the eyes of one or another trophy catches my eye for a fleeting moment. In an instant my spirit leaps to life thinking of the moments of our encounter.

Routinely, I deliberately take the time to commune with my

trophies—my comrades, my friends, my rivals who are now my guests of honor and my symbols of kindred spirit. I talk to them and imagine their answers with fond memories. When my eyes reach the far end of the wall, I see the three sheep I have taken in six hunts. Two of them are magnificent, with better than full curls. They look at me with stately elegance. They put to shame my first ram of the barely legal curls. But he is my favorite. I think of that bone jolting, flesh tearing fall down the mountain and the agonizing hike to camp. I still feel the pack straps cutting into my raw shoulders and my aching, buckling legs that could barely stand me up.

Then the same old question comes to my mind. All I can do is ask my ram. "Were my best efforts good enough for you, even a tiny bit? Please, tell me I did not let you down, after all." Someday, when we meet again on the other side, I hope he will answer my question and give me a passing grade.

Little Blackie

I t was April in Valdez. Alaska Spring exploded with a burst of fresh, yellow-green on lower mountain slopes. The tops were still blotched with snow. Our boat, a small but speedy craft, was making good time through Valdez Arm running out to sea. We had gone far enough to see the mountains taper into the horizon. Beyond was Prince William Sound—a bit of ocean that could be as mean and temperamental, when it wanted to be, as any Alaska waters. Out there, overhead, the sky was turning to an ominous black, and the wind told us that, before long, the brewing storm would be in our laps. We turned back with disappointment.

We scoured those slopes on our way out, looking for black bear. We were at the right place at the right time, for they were coming out of hibernation now and would be constantly on the move for food to sate their ravenous hunger. We had seen no sign anywhere. Now, returning to port, we looked over the same grounds we had already found barren of bear.

The wind picked up, whipping waves into jagged edges of white. Overhead, the skies were a sullen gray. When the boat's prow sliced through waves with higher crests, the bottom slammed down hard in the troughs. Swirling water felt like fluid potholes, jarring our teeth loose. Tom, who was manning the engine, smiled his optimism each time I looked at him with growing doubts. Our wives snuggled in their windbreakers and remained silent.

I crouched up front, scanning every inch of the slopes for a telltale spot of moving black. The odds of seeing a bear now were rather slim, but still, I hoped against hope. I wanted to undo my anguish over the bear at Manley 3 years earlier—for the bear's sake and mine. There had to be a bear somewhere in all this mountainous vastness spilling into the sea. To quench my doubts, I breathed the atomized salt mist in deeply when wind gusts sprayed foam across the prow. I recited Masefield to myself, "I must down to the seas again, to the lonely sea and the sky, and all I ask is a tall ship and a star to steer her by." It was one of my favorite poems, and its mood precisely fit the gray sea and sky around us.

Suddenly, my brain switched to a different circuit. My eyes had connected with a black spot about two-thirds of the way up the mountain side to our left. There, emerging spring green was patched with darkness under the gathering ominous clouds. I tried to hold my adrenaline in check. That black spot could be a boulder.

The women were offering coffee from the thermos, but I brushed it aside, grabbed my binoculars, waved to Tom and motioned to the beach. It was littered with huge black rocks, where waves shattered themselves into spray and receded into foam. Tom cut the engine, the boat bobbed erratically. I tried bracing my elbows on the gunnel to hold the glasses still enough to find that black spot in the moving, hazy field of view. It could be a boulder. I found it. What could have been a boulder moved, and my adrenaline freewheeled through my system.

It was a bear, all right. When it turned broadside, its head seemed small, tapering to a point that meant optical illusion. It seemed small only because the rest of the body was gigantic in comparison. I let out a low whistle of awe and turned around for a moment to check, and Tom, too, had his glasses trained on that behemoth. All he could say in response was, "Yeaah—ah."

That bear had to be bigger than the one at Manley. My heart wanted to pound out of its cage. By the time I lowered my glasses, I knew I had found the Golden Fleece, Jewel of Opar, das Rheingold, Kohinoor—the treasure of my wildest dreams.

Reality quickly frustrates newborn desire—it always does when desire is overly ambitious. I glanced at Tom, looking up nervously at the threatening sky. Maybe he was disappointed the black bear didn't turn out to be a black rock. I knew what he was thinking, and he had to be disarmed, quickly.

"I want him," I said.

In his soft-spoken way, he hammered at the obvious in case it had escaped my notice. "In 2 hours this place will be in the middle of a stormy nightmare," he said. "We'll have to make an overnight camp in some safe cove."

"I'm against it," I said, sneaking a glance at the women. Anxiety was spilling out of their furtive glances. Without question, their welfare came first, and an overnight camp in this weather, without proper gear, was too much to ask of them. Tom was trying to accommodate me against his better judgement.

"Let me jackass it on the mountain, and you can come back for me first thing in the morning," I said.

Tom seemed relieved for the women's sake, but his eyes bored into mine, questioning the sanity of my plan. He looked at my wife for support, mutely asking her to veto my decision. Her stare back to him was unfathomable—she was always kind that way, when she didn't give a damn. Then he looked at his wife, and she didn't have to say a word to tell him she thought I was insane. It was another triumph of democracy in action as the abstentions lost the day. Tom made one final plea, telling me the odds were too great against me, given the conditions. I knew that, but this was not just another bear. It was the very treasure I had first seen in my boyhood dreams. It was what had beguiled me to Alaska, and to take him under the existing conditions merely increased its value 10-fold, no matter the odds. Further words were futile.

The beach at the point of debarkation was covered with half-submerged boulders that seemed to come up for air every time the booming, spuming waves crashed and receded. It was going to be a tricky landing. My insistence may have been unfair to Tom, but he was a superb seaman.

Cutting his speed, he skillfully steered the craft between the larger boulders that were more widely scattered. We got through the first phalanx and reached smaller boulders forming a more disarrayed, broken chain to the beach. The craft floated closer to one of them. I asked Tom again to get the women back to port and safety and come for me in the morning. I checked my pocket for the folded sheet of plastic for my overnight shelter, grabbed my rifle, a handful of shells and raisins, and climbed the prow. It was a momentary wait until a receding wave exposed the top of a boulder and I leaped on it. When the swirling foam between the rocks dropped low enough, another leap, and yet another, carried me from tip to tip of the slippery bridging, until it was possible to jump into the water and race toward the beach ahead of the surf. I turned to wave good-bye, and it was tough telling whether they, or I, felt more deserted.

The beach was strewn with black, flinty boulders, jagged and sharp—obviously the result of avalanches that spewed part of the mountain into the water's edge. Ahead, there stood an embankment maybe 30 feet high, its still-frozen, muddy face eroded and gouged with innumerable trickles of meltdown seeping from a thick blanket of ice and snow. The blanket shot upward in a precipitous avalanche chute, to a sharp point. It was a huge, elongated triangle going up perhaps 800 feet from its funneled-out bottom on the embankment to its point of origin up the ravine.

There were many such ravines and avalanche chutes all along these slopes, but this one was higher and larger than most. Its embankment, at least 100 feet wide, tapered out at the sides into dense alder thickets, newly foliated. They seemed to run for miles along the beach. I studied all this carefully, sensing enormous problems, but my mind had not the slightest inkling how real the menacing appearance of all this would prove to be. All I knew for certain was, the bear of my dreams was up there, above the top of that icy triangle.

I could not see above the top of the embankment, but I easily recalled the topography I saw from the boat. Above that icy tip was a narrow, level shelf of bare ground at the base of a rocky tower, that reached up to a plateau of lush green grass. That's where the bear was sumptuously dining. With its rotting ice and snow, that avalanche chute was the shortest route to the green plateau above it, but climbing it was out of the question. Even with crampons and an ice axe, it would be too treacherous. Besides, there was plenty of ground hugging the edge of the icy chute all the way to its top, which was much less dangerous to climb. The only trouble with that was its covering of alders.

Alder thickets are the bane, the unyielding curse on the Alaskan hunter. They are to be avoided at all costs. Like giant, inverted umbrellas, their branches shoot upward and intertwine on top with those of other clumps. Rib-like trunks curve out and up, often to 12 feet or more. Several inches in thickness, the trunks are interlaced with saplings in a tangled undergrowth, all fighting for survival. They make any hunter who gets caught in them, also fight for survival. They become a living hell, no matter how short in duration, and, unlike jungle foliage, one cannot chop his way out. One can only twist, turn, squirm, crawl, and slither his way out, and the way out is often a long way off. It's like being caught in a giant ball of steel wool, locked up in an iron cage. Alders should be avoided like the plague, unless all else fails.

All else had failed. To walk along that beach to where the alders ran out was too far. It would force me to double back the same distance, once above them. There would not be enough time, because both the storm and darkness were closing in too fast. Besides, as soon as the storm hit, the chances were excellent that I would be forced to seek cover, even if the bear did not disappear. The sooner I climbed up and away from the beach, which would be under deeper water before too long, the better. How I hated the thought! But there was no choice. I walked past the embankment's edge of ice and snow, just a little way to my left. Then, I cut into the alders.

Barked shins, scraped knees, falls and stumbles, tortuous twistings and crawlings, welts and bruises from lashing, snapping switches were bad enough. The steepness up the slope through that tangled nightmare was worse. There was no visible direction through the undergrowth, but there was every sensation of it. Grabbing branches to pull myself up, hand over hand most of the way, with aching shoulders and legs, I didn't have to see to know which way I was going. It was up, all right. What was worse, however, was the dense, dead air that was barely breathable just when burning lungs needed gallons of oxygen.

Unrelenting squadrons of little flying things, shaken loose from the foliated tangles, came in clouds, biting with ferocity to humming, whirring, droning, buzzing sounds. My face, neck, and hands caught the full blast of the bites. I was wearing my parka, and over it a raincoat. It might not be enough protection during the night, but right now, it gave the rest of my body cover against the aerial bombardment. It was at the price of a straight jacket worn in front of a blast furnace. It bathed me in perspiration. All sense of time and distance had disappeared. Was it an hour or more to move through a couple acres or less? It felt like a century. Suddenly, the nightmare thinned out into wet, matted grass on a rising swell of mountain side.

Immediately, fresh, moving air revived me and I flopped down, propped myself against a boulder, and tried to regain my strength. Time was still of the essence.

With nothing to struggle against for the moment, memories romped around in my mind of many discussions I'd had with antihunters who always derogated the hunter's enterprise as inconsequential. All the hunter had to do was aim his "high-powered" rifle and just shoot. What was so tough about that? No one ever thought about what the hunter had to go through in the topographical preliminaries before he got to that moment of the "high-powered" shot—if he got there at all. I was still too close to the misery I had just been through not to ponder it. Much later, I was to do a lot of thinking about those "sporting moments" during the toils I had just experienced. The ideas that bore fruit were seeded during that brief rest.

My 5-minute rest period felt too short, but it would have to do. Climbing a bit higher around a promontory allowed me to cut to the right, bringing me to a clearing. From there, I could look down and see the icy tip of the avalanche chute a little below me. My position was now on a narrow shelf of rock and shale. From the center, a tall, rocky column towered above me. It surprised me. It was much higher than it had appeared from the boat. I gawked at it for several minutes. I couldn't step back far enough on that narrow ledge to accurately gauge its height. What difference did it make? I think I was looking for an excuse to try some other route and ignore the pressure of time nagging me. I got a little irritated with myself, also, since I had less confidence guessing heights as I did in guessing distances.

In gauging length or distance, I was surprisingly accurate, but there was no mystery. Nearly 4 years of my life had literally run out on the board and cinder track—5 days a week, 50 weeks a year, running 40-, 100-, 220-, and 440-yard dashes and sprints and high and low hurdles. Also triple and long jumps, and half-mile and one-mile runs to condition stamina for other events. At an average of 20 times a week, running or jumping gave me a conservative estimate of 3,500 times I had squinted out to the tape from the starting blocks, or to the mark from a takeoff jumping board. In the wilderness, I just looked for the imaginary tape from where I was standing. Even a chimpanzee could have made accurate estimates with that kind of training.

All of this went through my mind just standing there, somewhat dazed, while trying to guess the vertical height now in front of me, and I couldn't decide if it was 50 or 80 feet or somewhere between. Somehow, I didn't want to proceed until I knew the exact height. Why? I was playing a game of head-shrink with myself. Why? The moment I asked myself that, I got the answer. All this "calculating" was going on in my skull to divert my mind from another "calculation" going on in my guts. It was an old familiar feeling long since forgotten. I'd had it a few times during the war, and then I recognized the problem. Good grief! I was afraid! I didn't want to make that climb.

Admitting that, I got a little more calm and realistic about my evaluation of the tower. I ignored the height and studied the characteristics of that rocky wall that shot upward. It was part of an escarpment which extended on both sides of it, and an earlier waterfall must have cascaded down it. Its nearly sheer, gouged face was scoured with countless crannies, clefts, and ridges of outcropping stone and ledge. Here and there, a scraggly bush clung tenaciously to its rocky fissure. Icicle slivers resisted the spring thaw, dribbling water streaks that shone like black varnish on the gray rock. The whole thing looked like an impregnable fortress. It cowed me and like I say, I knew I was afraid.

The problem was, that the escarpment on both sides of that rock wall sported another line of alders fanning out to infinity again. What the binoculars from the boat had showed as a thin line of brush, now became another agony of alder thickets. I now had exactly the same problem up here that I had below when I faced the first barricade.

It would be ideal to get above the bear. If he became alerted and started to flee, he would run downhill (knowing danger was above him), giving me a few crucial moments to keep him in view. Otherwise, if he ran uphill, he would disappear from the angle of my view in an instant. To chase him up slope was impossible. Potshots, verbal and ballistic, notwithstanding, no man born of natural woman can chase after any animal on earth running uphill. Finally, there was a strong, steady air current rolling down the slope, and it would instantly give my scent away if I got above him. Any other advantage would be canceled.

He would have to be reached from below. The wind determined that. It would be in my favor. This mandated only one of two choices: the alders on either side of that escarpment or the frightening rock tower itself. I had just battled that alder barricade to near exhaustion below. I knew I could not go through another agony like that. Apart from the physical factor of tiredness, there was the emotional one. I loathed those alders. One encounter a day with them was more than enough. Besides, when the time came to double back toward the plateau above that tower, the bear would undoubtedly hear the switching, snapping brush as I blundered through. A quieter, quicker climb was right up that tower of rock, the fear of which was causing my paralysis of will. If I could make that climb, however, I was assured of the great advantage of surprise.

I scrutinized the details on the rocky surface once more and admitted that this was a task for an expert rock climber with proper gear. It was really beyond my ability. My head told me to turn back, but my soul throbbed with the memories, dreams, and yearnings of a lifetime. He was up there—my ultimate. If I gained nothing else in my life, the living before and after it, would make it all worthwhile. Rarely had I confronted myself so starkly. Was any dream, cherished as much as this, ever attained without risk— great risk? Well, here was the dream. I either grabbed it, or I did not. I had stalled long enough. Fear or no fear—I closed in on that monolithic nemesis.

My line of ascent was started beneath where there seemed to be the most hand and foot holds going up in as nearly straight a line as available. Quickly, the reality of limited vision broke upon me. Clinging to a sheer wall, like a fly, did not allow looking up, down, or sideways more than several inches at a time, if that much. Trying to look much further than that swept waves of vertigo over me, and that increased the fear gradient. The climb was mostly by feel, gingerly probing for foot and hand holds, testing each one carefully before entrusting my full weight to them. When my foot found the solid toehold, I clung to a grip with one hand, while the other caressed the surface overhead for another grip. Often, the absence of one forced movement sideways or back down for a new hold. Occasionally, good fortune let me grab a frozen root or a skimpy bush that guided more than it supported. Once, a sliver of rock on which my foot rested broke loose. Luckily the other foothold and my solid grip held. I thought loose a couple of curses, hoping the wind carried the clattering sound of falling rock out to sea.

Once, a slice of rock jutted out too far, right at my belt line. I bent in the middle, and slid past. I felt a little proud of that maneuver. It helped me think I knew what I was doing for a change. A little higher up, another rotting rock sliver crunched loose, and more fragments plummeted down. Two or three times, my toe-holds were so skimpy I had difficulty controlling my trembling legs to hold me up straight. It occurred to me, I had repeated an old folly. I had worn my hipboots that contributed to my difficulties, but on a boat, ocean-borne, what else does one wear for jumping in and out of landings? I would have given anything for my cleated hunting boots, but it was too late for regrets.

Somewhere along the line, a slight complication made things infinitely worse. My rifle sling slid off my shoulder and dangled it in the crook of my elbow. The weight imperiled my arm and hand movements. With my other hand holding on for dear life, I could not get the sling back to my shoulder and adjust it with one hand. That meant my right hand had to move the rifle up to find a niche or ledge above, cautiously rest the rifle butt on it, muzzle pointing up, and slanted forward, to make it secure. The next step upward had to be half the distance it would have been so I could barely reach down enough to grab the muzzle end and start all over again. This doubled the time, effort, and grief moving upward.

I do not have the slightest idea how long that foot-by-foot, minute-by-minute nightmare lasted. It felt like forever. Again, I reached overhead to feel the rocky surface for a hold, only there was nothing there. My heart skipped a beat. Was there a large hole into which my hand had poked, and what was next? Bracing myself for the wave of vertigo, I tilted my head back just enough to see the nearly black sky above the rim of rock. I was stunned with disbelief. I had made it—well, almost! I admonished myself not to get careless with joy, for there was a final hurdle to clear. My fingers clawed, scratched, and dug into the ground atop that ridge and grabbed on for one final toehold against which to push. My arms pulled forward, dragging my body along until my legs dangled over emptiness behind me when they, too, wiggled forward and, at last, my body—all of it, every bit of it—stretched out exhausted, but safe. I was too weak and nauseous to do anything but just lay there, feeling the wind and scattered raindrops sweep over me. I just didn't care what else happened.

During the several minutes it took to calm my system down, I studied the large boulders strewn across the green plateau which rose steeply upward. My prized colossus had to be between those boulders and the rise. The wind pelted me full blast in the face. So far, so good. The bear could not have scented me. Had he seen me? I'd find out in a moment. Crawling on my belly, diagonally, to a level spot shortened the distance and time the bear would have to move, making it easier to surprise him.

Easing up to a half crouch, I ambled like an ape, full speed, to the side of a bigger boulder, taller than I. My heart pounded my attention to the utmost alert. I expected to see him just as I turned the corner. There was nothing there. Scanning the ground showed no spoor. A stone, hurled against one of the further boulders, should have done the trick, but still nothing came. A few moments more, and it became obvious the bear was not here. Tension knotting up my insides had been for naught. A hurried study of the terrain showed why. The green sloping rise ahead had its top starkly etched against the ominous sky. There had to be another plateau up there. The 7-power binoculars from the boat had not picked up the detail of the ridge as being separated from the one above. It had looked like a single flat strip. Either that, or my judgement had been in error. Fortunately, the rolling slope ahead was not too steep, and I soon gained the top of it. Cautiously, my head came over the ridge to see without being seen. I saw more huge boulders in the middle of a lush green amphitheater a couple of a hundred feet in diameter. Now it began to make sense. Around the edge of that green, ran a dense strip of heavily foliated hedgerows, probably blueberry bushes not yet in fruit, outlining the top of the ridge.

With only my head barely showing above the rim of my vantage point, the wind was rattling my sinuses, bringing with it the pungent, sweet-sour odor of wet black bear. This was the place, all right! A short quick dash to the right brought a sense of tremendous relief. I had entered a large flat area. There was adequate footing here, ideal for both of us to make a good fight of it. He should be behind those boulders ahead. I stayed downwind.

Taking my position and releasing the safety on my rifle, I let out a shrill whistle imitating a marmot, a favorite bear food this time of year. When nothing happened in a few moments, I threw another stone at the far edge of the boulders. The clatter should have awakened the dead above the wind's sibilation, but still nothing came. Moving more rapidly among the boulders, my nervous scan took in the scene and there was no bear—but what a sight lay at my feet!

It was a stunning, breathtaking bit of mayhem that looked like some form of ursine abstract art. The grass had been torn and clawed out in countless clods. Their rich, dark brown undersoil showing ivory tips of hairy roots looked like a wig factory blown over by a cyclone. Holes and gashes in the soil showed where the bear had been rooting. It was a profusion of light-green clumps of a variety of baby skunk cabbage with their pale, creamy-yellow tips broken or chewed off. He was out of hibernation and obviously he was going to devour anything edible on the mountain range.

The entire area had been plowed or torn into streaks of dark brown against the yellows and greens of the Alaska Spring verdure. What made the whole scene so eerie was a jagged hole formed briefly in the black clouds, letting in stray sunlight that etched everything with a misty luminescence. It was a psychedelic masterpiece few modern artists, stoned or otherwise, could capture. The green strip of hedgerow outlining the ridge swung down to my left, and my eyes followed it to a gaping hole torn through the leaves. I walked to it for a closer look. As I had guessed, it was the opening of a tunnel through which the bear had made his hurried exit.

It was baffling. Tossing a stone over the edge of terrain I had just climbed, brought back no sound, the winds blowing it out to sea. Good. The bear couldn't have heard it, either. Crouching about 3 feet from the ground on the probable level of the bear's optical system and looking out, revealed nothing but the dark ocean. Good. The bear couldn't have seen me either, unless he had walked right to the edge and looked down. That was highly unlikely, so why, and where, had he moved? It became more and more certain, he could not have been alarmed by me since my climb began up that towering wall. Therefore, he had to be around here, somewhere.

I needed to review the situation, and with enough fatigue to justify it, I sat, propped up against a boulder in spite of fleeting time. I had not taken a bulky, bothersome canteen and, of course, I badly needed a long drink of water. I would look for a pool or stream, later. A few wet sops of squeezed-out moss only aggravated my thirst. The vista before me captivated my awareness. The seas in the channel were etched with white zig zags across the surface of the somber blue-black, wind-ravaged water.

A feeling of gratefulness surged through me knowing that, by this time, Tom and the women were safe back at port. Overhead, the skies were a pitch-black, unbroken expanse, clear to the mountain range across the channel. There, the black sky was shattered with purplish-gray streaks, raggedly smeared across the heavens edging the mountain peaks with a deep, blue tint. I was instantly reminded of El Greco's Storm Over Toledo. If that genius were here now, sitting beside me, how would he capture the feeling of the utterly awesome in this expanse of unfolding fury, power, and might?

Thinking of all the philosophizing about art that filled the books I'd read, my mind wandered back to one of my favorite ideas. There was an enormous connection between art and hunting. In fact, for centuries, hunting was known as the art of *venery*, or the *venatic* art. It was here that some new ideas were born, which 10 years later became one of the most crucial aspects to my philosophy of hunting.

The stray sunlight over the green plateau disappeared, and the fantasia around me changed back to its former gloom. Sitting still for so long, wind chilled to the bone, I noticed my line of ascent to the present point had been nearly a straight line. If I continued that line straight upward, the bear's tunnel through the brush would be to my left facing the ocean. The wind was still rolling straight down, and maybe that bear would not get a whiff of me yet if I climbed up that imaginary line. But whiff or no whiff, there was no alternative. I had to do something. If I climbed higher, I might see him lower down.

Another 50 feet up brought me to the hedgerow of green, sloping gently to the tunnel, and then plunging sharply down the escarpment's brow. At that point, the hedgerow formed a cantilevered awning that shot out into space. I was willing to bet that if there were a bear in there, I'd never know it. The hedgerow above me was now too close to take carelessly. If that bear circled me from above and then emerged through that underbrush, it would be he turning the scales of stunning surprise. There was no substitute for alertness.

I still refused to believe he had left the area. There was nothing to do but sit and wait him out. He must return. I sat facing the ocean to watch the amphitheater below. At regular intervals, I turned my head to glance quickly behind me to make sure there was no funny business going on. It was on one of those turns that I saw it. A patch of black fur slipped past a leafy opening, flashed again in a blurry streak further on, and then disappeared. My heart almost burst. My giant bear was back!

In an instant I was on my feet, the shell bolted in, and the sights to my eye. He was not in view due to the steepness of the slope, but in the hedgerow high above me, at one o'clock headed due west, the brush quivered spasmodically. Suddenly, the foliage began to move in an abrupt turn and started to unzip in a wavy line toward me.

I stood fascinated. The movement looked like a Hindu fakir's giant, slithering cobra in rhythm to the master's flute. That wavy line instinctively let me sense that it was not a straight, determined charge, but a rush in my general direction to find out what was going on in his rumpus room. Still, I had doubts. With the speed of an express train hurtling through all that underbrush surrounding him, why was he not going at the rest of the world? Why mine? When he broke into my clearing, would he shake my hand in a warm welcome? The thoughts had raced through my mind like lightning, until something inside said, "Never mind his intentions. Shoot now or pay later, even if you can't see him." I was totally positive I couldn't miss.

Aiming at the leading edge of movement in the foliage and dropping my sights a bit, I squeezed at an apparition of a thing unseen. Every hunter has experienced it in archetypal moments of a supreme hunt. I knew with absolute certainty that a millisecond before I squeezed the trigger and heard the solid thwack of the bullet, my bear was dead. I had hit him fair. He rolled down the slope, still unseen, and then the brush stopped him. Finally, it set up its telltale jerky spasms in the midst of the surrounding foliage swaying too rhythmically to the winds.

I leaped forward, instantly, a man possessed, all exhaustion gone, grabbing branches and pulling myself up the 10 or 20 feet to where he was, my heart exploding with delirium. I was in the throes of ecstasy, of truly being outside my self, and where outside, except in the firmament reveling with the gods! I had won against all odds. My agonies up that trail had been justified. By any standards it had been a classic, supreme stalk. It had been a superb contest against the elements. It had been perfect strategy, outwitting him all the way. It had been a perfect, impossible shot. It was an ultimate—my ultimate—my perfection! I wanted to soar off that mountain, defying the gods who were churning the world around me into a primordial struggle of elements, of which I was now a part. It was apotheosis, pure and simple. All of us secretly aspire to the beingness I had just created, godlike, at least once in our wretched lives. Only the means differ. Those who deny it either lie or have lost their souls.

I was still in the throes of rapture when I thrust through the brush and, suddenly, there he was laying at my feet. I stood above him looking at his crumpled form. I was thunderstruck, dumbfounded! My mind reeled, not believing the evidence to my senses. It was a bear all right, but hardly the behemoth I had dreamed about, seen from the boat, and agonized up that trail for. It couldn't be. I looked down at an average, 5-foot bear. My explosive joy spluttered and then fizzled out. The reality finally sank in. Somehow, this was a different bear. All that toil, hazard, emotional turbulence, and spiritual ecstasy—for this? This miserable, pitiful ball of fur? Slowly, I began to feel so very, very foolish, then sad, then numb.

Then guilt set in. Hemingway's thoughts crossed my mind. He had said that the matador in the arena does not take the life of the magnificent bull. He merely gives it death, godlike, as some kind of divine gift. It was like the hunter and his prey. But that was the musing of a giant, literary genius-Janus who pursued the life-style of the very decadent nobility he denounced in his politics with typical liberal cunning. Did he see himself as the matador when he hunted in Africa dispensing his gifts? If this is what I had done, could I now give back as a gift the un-death of this poor scrawny animal whose life I had taken in honest error, on which I had mistakenly gifted death? That would be godlike, indeed.

My throat tightened with sadness that turned into anger and resentment against a treacherous destiny that had made a shambles of my very best efforts and a mockery of my fondest dreams. It had been a perfect hunt for an imperfect trophy.

Do gods delight in making such wretched fools of us in our most exalted moments? Is exultation reserved only for them, and do we mortals pay the price when we encroach on their prerogatives? Did they know what it had taken out of me to stalk the trail for—this? Did they care? If only the quality of the prize had justified the quality of the hunt! Well, that's what destiny had decreed, and always it marred perfection within the hand's grasp— or as they say in the old country, "Just when I put the crust of dry bread to my mouth, something snatches it from my lips." I felt like an ersatz version of some Greek tragic hero punished by the gods for hubris. Well, I had felt godlike, hadn't I?

I knelt and opened his mouth. His teeth were black, full of caries, and worn down to the gum line. He was an old, wretched thing, this "monstrous trophy" of mine. He would have been lucky to survive another winter. I dragged, rolled, and pushed his carcass to the edge of the plateau to get him away from the amphitheater. I had decided to sleep there. There was no need to have his remains tempt some denizen into the area to disrupt my sleep—unless it was my monster for whom I would roll out the welcome mat. If I woke up in time, of course. Actually, this was as good a place to stay overnight as any.

Like a shot, something straightened me up with total surprise. No, it was not imagination. I heard the sound of a boat's horn from below. Three faint, but distinct toots equally spaced. Then I heard the same thing again. That meant only one thing. The universally recognized signal of SOS. My people were long gone. No one else knew I was up here. Someone was in heap big trouble down there. I went to the edge of the tower, put the rifle scope to my eye, turned it to high magnification and scanned. "Great Scot!", as they used to say in the old comic strips. It was Tom and the women in the boat! I had looked at that beach a few times, had seen nothing, and was dead sure they had gone to port. Where had they been? Was this some kind of joke?

What in blazes were they doing here? Were they crazy? The sky was black over the channel—and so was the water. The waves were pounding furiously against the boulders, and the beach seemed much narrower. The tide was coming in, and the boat seemed to have grand mal seizures among the rocks, twitching out of control. Obviously, with that SOS signal, there was something radically wrong with the boat. It had to be engine trouble, or they wouldn't be that close to the rocks. Maybe that's why they never left, and I had somehow missed seeing them. For whatever reason, they were telling me to make a mad dash down that slope.

If they wanted me down there sooner than yesterday, then it

rattled me. It would require a murderous pace to get down there in time. Did they think the way down that mountain was a roller-coaster ride? On the other hand, they were risking their lives in that maelstrom because of me. There was no other conscionable choice. I had to leave, and quickly.

What was really happening down there, they later told me. It so boggled my mind that I was glad to submit to electroshock therapy, and still am, whenever I think of it. Tom and the girls had decided it would be a fun thing, live entertainment, to watch real theater. They would look through binoculars as long as the storm permitted, and look they did—at every bloody move I made. All this was, of course, contrary to our agreement, or at least my understanding, that they would return to port as soon as they let me off. But no, they had changed their minds and opted for the theater, despite their improper dress for the evening performance. Tom thought, if things got too bad on the boat, they could make a mad dash to safety before the curtain came down on the final act.

They saw my giant bear about 50 feet below me and only a couple hundred feet to my left, well hidden to my view by the cantilevered lush foliage of the bushes. He was romping, swaggering, letting off sheer male bear steam. Who knows why? Then, he headed back to his dining salon in the amphitheater, where he would have been in full view directly below the plateau where I was sitting. He was almost there when I shot my bear in error. The big monster wheeled and fled in a blaze of speed. Had he been there 2 minutes earlier, or had the little guy I shot been there 2 minutes later, I would have had my real trophy!

There was more. At my single shot, which reverberated down the mountain side, the theater spectators saw still another bear dash off, directly above me, behind the bush curtains! Naturally, they thought my shot was at him and, therefore, a clean miss. Then, to their surprise they saw me dragging my bear to the edge of the tower. I had been virtually surrounded by three bears, and neither they nor I knew how close we were to the other's presence. If that little fellow had not rushed toward me and forced my shot, this story would have had a different conclusion.

The three toots from the boat were nothing more than a signal of congratulations, a nautical applause piped up in the wrong cadence. They were too excited by the drama to pay close heed to the other drama. The wild waters tossed the boat hard enough among the rocks to break the shear pin in the propeller. That is why the boat was in a fit of epilepsy in those roiling waters among the rocks when I saw it through my scope. What a tragicomedy was to follow from my misunderstanding of that faulty signal tooted up the mountain side!

Having decided I must get down the mountain as soon as possible in answer to their SOS, I now looked at the bear as an albatross around my neck. He would certainly slow me down when every minute counted. He really wasn't a trophy to begin with and I really didn't want him. But there was the hunting ethic and my code was the code going into operation the moment I squeezed the trigger. I had committed myself to the consequences of whatever followed the shot, at any cost. But surely every rule was tested by its exceptions. Surely, this time was an exception. Surely there was clearcut justification below, and they wanted or needed me.

By leaving that carcass, I could better tend to my needs and theirs. Surely, honor would permit this one deviation from my moral code—the hunter's code of which I was so proud an adherent. I could save 5, maybe 10, minutes. The more I justified my reasoning, the less I believed it, and in the end, I could not abandon my bear. Destiny would have to save us all 5 or 10 minutes past her schedule, because I had faith in Tom to wrestle her to a draw. Moving the bear's hulk to the edge of the tower, I shoved. He plummeted out of sight, and I was not going to lean over that treacherous drop to see how he landed. When I reached his position at the foot of that tower would be time enough to figure out my next move.

The scattered drops of rain had now become a drizzle, making every step slippery and treacherous. Naturally, going down that tower was out of the question. That left the abominable alders, and no matter my rebellion, there was no choice. The wet, rain-drenched leafy branches could hardly wait to enfold me in their clammy arms. The descent was merely dropping straight down through notches, crotches, and blotches of branches, trunks, and foliage.

My foot got caught in a slippery wedge of tangled roots and short-lurched me. The sharp pain told me the swelling in my ankle would soon follow. I finally got out of the wedges and pinions of the torture chamber and emerged on the plateau at the base of the rock tower.

I couldn't control my curiosity and turned to look at the wall of towering rock. It confirmed my suspicion. I had been insane to climb it, but didn't know it, until after I got my "monster" bear. Now it sat there, like it had for a million years, patiently waiting to silently mock me for the terror it had stirred in my soul. I shook my clenched fist at it and yelled, "I still whipped you, didn't I." I'm not sure, but I think it was afraid, now that I was safe on the ground.

Then, I turned to my bear, rolled into a pitiful ball of fur looking even smaller than he did up top. He knew perfectly well I would heed his audacious demand for a place of honor, he did not deserve, among the other trophies who, I hoped, would not throw him out for gatecrashing. I'm positive he knew he had me.

"You little bastard," I said, "you don't deserve it, but you're coming with me." I dragged him the few feet from his platform to the tip of the chute where the snow was rotten. I shoved. He rolled a little over the slush, picked up momentum over some hard-packed stuff and glissaded out of sight on his way to the beach, 800 feet down.

My moment of truth had arrived. I was on the last leg of my journey, and how I loathed those alders. They were on a steeper slope than the previous ones, very much longer till my next stop, and drenched with rain by this time. I plunged into the hateful, soaking green mass. My ankle didn't help matters any. I had not gone down a hundred feet, when I thought I would never make it by nightfall at this rate. I had to move faster, but neither ankle nor alders would let me. That's when my mind jumped onto a bold— or insane—idea, depending on how one views it.

There was one quick, easy, and painless way to get down to the beach. It was the avalanche chute itself, plunging right down alongside of me. Cutting to the side through the palisade of alders between us, I got to the edge of snow and ice.

No fooling. The idea was not as crazy as it might first appear. Countless times when ptarmigan hunting in winter on mountain slopes, I had tobogganed down by squatting on my snowshoes and letting gravity do the work. It was not only quick, it was lots of real fun and even exhilarating. There was always some scattered brush sticking up through the snow and grabbing them going past, braked the speed when it got too fast. I had done that routinely many times. The chute, full of snow and ice, was not much longer than those rides, although, admittedly, it was a lot steeper, and I was not on snowshoes. If it could be done now, it should solve my problems. To calculate that risk, however, required the proper perspective.

The proper perspective required getting on that ice, squatting on it to gauge the slope and the presence of bushes, to make that decision. This called for cautious judgement, not reckless derring-do. Given the circumstances, it didn't seem as wild then, as it might appear, now.

There was, of course, one thing wrong with my plan. My obsession with the idea, the pressure of time, and my throbbing ankle simply helped me to forget one critical fact—the 30-foot drop from the funneled out bottom of the chute to the sharp, jagged boulders on the beach. Had I remembered that, I would have gone through the hell of 10 alder thickets. I forgot all about it, however, and as Robbie Burns, the Scot, said, "The best laid plans of mice and men gang aft agly."

I moved sideways, gingerly, not more than four or five steps, and squatted on the icy patch. One look told me I couldn't do it. The white expanse before me suddenly dipped further on and continued downward at a much steeper decline than where I was crouching. I could not see the beach from my position. That is what told me there was no future down there.

It was that which led me to change my mind. Well, I calculated the risk. I had no choice but to hammer myself through the alders and hoped the crew would be all right in the boat until I got down the slow way. As I straightened up cautiously, it occurred to me it was going to be much more difficult getting off that ice than it had been getting on it. Getting on it had let me lead with my left foot. Getting off it led with my right foot. What's one foot, more or less, eh? My sprained ankle gave just a bit when my weight came down on the sideways motion, just enough to jerk out from under me, and that shot out the other foot. I did a running long jump scissors kick prone in midair and landed hard in a sitting-up position. Since gravity waits for no man, I started to move almost immediately in a slow motion slide.

I shall never forget those hip boots, with their hard rubber heels glazing over the surface. No matter how I tried to dig or jam them into the ice or snow, they just kept sliding. It felt familiar. My left hand was still clutching my rifle, so my right-hand fingers began to claw and scratch frantically into the surface. It was too glazed, so that didn't work either. Faster and faster grew my acceleration. I recalled wondering earlier if my boat people thought I would get down to them quickly on a roller coaster ride. What prescient thoughts, even if they didn't have them, and I didn't mean it that way! That's precisely what I was doing, now only faster than I could ever want. Ice and snow did to me what no roller coaster ever built could do.

Something inside barked a command to stay calm—there had to be a bush or something, anything, sticking out of that white, crusted surface that my rifle might snag or give my hand a grab-full. There was. In spite of the zooming speed, a heightened sense of perception made every detail visible in a bush, just ahead of me, stand out starkly. It was on my right-hand side, so I leaned over from my sitting position and grabbed the center, heavier switches. In such moments, human reflexes can do wonderful things, but this was not good enough. The handful of pencil-thin, denuded stems snapped or tore through my grasp, so fast was I moving, not slowing me down one bit. What it did was to make things worse. It yanked me back as I slid past and flattened me out prone on my back. I don't believe I straightened out from that moment on. My raincoat was now in full contact with the surface, and it acted like more space-age lubrication. It produced what was one of the eeriest sensations I've ever known.

The sky overhead was evenly black. There were no clouds or shades of color against which my brain could see motion, as I slid past in my prone position, with my eyes staring up, and I couldn't bend upright. Hence, it did not feel like my body zooming down, but the glazed snow and ice rushing up beneath me with a rasping, noisy friction against my rain coat! I could swear to it, but I won't, that I lay absolutely immovable while the mountain moved with dazzling speed during those few incredible moments. Honorable Mohammed, I can tell you there are times when you do not have to go to the mountain. The mountain will come to you.

Science says nerve impulses travel at the rate of 300 feet per second. But science cannot tell why we experience timelessness and eternity in spite of neural speed. During one of those eternal moments, a very recent memory trace broke into my mind from nowhere—the 30-foot drop from the embankment to the rock-strewn beach I'd forgotten all about. If Robert Browning had not said it, somewhere, I could have told him, yes, there are experiences where, in a single moment, we have insight into eternity, and this was one of those moments in my life.

No, my whole life did not flash before my eyes. What did flash, was a feeling of total, absolute, immutable, irreversible certainty that I would not get killed when I smashed into those rocks. I would survive. Rushing toward death at lightning speed, knowing that I would not die was not the only point, however. I could have felt that from sheer, desperate wish fulfillment. The important point was that I was certain, not only in feeling this, but in knowing that what I felt was a truth that would reveal itself in a moment. It left me with the calmest moment of tranquility and peacefulness I have ever known. To say this was unreal is an understatement. These images flashed by in milliseconds, undoubtedly. That's all I remember. The rest was awesome velocity. I know what eternity feels like between both ends of an 800-foot slope, steeply declined, in what could not have been more than a dozen or so seconds. And yet, it seems like it was over even before it began.

That zooming glissade suddenly ceased its tearing, sliding, frictional sensation on my back, and then, for a split second, I knew I was airborne. I know that reflexively my legs stiffened to take the impact, expecting the sheering, snapping crack from broken bones—something I had experienced during boyhood. All I can recall is landing (on my knees, as it turned out). I felt a thumping impact that bounced me into the air, and I heard a loud "ugh!" explode from my lungs. I must have bounced 3 or 4 feet, judging from the retinal images that tail-spun about me as the earth, ocean, mountains, and sky suddenly whirled like a giant pinwheel. I know I blacked out before I returned to the ground.

They had watched all this from the boat, horror stricken, and guessed that I was unconscious for about a half minute. When my blacked-out brain regained its awareness, the first thing that registered was the mud embankment several yards in front of me. I had gotten turned around, somehow, on returning to earth after I bounced. Tiny, bright-blue points of light were flashing on and off in my head, stroboscopically, making bizarre trick-photography of the embankment.

Reflexively, I tried to stagger up, pushing down with both hands for leverage. It felt like the boxing I'd done as a kid when I had to pick myself off the deck a couple of times when it wasn't standing still. Even through blurred senses, there was no doubt that I felt something soft, damp, and furry, under my hands. It was my bear. I had landed smack in the middle of my bear!

That's what had bounced me upward into the air. Getting to my feet unsteadily, my focus clearing, I could easily see his carcass firmly wedged between two jagged boulders. My glorious, gorgeous, adorable, incomparable little bear! He had saved my life from those twin rock cleavers with my number on them. No one could have escaped destruction smashing into those boulders with my speed and force. The bear I called a bastard and rejected as a trophy, gave me the greatest trophy I own after he was dead—my life.

The world began to take shape, bringing the boat into perspective. It was still having spasms in the shallow water, too close to the beach, rolling among the rocks. The engine was sitting in the boat with it's broken shear pin, and Tom was fighting the smaller auxiliary trying to get it aligned onto the stern plate. The rain was now fully upon us, the breakers had reached full omnipotent size, hurling their fury into creamy-white crests, as they spent themselves against the boulders, only to revive in a moment for the next onslaught. It was surprising the craft had not yet been smashed. Obviously, luck would run out soon unless Tom got that engine started. My heart went out to him. He was simply magnificent in the way he handled things, without losing his cool. How he eventually got us out of there, I will never know, but it was a tribute to his ability and character. His preoccupation with the auxiliary left me to my own devices.

The bear took some doing to tug and pry him loose from between those boulders, where he was so tightly wedged. The blue stars of light pinged on and off in my head again, as I lifted his limp form. He must have weighed around 160 pounds or so, emaciated from his hibernation. I thought he weighed that much, because I know I cannot lift more than that much above my waist, which is how high he was when I staggered into the sea.

My attempt to get him over the gunnel was the problem. First, the boat was bobbing crazily, and second, the gunnel was at my shoulder level even when it rolled down to its low point. The trick was to get that carcass up on that gunnel immediately, before the boat rolled up higher with the next rise, way above my reach. All I could get was the head and shoulders of the bear onto the gunnel, and the rest of his weight would come sagging down with the dip of the boat, and I needed more hands to grab him any which way.

A few waves, of course, swept over my head and shoved me around. I quickly tired of doing the tarantella on the ocean floor and drinking salt water at the same time. I made the heavy heave upward three or four times, and my steam was running out. Now the bear was too heavy for me, the boat too nervous, and the waves too merciless. Was I going to lose this bear after all that had happened? Man, but how I wanted this adorable mutt!

Two or three more attempts, and all my strength was drained. That bloody boat would not stay still for a moment. I tried one final heave and, unexpectedly, Tom's wife came through for me. Leaning over from her seat, so as not to stand and risk going overboard, she merely grabbed the bear at its point of balance on the gunnel, and hung on tightly for just a moment. It may not have been much, but it made all the difference in the world. She was magnificent, and saved the day for me. She gave me just enough time to duck under the rest of that beast, come up spluttering for air with a fresh purchase. Now that I had both hands free, and with a last do-or-die heave, I flipped the rest of the carcass into the boat.

Clambering onto the prow, I grabbed the emergency oar and began jabbing at the rocks to push the craft away from being smithereened. Finally, Tom had the engine ready to go. He yanked the lanyard a few times, revved up the engine, and roared out like a shot to escape that cemetery of boulders and the pulverizing force of the waves. I'll never know how the boat had survived the pounding it took. Tom weaved in and around the boulders and the waves until he reached open water, then curved sharply into the sea.

Meanwhile, I had been dancing again—this time an Irish jig—on that slippery covered prow trying to maintain my balance until the right moment so I could get into the boat. When Tom took that sharp curve into the waves, the motion knocked me off my feet, threw me flat onto the prow, and by some miracle I grabbed the brass cleat before I got pitched overboard. My lower legs trailed through the water for a few moments, until I somehow managed to grab the other cleat and pull all of myself onto the prow, spread eagle, and hold on for dear life.

Tom was busy getting the boat underway. He was unaware of my plight. His wife kept screaming for him to stop, and when he turned around to see me, I yelled back at him to keep going and get us out of this. His small auxiliary engine was barely able to cut the higher seas, and I knew what needed doing without getting in the way. When the craft finally straightened out to even keel so that it's pitching was less violent, I crouched up and before losing my balance again, I took a hasty dive, head first, over the glass windshield and landed amidships—but not before shattering the windshield as my feet flew over it on the way in. For the first time in a long while, I knew I was safe at last.

A few minutes later, Tom found protection behind a natural break water in a cove, changed the shear pin in the big engine, and we got it mounted on the stern plate. I was standing in the shallow water, the boat was fairly still, for a change, and level solid footing beneath gave me a surge of seasickness! I shoved my head into the brine, vomited, recovered instantly, and we were off again, this time with enough engine power to outrun the storm. The rain was nearly horizontal to our backs with the wind driving it like jagged bits of metal. The whitecaps tore free from the roiling waters, drenching us as the prow split its way through. Oh, what a wild, glorious, tempestuous ride it was, and how deliciously great to be alive!

I shall never forget that ride. It was another archetypal experience. A tempest of spirit was building inside me, complementing the one all around us. I was miraculously alive and utterly intoxicated with the life I'd nearly lost, now in the midst of the elements gone wild. My hunting had been perfect. The stalk worthy of the name, an uncanny and perfect shot, full challenge to my abilities, and unstinting commitment to the bottom line. Enough adventure to last a lifetime, a debt discharged, and a promise kept to my bear at Manley. My little bear, the wrong one at that, may not have been a trophy by the books, but he was the greatest prize I've ever won. He became the turning point for the rest of my life. How sweet life was, how great to have beaten the odds—all those pent-up emotions that had piled one atop the other so quickly had to go somewhere.

Standing up in the stern, head bared to the winds and stinging rain, I heard myself bellowing a lusty sea chanty I'd learned as a kid:

> "Come on all ye young fellows who follow the sea,
> With a yo-ho we'll blow the man down,
> Who shipped for good seamen on board the Black Ball,
> Give us sometime . . ."

I was reveling with the gods. The crew looked at me as though I was beside myself, and they were entirely correct.

As I drove home at high speed over an early morning deserted highway, I nearly ran over another enormous bear sitting right in the middle of the road! What an anticlimax, but this is another story already told. As I've said before, no hunt is ever really finished.

Little Blackie
Reflections

Sometimes, when we look at another person's life, we see it as a congeries of unrelated, irrelevant events all thrown together in any old way without making sense to either the observer or the person observed. It is as though a large picture has been torn into many tiny pieces and jumbled together in a senseless heap. Yet, we find a single pattern, a common denominator, or a major theme relating all those pieces together, giving us a fascinating tapestry. It needed courage to search for the right pieces, luck to find them, and patience to put it together.

If what follows is like that jumble of pieces and seem irrelevant or unrelated to my hunting experiences, I invite the reader to read with fingers crossed while I put those pieces together. Then, he can see how Little Blackie wove the tapestry of my life in the most unexpected way. He became the major crossroad connecting two junctions: one I had taken 25 years earlier, and one in which I was floundering when Little Blackie came into my life he had given, at the cost of his own.

What follows is deeply personal. It has taken its toll on me for a very long time, and, hopefully, the reader will be patient with my spiritual travails, but without this, the real meaning of my hunting career loses the point.

For me, my hunting trophies have been symbols in search of some ultimate. Little Blackie revealed the ultimate of all ultimates—God. I warn the reader, if such things turn him off, then perhaps he should stop now. Here, however, my story simply proves the observation, now trite, that truth is stranger than fiction. A good hunt never ends, I have said, making all sorts of connections with the future; and now I see that a good hunt often has its beginning long before the hunter takes to the trail.

In wartime, soldiers rarely know where they are, with battle-perimeters changing all the time. What they know is, they are in some foreign country. Strange sounding names of cities, towns, and villages are forgotten, if they were ever learned. Yesterday's battle lines become tomorrow's secured territories. After North Africa and Italy it was just "somewhere in France" for me before the final push into Germany. The thing happened not far from one of those battlefronts of World War II.

My longtime frustration was nearing its limits. I had refused Officer Candidate School, for which I qualified early in my basic training, because I volunteered for the infantry to get overseas and see action in Europe right away. I was mistakenly worried that the war might be over too soon! War is about fighting, isn't it? And where does one do that better than in the infantry? But they stopped me cold. I was over qualified, they said. It was an insult. How could anyone be over qualified to fight for his country?

Instead, I qualified for more "important" things like the medical corps, and they needed good men there at this point in the war, and I was a "good man." They lied. It was better to fight in the infantry. Action changed things constantly. The same old things did not drag on monotonously day after day, as in the medics. I was frustrated for most of the war. If I had used my head and lied, I should have asked for the medics. Then, I would have made the infantry. Instead, I got stuck as a surgical technician.

As I said, we were somewhere in France when it happened. My entire medical unit was exhausted with the unusually heavy casualties our guys suffered. Field ambulances were busy piling wounded and dying faster than we could assembly-line them through surgery and ship the survivors back to rear echelons to convalesce. We needed the bed space (actually, cot space) as quickly as we could empty them.

It had been 3, maybe 4 (well, who knows how many) weeks we had been at it, two 12-hour shifts a day, 7 days a week under smelly canvas tents, of unending, broken, blasted, torn, incomplete bodies log-jammed in their own trickles or seepages of blood right at our tent flaps. I, too, had taken everything in stride, stiff upper lip, and that sort of thing (eh, wot?), until that night on the literal graveyard shift.

I reported for duty scrubbed, capped, gowned, masked, and carrying my tray of sterilized surgical instruments to my assigned operating table to assist Major S . . ., who was as sharp a surgeon as the number 19 Bard-Parker scalpel blades we used to slice into human flesh. I enjoyed working with him because he taught me a lot, and he seemed glad to have me.

I was halfway through the narrow aisle, surrounded on either side with operating tables in our long, narrow, wall-tent surgical "ward." The generator had been knocked out again. This time from mechanical failure instead of stray enemy fire. The dim, circular blobs of battery-operated field lights made weird shadows.

Sergeant so-and-so, who knew I spoke French, side tracked me to the far end, where several wounded G.I.s, in varying degrees of unconsciousness, lay inertly on their litters, waiting their turns for an operating table. Thank heaven for sedatives, or their moans of pain would have been soul-shattering. On occasion, as a humanitarian gesture, our guys picked up a civilian or two, wounded in cross fire. The sergeant wanted to know what one of them was now saying.

I had seen and assisted on the surgery of more horrors inflicted on human flesh in a couple years than any three surgeons (with due respect) will see in a lifetime of civilian practice, and had a foolproof attitude of inurement. Nothing surprised me anymore about battlefield wounds and corpses until I reached that French patient. Then, I knew I had never experienced anything like this before. It was a little 7-year-old girl wailing through narcotized pain, "Je soif, Je soif."

"What's she saying?" asked the sarge.

"She's saying she's thirsty," I said.

The sarge asked if I would help him. I had been notified awhile back that my own daughter had been born, whom I'd not yet seen, and maybe that's why I took this child so personally. Besides, we had never had a casualty like this before.

The ol' sarge looked for the admitting tag on the litter (which would tell us what the wounds were) and could not find it in the dim light. Neither could I, but I could make out a blotch of blood seeping through the child's blanket halfway down. I drew the blanket back to ascertain that there were no abdominal wounds to prevent her drink of water.

Then, I saw it. Her legs were blown off at the knees by a land mine. There were two stumps wrapped hastily in blood-soaked bandages. She had been given only the usual, minimal field treatment to save her life, and a probable shot of morphine was now wearing off. I stood stunned for a moment.

Often, when my sainted mother, who was a believer, would invoke God's protection, my sainted father, who was not a believer, but loved mamma beyond all spiritual measure, would gently chide her with bitter memories. "Wife, if your Papa God was up there, and his eyes were open and he saw what the Turks did to us, how could he let it happen"?

In my stunned moments of silence standing there, now, trying to comprehend what I was seeing and hearing, I kept asking myself the eternal "Why?" No answers came, and then my father's old, familiar question broke through the recesses of my mind and soul. "God, if you are really up there and your eyes saw this, how could you let it happen"?

These soldiers, perhaps. But this innocent child? I knew she would never walk, run, or play again. "Why?" I inwardly raged, but again, the answer of silence and the feel of emptiness in my soul. Only the plaintive cry, "Je soif, Je soif," over and over again. I, who believed there was no God, now stood demanding an answer from that Absence. Nothing came.

There is no need to contrive a good front on the inexcusable misconduct of a 19-year-old dumb, confused, and distraught youth unable to control his emotions when serving his nation in another of democracy's endless wars. Maybe the unrelenting pressure of weeks of this nightmare had caught up with me, but there is no excusing it.

Suddenly, I didn't care about the consequences. I just

exploded into a bellowed stream of profanity and blasphemy against God. I didn't know who or what had really started this war, so who else could I blame? I knew that in my anger, I could have destroyed anyone and anything that got in my way. The sterilized instrument tray I had laid down got in my way. I picked it up, hurled it across the tent, and stalked out, oblivious to the dim battery lights, the cut and dying wounded, and the entire surgical crew, who stood in stunned surprise at my outrageous spectacle.

I made off to my tent to dig out the hoarded bottle of Calvados, the worst alcoholic beverage ever made in wartime France, now buried in my duffel bag. I took out my rage, against God, on myself, since I was reachable. They later told me I had stumbled to the pyramidal tent serving as a chapel and railed against the Almighty in the dark for a long time, until I passed out with my bottle nicely reduced in content. My buddies carried me to my cot. When I awoke the next day, with the worst hangover I've ever known, I dimly sensed that I was in for a court-martial and the stockade for deserting my post in the line of duty and engaging in "conduct unbecoming an American soldier."

It was a narrow squeak, but my Major had gone to bat for me and got me off the hook when the C.O. had called for my hide. When I found out about it, I went to thank Major S . . ., feeling like a sheepish idiot for what I'd done, and I told him so.

He just smiled and said, "Hey, kid (he always greeted me with "Hey-kid"), don't worry about it. There isn't a man here in this hell-hole, who hasn't blown his stack at least once. But if you do it again, I may not be able to get you off."

I was indelicate enough to ask him why he had done it in the first place, since the risk to him was obvious.

"You're one of the good men on my shift, and I don't want to lose you. You know what I mean, kid"?

I suddenly recognized this man as a true friend, a true officer and gentleman who had truly saved me from serious consequences.

"And do me a favor, will you, kid? Change the brand of booze you were drinking. Now, is there anything else?" he asked, letting me know the interview was over.

"Yes, sir," I said, "do you know about the girl? How is she? I mean, will she make it."

"Yeah, I think so," he said. "They shipped her out to a civilian hospital. I heard her prognosis looked good."

"Thank you, sir," I said, saluted one of the finest officers I knew in the 5th and 7th Armies, and wheeled out.

We never found out why, but shortly before the war ended, he was shipped out of the outfit. Rumors had it he wouldn't knuckle under to some of his superiors he didn't think much of. I can't prove it, but if some of us guys, who had often gotten into trouble over minor infringements of asinine rules, still got the Good Conduct Medal with our other citations, decorations and campaign ribbons, I guessed that Major S . . . could have set us up. Others guessed the same way.

───────── •◆━◆•━◆•─────────

No man survives a war and leaves it the same way he went in. The whole world had changed, and that included me. I had seen the other side of human nature in war and the heights of insanity it could reach.

We veterans flooded the universities to resume interrupted educations, or because we didn't know what else to do except "find ourselves" in the big hole of discontinuity in our lives left by the war. I entered college, hoping to learn, among other things, the causes for that demonic insanity that the world's political leaders on our side called, "the war to stop Hitler," while we gave Stalin the green-light. I never did find out until long after I left school.

However, I got an impressive start with a quotation pinned over my major professor's desk in experimental psychology. It was from the great Russian scientist, Ivan Pavlov, who put psychology on a solid scientific footing until Freud came along. It said, "I shall follow truth wherever science leads me." Freshmen (or fresh women or fresh persons) are easily impressed with such heroic statements. I was too. I adopted that vow for my own, and adhered to it through the years. Incidentally, I discovered later that the quotation was in Latin usage long before Pavlov.

It was in the advanced courses that we experimented with many aspects of the paranormal, like precognition, clairvoyance, telepathy, and the like. They were fascinating experiments, providing just enough answers to make one believe there might be something to it, but not conclusive enough to warrant sticking one's neck out. In graduate school, I stunned one of my professors with my knowledge of a rare and esoteric work on the extrasensory I had read. He thought no one else could know about the work. That got me in his good graces, and he asked me to help in a well-advanced experiment. After a year of hard work, and at the critical moment, we got the same results—intriguing promises with nothing conclusive.

Either no such phenomena existed, contrary to what many books claimed, or Western scientific methods were ill-equipped to deal with it. My prejudices against spiritual or supernatural notions helped me to opt for the first alternative. If any problem in the natural or physical universe is not amenable to scientific method based on mathematical analysis of observed and verified data, then authentic science and scientists leave it alone. What science can study is limited to its methods.

This leaves a vast array of human concerns which science rightly leaves in the care of others like, priests, poets, and philosophers who have all but sold out their perfectly valid and precious disciplines. They have "scientized," if I may, everything from art to zoolatry, but it cannot be done with scientific validity. It results in the new religious faith of *scientism* and promises humanity a new salvation based on pseudo-scientific nonsense. To believe it, requires greater fanaticism than the religious faiths which scientism denounces. I sensed all this coming, but really didn't care. I was overloaded with courses to finish a 4-year undergraduate program in 3 years, partially to make up for the years the war took out of my life.

The liberal arts attracted me and, indeed, liberated me, artfully. I took a second major, Sociology. It was truly an intellectually intriguing discipline, until the Marxists took it over for "social engineering" during the Viet Nam "protest." One way or another, most of my professors in my classes got the message across: God, religion, and metaphysics were a waste of time only for superstitious dullards; liberal humanism was the hope for the salvation of the world; Marx and Freud reigned supreme. It was the one kind of knowledge, actually secular religion, they all accepted. All this was exactly what I wanted to hear. It justified my battlefield denunciation of the supernatural power of which I never found a trace in my "paranormal" experiments. It also let me enjoy the great liberal conceit, that we liberals were more intelligent than others, though the only definition for intelligence was "what intelligence tests measured," and they measured "something." The test results were denounced by "others" as culture-bound, invalid, and prejudiced. But we boasted of the measured "something" that we couldn't define, anyway, though we couldn't distinguish between it and wisdom, which was more important but in much shorter supply. It did not occur to me that *Pan troglodytes*, the chimpanzee, was also "more intelligent than others' without the benefit of tests and measurements.

We were naive enough, at least I was, not to see what was really happening in higher education. Our intellectuals, most of whom had not seen a real war, were fighting a secret war at home against the country we had fought for, and died for, on foreign battlefields. It had been going on for some time, but we were too beguiled to see where it was really headed, and our professors did not un-beguile us. The state-funded universities were chipping away at the foundations of Western culture, civilization, and the Christianity that caused them.

With the war over, liberal arts programs became the recruiting grounds for lost souls, starry-eyed freshmen just out of high school, and disillusioned idealists like myself. We became the atheists, Marxists, Freudians, humanists, political liberals and activists for the professorates of the next generation.

When I entered university teaching, after a 12-year hiatus, (mounting debts, a growing family, and other circumstances interrupted my graduate studies), I stepped into the vomitive magma of the anti-Viet Nam demonstrations. Liberal doctrine, with which I was infatuated a bare decade ago, had become something else. According to one prestigious national poll (the American Association for the Advancement of Science), 97.3% of the professoriate in the social sciences, (especially sociology), humanities, and liberal arts, nationwide, were from liberal to radical left in their personal beliefs.

At first, I chuckled at my associates who wanted a one

world utopia and anathematized greedy capitalists who prevented it. They didn't have the least inkling that the Marxist dream of a new socialist one-world utopia was being supported by the very capitalists and industrialists who were denounced! There was money in it. In the 1964 Pugwash Conference, sponsored by the industrialist Cyrus Eaton, our spokesmen promised Khrushchev a no-win war in Viet Nam. Our "statesmen" straight-jacketed our fighting forces with asinine "rules of engagement" unknown to combat since the caveman wielded his cudgel. Our soldiers were forced into a deadly charade and prevented from winning by deliberate political strategy that had nothing to do with military tactics. The greatest secret counterintelligence the enemy had was our wide-open Department of State under the thumb of the Council on Foreign Relations.

The political, intellectual, and media power-brokers were going to save the world's humanity for another utopia by laying waste the soldiers of their own nation! It was a shameless sacrifice of innocents. Did the enemy betray its soldiers with such pompous perfidy?

The proclamations of the activists, students and faculties, alike, were against the "evils of war" in the name of lofty moral ideals for humanity's sake. But never a word was said about one of the highest moral ideals of all—loyalty to the men we had sent to fight and die. Whether the war was right or wrong was crying over spilt milk (all wars are wrong). The issue was the right or wrong of sacrificing our fighting men as pawns in the game of political power on the home front.

Whether or not the activists knew it (and some knew it very well), the counterculture was a continuation of the class war at home fostered by the campus Marxists for whom our soldiers were expendable. The shameful cry for "unilateral withdrawal" was the cover-up for the no-win war to further yet another step in the triumph of Marxist liberals at home and abroad. We had swallowed the liberal notion that we could be proud of losing the war, but winning it was a matter of shame, and we should embrace a one world order no matter who controlled it. Every two-bit dictator, thereafter, would gladly spit in our eye.

The destabilization of our society began the trend that gave us the degenerate, drug, sex, and crime culture 20 years later, and threatens our very existence. It was just as Jerry Rubin, one of the counterculture "heroes" boasted—they would "bring America to her knees."

My own generation had fought a war in which nearly a half million men were killed. Slightly more than a half million men and women were wounded, maimed, dismembered, and otherwise disabled. One way or another, nearly 16,000,000 Americans had served directly in that war effort. We destroyed the Nazi monstrosity in history's most devastating war. Our victory had preserved and maintained the traditions of a free nation and free people to serve as a polestar for others. That was the legacy we had given to our young generations, and they were doing to it what the battlefield enemy could never do. We had become two Americas, only one of which could survive the future.

The activists were barely 3% of all student populations, seemingly representing the rest. They were not necessarily the highly intelligent idealists as the media lionized them. Too many were simply draft-dodging hippy malcontents looking for any cause to vent their displeasure with a world not to their liking.

The younger faculty spoke of humanitarian ideals, but leveraged campus instability for higher salaries, administrative appointments (where the money and power were), more grants for research of doubtful value, and more travel funds to read monographs at conferences set up in luxurious surroundings, where they denounced filthy capitalist social systems. This gave them a half-dozen, short-term high-class vacations a year. One wag wrote a book encouraging students to become professors. I forgot the book's title but the subtitle was unforgettable—*It Sure Beats the Hell Out of Working for a Living*. It surely did for many of my liberal colleagues.

It was the activist students who really made out, however. They leveraged campus destabilization for fewer and easier course requirements, bigger student loans (most of which were never repaid), removal of all restraints on any kind of overdrive sex, legalization of booze and drugs on campus, and participation in administrative power politics to appoint professors to their liking, and get rid of guys like me. Their idealism ended abruptly, as soon as the war was over, as one-third of the male draft-dodgers walked out with their "educations" unfinished. So much for their higher devotions. Many of those who remained became the future academic officials, whose policies have made a joke of higher learning at the parasitized taxpayers' expense.

I knew from firsthand experience what our soldiers were going through in Viet Nam. They were my age when I went to war. My concern was for them on the battlefield, not political philosophy in the halls of ivy. I kept my professorial cool, until the draft-dodging activists began calling our soldiers "Nazis" and "animals." That's when I blew my top. Those who would call their compatriots such names were capable of doing worse. Those who could rob the fallen battlefield dead of the honor due them were capable of doing anything. A nation that permits this in the name of free expression cannot keep its freedoms for long, nor does it deserve them.

Surrounded on all sides by the enemy, I could attack in any direction. I wrote articles, made speeches, broke up a campus-wide demonstration, had my office ransacked twice, got into physical violence in self-defense, and while there were others who felt as I did, I think it fair to say that, when the chips were down in a public standoff, I stood pretty much alone. My colleagues did exactly what I knew they would. After all, I knew all about the California "F" scale. They branded me as the crypto-Fascist warmonger and right-wing reactionary with views uncharacteristic of mainstream sociologists. I knew all about the mainstream characteristics, too.

I could no longer subscribe to what liberal humanism had become at the hands of liberals who knelt at the altar of self-worship. Humanity was easy to love; it was people they hated. The former was an image dominated by our secret tyrannies. The latter were flesh-and-blood realities who always talked back. I turned against the whole phoney setup of social science, built on liberal left-wing lust for power, and told it like it was. My classes were jam-packed with non-activist students who knew the real world better than the pap we were feeding them. I made more collegial enemies.

Now, I was shorn of the values that had supported me for half of my adult life, and I could not return to them, ever. It left me empty inside. When perception of the external structure of the social world falls apart, the inner, private world of mental reality also falls apart. Its own structure is organized congruously with the perception of that external world. I had to unlearn a great deal of the old to learn very little of the new. That's when I stumbled on a mainstream book that had made a splash in the world of academe, but only a tiny splash, that soon rippled out. It was Professor Harlow Shapley's book. So man was no more important than Pre-Cambrian cockroaches, was he? That's when the images of my war came back to haunt me.

Is that what I had seen and heard—cockroaches? When our military vehicles carried us from one hell-hole to another, I had often seen long lines of tired and hungry women, children, and old men on the shell-torn roads trudging to nowhere from their ruined homes and villages. From descriptions I'd heard in my childhood, this is how my people must have looked when the Turks force marched them 300 miles to the desert of Deir el Zor to die of starvation. The phrase "starving Armenians" had become macabre humor, even to my 10-year old classmates who often teased me with it.

Then there were towns or cities reduced to bombed-out rubble covering the dead, but not covering the stench. There was infamous Dachau, where I went the day after our troops opened up that nightmare, to see with my own eyes what we had heard about. Well, I did see, and how I wished I hadn't. I opened the iron doors of the three ovens in the crematorium, and stood there in silent horror at a new kind of "cockroach" degradation—grisly human bones and ashes still glowing in rosy-red embers. Once they had been innocent human beings who had nothing to do with killing on the battlefield. The heavy-hanging stench forced me outdoors to retch and gasp for untainted air.

I went past a barbed-wire enclosure and, at arms-length, I saw the cadaverous caricatures of what were human beings scarcely able to wave their hands. Their sunken eyes staring right through me. Their grim, gaunt faces barely able to smile, but one of them did, and his eyes glistened with tears of joy in recognition of my uniform. He found the strength to mumble the most beautiful sound I could hear, when he uttered a single word of affirmation—"American." We stared at each other, each wondering if the other was real.

I went out a different way than I entered and chanced on some back road. Was I being damned to some eternal nightmare? As far as the turn in the road, a mile away, there was long line of immense, horse-drawn wagons. Their drivers' faces were covered with bandanas to fight off the stench. The wagons were piled high with stiff, wasted, twisted corpses, looking like wooden marionettes in some Punch and Judy show. Only no one could laugh. These were once human beings who had not made it to the ovens in time.

I thought of my countless G.I. compatriots, whose mutilated forms lay on our operating tables. I saw the dying of many and heard the cries of pain from many more. Some were battle-hardened veterans of the front-lines, calling for their mothers in infantile voices through drugged unconsciousness. They would be decorated for valor and heroism, if only we could save their lives.

They were American soldiers whose sons would fight and die later in the Viet Nam jungles from the same agonies of war, for the same country, the same ideals. Were they all the "animals" and "Nazis" their activist compatriots were calling them a quarter century later, living in a freedom purchased for them at the price these soldiers had paid?

Always, there came the plaintive wail of my little girl crying, "Je soif, Je soif," from the haunting past. By what mental trickery could I believe that the agony and horrors I have seen inflicted on human beings were of questionable importance, since Nature made no distinction between them and cockroaches? But that was the logical conclusion to believing that man was an accidental, chemical by-product of random chance without purpose, value, and design. Why, then, should it not be "natural" to dispose of him in the "survival of the fittest"? Nazism and Communism were only two of the latest tyrannies that did this sort of thing, quite "naturally."

I heard too much of this "Nature is All" business as the intellectuals defined it. But then I heard more "unsophisticated dullards," whom I had always turned off, talk mysteriously about a God who had created nature and man, separately, declaring man was of supreme value on this earth, not because nature or tyrants cared, but because God did—the God I had denounced some 25 years ago when a little girl cried for water. Somewhere along the route, my brain went numb with emotional overload.

I needed to escape all the madness around me to give my

mind a rest and embrace the joy of the wilderness that would calm my turmoil. I would go on a black bear hunt and embrace honest reality. Bears would be coming out of hibernation—in Valdez. I needed a good, solid dose of wilderness excitement to revive a tired and wounded spirit. I didn't know I would meet Little Blackie, and that he would heal my alienation. I didn't know he would answer the questions tearing me apart—but only after he died without saying a word. That was to be my Rubicon.

The euphoria after my Big Bounce on Little Blackie lasted for a while, during which time my flirtation with the supernatural and mystical disappeared. Who needed them? This time the *prima facie* evidence, as lawyers say, was indeed self-evident. The avalanche chute was a V shaped trough down which Little Blackie zoomed. If a head of cabbage, a pygmy elephant, or I fell into his trajectory, we would all land on the same spot. Right? Well, not exactly. Although socially, I was living in euphoria, enjoying my invincibility, a nagging doubt I had would not go away.

Some vague memory traces vibrated faintly, trying to focus on Newton's laws of gravity, motion, inertia, and other things. It was a long time since I first met Sir Isaac's axiomatic $F=MA$, or Force equals Mass times Acceleration. I checked with a couple colleagues in the physics and math departments at the university, who knew better than I about such things, just to make sure.

I posed the problem, hypothetically, of course, about objects making that slide, and they confirmed what I feared. There were no exceptions. The heavier object traveling the longer distance would have greater force at terminal velocity or at that point at which it became airborne. It would land further out than the lighter object traveling the same distance.

My colleagues were totally unbiased in their analysis, which is why I had used the word objects to make this as impersonal, objective, and abstract as possible. Then I loused everything up by revealing the true nature of the objects, using other words referring not to abstractions, but to flesh-and-blood realities—like bear and Sarkis. Or life and death. I saw an image in my mind of myself falling on top of that bear. I chuckled. Well, it did look funny long after the fact. Instantly, my colleagues became grim. Did they think I was slighting their responses?

They faltered at first, and then one of them said, with absolute certainty, "What you say happened could not have happened. It's impossible. There's something wrong, somewhere."

That's what I had thought, too—there is something wrong somewhere, which is why I was here. The question needing the answer was—"what is it that is wrong?"

But it did happen," I said. "I lived through it. I experienced it. How do I explain it"?

My other colleague said, also with absolute certainty, "It can't be explained, It's like trying to explain . . . " and here his voice trailed off. His hands juggled handfuls of air, as his shoulders seemed to shrug under the weight.

"A miracle?" I blurted to finish his sentence.

"Yeah Sarkis," he said with a hint of sarcasm, "if you believe in miracles."

But that was the whole point. I didn't believe in miracles; I believed in science and wanted its confirmation.

My first colleague, with squinting eyes under arched eyebrows, looked psychiatrically into mine without another word. It was exactly the kind of look I was afraid, of because it said: a) I was lying, b) I was hallucinating, c) I was showing off my ego with excessive machismo, d) all of the above. We resorted to small talk, and when it was discreet to do so, I thanked my colleagues and took my leave in turmoil.

I wanted scientific answers, and science obliged me with a formula. I knew two things for sure. Although I guessed that I weighed more than that emaciated bear, I felt certain we were not exactly the same weight. The second thing I knew with absolute certainty was where, before I shoved him on his way to the bottom, I had placed Little Blackie at the very tip of the avalanche chute just below the rock tower.

I guessed that I had walked through the alders to a point no less than 50, and no more than 100 feet below the bear's point of entry. I knew with absolute certainty that we had to have traveled different distances, whatever they were. Mine was the shorter one. One of us should have landed in front of, or behind, the other—the formula said so, and that was scientific reality. So how come I had landed right on top of him? A miracle? No way. There are no miracles in nature, only invariant laws. Water seeks its own level and that sort of thing. Something was wrong, somewhere, as my colleagues had said, corroborating my worst suspicions.

If only the Big Bounce and F=MA checkmated each other, it was not that bad. I could have shrugged my shoulders and walked away saying, "Forget it, such freak accidents happen." This was understandable just once, because life was full of just onces. Maybe twices. But there were five consecutive episodes in a 3-year period: the quicksand, the airplane crash, the fall after my sheep, the truck landing on top of me, and the Big Slide. These didn't occur anytime or anywhere else, except on one or another kind of hunt. Most important, there was nothing I could do to influence the outcome once the action patterns had begun. I was totally in their power.

Accident, luck, chance, and coincidence were exceptions to the rule or law of averages by definition alone. But five times in a row? How often could an exception become routine and still remain exceptional? There is a saying that the pitcher that goes to the well too often gets broken. The question was how often is too often? How many more times could I tempt finality with the Great Shadow that quickly passes by?

As pollsters say, there was a trend emerging here. I didn't want it to become the fashion. Those other four close calls, one after another were all different, but each was like the other in one critical respect. Each had only one of two possible outcomes for me. Either I got killed or I survived. There were no other possibilities. It was a 50-50 chance. Not once, but five times in a row coming out the same way in my favor, oh, goody gum-balls.

Science doesn't like to deal in possibilities, because we don't know all the things that are possible. That's why we say anything is. When science has insufficient proof of specific causes that preceded an event, it resorts to probability theory. What is the ratio of chances favoring an event out of the total number of chances for and against it? This is a nice way of saying that much of science is a gigantic crap game with Mamma Nature, in which nothing is certain, but only probable. One gambles on the odds.

I played the numbers game out of sheer desperation. If I tossed a balanced coin, what were the odds that I could toss heads five time in a row? There was a 50-50 chance, or one half, on each toss. Multiplied by itself five times, I had 1 chance out of 32 or .03125 in my favor. The $\frac{1}{2}$ or .5 already looked like Mt. Everest in comparison. But that wasn't so bad. What really scared me were the other odds—the 31 chances out of the 32 against me or .96875 worth of tails.

Probability theory cannot say if the one chance in my favor would come at the start or the finish or somewhere else in between the total chances. Mamma Nature had all sorts of opportunities between 1 and 31 chances to send me to Cimmeria, which, according to Homer, was the underworld of mist and shadow where no one ever sees a sunbeam. Was Mamma Nature fast asleep in the middle of the day?

A terrifying thought fell into my mind, as they say in the old country. What if I went on my next or sixth hunt and the trend continued? The odds would drop to 1 in 64 for heads or .015625. Mt. Everest began to look like a molehill. Again, as they say in the old country, let's sit crooked and talk straight. The tails increased to 63 chances out of 64 against me or .984375 which was relatively absolute enough to use another popular liberal oxymoron of the day.

Of course, all this was a theoretical game with little relationship to reality. There is a vast difference between an inanimate coin flipped with no intervening variables, while a man and a bear on an avalanche chute confronted a whole bunch of them. On my Big Bounce caper alone, there were hosts of details, like mass, height, length, velocity, distance, angle inclinations, differences in body temperature, varying wind resistance, surface differentials, friction coefficients, and who knows what else I had carelessly neglected to observe or measure during rapid transit to final ends. These variables were so many, that if they could be accounted for, the mathematical odds would increase in astronomical proportions to my meager calculations, which were bad enough.

Moreover, the variables, which were common to all five events, differed in timing, duration, and degree. I was not about to replicate the events, experimentally, for precise measurements even if I could. After all, if that coin flipped to tails just once more the next time, instead of heads, the consequences to me could be very sad. If it was foolhardy to bet even money for heads five times in a row, it was insanity to bet my life on it. I admit it was rather cowardly not to put theory to a real test by falling off anything again, at the rate I was going.

No doubt, there were many ways to interpret the facts and numbers that seemed significant to me. It was that supreme actor who beguiled us into World War II, Winston Churchill who correctly pointed out that there are liars, damned liars, and statisticians. Of course, he did not credit Disraeli who said it originally. Every day, government made momentous decisions of virtual life and death involving entire populations, based on probability odds far more fictitious and deceptive than anything I had devised for myself.

I desperately wanted believable figures so that, in the name of science, I could turn my back on the real problem plaguing me. But science pushed me into exactly the opposite direction. All I had left was the growing mystery that somehow, when I hunted, something unknown or unknowable was saving my life, or threatening it with death, by closer and closer margins of inches or seconds. Yet, I had survived—so far. I had tried to be rational and scientific about the whole thing. Now, I could either walk away from the something unknown, or face it with whatever consequences, at all costs. I knew the popular adage that, "He who runs away today will live to fight another day," but considered it an excuse for timid souls who preferred to keep running. My rebuttal to that had always been, "He who runs away today, will he fight on any day?" I had to fight the something unknown, now.

My real problem was the flash of experience in a split second, somewhere during my roller-coaster ride, when I remembered that there was a 30-foot drop to the beach. The only probabilistic answer I had forced me to the extrasensory I had abandoned so many years ago. How can I ever forget what flashed through my mind and inscribed itself indelibly in my memory? I knew with absolute certainty I was not going to die. Moreover, I knew this was not wish-fulfillment born of a desperate desire to survive, because survival was a foregone conclusion. I knew in advance that it would be proved when I hit bottom. This was precognition, if it was anything.

The strangest sensation of all was feeling that this fore-knowledge was not a thought originating inside my head. It was not mine. It felt foreign, alien. It was an awareness permeating my entire being, coming from somewhere outside me that had nothing to do with my head or brain. It was not subconscious. I was not thinking or imagining anything, yet I was totally aware, with stark clarity, that I was knowing all this. Everything was being thought for me, as a warmth and timeless sense of being gripped me. Total peace and serenity held me. I didn't want it to end for a moment. If this was the Biblical "peace that passes all understanding," of which "superstitious dullards" talked a great deal, then I've experienced it. Most incredible was my awareness that I was knowing these separate thoughts at the same time, and recognizing the differences, although they appeared as one. This is the only way I can describe what must have lasted for a moment or two, but seemed like forever. I know beyond a shadow of doubt that this was a supra-sensory phenomenon of a transcendental kind. It had nothing to do with nature. Dare I say it? This must be what is known as revelation, or the revealed knowledge of which shamans, holy men, theologians, and saints have talked about for centuries.

Science, properly applied with its rigorous investigative methods, is a superb achievement of the human mind for understanding the physical world of nature that we experience. But there are many things we humans experience as natural, about which science can tell us little or nothing. No laboratory experiments can operationally define and quantify such terms as love, loyalty, or lechery for example, yet we all have experienced them or the lack of them. Science can tell us what electricity is and how it functions, but whether we ought to make electric shavers or electric chairs, has no scientific answer. Science could not answer my questions. Neither could scientism, with all its claims that only science has all, and the best, answers. No authentic scientist will subscribe to this perversion that functions with religious fanaticism.

The questions all this raised is exactly what I wanted to avoid when I looked for probability odds and scientific explanations to lead me into an opposite direction. It had been a vain hope. Now, I looked into the void of my soul and admitted that the accumulated, musty thoughts of my mind were limited and powerless to find an explanation. I could only admit one of two things: I had either experienced all this or I hadn't. The fact that I had did not permit suspension of judgement or belief, which would be a cowardly cop out. I either accepted or rejected the implications.

Unable to deny the reality of what I had experienced, and unable to explain them scientifically, I faced the only alternative left to me—Miracles. The few miracles I had read about were unverifiable. The ones I'd heard about smacked of hobgoblins, spooks, and things that moaned after midnight in children's fairy tales, or smelled of incense and echoed like subterranean chanting in dim candlelight and wispy smoke.

I assumed that since miracles contradict Nature, they could not be real. In my voracious reading to get answers over the next 2 years, I made a troubling discovery. More than 1,500 years ago, St. Augustine had enunciated a doctrine that miracles do not contradict nature. They only contradict our understanding of nature. That made sense since what we scientifically know of nature, substantial though it may be, is only a drop of water to the Atlantic and Pacific Oceans combined compared to what we do not know. Moreover, recent discoveries so contradict our understanding of science, that a logically coherent system of thought is on very shaky grounds.

We are always in search of what is real, and because we are sight-oriented we "see" the "real" in nature. In fact, we do not even see the real sun. It takes nearly 9 seconds for its rays to reach our planet, by which time it has moved two diameters away from the place where we "see" it. Yet, we say that "seeing is believing." A thing unseen is not as "real." I would often pound the top of my lectern to demonstrate its inanimate, solid, and immobile properties to make a point to my students, (and even if I didn't succeed, at least the pounding awakened some of the light sleepers with a jolt).

Then, I'd remind them that if we sliced off a single square inch of ultramicroscopically thin wooden surface, we would find trillions of vibrating atoms, consisting of mobile particles, moving at enormous speeds. Reduced to its smallest level of reality, what seemed like solid, inert matter was energy in motion unseen by the eye. Matter is energy and energy is matter. "Your minds can understand the presence of something the evidence to your senses denies," I would say.

We are confounded at every turn by nature's contradictions and realities that defy logic, so we create concepts that help us understand what might be real, but cannot be mistaken for it— like the Law of Gravity, for example. While gravity is real, the law explaining it is fiction, no matter how useful. The law is an abstraction based on falling bodies in a vacuum to make uniform or constant the condition in which it applies. But there is no vacuum in nature because there is no constancy or uniformity in it.

The "law" is a reference point, taken out of context, to help understand one tiny part of nature's reality that is a vast complex of chaotic occurrences. The law is an artificial construct that applies only if all other things are equal, which we know in advance they are not. This is why nature is studied to create some order and logic out of it. But this is our creation, not nature's. A few years or months later, another discovery alters all our understanding of its order, and we are forced to impose a different orderly creation.

While the fictive law helps us to understand nature, it cannot be mistaken for it. Alas, any law, by definition, is a generalization that stands alone against a myriad of exceptions testing and assaulting it. But unless we generalize a law, we have no guideline to help us deal with the exceptions. Ask any governmental bureaucrat, surrounded by manuals of endless laws, rules, and regulations, and he will tell you that when trying to apply a rule against a particular case, rarely does he find a neat congruity. The next rule, in that event, will tell him how to reach the next higher level of authority that judges how to resolve the discrepancy despite the rules.

If nature is loaded with inconstancies, inconsistencies, contrarieties, and contradictions, what explains these exceptions? All too often we don't know. We see the regularities and normalities by arbitrarily ignoring the exceptions, or we would get no laws. The exceptions are unpredictable, inconsistent, inconstant, ununiform irregularities. These words become palatable synonyms for the suspicious word "miracle" that is inherent in nature. She contains the possibility of the irregular or the miraculous, but lacking intelligence, design, and purpose, which we illicitly read into it, it cannot distinguish between the general and the particular, nor activate them as the miraculous—a term at which unbelievers bristle.

If the exceptions to nature's regularities laws are miracles, and those exceptions are potentially inherent in nature, then her invariant laws cannot create miracles without self-contradiction. Then, how are miracles activated, caused, or brought into being? Miracle is not an event without cause or effect. Its cause cannot be nature without the capacity to reason between logical consistency and contradiction, but an activation by some other intelligent source. If I believed in miracles, then I had to believe in the cause behind them. Since that ruled out nature, only one other thing with conscious intelligence could be inferred—God.

I was back to Aristotle's First Cause, Uncaused, which we moderns transfer from God to nature or the probable, with disastrous results. Then, we forget that, even if we are not certain that God exists, it is most highly probable that He does, even by our own probability theories, which we contradict by asserting that He does not.

Only God, without contradicting the actions of His laws in the very nature He created, could routinely select those appropriate exceptions with qualities of the miraculous. Why and how did He do it? If I knew that, I would be He. That was His business and my mystery. All I had to know was what I think He did as nearly as I could figure it.

I do not palm all this off as a contribution to knowledge. I present it as a psychological explanation of why and how my mind worked, for better or worse. I could not wait for the final answer on doomsday. I wanted understanding, not the Nobel Prize. And I found enough truth to calm the tempest in my soul with the best I could do.

Why was it so difficult for me to believe in the miraculous? Because the miracle is a unique, unrepeatable, one-shot occurrence whose results cannot be traced back to its origin for measurement and verification. Did that make them less real? Did this mean that I couldn't believe in the reality of the planet Earth on which I stood because it, too, was a one-shot, unrepeatable occurrence not traceable to its origins for verification, as conflicting theories and hypotheses testified?

We adore nature because she cannot hold us accountable to anything. She showers us with joy or terror without rhyme or reason and let's us get away with anything we can. In fact, not having reason, she has no morality or purpose. She moves in meaningless and eternally recurring cycles so beloved by pantheists. She cannot distinguish between man or Pre-Cambrian cockroaches, between right and wrong, good and evil.

God is different. He knows what we are about and holds us responsible for what we do, which is why we have reason, will, choice, and a sense of right and wrong. We are forever caught between what we want to do and what we ought to do. We have the freedom to choose and often trap ourselves in regrettable choices. But then, we can try to make amends. It is we who can think and create in imitation of our Creator, not nature.

My problem was a lifetime of adherence to the logico-positivistic branch of philosophy on which modern liberal humanism built its bastions. Auguste Comte, the founding father of sociology, the discipline in which I spent a lot of time, developed positivism to a new religion, and boasted of it as such in the New Age of his time. He was, admirably enough, trying to put the pieces together of the mess left by the French Revolution that had ushered in a scientific new age and quickly become contentious scientism.

The new order resorted to old techniques and made generous use of the guillotine to dispatch controversial theories by dispatching the theorists. Perhaps that's why Comte insisted that only those things readily available to the senses could be knowable with scientific certainty. As the French said, "The more things change, the more they remain the same."

Man can have no positive, or scientific, knowledge of original causes or ultimate ends, he insisted, and speculation about them was religious quackery. Despite this, he insisted on establishing the causes and origins of society and their development to a final utopia through his "Law of Three Stages," no less. As undergraduate students, we all chuckled at his claim that sociology was the new religion, after denouncing religion; sociologists were the new priesthood and Comte was the new god. We chuckled, but believed it, anyway. His scientism had made sociology into social engineering nearly a century later in our campus activisms. It also gave psychology and psychoanalysis their underpinnings.

Some of us had begun to act like gods in these disciplines, especially sociology, because it was one of three things we could do with it. The other two were to teach or enter governmental service to engineer voter support for the incumbents. The psychologists were more clever than we. They shrank one head at a time with the inducements of freewheeling sex to change society to their liking. We sociologists wanted to change society all in one shot, and when it didn't listen to our omniscience, we rammed it down the societal gullet at the first opportune moment for us—in the guise of protesting the Viet Nam War.

What I hadn't realized, was that in trying to explain reality, I had explained it away with positivism. I realized this when Bertrand Russell, one of the world's leading left-wing atheistic positivists, who had been a pacifist until he became a hawk on behalf of world socialism, supported Viet Nam and denounced the American soldier as an animal and a Nazi, while the flag of the enemy was flown above our own. The American left emulated and cheered him. If this was the birth of the New World Order, then I preferred to die in the old one. That's when Little Blackie came into my life and forced me to reconsider the things available to my senses and the realities behind them.

I knew that the answers I came up with in the foregoing would seem primitive and full of holes to learned physicists, theologians, and philosophers. I obviously had no way of knowing how life had tested their thinking. I only know how it had changed mine. God really existed, although science could not quantify him, scientism falsifies him, liberalism denies him, and humanism buries him. I had subscribed to each of those "truths" with impassioned faith ever since my formal schooling. Now that Little Blackie had put me to the test and all else failed, I either believed in the only answer I could find—God—or I didn't, and now I knew what the leap of faith was all about.

I hesitated. No, it was not what would happen to my professional reputation when (not if), word got out that I had become a believer. That price I would gladly pay. I hesitated because, through the labyrinth of memory and the agony of soul, I heard the faint echo, "Je soif, Je soif." I had tried and failed to forget that night in wartime France when I denounced the God who let that little girl symbolize all the innocent children of this world who suffered the barbarities of man.

To believe in God now was to eat humble pie and deny everything I had believed in all these years. Humility does not sit well with professorial pride. It is the torrent of water that drowns the wildfire of hubris, but it is the beginning of wisdom. In my high school senior year, as captain of my track team, I had reveled in the glory of an undefeated season with broken records in the long jump. Now, I had to make another leap far more important, running down a different kind of track, not with exultation, but with trembling uncertainty. I leaped from that spiritual takeoff board as I had never done before, not knowing if I would bridge that gap to the other side.

My gods of science and reason, despite my fondest hopes to the contrary, had brought me face to face with the Sciential God of All Reality. My vaunted ego recoiled at the self that now stood helpless before Him who was the Great I Am. I could leap no further.

There was a thing that left-wing intellectual malcontents always derided. It was called "soul" in the old days. I had also derided it. We had taken it from God and called it the subconscious, Ego, Self, I, Me, Generalized Other, Super Ego, etc., so we could hog it all on our terms. It was really the greatest theft in all human history. Dr. Faustus lost his soul in his bargain with the Devil. I was fortunate. I found mine when I returned it to its rightful Owner. Let the others scoff, as I had. I cannot, and will not deny, what I have experienced.

It was another 20 years or so after the discovery of DNA, the hereditary basis of life, that David Foster made some arresting calculations.[1] The reality of that DNA, its elements, and the way they were put together on the basis of chance were finally stated mathematically. If the DNA specifics of the simplest T4 bacteriophage (forget anything as complex as man) were tossed at random once every second to make it come out the way it did based on chance, there would be one chance in $10^{(78,000,000)}$, or 10 times itself for 78,000,000 times. The real problem is that the universe is only $10^{(18)}$ seconds old. There has not been enough time, by a very, very long shot, for chance to have done its work.

While evolutionary theory is tentatively acceptable as theory, Darwin's particular account of it is already embattled on many fronts. Foster concludes that, not only Darwin's theories of natural selection based on random mutations is impossible, but that there is a God who works things apart from Nature's laws. The renowned astronomer, Sir Fred Hoyle, not known for religious zealotry, had his own probability odds based on different evidence and said (before Foster) there is "???" or "God." (Take your choice.)

The evidence continues to mount, as does the irrational opposition to it. How easy things would have been for me back then if only I had these recent findings. But then, faith would have been a simple intellectual exercise. Faith based on knowledge is redundant, unnecessary. No faith earned without suffering will stand by us when we need it most. Faith is the affirmation of what the soul understands. It is always more than what the head can think. I had long since made my peace with God, when the new findings in science emerged, and all I could do was smile and say, "Yes, I know."

We are born rebels and, ultimately, all human revolutions, rebellions, wars, personal hatreds, and utopias are against the only certainty we have—death. I came out of my tortured travail of spirit with the conviction that science is not only one of God's great gifts to man, but there is no real conflict between science and religion. The two are complementary. The conflict is between men of ill-will, each misrepresenting the integrity of his own calling. Once I crossed my Rubicon, all the rest fell into place.

One of the most intense spiritual crisis of my entire life originated with a sweet, innocent child on a battlefront in France, and was resolved by a black bear in Alaska, who saved my life some quarter century later, then forced it into a confrontation with the Creator of the three of us. That was another miracle.

A final odd incident occurred in this long saga. Long after I had made my peace with God and no more death defying episodes occurred (though I hunted with no more caution than before), I made a heart-wrenching discovery. One day, the muse turned me on during a brief respite, and I picked up the freshman copy of my English literature text, *British Prose and Poetry*. It sat on one or another of my library shelves for nearly 50 years, during which interim I had referred to it less than a dozen times. As a student, I had faithfully done all the assignments my professor had doled out from the book's 1,346 pages. A few things had been omitted at the professor's discretion. Now, I discovered, quite by accident, one of those omissions at the end of the book. It was a poem that had been sitting at arm's reach all these years, and I hadn't known it!

It was written by Francis Thompson, a thing he called, *The Hound of God*. It was recognized as one of the finest lyric poems in the English language, whether or not one agreed with its theme. To my amazement, I found the unbelievable parallel between his anguish and mine, no matter how different the experiences, in our attempted escape from the Creator of Heaven and Earth, and all that is seen and unseen. How well I understood the agony in his soul as I read, through choked-up emotion, the beauty and poignancy of his verse that also described the stark reality of my travails. It began,

> I fled Him, down the nights and down the days;
> I fled Him, down the arches of the years;
> I fled Him, down the labyrinthine ways
> Of my own mind; and in the mist of tears
> I hid from Him, and under running laughter.
> Up vistaed hopes I sped; and shot, precipitated,
> Adown Titanic glooms of chasmed fears,
> From those strong Feet that followed,
> Followed after.
> But with unhurrying chase,
> And unperturbed pace,
> Deliberate speed, majestic instancy,
> They beat—and a Voice beat
> More instant than the Feet—
> *"All things betray thee, who betrayest Me."*

The last line decked me—"All things betray thee, who betrayest Me." So that's what had happened! In a single, neatly placed shot, that one line gave me more understanding than all the books I'd read on the subject matter. Had I not fled Him under running laughter in the mist of tears after denouncing Him in a fit of drunken blasphemy? Had I not hid from Him in the labyrinths of my mind all those years when schools, professors, and text books could not give the answers of the hunting trail? Had I not literally shot down chasmed fears on mountain sides, refusing to listen to the unperturbed pace and the Voice of the Hunter who hunted me, not betraying me as I had betrayed Him? Of all the betrayals, was this not the greatest of all? When I hunted on those countless trails, now long forgotten, searching for ultimate treasure, who was the real hunter and who the hunted?

And so it was that my little bear, whom I nearly betrayed on that mountain, completed the circle I had journeyed over. It had started that day with the cries of an innocent child maimed by war, who was somebody's daughter, and could have been mine. I have wondered if she is still alive, who and where she is, and if she remembers anything of that night somewhere in war-torn France when a young American soldier denounced God for what man's inhumanity to man had done to her. Injustice is the suffering of the innocent.

My journey ended in the midst of higher education gone insane with anti-Viet Nam dissent tearing me and my country apart, when an undersized black bear came into my life and forced me to meet the Maker of my soul.

I named my bear Little Blackie, which I know is so prosaic. But it has an affectionate ring to it and teases away the affected look of false ferocity put there with good intent by the taxidermist who did not know my adorable mutt as I do.

To me, he will always look mischievous, with a sly twinkle in his eye. He knows how helpless I feel when guests ask me which is my most important trophy of all and I point to him, poking out his little head amidst the trophies of grandeur on that wall, most of whom are in one or another world record book. And standing there, my guests are silent with incredulity when they ask me why, and I tell them how he turned me to God long after I had denounced Him. Once a guest retorted, "How can a man like you be a believer?" in such a way that "a man like you" meant killer of animals. I did not repeat the trite , but true quote, "God moves in mysterious ways . . ." I knew how

He had moved in the only way I would understand—the hunting trail.

All I could say was, "How can any man, even unlike me, not be a believer?"

So I have stopped trying to explain unless they, too, have slid 800 feet and landed on a bear. Or have read *The Hound of Heaven*. Or watched a wounded, thirsty child crying in agony because of war.

Often, when I see Little Blackie trying to catch my eye, I wink at him, and I swear he winks back at me. I know what he's thinking, and I know he's right. He knows me better than I know myself. I'll see him romping around on that Celestial Mountain somewhere in the Happy Hunting Grounds when we meet again, and all I want to say to him is "Thank you for introducing me to Him, Who created us both, and a little girl in war-torn France with whom this whole story began.

Index

Portrait © 1995 by Betts Photography

S arkis Atamian, the son of immigrant parents who miraculously escaped the genocide of the Armenians by the Turks after World War I, was born in Providence, Rhode Island. As captain of his high school track team, he lead the team to state and New England championships. In nonscholastic amateur track and field, he established a triple jump record, which stood for 27 years. Upon graduation from high school, he served in the United States Army in four campaigns during World War II: Italy, France, Germany, and North Africa. Following the war, Sarkis, received his cum laude education at the University of Rhode Island, Brown University, and the University of Utah. The Armenian genocide, and his parents escape, led him to publish his academic thesis, *The Armenian Community*, as he completed his university education.

After a brief stint with Civil Service, he moved to Alaska and joined the faculty at the University of Alaska, Fairbanks Campus. There he served for two terms as head of the Department of Sociology and Psychology. Sarkis was a founding charter member of the University's National Honorary Society of Phi Kappa Phi. His main reason for going to Alaska was to hunt, and hunt he did—throughout the length and breadth of the Greatland. He has also hunted in other states, twice in Africa and once in India.

His numerous academic research papers and articles, concerning the philosophy and psychology of hunting, has contributed to Mr. Atamian being a recognized authority in that field. He has been a popular speaker at conventions of the Safari Club International, The North American Federation of Sheep Hunters, Alaska Professional Hunters Association, and many other associated organizations. He has had membership in many professional societies including the Egypt Exploration Society, and has guided several student tours to the Land of the Pharaohs. He keeps active membership as a Fellow of the Explorers Club.

Sarkis is happily married to Alison C. Betts, a former student, who, he says, is really an angel in mortal disguise. He has retired from University life, and currently resides with his wife in Wasilla, Alaska. Although he admits to slowing down, he continues to be an avid hunter.